T0304106

The Global Financial Crisis and the New Monetary Consensus

The Global Financial Crisis has reshuffled the cards for central banks throughout the world. In the wake of the biggest crisis since the Great Depression, this volume traces the evolution of modern central banking over the last 50 years. It takes in the inflationary chaos of the 1970s and the monetarist experiments of the 1980s, eventually leading to the New Monetary Consensus, which took shape in the 1990s and prevailed until 2007. The book then goes on to review the limitations placed on monetary policy in the aftermath of the global meltdown, arguing that the financial crisis has shaken the New Monetary Consensus.

In the aftermath of the worst crisis since the Great Depression, the book investigates the nature of present and future monetary policy. Is the Taylor rule still a satisfactory monetary precept for central bankers? Has the New Monetary Consensus been shaken by the Global Financial Crisis? What are the fundamental issues raised by the latter cataclysmic chain of events? How should central banks conceptualize monetary policy anew in a post-crisis scenario?

Existing books have dwelt extensively on the characteristics of the New Monetary Consensus, but few have cast light on its relevance in a post-crisis scenario. This book seeks to fill this gap, drawing on the lessons from five decades of contrasted theoretical approaches ranging from Keynesianism, monetarism, new classical macroeconomics, inflation targeting and, more recently, pragmatic global crisis management.

Marc Pilkington is Associate Professor of Economics at the University of Burgundy, France.

Routledge international studies in money and banking

The Global Financial Crisis and the New Monetary Consensus

Marc Pilkington

Routledge
Taylor & Francis Group

LONDON AND NEW YORK

First published 2014
by Routledge
2 Park Square, Milton Park, Abingdon, Oxon OX14 4RN

and by Routledge
711 Third Avenue, New York, NY 10017

Routledge is an imprint of the Taylor & Francis Group, an informa business

© 2014 Marc Pilkington

British Library Cataloguing in Publication Data
A catalogue record for this book is available from the British Library

Library of Congress Cataloging in Publication Data
Pilkington, Marc.
    The global financial crisis and the new monetary consensus /
Marc Pilkington.
    pages cm
    1. Financial crises–History–21st century. 2. Banks and banking,
Central–History–21st century. 3. Monetary policy–History–
21st century. I. Title.
    HB3722.P55 2013
    332.1'1–dc23

                                                           2013010914

ISBN: 978-0-415-52405-6 (hbk)
ISBN: 978-1-315-88725-8 (ebk)

Typeset in Times New Roman
by Wearset Ltd, Boldon, Tyne and Wear

Contents

PART III
Monetary policy after the GFC 103

Illustrations

Photographs

Map

Tables

Preface

Starting in the 1990s, a 'New Monetary Consensus' (NMC) emerged in the world of central bankers. Alan Greenspan was soon acclaimed as the world's greatest central banker ever, even though a few dissonant voices were to be heard in academia at the peak of his career. After discovering the NMC as a pragmatic response to the demise of monetarism, he sought to manage expectations in order to control real-world outcomes by building credibility and transparency to ensure price stability and low inflation.

Prior to the Global Financial Crisis (GFC), Ben Bernanke, Alan Greenspan's successor, proclaimed the era of 'the great moderation' characterized by lasting macroeconomic stability. Until the GFC, there was a remarkably strong consensus among academics and professional economists that central banks should adopt explicit inflation targets and that all key monetary policy decisions should be subordinated to price stability and low inflation. Since its introduction in New Zealand in 1989, inflation targeting has gained prominence in the central banking community.

The subprime crisis broke out in August 2007. Following the demise of Lehman Brothers, it mutated one year later into the first global crisis of the twenty-first century, the latter episode of which being the enduring Euro sovereign debt crisis. The aim of this book is to assess whether the latter cataclysmic chain of events has shaken the New Monetary Consensus. It is indeed difficult to convey how much doubt has been thrown on the entire corpus of central banking theory by the current global crisis. Macroeconomic indicators have become unpredictable, rare (so-called black swan) events have become common and accepted orthodox frameworks have lost their appeal.

Following an overview of the situation, our introductory chapter briefly depicts the evolution of central banking practices over the last half century, with the underlying theoretical frameworks and the corresponding macroeconomic outcomes. We then thoroughly analyse the mantras of the 1990s, leading to the worldwide configuration of monetary policy until 2007. In the aftermath of the worst crisis since the Great Depression, we try to understand the unconventional policy responses of central banks, and we sketch out the nature of future monetary policy. Is the Taylor rule still a satisfactory monetary precept for central bankers? Has the New Monetary Consensus been shaken by the Global

Financial Crisis? What are the fundamental issues raised by the latter cataclysmic chain of events? How shall central banks conceptualize monetary policy
anew in a post-crisis scenario?

Existing books have dwelt extensively on the characteristics of the NMC.
Very few authors have cast light on its relevance in a post-crisis scenario,
drawing on the lessons from decades of contrasted theoretical approaches
ranging from Keynesianism, monetarism, new classical macroeconomics, inflation targeting and, more recently, pragmatic global crisis management. It is precisely this gap in the literature that this book intends to fill.

Abbreviations

ABM	agent-based modelling
AMLF	Asset-Backed Commercial Money Market Mutual Funds Liquidity Facility
BIS	Bank for International Settlements
BoE	Bank of England
CPFF	Commercial Paper Funding Facility
CPI	Consumer Price Index
CW	Collected Works
DB	Deutsche Bank
DRIVE	Do – Restrictions – Investments – Values – Essential
DSGE	dynamic stochastic general equilibrium
ECB	European Central Bank
EMH	Efficient Market Hypothesis
EMU	European Monetary Union
ESCB	European System of Central Banks
ESRB	European Systemic Risk Board
EU	European Union
Fed	Federal Reserve
FOMC	Federal Open Marker Committee
FTPL	Fiscal Theory of the Price Level
FX	Foreign Exchange
GDP	gross domestic product
GEM	Global Economy Model
GFC	Global Financial Crisis
GG	Grundgesetz
GPL	General Public Licence
HET	History of Economic Thought
HICP	Harmonized Index of Consumer Prices
HIV	human immunodeficiency virus
ILO	International Labour Organization
IMF	International Monetary Fund
ISDA	International Swaps and Derivatives Association
IT	Inflation Targeting

ITers	inflation-targeting central banks
JAMEL	Java Agent-based MacroEconomic Laboratory
LATW	lean against the wind
LB	Lehman Brothers
LSAP	Large-Scale Asset Purchases
LTRO	Long-Term Refinancing Operations
MP	Member of Parliament
MPIP	Monetary Policy Ineffectiveness Proposition
MTFS	Medium-Term Financial Strategy
NBFI	Non-Financial Banking Institutions
NEMO	Norwegian Economic Model
NKPC	New Keynesian Phillips Curve
NMC	New Monetary Consensus
OCA	Optimal Currency Area
OECD	Organisation for Economic Co-operation and Development
OTC	over-the-counter
POWER	Positives – Objections – What else? – Enhancements – Remedies
PPP	Purchasing Power Parity
QE1	Quantitative Easing 1
QE2	Quantitative Easing 2
RAMSES	Riksbank Aggregate Macromodel for Studies of the Economy of Sweden
RBC	Real Business Cycles
RBNZ	Royal Bank of New Zealand
SDRM	Sovereign Debt Restructuring Mechanism
SOMA	System Open Market Account
TAF	Term Auction Facility
TBTF	too-big-to-fail
TFEU	Treaty on the Functioning of the European Union
TIPS	Treasury Inflation-Protected Securities
VAR	vector autoregression
VPS	variable payments system

Part I
Overview

1 The Global Financial Crisis
An unprecedented configuration for monetary policy

Introduction

In 2008–2009, the world experienced 'by far the deepest global recession since the Great Depression' (IMF, 2009). Regardless of the existence of varying policy objectives assigned to central banks, it is a truism, five years after the beginning of the crisis, to state that significant limitations have been imposed upon monetary policy. The Global Financial Crisis (GFC) has undoubtedly shaken the world of central bankers and taken monetary policy into unchartered territory. This overview announces the structure of the volume. In the first part of the book, we will examine the mantras of the 1990s embedded in the NMC, before examining, in a second part, how monetary policy has been transformed in the aftermath of the GFC.

The Global Financial Crisis: what future for monetary policy?

The subprime crisis broke out in August 2007. One year later, following the demise of Lehman Brothers in September 2008, the crisis mutated into the first global crisis of the twenty-first century, the latter episode of which being the enduring Euro sovereign debt crisis. The aim of this book is to assess whether the subsequent cataclysmic chain of events has shaken the New Monetary Consensus. It is indeed difficult to convey how much doubt has been thrown on the entire corpus of central banking theory by the current global crisis. Macroeconomic indicators have become unpredictable, rare (so-called black swan) events have become common and accepted orthodox frameworks have lost their appeal.

Stated objectives

Following an overview of the situation, we depict the evolution of central banking practices over the last half century, with the underlying theoretical frameworks and the corresponding macroeconomic outcomes. We then thoroughly analyse the mantras of the 1990s, leading to a worldwide configuration for monetary policy up until 2007. In the aftermath of the worst crisis since the Great Depression, we scrutinize the unconventional responses of central banks, and we sketch out the nature of future monetary policy by addressing the following questions: Is the Taylor rule still a satisfactory precept for central bankers? Has the crisis irreversibly tarnished the NMC? What are the fundamental issues raised by this cataclysmic chain of events? How much reliance should we put on formal models? How should central banks conceptualize monetary policy anew in a post-crisis scenario?

Structure of the volume and methodological considerations

An extensive literature existed on the NMC (under the inflation targeting umbrella term) prior to the crisis. The claimed novelties of this book are twofold. Because we begin this volume with a historical overview, it therefore becomes natural to view the NMC as a historical moment in a long-term perspective *à la* Braudel. Therefore, this first part (which could *not* have been written before the crisis) must be read through the lenses of the economist *and* the historian. Chapter 1 begins with a brief overview and a statement of objectives. Chapter 2 contains a brief introduction to monetary policy spanning over several decades until the inception of the NMC. Chapter 3 is didactical in essence, and presents a simple three-equation model of the NMC in closed-economy analysis. A slightly more complex six-equation model is sketched out for an open economy. The following chapters offer a rigorous and critical analysis of the NMC mantras, understood as catchwords with an axiomatic dimension, namely transparency (Chapter 4), credibility (Chapter 5), price stability (Chapter 6), interest rate rules (Chapter 7) and finally inflation targeting (Chapter 8).

Although the first part of the volume proposes a seemingly diachronic analysis of the NMC during its existence, no deliberate attempt is made to undermine the NMC from the onset in synchronic terms. This would be way premature. However, in the first part, the reader, almost imperceptibly comes across brief reflections that start to shed light on the NMC in a critical post-crisis (and historical) perspective.[1] We prefer to talk about rather dim, and not dazzling, light here. The second part is less ambiguous, as it investigates a straightforward question. Does the GFC constitute the end of an era for monetary policy and, if so, in what sense? Chapter 9 focuses on the statutory missions of the Fed and the ECB; the impact of the GFC on these two institutions is apprehended through the lenses of the 'new normal'. Further limitations of the NMC are examined in the light of the problematic issue of the US dollar. Chapter 10 examines issues of exchange rate movements and international monetary coordination in a post-crisis scenario. The unavoidable problem of the zero bound on nominal interest rates is discussed in Chapter 11. Chapter 12 is a rather original end personal essay on the austerity versus growth conundrum that aims to depart sharply from commonly held views in mainstream economics. Chapter 13 looks at the Federal Reserve's quantitative easing programmes, by examining their nature, their scope and their effectiveness. It is argued that these unconventional monetary policy measures do not fit well into the NMC apparatus. Chapter 14 aims to single out the learning lessons for the contemporary period, derived from the theory of optimal currency areas developed by Robert Mundell more than fifty years ago. Chapter 15 focuses on the Euro sovereign debt crisis for which, we argue, the NMC has little, if nothing, to say. Chapter 16 concludes this volume, by broadening the reflection to post-crisis methodological considerations in central banking theory.

In this book, we have decided to devote little space to the narrative of the GFC, which has been extensively covered elsewhere. Instead, we shall focus on the transformative paradigmatic dimension of the GFC as regards the NMC. We will eventually let the readers decide, whether or not our conclusion phrased at the end of the book is warranted, both for the economist and the economic historian.

Part II

The new mantras of the 1990s

2 Introduction
Monetary policy prior to the NMC

Introduction

In this chapter, four historical Moments are singled out in the post-war period, to help put the emergence of the NMC into perspective. After briefly describing the ineffectiveness of monetary policy throughout the 1950 and 1960s, we look into the 1970s, a chaotic decade in which monetary policy was temporarily defeated by the inflation spectre. Then, we discuss the monetarist experiment, with a focus on the UK. Finally, we present the transitional period towards the NMC with the pioneering inflation-targeting experiment conducted in New Zealand from 1989 onwards. The pivotal role of the Maastricht treaty and the influence of supply-side economics on the birth of the NMC are discussed, before finally phrasing the theme of the book.

Monetary policy ineffectiveness in the 1950s and 1960s

The interdependence of policy objectives

The post-war period was characterized by a policy mix endorsing the interdependence of policy objectives in which inflation was interwoven with employment, the balance of payments and economic growth (Greenaway and Shaw, 1988, p. 379). However, this interdependence of objectives would soon come in contradistinction with the Tinbergen rule that we will briefly evoke.

The stop and go policies

Prior to the late 1970s, monetary policy was encapsulated in a surprisingly reductive dialectic between unemployment and inflation, notably symbolized by the stop–go policies and the Phillips curve. The economy was stimulated by low interest rates in the go phase, until overheating inevitably gave rise to inflationary pressures, and triggered the stop phase characterized by a restrictive monetary stance. The business cycle was narrowed down to its simplest form, and the resulting policy response was made entirely predictable for economic agents.

The Phillips curve

Charles Bean (2007) has provided an interesting historical overview of the past half century. He begins his survey with Phillips' pioneering work (1958), written at a time when policy makers believed that there existed an exploitable inverse trade-off between unemployment and inflation. It was believed at the time that the government was able to lower unemployment, in case it was willing to tolerate higher inflation. If excess demand pressures showed signs of spilling over into excessive inflation and a deteriorating balance of payments, a restrictive fiscal policy was the chosen tool, in order to mitigate inflationary pressures.

The non-compliance with the Tinbergen rule

Tinbergen (1952) argued that the number of policy objectives should not exceed the number of instruments.[1] Each instrument should therefore be assigned to the objective upon which it has the greatest impact. The Tinbergen approach exercised considerable influence upon policy discussion during the 1970s, and later became the favoured approach of policy makers. Before making its way in policy circles, the Tinbergen rule was repeatedly violated throughout the 1950s and the 1960s. Policy makers believed at the time that fiscal policy could simultaneously target low unemployment and achieve price stability.

The primacy of fiscal policy

Fiscal policy is one of the tools of economic policy. It affects the level, composition or timing of government expenditures, and can modify the burden, structure or frequency of taxation. Fiscal policy matters in the sense that it needs to be commensurate with macroeconomic expenditure flows. Fiscal policy alters aggregate output, whether directly (through the Keynesian multiplier effect) or indirectly through tax and transfer changes. Bean (2007) argues that fiscal policy was the primary macroeconomic stabilization tool in the post-war period. Greenaway and Shaw (1988, p. 381) aimed to explain the downgrading of UK monetary policy during this period. They argue that British economists were paying inordinate amount of attention to Keynes's special cases, such as the liquidity trap and interest inelastic investment (ibid.). Greenaway and Shaw (ibid.) also emphasize the Radcliffe Report (1959), which undermined the effectiveness of monetary policy in achieving short-term demand management.

The IS/LM framework and the inflationary gap

In the IS/LM construct, the inflationary gap denotes an abnormal discrepancy between equilibrium aggregate production and full-employment aggregate production, when the former is greater than the latter.

An inflationary gap arises when the economy has been expanding on the back of a high level of aggregate demand. Total spending and the economy's ability

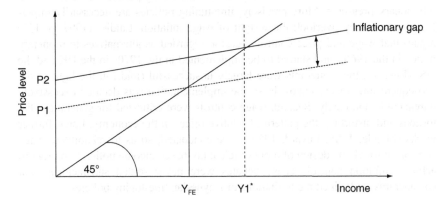

Figure 2.1 The inflationary gap on a Keynesian 45 degree line diagram.

to supply goods and services no longer move in concert, the former outpacing the latter. As a consequence, actual GDP exceeds potential GDP. Interestingly enough, the inflationary gap, couched in modern language, is the alter ego of the output gap:[2] 'just as today, the conventional view of inflation was that it was caused by an excess of aggregate demand at or near the "full employment" level of output' (Thornton, 2010, p. 91). The inflationary gap is combatted by a restrictive fiscal policy (higher taxation) or monetary policy (higher interest rates), through its impact on aggregate spending.

Demand management manipulation

Supply-side economists sometimes argue that productivity gains and enhanced efficiency lead to a rise in aggregate supply, thereby reducing the amount of excess demand in the long run. In theory, inflation control can thus be achieved by supply-side policies. However, the prevailing orthodoxy between the early 1950s and the mid 1970s, was in the Keynesian tradition of demand management manipulation as a determinant of inflationary control (Greenaway and Shaw, 1988, Ch. 18). Whether monetary policy affects the economy through supply or demand effects is a question of utmost importance. The Monetary Policy Committee (1999) discarded the supply-side effects of monetary policy, as its impact can only be apprehended via its influence on aggregate demand. In a surprising lineage with the Keynesian orthodoxy of the 1950s and 1960s, the emphasis on demand management will become a key feature of the NMC in the 1990s. Only the policy instrument will differ.

Wage controls

Greenaway and Shaw (1988, p. 384) critically assessed the performance of the UK economy during the Keynesian years, when demand management policies were at the heart of inflation control. They argued that fine-tuning policies failed to contain inflationary pressures. More precisely, fine-tuning policies are necessarily imperfect, because they overlook the weight of wage inflation. Laidler (1997, p. 153) argues that wage and price controls became regarded as alternatives to monetary policy in the 1960s, and started to be implemented in the 1970s in the UK and the US. However, these attempts were largely unsuccessful (ibid.) in the light of the subsequent inflationary chaos. First, the implementation was deemed excessively bureaucratic and costly. Second, wage controls were criticized for generating distortions and disturbing the pattern of relative prices in the economy. Later, further works (Meade, 1985; Layard, 1986) were conducted, so as to rehabilitate wage controls, through the design of more efficient tax-based income policies, in order to achieve inflation control. These debates were never settled satisfactorily, but considerably underlined the limitations of Keynesian fine-tuning policies.

The triumph of the Monetary Policy Ineffectiveness Proposition (MPIP)

The MPIP: the orthodoxy of the 1950s and 1960s

Although we draw a parallel between the emphasis on macroeconomic demand management in the Keynesian post-war era and under the NMC, starting from the 1990s until the GFC, one major difference lies in the diametrically opposed validity given to the MPIP. The MPIP states that monetary macro-policy is of little help in achieving effective demand management. The MPIP was very much an accepted dogma during the post-war period. Why was monetary policy so allegedly ineffective in the 1950s and 1960s? Why did Keynesian orthodoxy discard this policy option? First and foremost, one must understand the ancient linkage between monetary policy and the quantity theory of money. However, the quantity theory lost its appeal, and had little intellectual aura in the 1950s and 1960s. Cagan (1978, p. 85) states that it was utterly absent from central banking control variables at the time, as it did not fit well into the prevailing Phillips curve and IS/LM frameworks. Another justification for the prevalent MPIP was the subtle characterization of agential behaviour, foreshadowing the rational expectations revolution. Policy makers allowed inflation to drift temporarily throughout the stop-and-go policy era, by resorting to a loose fiscal response to inflationary pressures in the hope that it would bring down unemployment, but the interdependence of policy objectives precluded the stabilization of output and inflation. It was believed (Goodfriend, 2005) that households (price-takers) were in fact incorporating monetary stimuli by making inflationary wage claims in the go-phase, while firms (price-setters) were simultaneously raising prices above the equilibrium level of the previous phase, thereby negating the policy change. This learning curve had far-reaching consequences in the bond market, where lenders espoused the business cycle by requiring additional inflation premiums (ibid.). This resulted in increased volatility of both output and inflation, which rendered monetary policy ineffective.

A modern appraisal of the MPIP: the heterodox Keynesian literature

It is vain to attempt to present an exhaustive survey of heterodox Keynesian literature on monetary theory. Nevertheless, it is worthwhile stressing the seminal contribution of Moore (1988) and his book entitled *Horizontalists and Verticalists*, which laid the foundations of a consistent alternative post-Keynesian monetary theory throughout the 1990s. The key idea is the endo-genous nature of money that is credit-driven and demand-determined. In this framework, banks accommodate the demand for money at the rate set by the central bank, provided that non-financial economic agents are deemed credit-worthy by lenders. Post-Keynesian horizontalists stressed that the central bank cannot control the quantity of reserves supplied to the economy, but only the price thereof (Moore, 2003). This horizontalist theory of central banking posits the central importance of the interest rate, although Moore (ibid.) admits that the interest-rate setting procedure of the central bank is indeed constrained by a range of variables that substantially restrict its room for manoeuvre.

Monetary policy in disarray: the 1970s

Why so much confusion in the 1970s?

Inflation statistics and latent ideological transformation

Regardless of spatiotemporal conditions, mainstream orthodox thinking is bound to be defeated by a rival school of thought, when the former no longer satisfact-orily explains the reality it endeavours to influence (Kuhn, 1962). Keynesianism played the role of the mainstream in the 1950s and the 1960s (C. Taylor, 2011, p. 28). DeLong (1995) hammers this point home, when he argues that, until the 1970s, the post-war era was more or less structured around Keynesian macro-economic specifications. In the background of Keynesian orthodoxy, monetar-ism had been a burgeoning school of thought, and a powerful alternative in the making, ever since the Chicago School established itself as a strategic hub for free-market economic principles, in the tradition of nineteenth century neoclassi-cal economics. It took a full reversal of priorities and economic conditions to alter the ideological landscape in the 1970s. This fundamental shift of twentieth-century macroeconomics has been extensively examined in the literature by eco-nomic historians and theorists, and we do not aim to reopen the fascinating doctrinal debate as to which factors were the most decisive in explaining this ideological transformation. For the purpose of our book, it suffices to refer to inflation statistics in the 1970s, as the latter decade is certainly the one that saw concerns about inflation come to the fore (ibid.). Paul Volcker broke away with the formerly lenient approach to inflation, when he took office as Chairman of the Federal Reserve. In what would later be characterized as a full reversal in priorities, the objective to halt inflation became the highest priority of economic policy. Since the end of the Second World War, inflation only afflicted America during the 1970s. Microeconomic variables were filled with uncertainty, because business decisions were contingent on monetary policy decisions (that are macroeconomic, in essence).[3] The inflation rates observed in the 1970s were indeed comparable to wartime rates (ibid.).

The decline of Keynesian ideas

C. Taylor (2011, p. 29) rightly points out that countries, such as Germany and Switzerland, had adopted regimes with a monetarist lineage well before 1970. These precursors had arguably been influenced by Austrian economists such as Friedrich von Hayek (ibid.). However, clouds on the Keynesian horizon became increasingly visible during the 1970s. At this time, inflation became the elephant in the room of economists and policy makers. Goodfriend (1997, p. 50) analysed the decline of Keynesian ideas in the 1970s in terms of widening divisions within academia and questions that became more and more pressing, such as the link between central bank credibility and the management of expectations (Chapter 5). Attacks against Keynesian ideas flourished in the years before the sea change in orthodoxy (see next section) in the mid 1970s. Hence, Milton Friedman (1968) introduced the NAIRU (or 'natural' rate) that would later revolutionize monetary policy. Indeed monetarist economists, under the aegis of Friedman, gained prominence in the 1970s (Goodfriend, 2007). They argued that a short-run Phillips curve existed but, in the long run, its shape was vertical, meaning that there was no trade-off between unemployment and inflation. In the long run, only a single rate of unemployment was thus consistent with a stable inflation rate. Likewise, Phelps (1967) and Lucas (1973) improved the microfoundations of the Phillips curve, and discarded the long-term exploitable trade-off between unemployment and inflation.

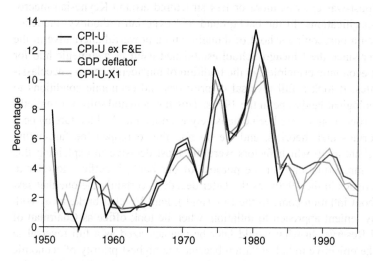

Figure 2.2 Inflation in the United States, 1951–1994 (source: DeLong, 1995).

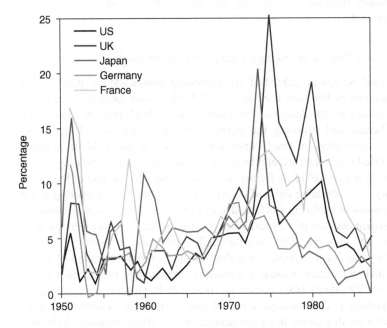

Figure 2.3 Inflation in the G-5, 1950–1994 (source: DeLong, 1995).

The sea change in orthodoxy after 1975: hints of a paradigm shift

By 1974, the acceleration of inflation in the developed world, along with the failures of conventional Keynesian policies, was conducive to a paradigm shift that was nevertheless gradual throughout the second part of the 1970s.

Callaghan, British Prime Minister (September 1976)

A noteworthy speech was given by British Prime Minister James Callaghan in September 1976. Below is an excerpt that sums up an ideological transformation, which was all the more surprising as Callaghan was leader of the Labour Party at the time:

> We used to think that you could just spend your way out of a recession and increase employment by cutting taxes and boosting Government spending. I tell you, in all candour, that that option no longer exists, and that insofar as it ever did exist, it only worked by injecting a bigger dose of inflation into the economy followed by higher levels of unemployment as the next step. That is the history of the past 20 years.

Without anticipating on our post-crisis analysis of the NMC in the second part of our book, we briefly venture into comparative historical territory, as the above words certainly resonate in a striking manner almost four decades after they were first uttered.

The 1976 Nobel Prize: a milestone for the economics profession?

In 2007, Paul Krugman published an interesting non-academic paper about Milton Friedman in the *New York Review of Books*. After cautiously using the religious metaphor to describe Friedman's methodical role in destroying Keynes's heresy and restoring the purity of the Classical School, Krugman argued that, regardless of one's knowledge claims in the field of political economy, Friedman must certainly be given substantial credit for helping classical economics regain 'all of its former dominion' (ibid.) by the end of the twentieth century. This stunning twist of doctrinal fate did not happen overnight, for the long-drawn-out intellectual efforts deployed by the Chicago School throughout the post-war decades of Keynesianism (C. Taylor, 2011, p. 28) were particularly slow to translate into institutionally grounded orthodoxy. Unlike contemporary dissident schools struggling to find common ground (Lavoie, 2006a) in their fight against today's orthodoxy, monetarism never claimed any heterodox (or dissident) label during the post-war Keynesian reign (the neoclassical synthesis). The subsequent rise of monetarism was nevertheless spectacular. Although this theme has been debated on countless occasions in books, academic journals and conference papers throughout the world, it is worthwhile stressing, for the purpose of our demonstration, the role played by institutional and visibility-enhancing signs of recognition sent by the economics profession at the highest level of prestige and influence. In this respect, awarding the Sveriges Riksbank Prize in Economic Sciences in Memory of Alfred Nobel (sometimes mistakenly named the Nobel Prize in economics) to Friedman was far from neutral in reshaping the ideological and socio-professional forces of economic science in the international arena. Thence, with hindsight, 1976 was certainly a landmark year for the profession.

Monetarism: the 1980s

The acceptance of the Tinbergen rule

The essence of monetarism is best understood in terms of its macroeconomic policy formulation. In this respect, Tinbergen's approach, also known as the fixed target approach, deserves further examination.

First and foremost, the role of decision-making authorities is to define a set of mutually consistent objectives from which no departure is permitted. Second, once these objectives have been expressed in terms of numerical targets, the policy maker selects the most appropriate instruments to secure attainment. The Tinbergen rule can therefore be expressed as follows: policy makers need as many *independent* policy instruments as targets. This principle starkly departs from pre-1970s Keynesian orthodoxy, which had acknowledged the interdependence of policy objectives. Central banks seem to have retained Tinbergen's classification in the conduct of monetary policy, for the short-term interest rate is now used as the sole policy instrument to control inflation.

Monetarism: main message and legacy

The quantity theory of money in new clothes?

THE FILIATION BETWEEN MONETARISM AND THE QUANTITY THEORY

C. Taylor (2011, p. 29) traces back the origin of the monetarist experiment to a set of ideas that 'finally crystallised in the form of the quantity theory of money towards the end of the 19th century'. He explains how the idea of monetary control is couched in the famous Fisher equation of exchange (ibid.). For the purpose of our argumentation, let us note that the quantity theory is nothing short of the monetary pillar of classical economics, whose successful reversal has opened new doors for the understanding of credit money and monetary macroeconomics.

MONETARISM: WHAT'S IN A NAME?

Meyer (2001) provided a threefold description of the essential features of monetarism. From the perspective of the history of economic thought, it is 'the reincarnation of classical macroeconomics, with its focus on the long run properties of the economy as opposed to short-run dynamics' (ibid.). Meyer also insists on neutrality and the filiation with the quantity theory of money. Further, monetarism is a rule-based approach to monetary policy that is sceptical of its short-term effects: 'given the widespread commitment to price stability, monetarists believe that they should give appropriate attention to money growth in the conduct of monetary policy' (ibid.). In an informative account of British monetary policy in the 1980s, Pepper and Oliver (2001, p. xvii) cogently distinguish between genuine, political and pragmatic monetarism. The difference between the first two types lies in the degree of conviction held by central bankers, as to whether money supply should be strictly controlled on theoretical grounds or merely targeted (through public announcements), in order to anchor expectations and stabilize the price level. Finally, the pragmatic approach questions monetarism's empirical validity (without, however, rejecting its primary postulates).

Principles having outlived the monetarist experiment

Tinbergen would certainly have agreed that the monetarist experiment was inconclusive, as it consistently failed to reach its publicly stated numerical targets. However, other commentators are much more severe, as they go as far as characterizing the monetarist experiment as a disaster in macroeconomic terms.[4] Strong and definitive evidence might now exist against monetarism, that is, the undesirable nature of strict money growth targets in the light of the poor operating procedures for controlling M1 money growth.

On the ideological front, the assessment is far more complex. We adopt the thought-provoking view that monetarism, in spite of its undeniable theoretical demise, has paradoxically won, against all odds, the ideological battle in the early twenty-first century. Although the irremediable weaknesses of monetarism account for its retreat from policy practices as early as the 1980s, this policy setback was certainly not the end of the ideological game. In the aftermath of monetarism's decline, policy makers had to fill an immense doctrinal void, and did so quite brilliantly with the emergence of the New Monetary Consensus (NMC), whose post-crisis assessment is the justification for the present book. However, the crucial point is that the transition could only be ensured by 'key elements of monetarist thinking that survived to influence policymaking in the last decade of the century' (C. Taylor, 2011, p. 47).

The monetarist legacy is enshrined in the following principles (ibid., p. 48):

• Rules rather than discretion in the conduct of policy.
• No commitments to full employment (or even any output targeting).
• Nominal targets are preferred (money growth, CPI growth rate etc....).
• The self-regulation argument (i.e. self-stabilizing effects of the market).
• Rational expectations as an overarching theoretical framework.

Taylor (ibid.) is also right to point out that these are well-known neoclassical precepts, monetarism being only a subset of neoclassical theory.

Paving the way for the NMC

New Zealand: the motherland of the NMC?

New Zealand is the country that pioneered inflation targeting in the late 1980s. It comes as no surprise that it was later labelled the mother of all inflation targeters (Schmidt-Hebel, 2010, p. 59).

On Figure 2.4, it is uneasy to conclude whether New Zealand has unambiguously anticipated international trends by giving the impetus, or rapidly converged towards OECD average inflation rates in the 1990s. By all means, it appears that New Zealand initiated a steady downward trend slightly before other industrialized countries (without implying causation). Importantly enough, before its conversion to inflation targeting, inflation in New Zealand was a more pronounced ill than in most OECD countries (Orphanides, 2010a, p. 15), with alarming two-digit rates in the mid 1980s and a peak at 16 per cent in 1985. The disinflationary trends occurred at a faster pace than average between 1990 and 1992, the ultimate victory other inflation being confirmed afterwards. Brash (1999, p. 36) explains the poor performance of the RBNZ prior to the shift to inflation targeting by the multiplicity of goals pursued by the central bank. The effectiveness of monetary policy was also hampered by the lack of operational

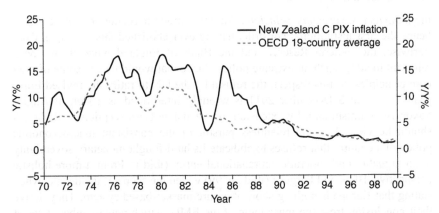

Figure 2.4 Inflation rates in New Zealand and selected OECD countries (source: Brash, 2000).

independence of the central bank, whose role was circumscribed to a mere advisory body to the minister of finance (Orphanides, 2010a, p. 15).

About the performance of New Zealand ten years after the beginning of inflation targeting, Brash (2000) wrote that the country had not driven his inflation rate markedly below that of other developed countries, but that it had successfully joined the mainstream of low-inflation countries. Although Brash conceded that, in terms of unemployment, the cost of bringing inflation down to 15+ per cent in the mid 1980s to the 0–2 per cent range in 1991 was substantial, he praises the economic performance of his country, once it started functioning smoothly under an IT regime. Between 1991 and 1997, New Zealand enjoyed a real GDP growth rate of 3.5 per cent; it slightly outperformed the United States (in fractional terms), and outpaced Japan and continental Europe (ibid.).

1992 and the Maastricht treaty: the new institutional apparatus

The ratification in 1992 of the Maastricht treaty laid out a blueprint for the European Monetary Union (C. Taylor, 2011, p. 50), and constitutes another institutional landmark in twentieth-century economic policy. The resulting institutional framework was an unprecedented architecture in the history of capitalism and monetary policy. Taylor does not refer explicitly to the New Monetary Consensus in his book, but instead to the 1990s synthesis (ibid., p. 50).[5] After listing its essential principles, Taylor (ibid., p. 53) goes as far as stating that the Maastricht treaty is the only document wherein these principles were ever unambiguously embodied. In their article on inflation targeting in the *Journal of Economic Perspectives*, Bernanke and Mishkin (1997, p. 98) mention the Maastricht treaty and its price stability mandate as the primary objective of the European Union. Further, Bliek and Parguez (2006, p. 98) have carefully examined the self-imposed constraints of the Eurozone through the lenses of monetary circuit theory. Within the latter framework, the modern analysis of the State stems from the *monetary sovereignty principle*. Amongst modern economies, the EMU is hence the first institutional construct having ever abolished this principle. Contrariwise, the Federal Reserve and the Bank of England have always been reluctant to adopt such an extreme policy stance that would negate some of their core principles. In this respect, the refusal by the UK to ratify the revised European Treaty on 8 December 2011 is wrongly interpreted as a sign of Anglo-Saxon isolationism and, by extension, of ostensible Euro-scepticism. Rather, it should be viewed as the relentless pursuit of the consistent macroeconomic policy of a country that refuses to abdicate its hard-fought monetary sovereignty to an arguably undemocratic supranational entity (ibid.).[6] From a more holistic perspective, Bliek and Parguez (ibid., p. 99) widen the scope of the debate, when stating that Europe is nothing short of a pure market-based system. They derive their conclusion from the inner logic of the EMU, which puts member states at par with private banks as far as their endogenous refinancing is concerned. The crucial difference with previous regimes is that the central bank does not intervene at all in this process, although this is a sine qua non for the coherence of the monetary circuit. Henceforth, Eurozone countries borrow the totality of the funds they require on sovereign bond markets to which they pledge allegiance through the pervasive supervision of a handful of rating agencies that unilaterally determine their borrowing conditions.

The implicit triumph of supply-side economics

Supply-side economics gained a wider audience in the aftermath of the monetary chaos of the 1970s. Its proponents literally left money and monetary policy aside. Instead, they focused on real factors that assumed to explain business cycles. The latter real factors included productivity, fiscal policy and international terms-of-trade shocks (Goodfriend, 2007, p. 59). The emphasis on real factors is reminiscent of the neutrality of money that was the landmark of monetarism and, by extension, of neoclassical economics. Likewise, Bliek and Parguez (2006, p. 99) explain that the mission of the European Central Bank since its creation, has been inspired by the new consensus emphasizing so-called supply factors, such as labour productivity, demographic patterns and the accumulation of capital (with saving assumed to determined investment). Parguez hammers this point home by stating the dual theory upon which the new consensus rests: demand shocks (wage increases, budget deficits) affect the economy in the short run, but in the long run, only supply-side factors matter (ibid., p. 100). Lavoie (2004, 2006b) introduces a fourth equation in the three-equation model of the NMC, so as to show that the natural rate of growth is determined by supply-side factors only. Another similar pre-GFC analysis is made by Arestis and Sawyer (2005, p. 17, emphasis added), who stresses the 'separation of real and monetary factors, namely, the assignment of monetary policy to the nominal side of the economy, and specifically to inflation, and *supply-side policies to address the real side of the economy*'. If monetary policy is solely concerned with nominal magnitudes, it is precisely because it does not affect real factors. Put differently, the core assumption of supply-side economics is money neutrality. As Goodhart (2005a, p. 7) notes, the essential contribution of central bankers to the economy is to provide a context of price and financial stability. The link between supply-side policies, price stability and inflation expectations is stressed by Cagliarini *et al.* (2010), who argue that monetary policy can help foster supply-side macroeconomic policies along with a stable low-inflation environment, thereby enabling the increased visibility of relative price signals for economic actors. This macro-stabilization is always achieved by means of anchoring inflation expectations (ibid.).

Yet, the verdict on monetary policy of the last decade is dazzlingly dichotomous. Whereas price stability can be seen as the ultimate triumph of monetary policy since the early 1990s, it can be argued that the financial stability objective, already seriously challenged by the recurring financial crises observed worldwide since the 1980s, has disintegrated in the chain of cataclysmic events experienced during the GFC. Pre-crisis mainstream analysis had certainly overlooked the possibility that excessive private demand in the USA, fuelled by sky-rocketing household debt, overwhelming financialization trends and the frenzy securitization of subprime mortgages, could possibly create the conditions of unsustainable demand (both domestically in the US and internationally through global macroeconomic imbalances). The breaking point would mark the beginning of the biggest recession since the Great Depression (see Table 2.1) with 8.8 million jobs lost and \$19.2 trillion lost household wealth (2011).[7]

Ironically, in spite of unprecedented growth rates observed worldwide in the years preceding the GFC, the reigning supply-side economists had ignored the warnings of their glorious predecessors (Say, 1971, p. 139):

> The encouragement of mere consumption is no benefit to commerce; for the difficulty lies in supplying the means, not in stimulating the desire of consumption; and we have seen that production alone furnishes those means. Thus, it is the aim of good government to stimulate production, of bad government to encourage consumption.

Indeed, the extensive deregulation of the US credit market, prior to the crisis, fuelled household debt that might appear, with hindsight, as an ill-advised attempt to stimulate US consumption.

Table 2.1 Magnitude of world recessions since 1974

Recession	% fall from pre-recession peak (expressed in real GDP at the trough of the recession)
1974	−3.2
1980	−2.2
1981–1982	−2.9
1990–1991	−1.3
2007–2009	−5.1

Sources: Bureau of Economic Analysis, Bureau of Labor Statistics, Federal Reserve.

Phrasing the theme of the book

A detailed historical account of monetary policy in the last decades of the twentieth century was not the declared purpose of this chapter, as this topic has been
extensively dealt with by mainstream and heterodox scholars alike. It nevertheless laid fore the ambition of this book, which is to comprehend, in a post-crisis
perspective, the nature of the New Monetary Consensus, defined as a moment in
History, after orthodox Keynesianism in the 1950s and 1960s, the inflationary
chaos of the 1970s viewed as a transitional period of decline for Keynesianism,
followed by the triumph of monetarism and neoclassical ideology in the early
1980s. The genesis of the NMC (sometimes termed 'new consensus macroeconomics' or '1990s Synthesis') was apprehended through the lenses of the
pioneering experiment in New Zealand and the set-up of a new institutional
apparatus by the Maastricht treaty.

The next chapters will be devoted to further the analysis of the New Monetary
Consensus. Although the transforming power of the GFC lies in the background
of our ongoing reflection, our implicit objective, at this early stage, is to cast
light on its pre-crisis defining features, albeit from a novel burgeoning post-crisis
perspective. It will also be argued that the implicit aim of the NMC was to
provide a form of stability (albeit not in the financial sphere) to the capitalist
system, and to ensure the ideological success of supply-side economics, in spite
of evident neo-Keynesian ramifications (Woodford, 2003).[8] The impressive track
of record high growth rates, low inflation rates and tamed business cycles, of
inflation-targeting regimes in the 1990s, up until the outbreak of the GFC, gave
economists a false sense of security. Bernanke (2004a) and Lucas (2003) proclaimed the Great Moderation and the end of depression economics. A similar
conclusion was reached by Chari and Kehoe (2006) in a paper entitled 'Modern
Macroeconomics in Practice: How Theory Is Shaping Policy', published in the
Journal of Economic Perspectives:

> Over the last three decades, macroeconomic theory and the practice of
> macroeconomics by economists have changed significantly *for the better*.
> Macroeconomics is now firmly grounded in the principles of economic
> theory. These advances have not been restricted to the ivory tower. Over the
> last several decades, the United States and other countries have undertaken
> a variety of policy changes that are precisely what macroeconomic theory of
> the last 30 years suggests.
>
> (ibid., p. 3, emphasis added)

Unfortunately, macroeconomists were ill-prepared for the unprecedented events
that unfolded a year after Chari and Kehoe's article. With hindsight, hubris probably paved the way for the GFC,[9] whose consequences on this wide-ranging
framework will be examined in Part II.

3 A simple macroeconomic model of the NMC

Introduction

In the course of policy implementation, central banks might be tempted to follow mechanical rules, because the latter make it possible to observe monetary policy actions more accurately. The rules versus discretion dichotomy is certainly not a recent one, as nineteenth-century controversies can be meaningfully analyzed through the lenses of this recurrent debate in the History of economic thought (Asso and Leeson, 2012, p. 7).

A simplified monetary policy rule can also serve as an introduction to the NMC. Building on Arestis and Sawyer, and also Lavoie, a simple macroeconomic model with three equations is presented; we start with the aggregate demand and inflation equations (akin to the well-known IS and LM curves of the neoclassical synthesis). The third equation is described as an interest rate rule that translates into the Taylor rule (McCallum, 2001), which is discussed in more detail in Chapter 7.

Rules versus discretion: a recurring debate in monetary economics

The 1970s: a shift from discretion to rule-based policy making?

Rules versus discretion: a preliminary assessment

Monetary economics has been the recurring stage for a long drawn-out debate about the best way to conduct policy. In Chapter 2, we characterized the policies of the 1950s and 1960s that were systematically non-compliant with the Tinbergen rule, while seemingly successful at the same time, as unemployment levels were indeed kept quite low throughout this period. These stop–go policies, however, were deliberately expansionary and guided by short-term considerations. The adoption of the Tinbergen principle in the 1970s brought forward the idea that the long-term structural (and potentially inflationary) consequences of discretionary policies had previously been neglected in the maze of interdependent policy objectives. This complacency and inordinate amount of attention given to short-term objectives were conducive to subsequent disorders. In the wake of unsustainable inflationary pressures, monetarists started to vigorously advocate a money supply growth rule *à la* Friedman, whose institutional legitimacy was endorsed after 1979 in the UK. The shift from discretion to rule-based policy making was one from the short-termism that prevailed in the 1960s to the slow recognition that the purpose of monetary policy was primarily to anchor inflation expectations in the long run (preferably through a rule-based approach). This redefinition of monetary policy entailed renewed concerns about the role of transparency (Chapter 4) and credibility (Chapter 5) in central banking. One landmark in academia was the publication of a paper by Barro and Gordon (1983), who developed a model based on rational expectations and money neutrality, in order to prove the inflationary bias inherent in discretionary policies. Barro and Gordon's paper showed how monetary policy was impotent, when used in an activist countercyclical fashion. What is more, discretionary policies entail higher money growth rates than what would be consistent with the economy's long-term growth trajectory, which is determined by real factors, as in the real business cycle (RBC) approach (Pilkington, 2011a). The Barro and Gordon paper did not, however, put an end to this long-standing controversy. Proponents of discretionary policies have continued to argue that the uncertainty surrounding the macro-environment prevents decision makers from anticipating external shocks to the economy, let alone from foreseeing structural change (such as labour market evolutions, financial innovation or unexpected regulatory reforms, often contingent on the political climate). This situation of radical uncertainty (Davidson, 1986) leaves policy makers with no choice, but to try to do the right thing, not necessarily for political gain (as repeatedly argued by critics of activist countercyclical policies), but to design the most suitable policy response in the face of changing and unforeseen circumstances.

A misleading debate?

Bernanke and Mishkin (1997, p. 104) have criticized the dichotomous framing of these recurring debates. For these authors, the two polar strategies, when plainly stated, spur major confusion on what monetary policy is about: 'the traditional dichotomy of monetary policies into rules and discretion is itself misleading'. Mishkin and Bernanke therefore characterize the inflation targeting regimes of the 1990s in a subtle way in terms of a framework for constrained discretion. Woodford (2010, p. 24) argues that the long-standing rules-versus-discretion debate briefly evoked in the introduction of this chapter stems from two seemingly antithetical ideals of monetary policy. The first one pertains to the quest for a monetary standard, tantamount to securing an effective institutional arrangement that guarantees the stability of the monetary unit of account (Keynes, 1930a). The second one amounts to the natural aspiration of monetary authorities to engage in stabilization macro-policies, to mitigate the adverse effects of exogenous shocks affecting the real economy. Woodford (2010) goes as far as stating that the seemingly irreconcilable nature of these two ideals, one merely consisting of a denial of the other, rests on a misconception. Woodford (ibid.) sketches out an audacious synthesis, by arguing that a well-functioning monetary standard facilitates the management and anchoring of expectations, thereby providing more scope for effective short-run stabilization macro-economic policies.

A new framework for 'constrained discretion' in the 1990s

Inflation targeting is discussed in more detail in Chapter 8. At this introductory stage, it suffices to delineate its epistemological dimension as a new framework for constrained discretion, as in Bernanke and Mishkin's seminal paper. The two authors rightly reject the idea that inflation targeting comes down to a rigid policy rule *à la* Friedman. Although the primacy of price stability is reaffirmed (Bernanke and Mishkin, 1977, p. 104), the existence of other legitimate (albeit secondary) goals cannot be discarded. The degree to which these alternative goals such as output, employment, exchange rates and other variables besides inflation (ibid., p. 105), may come in the picture cannot be unequivocally couched in a monetary policy rule. Bernanke and Mishkin curtail the criticism directed towards inflation targeting (notably the loss of flexibility incurred by ironclad rules). They assert that '[inflation targeting] does not qualify as a policy rule in that it does not provide simple and mechanical operational instructions to the central bank' (ibid.). They emphasize the role of the structural and judge-mental models (ibid., see also Chapter 16) and all relevant information affecting policy choices. Thanks to this clever oxymoron, inflation targeting performs the discursive and practical feat of constraining policy in a long- or medium-term low inflation target, while leaving 'considerable scope to respond to current unemployment conditions, exchange rates and other short-run developments' (ibid., p. 116).

Two simple macroeconomic models of the NMC

The merits of simplicity in macroeconomic theory

We have briefly touched on the New Monetary Consensus so far. Although we mentioned in Chapter 2 the existence of a new synthesis in the 1990s (C. Taylor, 2011) and discussed in the previous section the nature of inflation-targeting regimes in terms of the rules versus discretion dichotomy, no overarching consen-sus has yet been singled out. The NMC is often presented, for introductory pur-poses, as a set of equations incorporating more or less sophisticated policy rules. Following major post-Keynesian economists (Lavoie, 2004; Arestis, 2007) and mainstream authors of textbooks (Carlin and Soskice, 2006)[1] and academic papers (Carlin and Soskice, 2005) faithful to the NMC, we retain this didactic device here-after without understating the existence of a tension within the confines of the infla-tion targeting literature concerning both its constrained and discretionary scope. We do not underestimate the idiosyncratic features or the complexity of policies under the NMC. Rather, we adopt the approach embraced by Keynes (1936), Krugman (2000), Romer (2000) and Woodford (2003) praising the merits of simplicity in macroeconomic theory. We present two simple models of the NMC suited respectively to closed-economy and open-economy analysis

The NMC model with three equations

The model

The consensus three-equation model can be attributed to McCallum (2005) following Meyer (2001). Other authors include Arestis and Sawyer (2005), Goodhart (2005a) and Lavoie (2004). The three equations stand respectively for the IS-type curve, a dynamic Phillips curve and a monetary policy rule. The model is micro-founded and derived from individual optimizing behaviour with neo-Keynesian features. Price and wage stickiness come in the picture via the control of the real interest rate through the nominal rate. The control over the interest rate thus affects aggregate spending and the level of output.

SUMMARY OF THE THREE EQUATIONS

The salient features of the three-equation model have been described by Laidler, who argues that it posits the existence of an 'as if' direct relationship between the interest rate and aggregate demand (2006, p. 1). The methodology is reminiscent of the one put forward by Friedman (1953) known as scientific instrumentalism. By no means can it be argued that this relationship must be realistic. The three-equation model is supplemented by an expectations augmented Phillips curve with assumed causation running from aggregate demand to inflation. The three-equation model also requires a Taylor rule (Chapter 7), which is nothing less than a policy rule linking the interest-rate setting behaviour to the inflation rate. For Laidler, the aggregate demand function is excessively simplified, so as to suit the purpose of the model. Let us review briefly the three equations below:

Equation (3.1): dynamics of changes in the output gap

$$Y_t^g = a_0 + a_1 Y_{t-1}^g + a_2 E_t (Y_{t+1}^g) + a_3 [R_t - E_t(p_{t+1})] + a_4 (rer)_t + s_1 \qquad (3.1)$$

Y_t^g: (domestic) output gap at time t
R_t: nominal interest rate
a_0, a_1, a_2, a_3, a_4: regression coefficients
s_1: stochastic shock
p_t: rate of inflation at time t
E_t: expectations held at time t
$(rer)_t$: real exchange rate at time t (in the open-economy framework)

The first equation is an aggregate demand function reminiscent of the IS curve that populated the neoclassical synthesis; it is supplemented by inter-temporal maximization of sophisticated utility functions reinforcing the micro-foundations of the traditional IS curve. The current output gap is determined by past and expected future output gaps, while the aggregate demand function is negatively correlated to the real interest rate with forward-looking expectations. The impact of the real exchange rate is an additional constraint integrated ahead of open-economy analysis.

Equation (3.2): dynamics of change in the inflation rate

$$P_t = b_1 Y_t^g + b_2 P_{t-1} + b_3 E_t(p_{t+1}) + b_4 [E_t(p_{wt+1}) - E_t \Delta(er)_t] + s_2 \tag{3.2}$$

Y_t^g: (domestic) output gap at time t
b_1, b_2, b_3, b_4: regression coefficients
s_2: stochastic shock
p_t: domestic rate of inflation at time t
$p^w{}_t$: world rate of inflation at time t (in the open-economy framework)
E_t: expectations held at time t
$(er)_t$: nominal exchange rate at time t (in the open-economy framework)

The second equation is a sort of dynamic (or inflation-augmented) Phillips curve, wherein inflation is determined by the current output gap (instead of the output level in the static version of the Phillips curve) as well as expected future inflation rates. World inflation and nominal exchange rates are additional constraints included ahead of open-economy analysis. This second equation is thus a good indication of the degree of commitment of the central bank to future price stability (Chapter 5).

Equation (3.3): interest rate policy rule (Taylor-like)

$$R_t = (1 - c_3)[RR* + E_t(p_{t+1}) + c_1 Y_{t-1}^g + c_2(p_{t-1} - p^T)] + c_3 R_{t-1} + s_3 \tag{3.3}$$

R_t: nominal interest rate
$RR*$: equilibrium real rate of interest consistent with zero output gap
Y_t^g: (domestic) output gap at time t
c_1, c_2, c_3: regression coefficients
s_3: stochastic shock
p_t: domestic rate of inflation at time t
p^T: inflation rate target
E_t: expectations held at time t

The interest-rate setting procedure in the NMC is presented in more detail in Chapter 7. It suffices to say that the third equation is akin to a standard Taylor rule with current output gap and the deviation of the actual inflation rate from the inflation target (Setterfield, 2004, p. 37). The reason why Equation (3.3) is a flagship of the NMC is that it merely replaces the old LM curve. Money aggregates are replaced by the interest rate as the main control variable of the central bank. As King (2002) argues, price stability has become the central

objective of central banks, thereby reducing the attention paid to the money
stock by central banks.

The elusive quest for a neutral interest rate in the NMC

The Wicksellian nature of the NMC is examined in Chapter 6. At this stage, let
us emphasize the role played by the equilibrium real rate of interest (or neutral
rate noted RR* in the three equations above). The definitions of the neutral rate
vary with the methods of calculating them. The neutral rate also varies with
macroeconomic conditions. Alan Greenspan (2004) said: 'You can tell whether
you're below or above, but until you're there, you are not quite sure you are
here.'

The transmission mechanism of the model

The NMC model is best understood by starting from a position of equilibrium
with inflation on target and no output gap that is an economy growing at its long-
term natural rate (C. Taylor, 2011, p. 68). Let us consider the following
scenarios:

THE ECONOMY SUFFERS A POSITIVE DEMAND SHOCK
(E.G. UNEXPECTED WAGE INCREASES OR SUDDEN BOOST IN
CONSUMER CONFIDENCE)

Aggregate demand rises above its long-term equilibrium level (output exceeds
its natural rate) leading to inflationary pressures on the economy (i.e. demand-
push inflation). The central bank decides to tighten its monetary policy by
increasing its short-term nominal interest (it simply follows a Taylor rule
inscribed in its reaction function). Provided that inflation expectations are neu-
tralized, the interest rate hike also raises the *real* interest rate, which brings back
aggregate demand to its desired (non-inflationary) level.

THE ECONOMY SUFFERS A NEGATIVE SHOCK

Although central banks have resorted to unconventional policies since
2007–2008, we describe hereafter the pre-crisis sequence in the NMC model.
We assume that aggregate demand is lowered under its long-term equilibrium
level (output lies below its natural rate, or, put differently, the output gap is positive). The central bank opts for a more accommodating monetary policy by lowering its interest rate. The same way the IS curve would have been shifted to the
right in the old IS/LM model, aggregate demand is here stimulated so that the
negative shock is cancelled out. This sequence is a classic example of fine-tuning
macroeconomic demand management using monetary policy. These two scenarios are deliberately simplified. It would be misleading to assume that the central
bank only responds to unanticipated shocks (whether positive or negative) in the

short term, and neglects medium- to long-term evolutions. ECB policy decisions can now be apprehended through its medium-term orientation, which has been thoroughly presented by the ECB on its website (2011). The medium-term orientation is flexibility enhancing, as it enables the central bank to respond adequately to a range of exogenous shocks. The price stability objective is the central one over the medium term; it therefore discards the soundness of short-term fine-tuning monetary policy. Developments in prices over a few weeks are irrelevant to the medium-term orientation of the ECB. Yet, concerns about output fluctuations can legitimately be taken into account by policy makers, without jeopardizing the price stability objective. The medium-orientation also stresses the existence of variable and uncertain time lags in monetary policy (ibid.).[2] This approach departs from previous statements issued by the ECB (Athey *et al.*, 2004, p. 54) regarding the optimal monetary policy response to external shocks. The nature and the shocks under scrutiny determine the decision-making process of the central bank that must determine whether the most appropriate policy response is a prompt (i.e. aggressive) or a gradual one. In fact, the desirability of short-term fine-tuning depends on the nature of the shocks affecting the economy and on the robustness of the in-built credibility mechanisms developed by the central bank (Chapter 5). Because the model is intrinsically micro-founded with economic agents displaying utility-maximizing behaviour and forward-looking rational expectations, a sudden change in policy regime can be damaging, if the central banks lacks credibility (Sargent, 1983). Therefore, the choice between a prompt and a gradual move is dependent on the celerity with which expectations of future inflation are adjusted downwards by individual agents, and is not simply a matter of fine-tuning policy. Moreover, anticipated adverse consequences of output volatility and rampant uncertainty in financial markets often require the adoption of a longer-term time horizon. This deliberate medium-term outlook undermines the mechanical nature of the two above-depicted scenarios to characterize the transmission mechanism. The latter point is central, as it shows that simplified NMC models are potentially misleading (and may impede our understanding of the essence of the NMC, viewed as a meta-approach to policy), if their inner mechanics are interpreted too narrowly in quasi-physical science terms.[3] Of course, this reflection echoes the analysis presented in the first section devoted to the rules versus discretion debate.

The NMC model with six equations: a critical post-crisis view

Arestis (2007, 2009) has elaborated a more realistic open-economy model with six equations. In the first three equations, we already anticipated on open-economy analysis, so the first three equations of the six-equation model are identical.

In Equation (3.1), the real exchange rate that is negatively correlated to total output through its effect on competitiveness and on the net trade position (X–M). This addition is reminiscent of the IS/LM model in an open economy (i.e. Mundell–Flemming model).

Equation (3.2) includes expected world inflation, as the differential depends on the nominal exchange rate that will influence the competitiveness of exports and the price of imports expressed in domestic currency.

Equation (3.3) is unchanged from the closed-economy model. However, this choice is objectionable in several respects. Some authors (Brender *et al.*, 2009) have shown that Taylor-rule fundamentals can be used as determinants of exchange rates, with feedback loop effects on the reaction function of the central bank. Hence, Clarida *et al.* (1999) assume that the central bank includes the difference between the exchange rate and the target exchange rate, defined by purchasing power parity in its monetary policy rule. If the inflation-augmented Phillips curve incorporates the nominal exchange rate, equation (3.3) can no longer ignore the effects of exchange-rate dynamics on the net trade position (and on the output gap in equation (3.2)). Equation (3.3), in the open-economy framework, can be criticized on the grounds of neutral rate indeterminacy, the latter variable being more elusive than in closed-economy analysis. In fact, the idea that purely real forces may suffice to determine a dynamic equilibrium consistent with a zero output gap, seems even less plausible in our globalized, interdependent and crisis-prone world wherein the interplay of monetary forces cannot be overstated. The exclusive reliance on real forces in the NMC is simply not warranted, notably in the light of the monetary turmoil caused by the infamous currency war of 2009–2011.[4]

Dollar exchange rates since January 2009

Index: January 2009 = 100

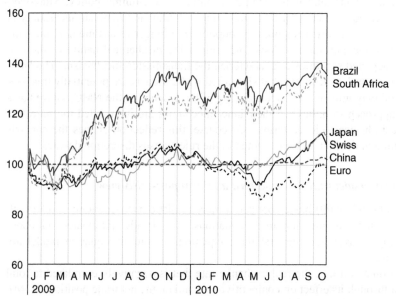

Figure 3.1 The currency war during the GFC (source: Federal Reserve).

Comment

The monetary forces unleashed since the outbreak of the GFC have been conducive to wide amplitudes in exchange rate movements, seemingly independent of
real factors.

The novelty of the open-economy model is in Equations (3.4) and (3.5).

$$(rer_t) = d_0 + d_1[[(R_t - E_t(p_{t+1})] - [(R_{wt}) - E(p_{wt+1})]] + d_2(CA)_t +$$
$$d_3 E(rer)_{t+1} + s_4$$
(3.4)

rer_t: real exchange rate at time t
d_0, d_1, d_2, d_3: regression coefficients
R_t: nominal interest rate
R_{wt}: world nominal interest rate
s_4: stochastic shock
p_t: domestic rate of inflation at time t
p_{wt}: world rate of inflation at time t (in the open-economy framework)
E_t: expectations held at time t
CA: current account of the balance of payments

Equation (3.4) is tantamount to a simplified theory of exchange rates, including
the traditional endogenous variables (interest-rate differential, current account
and exchange rate expectations) and exogenous variables (linked to supply-side
factors), used in standard exchange rate forecasting. Such deliberate simplifications in the light the complex and unpredictable exchange-rate dynamics
observed since 2007–2008 (Brender *et al.*, 2009) does not warrant the validity of
the open-economy model.

$$(CA)_t = e_0 + e_1(rer)_t + e_2 Y_t^g + e_3 Y_{wt}^g + s_5$$
(3.5)

CA: current account of the balance of payments at time t
Y_t^g: domestic output gap at time t
Y_{wt}^g: world output gap at time t
rer_t: real exchange rate at time t
e_0, e_1, e_2, e_3: regression coefficients
s_5: stochastic shock
E_t: expectations held at time t

Equation (3.5) puts the emphasis on the determinants of the current account
balance (that is, international trade factors), and is subject to the same criticism
as equation (3.4).

$$er_t = rer_t + P_{wt} - P_t$$
(3.6)

er_t: nominal exchange rate at time t
rer_t: real exchange rate at time t

Pw$_t$: world price level at time *t*
P$_t$: domestic price level at time *t*

Equation (3.6) is definitional in essence, and is hardly objectionable in its static form. A more dynamic framework remains needed to capture long-term exchange-rate dynamics. For instance, any comprehensive analysis of the euro crisis (Chapter 15) can hardly do away with the long-term evolution of the euro vis-à-vis the dollar.

Post-crisis assessment of the simplified model of the NMC

Strengths

Two transmission channels are acknowledged in the literature: aggregate demand shocks and inflation expectations. The simplified model is rigorous and robust to the Lucas critique. It is micro-founded and can be translated into game-theoretic terms (the economy is composed of two players: the central bank and the private sector).

Weaknesses

Notwithstanding the undeniable merits of the model, a few weaknesses must be noted. First and foremost, the role and nature of fiscal policy is neglected by the simplified model. There might be an implicit negative relationship between expansionary fiscal policy and the output gap. However, if increases in demand push the economy beyond full capacity output, fiscal policy necessarily becomes inflationary. Therefore, fiscal policy will not crowd out aggregate demand by higher interest rates, provided that the economy is below full-employment equilibrium. Unfortunately, the simplified model provides no indication regarding the unemployment threshold that makes fiscal policy acceptable or even desirable. In the case of fiscal policy, the impact on nominal output depends on the size of the fiscal policy multipliers. However, aggregate demand management only pertains to the short run; the long-run neoclassical equilibrium properties of the model explain that macroeconomic policy has no real effect on long-run (supply determined) equilibrium values. The simplified model of the NMC leaves no role to the public sector, which is problematic. Moreover, creditworthiness issues are not dealt with.

Conclusion

Simplified models of the NMC feature both strengths and weaknesses that we briefly reviewed. In spite of undeniable scientific qualities, the three-equation and six-equation models suffer from serious weaknesses all the more apparent in the light of the GFC. Indeed, massive bailout plans, fiscal stimulus and bank bankruptcy are hardly accounted for. However, these simplified models remain a satisfactory introductory description of monetary policy practices during pre-crisis fair-weather macroeconomic conditions.

4 Transparency
An essential feature of the NMC

> If you understood what I just said, you must not have heard me correctly.
> (Alan Greenspan, Chairman of the Federal Reserve (1987–2006))

Introduction

This chapter is devoted to the examination of the role played by transparency in the NMC and beyond. In the last two decades, the transparency of central banks has been greatly enhanced.[1] Kahn (2007, p. 25) acknowledges that the majority of central banks today provide regular reports on macroeconomic conditions, the stance of monetary policy, and the outlook for inflation and other key economic variables. Transparency is the first of the six core principles that define the NMC, according to Wray (2004, p. 8). For Dincer and Eichengreen (2007, p. 1), central bank transparency is the hallmark of modern central banking, as opposed to earlier historical periods. Hereafter, we tackle the definitional aspects, along with the study of the multidimensional nature of the term.

Defining central bank transparency: an uneasy task?

At the simplest level, central bank transparency may be defined as the modus operandi of the central bank enabling other economic agents to see what, how and when monetary policy actions are performed. As argued by Eijffinger and Geraats (2005, p. 2):

> Transparency of monetary policy can be defined as the extent to which central banks disclose information that is related to the policymaking process. It is a multifaceted concept that could pertain to any aspect of monetary policymaking ... transparency is qualitative concept that is hard to measure.

According to Orphanides (2010a, p. 20), transparency has replaced the opacity that once characterized monetary policy practices. For the European Central Bank, '[t]ransparency means that the central bank provides the general public and the markets with all relevant information on its strategy, assessments and policy decisions as well as its procedures in an open, clear and timely manner'.[2] Rogers (2010, p. 35) thinks that transparency is about explaining the transmission mechanism, the macroeconomic outlooks and the underlying risks and uncertainties related to policy; it is also about providing a clear picture thereof to the public. Further, Rogers (p. 32) argues that policy accountability and communications arrangements appear to be converging on an increasingly transparent model.

Information asymmetry

Information asymmetry is defined as the situation wherein some relevant information is known to some but not all parties involved. This concept is of utmost importance in order to capture the meaning of central bank transparency. As Geraats (2002, p. 1) argues, central bank transparency amounts to the absence of asymmetric information between monetary authorities and the public. In established frameworks, such as transaction-cost theory and neo-Keynesian economics, information asymmetry leads to non-efficient outcomes. In our examination of transparency in the NMC, the question therefore concerns the identity of the relevant parties under scrutiny.

Between policy makers and financial markets

This first pair is perhaps not the most instinctive pedagogical choice to explain asymmetric information in standard macro-theory. However the current global context easily explains the reversal in priorities. What is more, Jeanne (2011, p. 1) reminds us of the genesis of central banking, which is the outcome of the collusion between sovereigns and financial markets. Jeanne draws on a historical example, the financing of Napoleonic wars, and explains how bank note issuance funded the flow of expenditure of the Treasury at the time. Jeanne's subsequent depiction of the evolution of central banks shows how the latter institutions progressively undertook a more prominent macroeconomic role, primarily expressed in terms of inflation control, and, secondarily, in terms of output and employment objectives.[3] More recently, Tomljanovich (2007, p. 79) provides econometric estimates, to demonstrate that the quality of information released by central banks to the public has an impact on financial markets (their smooth functioning and their efficiency). Focusing on seven selected industrialized countries, he studies the effects of central banks' move towards more open disclosure in the 1990s on the predictability of national financial markets, in order to understand how the shift towards enhanced central bank transparency has influenced financial variables, rather than macroeconomic factors. He further argues that transparency is conducive to credibility, and helps channel clear and accurate information to financial markets (ibid.). Historically, the trend towards enhanced transparency perfectly coincides with the emergence of the NMC, endorsed by the principal central banks. The Bank of Canada, the Bank of Japan and the Bank of England became more and more transparent in the 1990s. The shift for the US Federal Reserve occurred in 1994 (ibid.). Tomljanovich (ibid.) nonetheless notes that the ECB constitutes a major exception.

Its preference for limited transparency is justified by internal cohesion and the fear of publicizing internal dissensions during ECB board meetings, which would weaken its credibility in the eyes of the public (Chapter 5).

Between central banks and the public

COMPLETE TRANSPARENCY WITH THE PUBLIC: A DIFFICULT CONCEPT

Transparency is about the central bank's communication vis-à-vis the public, in the broad sense. It is as much about the quality and the completeness of the information disclosed than the pedagogical skills displayed by the central bank. This conception is indeed shared by the ECB:

> [t]ransparency helps the public to understand the ECB's monetary policy. Better public understanding makes the policy more credible and effective. Transparency means that the ECB explains how it interprets its mandate and that it is forthcoming about its policy goals.[4]

Complete transparency between the central bank and the public therefore means that they both have access to the same information. However, this approach does not go without difficulties. Drawing on basic communication theory, the central bank is viewed as the sender of policy-relevant information, while the public is the receiver. Transparency therefore comes down to the full and accurate transmission of information between the central bank and the public. However, this argument says very little about the meaning of accuracy in central bank communication.

WHAT IS INFORMATION?

This simple and thought-provoking question conceals rather difficult issues for central banks. Indeed, what constitutes accurate information is not always clear. Because central banks process huge amounts of quantitative and qualitative information on a daily basis, flooding the public therewith could be considered as a transparent policy at first glance, but it is likely to cause much more confusion than clarity in the end. A good example could be the study of central bank websites. Can a non-expert reader comprehend the determinants, the nature and the prospects of monetary policy? Is academic expertise a pre-requisite for sound decision making? Can the average owner of, say, a small business make an informed decision without having to sift through the mass of information provided by the policy makers (ibid.)?

Transparency: a multidimensional concept

Transparency may apply to policy objectives, outlooks and strategies.

Geraats (2002) cogently distinguishes between five types of transparency:

1   Political transparency refers to openness about policy objectives and institutional arrangements.
2   Economic transparency focuses on the disclosure of information (data, models, forecasts...).
3   Procedural transparency refers to the central bank's decision-making process.
4   Policy transparency refers to the communication of the central bank (announcement, explanation of policy decisions and future policy inclinations).
5   Operational transparency concerns the implementation and the follow-up of monetary policy actions.

The rationale behind transparency

Influencing future inflation

In the three-equation model, the interest-rate policy rule includes an element of transparency (Arestis and Sawyer, 2005, p. 9), stressing the role of 'expected inflation'. Targeting and forecasting future inflation rates (Chapter 8) are thus a mark of transparency insofar as these targets and forecasts are made public by the central bank.

Although we take a critical view, the standard exposition of the macro-economic stability properties of a transparent central bank regime are summed up as follows:

> Transparency about monetary policy objectives, outlooks and strategies is necessary for effective communication with the markets, and effective communication is necessary for monetary policy to have stabilizing effects. Policy transparency makes it easier for observers to anticipate central bank actions and minimizes disruptions when policies change.
>
> (Dincer and Eichengreen, 2007, pp. 1–2)

Another property of transparency under the NMC is that it 'enhances the ability of policy makers to manage expectations, which is a key channel through which monetary policy affects outcomes' (ibid.).

The minutes of the Federal Open Market Committee feature an important statement on longer-run goals and monetary policy strategy, which is totally in line with the principles of the NMC:

> The Federal Open Market Committee (FOMC) is firmly committed to fulfilling its statutory mandate from the Congress promoting maximum employment, stable prices, and moderate long-term interest rates. The Committee seeks to explain its monetary policy decisions to the public *as clearly as possible*. Such clarity facilitates well-informed decision-making by households and business, reduces economic and financial uncertainty,

increases the effectiveness of monetary policy, and *enhances transparency and accountability*, which are essential in a democratic society.

(FOMC, 2012, emphasis added)[5]

Hence, if the central bank is committed to price stability, it will have a dissuasive influence on wage earners, who will refrain from demanding higher wages by fear of future costly and painful wage reductions (ibid.). This cognitive and rationalistic interpretation of the determinants of wage bargaining, in a credible and non-inflationary environment (Chapter 5), is in line with the view that considers central bankers as managers of expectations (Woodford, 2003, p. 15). If the central bank is more open, it shapes expectations more easily by providing the markets with its own views as to which fundamental forces condition its monetary policy stance (Blinder, 1998).

Forward guidance: transparency about the policy path

Forward-guidance policies are designed to influence the term-structure of interest rates. They rest on the formulation of a policy path defined as a sequence of current and expected future settings of the short-term interest rate that central bankers believe are consistent with achieving their goals (Kahn, 2007). Kahn believes that the clear formulation and the communication of a policy path is the next frontier in monetary policy transparency, as it enhances central bank accountability. The way this policy path is communicated to the public does, however, pose a problem. Should one retain the exposition of the favoured model(s) and forecasts used by the central bank? Should an objective function be communicated, or does a simple policy rule suffice? These questions take us back to the rules versus discretion debate. Another serious limitation is that monetary policy committees are generally composed of a number of members holding very heterogeneous views with regard to policy objectives, outlooks, models and forecasts. Therefore, reaching a consensus might prove extremely challenging (ibid.). Central banks endeavour to influence long-term interest rates through the management of market expectations concerning the future stance of monetary policy (ibid.). Likewise, Bernanke *et al.* (2004, p. 84) think that monetary policy works mainly by influencing the prices and yields of financial assets, which in turn affect future economic decisions. Therefore, transparency about future policy actions seems to matter as much as the analysis anchored in the present or expressed in terms of mere outlooks. This recent approach was first experimented by the Fed in 2003,[6] when Bernanke gave his support to forward-guidance policies:

> if the policy is one in which we essentially try to lower the whole path of long-term interest rates and we enforce that with a package of complementary actions that includes trying to manage expectations along the term structure and taking a series of other actions such as purchasing long-term bonds and other kinds of instruments, I think that's one of the things we ought to be doing.
>
> (FOMC transcript, 2003, pp. 45–46)

Clarity of economic forecasts: a quick comparison between Europe and the USA

Yet, the effectiveness of forward-guiding policies is dependent on the clarity of the message of the central bank. In the following extract (FOMC, January 2013, p. 9), forward-guidance policies are rather well described, although the FOMC's statement is consistent with a broad set of desired growth paths for the US economy:

> [t]he Committee decided to keep the target range for the federal funds rate at 0 to ¼ percent and currently anticipates that this exceptionally low range for the federal funds rate will be appropriate at least as long as the unemployment rate remains above 6½ percent, inflation between one and two years ahead is projected to be no more than a half percentage point above the Committee's 2 percent longer-run goal, and longer-term inflation expectations continue to be well anchored.

Although market participants do get a clear idea here that interest rates will remain close to the zero bound (Chapter 11) for a prolonged period, they do not have enough central bank information to form clear expectations based on a precise desired growth path (i.e. narrow target range for the US unemployment rate and inflation in, say, mid 2014 or early 2015). This deliberately vague projection, not so much for interest rates, but for key macroeconomic outcomes can be explained rather easily hereafter.

What if the Fed did not want to commit to too precise a projected growth path for fear of having its economic projections compared with future outcomes, thereby providing the market with a benchmark against which its effectiveness might be assessed?

This policy stance contrasts with the detailed forecasts for the Eurozone and the EU27, published by the European Commission (2013) in its Winter 2013 report. Perhaps, this is so because the European Commission is a governance body, which is distinct from the ECB; it does not directly aim at influencing market expectations. Yet, this assertion is not entirely warranted, as the European Commission is indeed a key actor of the complex economic governance of the European Union and, much less officially, of the euro area, which is still lacking a clear plan for future fiscal integration (Chapter 14).

Transparency: a mantra concealing a broader debate?

In Hinduism, a mantra is a sacred verbal formula repeated in prayer; it takes the form of an incantation, such as an invocation of a god, a magic spell or a syllable or portion of scripture containing mystical potentialities.[7] Friedman and Sims (2005) draw a parallel between Hinduism and the belief in the miraculous healing power of transparency. The reason for such a metaphor is the perception that the economics of monetary policy has become more of a religion than a science. In order to illustrate the tension between these two dimensions of monetary policy, let us refer to an article entitled 'Religion and Science' by Albert Einstein. For Einstein (1930, p. 1), it is primarily fear (of hunger, natural disasters, illnesses…) that evokes religious notions in primitive societies. For Einstein (ibid.), the organization of primitive societies have been conducive to the emergence of a '[religion of fear] stabilized by the formation of a special priestly caste which sets itself up as a mediator between the people and the beings they fear, and erects a hegemony on this basis'. An interesting parallel may be drawn with the non-expert receiver of central bank communication in modern times (for the sake of our argumentation, let us name this mysterious and fictitious character 'the public'). The focal point of the public's anxiety today concerns macroeconomic ills such as inflation, unemployment, recession or deflation. Under the NMC, central bankers have acquired tremendous economic power, simply because they have accepted to perform this social function of mediator between the (non-expert) public and the economic phenomena they fear. The hegemonic power of central bankers results from this situation. It is therefore legitimate to define central banking anew as a religion of fear with tremendous political implications, thereby echoing Einstein's description of the religious order in primitive societies:

> [i]n many cases a leader or ruler or a privileged class whose position rests on other factors combines priestly functions with its secular authority in order to make the latter more secure; or the political rulers and the priestly caste make common cause in their own interests.
>
> (ibid.)

Further, Friedman and Sims (2005) also explain that the asserted wonders of transparent central banks merely amount to a fallacious rhetorical device that assumes away the need for a thorough monetary reflection grounded in a historical setting. Central bank transparency is arguably about cutting corners in monetary policy, in order to conceal the deeper political, social, historical and institutional dimensions of the analysis. The most thought-provoking argument put forward by Friedman and Sims is that the discussion revolving around the claimed merits of transparency ought to be reinterpreted in the context of the debate surrounding the self-regulation argument and the desirability of unfettered private market behaviour (ibid.). Put differently, one may wonder whether the transparency phraseology is not part of the hidden agenda of market fundamentalists (Pilkington, 2012b). This question is of utmost importance in our critical evaluation of the NMC, as transparency constitutes one of its core principles (Wray, 2004, p. 8).

Non-optimal outcomes and government-induced communication failures

The critical evaluation of transparency has far-reaching implications for policy makers. If, as Friedman and Sims (2005) argue, the transparency mantra is nothing short of an avatar of the self-regulation argument (or the efficient market hypothesis), it is because non-optimal economic outcomes must be explained by misplaced government action (where the central bank is viewed as a government agency).[8] In this framework, non-optimal private decisions are the outcome of government-induced communication failures. This conception is in phase with the well-established NMC principle that views the central bank as a manager of expectations; the ability to influence expectations is facilitated by central bank transparency, and constitutes a key channel through which monetary policy affects macroeconomic outcomes (Dincer and Eichengreen, 2009). This approach therefore sheds light on the hidden agenda purported by proponents of the so-called transparency mantra. Drawing on Morris and Shin's (2005) contribution in the same issue, Friedman (Friedman and Sims, 2005) presents a blatant contradiction inherent in monetary policy. While central banks are trying to learn about the state of the economy by observing market prices set by private economic agents acting atomistically in a decentralized price system, these same private economic agents are continuously relying on the signals sent by monetary policy makers, in order to justify their decisions. The problem can be apprehended in game-theoretic terms, where the central bank voluntarily reduces the disclosure of policy-relevant information, in order to strengthen the information value (of price signals) observed in the market. The corresponding strategic interaction may be modelled with the appropriate tools available in game theory. However, what seems to matter here is that there exists a rationale for the central bank to be *less* transparent.[9] Moreover, Morris and Shin (2002, 2005) have argued that the diversity of sources of information used by economic agents (the media, price signals, government reports, etc.) are conducive to an overreaction to the signals sent by the central bank. An interesting parallel may be drawn between the ideas of Morris and Shin and the beauty contest described by Keynes in the *General Theory* (1936). Crowe (2010, p. 362) hammers this point home by arguing that whenever private sector agents try to 'second guess' themselves, high quality information held by private agents can be crowded out by public (i.e. central bank) information. Consequently, private sector forecasts might become more volatile rather than the other way round.

The macro-stabilizing effects of transparency: a critical view

In his remarks pronounced at the 56th Economic Conference at the Federal Reserve of Boston in October 2011, Ben Bernanke made the difficult assessment of the state of central banking theory. First commenting on its pre-crisis features, Bernanke stated:

> During the two decades preceding the crisis, central bankers achieved a substantial degree of consensus on the intellectual and institutional for monetary policy. The consensus policy framework was characterized by a strong commitment to medium-term price stability *and a high degree of transparency* about central banks' policy objectives and economic forecast.
>
> (Bernanke, 2011b, p. 2, emphasis added)

The emphasis on transparency is evident in this short description of accepted pre-crisis central banking doctrine. Bernanke (ibid.) adds that this approach has improved the scope of monetary policy for output and employment stabilization. He extrapolates, in a quantum leap forward, by forecasting that 'the ability of central banks to communicate with the public will remain the standard approach, as *its benefits in terms of macroeconomic stabilisation have been demonstrated*' (emphasis added). The underlying idea is that central bank transparency may have been the ideological coping stone of the Great Moderation.

Central bank transparency, the NMC and the Great Moderation

Let us adopt two lines of reasoning, in order to criticize the explanatory power of central bank transparency on the worldwide macroeconomic stability observed worldwide prior to the GFC. The first one is attributable to Friedman and Sims (2005), and refers to the lack of focus on real outcomes in the NMC.[10] The second critical inquiry is presented by Quiggin (2010), who goes as far as questioning the very terminological relevance of the Great Moderation.

The lack of focus on real outcomes under the NMC

Already briefly discussed previously, Morris and Shin's paper (2005) provides a tentative explanation for the erosion of forecasting accuracy in central banking research departments. However, far from relying on radical uncertainty or non-ergodicity concepts *à la* Davidson (1986), the authors remain in the confines of the mainstream, and put forward a game-theoretic interpretation of the strategic interaction between the central bank and the public. When the former is reluctant to disclose too much information about its thinking and deliberative process, the latter is necessarily compelled to augment the information value of the price signals originating in the market, which are made visible for central bankers. B. Friedman questions this narrow interpretation of central bank transparency, although the latter provides an unusual case for *less* transparency. He asks two questions of primary importance:

1   What are central banks actually transparent about?
2   Are non-disclosed objectives conducive to predictable real outcomes?

The answer to (1) is straightforward. Central banks try to anchor long-term expectations of inflation by trying to influence expectations of future macroeconomic conditions and policy. This is an established result in the NMC literature. However, what about alternative macroeconomic objectives? Friedman and Sims (2005) are critical of the central bank operating under the NMC that

> normally goes to great lengths to conceal any objectives other than inflation
> – for example, by rifting its public reports on monetary policy 'inflation
> reports',[11] as if inflation were the only aspect of the economy that mattered

for policy purposes, or by issuing public statements that typically make no mention of any tension, at any horizon, between the bank's inflation goal and its other economic aims.

In a nutshell, under the NMC, objectives that differ from the sacrosanct inflation are cleverly and skilfully evasive to the public. This leads to an acid comment made by Friedman and Sims (ibid.) about the

> [r]esulting 'transparency' [which] is like that of a polarised glass: one dimension of what the central bank is doing is fully transparent, or at least as transparent as one dimension of a multiobjective optimization problem can be when treated in isolation, while the other is fully opaque.

This critique is rather powerful. Transparency is perhaps just a misnomer after all: put differently, would central banks only let us *see* what they want us to *think*?

The Great Moderation: a (not so transparent) discursive device?

The Great Moderation is a term coined by Stock and Watson (2002). These authors argue that, between 1960 and 1983, the standard deviation of annual growth rates in real GDP (measuring the volatility of output) in the United States was 2.7 per cent. Between 1984 and 2001, it was only 1.6 per cent. According to Bernanke (2004b), the world economy has been experiencing a decline in macroeconomic volatility since the mid 1980s. Many academic sources have documented the reduced variability of quarterly growth in real output and quarterly inflation. Central banks have often been vocal (transparent?) about this alleged long-term evolution in macroeconomic aggregates. We do not aim to assess the thought-provoking claim that output volatility observed in the 1990s was not, after all, significantly lower than during the Keynesian heyday, the three post-war decades of sustained prosperity, with much higher average rates of economic growth recorded than during the Great Moderation, calling for a cautious statistical interpretation of what the standard deviation of output growth rate actually means.[12] This constitutes a fascinating econometric research agenda that lies beyond the scope of this book that deserves further inquiry.

Quiggin (2010, p. 13) goes as far as stating that the Great Moderation paved the way for a research programme embraced by a whole academic industry, whose participants 'displayed the disagreements for which economists are notorious'. He notes that commentators, trapped in their ivory tower, were enmeshed in highly technical discussions about alternative interpretations, causal hypotheses and projections for the future (ibid.), but utterly failed to address the most important question of all, that is, rather than the end of the business cycle, was not the end of the Great Moderation itself a more likely prospect (ibid.)?

The hubris displayed by central bankers under the Great Moderation is supported by Bernanke's strong, albeit admittedly temporary, 'assumption that monetary policymakers have an accurate understanding of the economy, and that

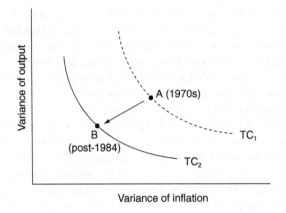

Figure 4.1 Monetary policy and the variability of output and inflation (source: Bernanke, 2004).

they choose policies to promote the best economic performance possible, given their economic objectives' (2004b). This echoes Goodfriend's claim (2007, p. 61) that the NMC makes actual output conform to potential output. To a certain extent, 'as an operational matter a central bank can make the economy conform to its underlying core', but 'monetary policy should not try to counter-act fluctuations in employment and output due to real business cycles' (ibid.).

Previously, we have evoked B. Friedman's assertion that central bank trans-parency carries a hidden agenda purported by market-fundamentalist economists, implicitly blaming non-optimal economic outcomes on government communica-tion failures, thereby emphasizing the sheer capabilities of private agents to coordinate their economic decisions in an optimal fashion, with the help of unfettered, self-regulating and efficient markets. Likewise, Quiggin (2010, p. 13) describes the Great Moderation as an ideological apparatus tantamount to a testi-mony of the success of market liberalism (i.e. free-market economics). Follow-ing the demise of Keynesian economics in the 1970s, the arguably exceptional period of stability between 1981 and 2007, marked by long expansions and short recessions (ibid., p. 12), overshadowed 'whatever inequities and inefficiencies involved in the process'. It felt like the theorists of the Great Moderation had managed to establish the success of market liberalism and the ineffectiveness of Keynesian polices (ibid.) in mainstream academic and policy circles. Quiggin (ibid., p. 12) is certainly right to interpret this affirmation with the greatest caution. The only two recessions observed during the Great Moderation, respec-tively in 1990–1991 and 2001, were not significant enough to warrant any trans-historical conclusion, and this fact should certainly have called for more humility on the part of macroeconomists: '[i]n the light of past experience of failed claims, it might seem premature to proclaim the end, or at least the taming, of the business cycle on the strength of two good cycles'.

However, it is a diametrically opposite stance that leading mainstream economists decided to adopt. In a widely acclaimed *New York Times* editorial, Paul Krugman (2009) referred to a paper entitled 'The State of Macro' (Blanchard, 2008) by IMF chief economist, who was overconfident that 'the state of macro [was] good' (ibid.), the battles of yesteryear being over, leading to a 'broad convergence of vision' (ibid.). Krugman (ibid.) also quoted Lucas stating that 'the central problem of depression-prevention has been solved (sic)'. Well, so much for the end of History (Fukuyama, 1992) in macroeconomic theory today![13]

In a special issue of 'On the Horizon', Pilkington (2012b) wrote a paper entitled 'Economics as a Polymorphic Discursive Construct: Heterodoxy and Pluralism'. He puts forward the novel idea that the convergence between language for specific purposes and economics may help us enhance pluralistic representations of economic reality, thereby fostering critical discourse, by analysing the nature and the purposes of the discursive devices used by economists. Yet, any discursive device that fails to coherently account for reality logically mutates into a terminological fallacy. One may wonder whether the Great Moderation constitutes a subtle (albeit erroneous) discursive device concealing an unspoken ideological agenda. This seems to be the line of reasoning adopted by Quiggin (2010, p. 24), who refers in his book to the standard Great Moderation story, implicitly acknowledging the discursive nature of his own interpretation.

When central bank transparency is not the priority

Transparency before monetarism

Transparency was not of paramount importance under the gold standard, whose demise paved the way for the spread of modern central banking (Dincer and Eichengreen, 2009, p. 5). Goodfriend (2007, p. 60) argues that central banks had little incentive to be transparent under the gold standard, as monetary policy merely consisted of maintaining a fixed currency price of gold. The chaotic decade that ensued was characterized by little transparency, mostly due to the somewhat embryonic policy reflection of central bankers in a world wherein currencies were delinked from gold: 'central banks remained secretive after the gold standard collapsed, in part out of habit and in part because they lacked a coherent monetary policy strategy within which they could communicate productively' (ibid.).

The secrets of the Fed

The Federal Reserve's Secrets of the Temple *(1987)*

As journalist Peter Fenn put it, '[a] basic tenet of a healthy democracy is open dialogue and transparency'.[14] This quotation sheds light on the intricate nature of power and knowledge within social structures. In this respect, the best seller, *The*

Secrets of the Temple (Greider, 1987), provides us with valuable insights into the opaque workings of the Federal Reserve. The title of the book suggests that transparency is, at best, a remote prospect for central banks, and, at worst, an impossible goal. A non-academic book should not be discarded in a sweeping statement, provided that it contains relevant elements that may be translated into a more academic discourse. Based on extensive interviews, which constitute an acknowledged form of scientific inquiry, under Paul Volcker's mandate with major stakeholders of the Federal Reserve, endowed with substantial insider knowledge, the book is a fertile ground for economists, political scientists and Historians alike.[15] The subtitle *How the Federal Reserve Runs the Country* is both a positive statement and a knowledge claim in the making, with tremendous potential implications for the understanding of our object of study. We cannot draw any definitive scientific conclusions from this valuable book, albeit written in a slightly populist prose, thereby undermining its academic force of persuasion. However, one may retain the author's innovative transdisciplinary outlook on central banking practices, a fruitful approach leading to valuable insights in a post-crisis perspective (Pilkington, 2011b).

The burning secrets of the Fed: unveiling the biggest bailout in US History

In this section, we venture into the very recent period, which should logically be dealt with in the second part of this book. However, because of the nature of the central theme under scrutiny in this chapter, that is, central bank transparency in the NMC, we have decided to introduce a discontinuity in our seemingly dia-chronic treatment of the NMC, in order to cast light on one of the best kept secrets of the Fed in American history: the bailout of the *haute finance* sector[16] in 2008–2009. The detailed narrative thereof remains uneasy, given the unofficial nature of the information disclosed by the Fed at the time of writing. However, these secrets, kept by the Fed during the GFC, put into perspective the perspicacious and foretelling interrogation of Friedman and Sims (2005) as to what central banks are transparent about (as opposed to what they are *not*). After the collapse of Lehman Brothers in September 2008, little was known until recently about the rescue of Morgan Stanley, a legendary Wall Street institution, whose bankruptcy could have precipitated the global economy into the abyss. It took Bloomberg almost three years to gather crucial information about this avoided debacle.

On Figure 4.2, line (1) represents Morgan Stanley's market capitalization between late 2007 and early 2010. Line (2) is the outstanding negative balance of Morgan Stanley's account at the Federal Reserve on any given day – which peaked at $107 billion on 29 September 2008. The skyrocketing line (3) represents Morgan Stanley's total debt to the Federal Reserve, expressed as a percentage of its market value. The ratio between Morgan Stanley's outstanding debt to the Fed, and its capitalization exceeded 750 per cent at the height of the crisis, which defies any prudential imagination.

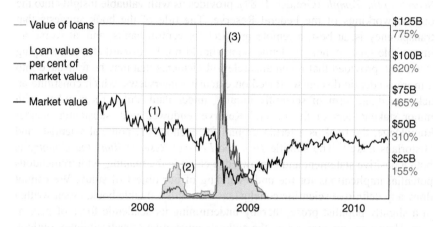

Figure 4.2 Morgan Stanley's debt to the Federal Reserve and capitalization during the GFC (source: 'Secret Fed loans gave banks $13 billion – undisclosed to Congress', reproduced with permission of Bloomberg, 2011, after some intense negotiations with Fed officials).

It is plausible that, in times of unprecedented financial turmoil such as in autumn 2008, the Federal Reserve decided not to disclose excessive information, in order to ward off the most pessimistic expectations of a total breakdown of the global financial system. In this respect, the Fed was consistent with its role of manager of expectations under the NMC. However, one cannot help thinking that the transparency mantra, in retrospect, was never really what it seemed. The vacuity of the term now strikes us as evident and even disturbing.

Widening the scope of central bank transparency

We continue hereafter to venture into a post-crisis world, so as to widen the scope of transparency in monetary and financial policies. The debate on transparency is too often circumscribed to the interest-rate setting procedure (Chapter 7), with central banks merely responding to changes in inflation outlooks. In September 2011, the IMF adopted a post-crisis supervisory role, and issued a set of new recommendations, in order to enhance transparency in monetary and financial policies. It is also worthwhile stressing the involvement of the Bank of International Settlements. The IMF has developed its assessment in a *Code of Good Practices on Transparency in Monetary and Financial Policies*.[17] The following principles were stated therein:

Clear roles, responsibilities and objectives

What is the central bank trying to achieve? B. Friedman (Friedman and Sims, 2005) was critical of the mantra-like mission of central banks, and compared the

NMC version to a polarized glass conducive to a rather ambiguous conception of transparency. Furthermore, the specification of roles, responsibilities and objectives (all of which must be written in law) hardly constitute novel features. The major breakthrough inscribed in the IMF report is the following sentence: 'the institutional relationship between monetary and fiscal policies should be clearly defined, as should any agency roles performed by the central bank on behalf of the government'. This statement should certainly not be underestimated. Abstracting from the international policy aspects (Part II), it is the most significant proposition formulated by the IMF[18] since 2007–2008, in order to fight off the GFC.

The innovations of the IMF Report (2011)

Transparency and the pedagogy of central banks

All five types of transparency made explicit by Geraats (2002) are reaffirmed by the IMF Factsheet (2013). The novel feature of policy transparency is the establishment and maintenance of public information services, explaining the issues to the public and the procedures put into place by the central bank, in order to monitor the latest developments in the financial system. The emphasis is as much on the disclosure of policy-related information as on the pedagogical skills required to reach the public:

> Financial agencies should issue periodic public reports on major developments in the financial system, report aggregate data on a timely and regular basis, make texts of regulation and directives readily available to the public, and publicly disclose special protections, such as deposit insurance schemes and consumer protection arrangements.
>
> (IMF, 2013)

After reading this recommendation, one question nevertheless comes to mind: when it comes to central bank pedagogy, how much is enough? This interrogation is particularly relevant at a time when financial literacy worldwide is the source of renewed concerns.

Transparency and the integrity of central banks

There is an ongoing reflection on the nature of ethical decision making and the need for new codes of conduct in the financial sector:

> The failure to understand and manage ethical risks played a significant role in the financial crisis and recession of 2008–2009 ... there is also a fine line between the ethics of using only financial incentives to gauge performance and the use of holistic measures that include ethics, *transparency*, and responsibility to stakeholders.
>
> (Ferrell *et al.*, 2011, p. i, emphasis added)

However, little is said in this debate about the ethics of central banking, which is too often equated to accountability (Chapter 5). In this respect, the IMF Factsheet (2013) states that: 'the central bank should provide assurances of the integrity of operations and the standards of conduct for its officials'.

Ethics and central banking: the example of the ECB

The ECB recently adopted a new ethics framework that came into force on 1 April 2010.[19] What proves utterly disappointing with this code of ethics is that it is *exclusively* devoted to the prevention of self-enrichment amongst central bankers. However, if we retain the definition of ethics as a philosophical discipline with a dual practical and normative dimension (Pilkington, 2011b), there is nothing that circumscribes the domain of ethics to mere self-enrichment. In fact, if we look at the mandate of the ECB,

> The main objective of the Eurosystem is to maintain price stability: safeguarding the value of the euro. We at the European Central Bank are committed to performing all central bank tasks entrusted to us effectively. In so doing, we strive for the highest level of integrity, competence, efficiency and *transparency*.[20]

> (emphasis added)

Whenever the EBC is not transparent, it negates its own stated mission. Furthermore, if transparency is an ill-defined concept, it is *also* the mission of the ECB (as well as its ethical duty) to put forward a precise definition of transparency, *which it does not* to date. The mission of the ECB therefore sets the bar extremely high. Both the positive and normative dimension of ethics seem to be violated whenever the ECB makes a monetary policy decision that is not *made explicit* to the fullest extent. What, then, is the meaning of an explicit decision? In a paper entitled 'The Process of Problem Finding', Pounds (1965, p. 3) states: 'the essential process by which important decisions are made may be carried out satisfactorily by simple explicit decision rules which are easy to teach and execute and easy to improve through analysis, simulation or experimentation'. Do monetary policy decisions made by the ECB follow an explicit monetary policy rule? Are these decisions easy to teach to the public? Does the decision-making process follow a learning curve based on analysis, simulation and experimentation? We shall let out our readers decide whether ECB decisions have complied with this definition since its inception. But if the answer proves negative, that is, if the ECB monetary policy is not rigorously structured around explicit decisions, the transparency mantra, by extension, would be considerably weakened.

The paradox of the IMF and its own lack of transparency during the GFC

Although the IMF is not a central bank, the fundamental role played by this institution in the world economy, as well as the post-crisis supervisory role it has endorsed since 2011, deserve further enquiry as far as its conception of transparency is concerned, notably as regards the financial policies it recommends and puts in place worldwide. In this respect, the following story is far from anecdotal. IMF senior economist Peter Doyle resigned in June 2012. In a letter dated 18 June, to Shakour Shaalan, dean of the executive board of the IMF, Doyle (2012) had these bitter words: '[a]fter twenty years of service, I am ashamed to have had any association with the Fund at all'. Doyle evokes the warnings the IMF had received about the crises of the Eurozone (Chapter 15) and the global financial system: 'substantive difficulties in these crises, as with others, were identified well in advance *but were suppressed here*' (Doyle, 2012, emphasis added). Doyle (ibid.) blames the lack of IMF response, which was 'a failing of the first order'. For Doyle, the lack of transparency of the IMF, and its refusal to disclose knowledge about the state of the economy, clearly amount to a negation of its mission to preserve global public interest. This failing has had enormous socio-economic consequences, such as the impoverishment of the Greek people, not to forget that the second world reserve currency is now on the brink of collapse (ibid.). If these controversial statements are further evidenced,[21] the IMF would soon be confronted with an ultimate paradox, that of a widely regarded institution that is vocal about the merits of transparency and integrity in its relations with the public (IMF, 2013).

Should central banks be transparent about the limitations of their knowledge?

This interrogation is in phase with our discussion of ethics and integrity in central banking practices. As Bernanke and Gertler (1995, p. 27) noted, there is little agreement on exactly how monetary policy exerts its influence on the real economy. We are therefore left with a set of unanswered questions. Should central bank communication hint at its own knowledge limitations, and should a clearly formulated conception of uncertainty be put forward as part of a renewed approach to transparency?

Conclusion: explaining the new priorities

The NMC never really put forward the idea that transparency was the ultimate goal of monetary policy. Transparency should not be viewed as an end in itself, because the essence of central banking cannot be equated to mere communication with the public (Issing, 2005). Yet, in the NMC, transparency is key to achieving the overriding goal of monetary policy, namely price stability (Chapter 6), by helping ensure accountability and efficiency. Thus, in a post-crisis scenario, the shifting meaning of transparency should not be overlooked. For instance, Eichengreen *et al.* (2011) are highly critical of the framework underpinning modern central banking in the run up to the crisis, namely the NMC. They therefore advocate the introduction of a new mandate for central banks featuring a well-defined financial stability objective. Price stability and inflation targeting are further discussed in Chapters 6 and 8. At this stage, it suffices to state that the NMC has been overwhelmingly concerned with objectives over-looking financial stability. As soon as the latter priority is reaffirmed and institu-tionalized in a post-crisis scenario, central banks will be confronted with a dilemma, insofar as legitimizing their actions will require enhanced pedagogy and improved communication:

> The public and its elected representatives may not be happy, for example, if the central bank curbs credit growth in the interest of financial stability, causing asset prices to fall. This makes it important for the central bank to clearly communicate its assessment of the risks and the rationale for its policy actions. It needs to explain how it seeks to balance the objectives of price stability, output stability, and financial stability.
>
> (ibid.)

5   Credibility in the NMC

Introduction: credibility in the 1970s, a lost paradise

Goodfriend (2007, p. 47) describes monetary policy as being in a state of disarray in 1970s. The high inflation rates recorded throughout that decade were a testimony of the prevailing pessimism of central banks, as to whether or not these institutions could effectively control inflation. Price stability was, at best, a remote prospect and, at worst, a lost paradise. So was credibility, both in the eyes of central bankers and the public. Blinder (2000, p. 1422) once stated that 'a central bank is credible if people believe it will do what it says'. Likewise, Gomme (2006) defined credibility as what 'concerns people's beliefs about what policymakers will do in the future'. These rather instinctive definitions conceal a set of rather different conceptions of credibility over the last few decades. We are interested hereafter in the historical evolution of the credibility mantra from the early 1970s up to the inception of the New Monetary Consensus in the 1990s.

Credibility under monetarism and beyond

The links between monetarism and credibility

Political monetarism and credibility

MONETARISM: A CREDIBLE ALTERNATIVE TO KEYNESIANISM?

According to Cagliarini et al. (2010, p. 17), the 1970s were crucial for proclaiming that monetary policy and inflation expectations did in fact matter. The postwar Keynesian policy arrangements had proven ineffective by the middle of the decade, but a credible alternative was yet to emerge. The strength of monetarism was to dress the demand for money in the clothes of the quantity theory of money (Friedman and Schwartz, 1963), and reassert its empirical validity. Chicago economists Milton Friedman, Karl Brunner and Allan Meltzer had been relentlessly trying the restore the aura of monetary policy since the early 1960s. Their strict obedience to the quantity theory of money translated into the theoretical proposition that long-term inflation was the outcome of excessive money growth (Goodfriend, 2007, p. 50). Hence, gaining the ideological ascendancy in mainstream policy circles was tantamount to winning the battle of credibility.[1] A decisive characteristic of the monetarist strategy was thus to operate 'a shift towards the "rule" end of the "rule-discretion" spectrum' (Cagliarini *et al.*, 2010, p. 18). This feature is emphasized by Cagliarini *et al.* (ibid.), who claim that there was a latent 'instinct for rule-like behaviour' in Europe that later paved the way for the abandonment of monetary policy sovereignty, with the ratification of the Maastricht treaty in 1992, an institutional framework designed to lock up and enjoy the benefits of the credibility acquired by the Deutsche Bundesbank in the second half of the twentieth century.

POLITICAL MONETARISM: THE ART OF MANAGING EXPECTATIONS

Peter Middleton was the Permanent Secretary of the UK Treasury from 1983 to 1991. Although Middleton was believed to be a fervent advocate of money supply targets throughout his career, Pepper and Oliver (2001, p. xviii) argue that he was in fact a political monetarist.[2] Political monetarism can be defined as the art of managing inflationary expectations by publishing a monetary target.[3] In this respect, the following quotation is most instructive, and could pertain to a post-GFC world:

> Economic policy is heavily constrained by the nature of the world we live in. Policy-makers have to be sensitive to changes in the environment and ready to adjust their policies as appropriate. With global financial markets *the main effort must be directed towards maintaining the credibility and reputation of macroeconomic policy so that financial markets behave in a way which generally supports it.* It is not possible to intervene in financial markets to produce directly the results the government wants. More generally, the power of governments to influence the economy is limited.
>
> (Middleton, 1989, p. 51, emphasis added)

The modernity of Middleton's argument pertains to the articulation between financial markets, credibility and the management of expectations.[4] Middleton (1989, pp. 48–49; Pepper and Oliver, 2001, p. 15) was adamant that what financial markets and the public at large *believe is happening* matters infinitely more than what actually *is* happening.

A political shift: the Medium-Term Financial Strategy (March 1980)

The adoption of the Medium-Term Financial Strategy (MTFS) in the UK by the new Conservative government led by Margaret Thatcher was a landmark in British politics. It is embodied in the White Paper published in March 1980, which reaffirmed the role of economic policy as a steady reduction in the rate of inflation between 1980 and 1984, through the preannouncement of target ranges of growth for monetary aggregates to ensure policy credibility. The favoured target was the public sector borrowing requirement. The MTFS consisted of a radical departure from previously held ideas about both the objective and the strategy of economic policy.[5] With the advent of monetarism, it symbolizes the demise of the British Keynesian policy regime in the twentieth century. The link between the MTFS and credibility was pinpointed by Middleton (1989, p. 49, emphasis added), who argued that 'the medium-term dimension to policy itself *added greatly to market credibility* and the chances of success'. The rise to power by Margaret Thatcher should be seen as a wide-ranging ideological transformation of the British landscape:

> I see that the last occasion on which you invited a British politician to address you was some four years ago, when your guest speaker was Margaret Thatcher ... Her theme on that occasion was – and I quote – 'the fundamental change in direction which I believe is about to occur' in the Western world in general and in the United Kingdom in particular. Two years later Margaret Thatcher was elected Prime Minister – achieving, incidentally, the most decisive election victory secured by any Party in Britain since the Socialist landslide of 1945.
>
> (Lawson, 1981)

'The fundamental change in direction,[6] which I believe is about to occur' is a prophetical sentence attributable to the future Iron Lady, paving the way for her rise to power. In 1981, Nigel Lawson (ibid.), made a case for monetarism. He proposed a full-fledged demolition of the policy conceptions that had prevailed throughout the Keynesian heyday. He thoroughly argued that post-war British policy had been based on the premises that full employment was the primary objective of the government, and that inflation was a phenomenon that should be dealt with separately (for instance, through the use of wage controls or voluntarily imposed price restrictions). Lawson (ibid.) clearly stated the idea that, although the favoured way of securing the full-employment objective during the 1950s and 1960s was an appropriate mix of fiscal and monetary policy, his critical assessment thereof was very negative. The acceptance of the failure of standard Keynesian remedies foreshadowed the abandonment of expansionary monetary and fiscal policies through the amplification of the monetarist credo and its well-known money supply targets, designed to restore the credibility of economic policy.

The emergence of the credibility literature

Forder (2000) traces back the emergence of the credibility literature to the shortcomings of the time-inconsistency framework put forward by Kydland and Prescott in 1977. One may also mention the work of Calvo (1978) linking surprise inflation to tax policy, thereby stressing the (time-inconsistent) incentives of governments to change tax rates unexpectedly. Within the confines of the NMC, the strategy of credibility is defined as a modus operandi adopted by the central bank, whereby the latter follows a preannounced model of behaviour. In a nutshell, the central bank says what it does and vice versa.[7] For Le Heron (2005), the credibility framework started as a synthesis between monetarism and new classical economics. The merit of Kydland and Prescott (1977, p. 473) is to have initiated a game-theoretic approach to monetary policy: 'economic planning is not a game against nature but, rather, a game against rational economic agents'. But the real starting point of the credibility literature is to be found in the works of Barro and Gordon (1983), with the emphasis on reputational equilibrium and the institutional anchoring of expectations. But the reputational equilibrium too, will come under attack in the 1990s, long after the end of the monetarist experiment and well into the NMC era, notably by Walsh (1995), who developed the idea of an optimal incentive contract within a principal–agent model. Walsh's ambition was to show that it was possible to eliminate all inflationary bias in monetary policy, thereby simultaneously ensuring credibility and flexibility (ibid., p. 153).

Has a lack of credibility irremediably tarnished monetarism?

A critical evaluation of the monetarist experiment was briefly presented in Chapter 2. We focus here on the assessment of the credibility deficit that monetarism has suffered. C. Taylor (2011, p. 39) explains that the sheer disillusion with monetarism was not circumscribed to the UK. Looking at the costs in terms of employment, the monetarist experiment can hardly be regarded as a success (ibid., p. 40, Table 3.1). For Goodfriend (2007, p. 52), the verdict is much more severe, as he deems the result of monetary policy in the 1980s literally disastrous. However, a few monetarist countries, such as West Germany, did manage to control inflation throughout the 1980s, but, even then, the targeting of monetary aggregates proved ineffective, if not irrelevant (ibid., p. 39). Generally speaking, monetarism failed, because it was not credible.[8] Inflation was sometimes under control, but its successful reduction owed to macroeconomic factors other than strict monetary control (ibid., p. 40). In this respect, it is worthwhile quoting the words that Friedman (*Financial Times*, 2003), the father of monetarism, conceded to the *Financial Times* on 6 July 2003: 'The use of the quantity of money as a target has not been a success, I'm not sure I would as of today push it as hard as I once did.' All in all, this confession speaks louder than any econometric estimation of the robustness of the quantity theory of money.

The importance of credibility for low inflation

Credibility as a core tenet of the NMC

For Goodfriend (2007, p. 56), credibility came to be regarded as pivotal in ensuring the effectiveness of monetary policy, because it shields the economy against inflation scares. It enhances the flexibility of monetary policy, with stabilizing macroeconomic effects over the business cycle. This claim is, in fact, a core tenet of the NMC, and thus justifies the present chapter fully devoted to credibility matters. It can be divided into two central arguments:

- The pessimism of the 1970s was defeated: monetary policy *is* effective in controlling inflation, provided that it is credible.
- The credibility and the flexibility of monetary policy are intertwined. These two principles are at the heart of the Great Moderation (Chapter 4).

The intellectual roots of the credibility mantra

To understand Goodfriend's aforementioned emphasis on credibility for the purpose of low inflation, one may turn the clock back a decade earlier when he co-authored an NBER paper with King entitled 'The New Neoclassical Synthesis and the Role of Monetary Policy'. Goodfriend and King (1997) meticulously described the genesis of the NMC, which has sometimes been labelled differently elsewhere.[9] The terminological variation is particularly interesting, insofar as it unveils the ideological structural apparatus behind the macroeconomic shift operated in the 1990s. The *New Neoclassical Synthesis* embodies the classical legacy of the rational expectations schools, with its emphasis on the dynamic micro-foundations of macroeconomics (ibid., p. 232) and inter-temporal utility maximization as a guiding behavioural rule at the individual level (ibid.). The Keynesian component of the synthesis is couched in the pure neo-Keynesian tradition, with its emphasis on price stickiness and information asymmetries affecting pricing decisions relative to output. This constitutes the backbone as well as the ideological superstructure of the New Neoclassical Synthesis. Foreshadowing the credibility mantra in the NMC, Goodfriend and King (ibid.) state that the New Neoclassical Synthesis implies that credibility plays an important role in understanding monetary policy and its consequences; credibility thus requires the clear formulation of a simple and transparent rule. In the same paper, a whole paragraph is devoted to credibility matters (ibid., pp. 242–243), tracing back the analysis to the well-known Lucas critique (1976) and its established unpredictability of policy actions in the light of fluctuating policy regimes, as well as to the ideas put forward by Sargent (1986), who linked inflation levels to the public's expectations of future government policies. Credibility is further examined (Goodfriend and King, 1997, p. 274) in the light of the practicality of inflation targeting (Chapter 8). They argue that the effectiveness of low-inflation targeting in the New Neoclassical Synthesis[10] can be explained by resorting to a simple model of price-setting behaviour taking into account the predictability of the price level and real marginal costs. The authors stress in their model the self-enforcing nature of central bank credibility for low inflation. Credibility is linked to the confidence that economic agents place in price stability. This is reflected by firms' lack of nervousness concerning inflation scares, in the course of pricing decisions at the microeconomic level. Nonetheless, inflation scares do occur sometimes (Goodfriend, 2003); Goodfriend and King (1997, p. 274) even identify a rationale for a central bank to cheat[11] its commitment to price stability[12] in the short run by altering the mark-up distortion, in order to reduce unemployment (in other words, to exploit a trade-off on the expectations-augmented Phillips curve). However, they (ibid., p. 275) rapidly dismiss this gloomy scenario by arguing that the long-term costs of cheating were internalized by central banks after Volcker's Fed took responsibility for keeping inflation under control. There was no turning back because central banks had irreversibly become responsible for inflation. This powerful assertion reinforces two core beliefs at the heart of the NMC. First, central bank credibility is always the outcome a long drawn-out battle against sceptics, with a landmark victory in central banking history, namely the well-known Volcker episode. Second, central banks must be held responsible for inflation control. It is an undisputed contemporary fact of economic policy. It is yet regrettable that the term 'responsibility' occults the distinction between credibility and accountability.

Central bank accountability: a critical outlook

Central bank accountability and transparency

Transparency was examined in Chapter 4 as a full-fledged central bank principle and core constituent to the NMC. Additionally, transparency may be seen as a very important element of accountability (Eijffinger and Hoeberichts, 2000, p. 2). The institutional arrangements designed to ensure central bank accountability are certainly dependent on the quality of information disclosure, without which the critical evaluation of its performance is necessarily hampered (ibid.). Transparency and accountability become intertwined when the former is embedded in law, in order to ensure the latter (Bini Smaghi, 1998). This might have been a genuine source of concern when the Maastricht treaty was first drafted more than twenty years ago. A crucial aspect of the articulation between the two concepts is the mandatory publication of minutes by the central bank. This requirement enables the communication to the public of the underlying reasoning of the central bank committee behind a monetary policy decision[13] (Eijffinger and Hoeberichts, 2000, p. 3). While the minutes always give a flavour of the policy debate, in early 2012 the Fed provided for the first time a qualitative assessment of the details on officials' views on its near-record $2.9 trillion balance sheet. This new information follows the first-ever interest rate projections released in January 2012; these forecasts concern expected interest rate levels in late 2012, in future calendar years and beyond that. Alongside their projections, the Fed's policy makers planned to release, on a quarterly basis, when they expect the first change in the central bank's official short-term interest rate to happen. The move is designed to enhance central bank transparency in the eyes of market participants. The evolution marks a milestone for Ben Bernanke, a proponent of the NMC and an advocate of greater transparency.

Central bank accountability and responsibility

DEFINITIONAL ASPECTS

Goodfriend and King's quote (1997, p. 295) states that the Fed is widely held *responsible* for inflation. Although the term conveys powerful semantics, one might argue that the word is polysemous. The *Collins English Dictionary: Complete & Unabridged* defines it as follows:

responsibility
1. the state or position of being responsible
2. a person or thing for which one is responsible
3. the ability or authority to act or decide on one's own, without supervision

The first definition is circular, and adds little to the discussion; responsibility is merely the state of being responsible. The second one focuses on the object of responsibility (one is responsible *for* someone or something), but fails to cast light on what responsibility means. The third one carries a political dimension combining power and freedom (responsibility is tantamount to being free to act without supervision). Paradoxically, the missing link is found in the definition of another word, 'accountability'; to be accountable is to be 'obliged to give a reckoning or explanation for one's action, *responsible*' (*Oxford English Dictionary*, emphasis added). It seems that 'accountability as obligation' (or 'responsibility as duty') is nothing less than the alter ego of 'responsibility as freedom'; the very term 'responsibility' is thus two-sided. Extended to the realms of monetary policy, *central bank responsibility* (1) concerns 'the decisions about the explicit definition and ranking of objectives of monetary policy' (Eijffinger and Hoeberichts, 2000, p. 2). This is the 'responsibility as freedom' side of the coin. *Central bank accountability* (2) is the specification of 'who bears final responsibility with respect to monetary policy' (ibid.).

The freedom/obligation (or the responsibility/accountability) dialectic ought to be reframed and analyzed through the lenses of political science and economic history. In principle, (1) is the prerogative of elected politicians in a democratic society (ibid.). Leaving monetary policy decisions in the hands of an unelected body (i.e. an independent central bank) poses the burning, and yet unresolved, question of political legitimacy in a democratic society. In the face of this conundrum, (2) is the answer put forward by proponents of the NMC.

CENTRAL BANK ACCOUNTABILITY IN A HISTORICAL CONTEXT

Bliek and Parguez (2006, p. 98) note that the Fed is not even an autonomous component of the Federal Government, as it is accountable to the Congress. In fact, the Fed itself is a 'creature of Congress' (Woolley, 1984, p. 153) established in 1913 (Waller, 2011), which translated into an extraordinary institutional tension, whose effects still reverberate today. How does an independent central bank remain democratically accountable to the electorate? As argued by Buiter (2005, p. C1),

> Central bank operational independence and other institutional arrangements
> and ongoing developments relevant to the conduct of monetary policy
> should not blind one to the fundamental truth that monetary policy is but

one component of the fiscal-financial-monetary programme of the state – the sovereign. Fundamentally, there can be no such thing as an independent central bank. For the central bank to perform well, it needs to be backed by and backed up by an effective fiscal authority. In this relationship, the central bank is, inevitably, the junior partner.

The articulation between monetary policy and fiscal policy is still one of the most sensitive questions of modern central bank thinking. Having placed the debate on the field of political science, we pursue hereafter our conceptual effort to clarify the meaning of accountability. The creation of the Fed generated a tension between independence and accountability that was superimposed to a second one between the State and the Federal Government (Waller, 2011, p. 297). This called for a system of checks and balances in order to protect the interests of the two levels of political decision making; logically, a similar system was implemented to preserve the interests of the nonelected officials in charge of monetary policy and those of the public at large. One must mention the institutional architecture of the Fed with the Board of Governors and the twelve regional reserve banks (ibid., p. 298); the rationale behind this architecture was to disentangle monetary policy decisions made on economic grounds and political pressures originating from the Federal level. Somehow, there was an early form of democratic accountability in this regionalization of monetary policy balance by a Board of Governors ensuring the maximization of the welfare of the nation as a whole. A vast literature is devoted to the evolution of the institutional architecture of the Federal Reserve, throughout its history, as regards its independence and accountability. But these questions have often been enmeshed either in subtle rhetorical terms or inconclusive quantitative analysis. All in all, when it comes to the Fed, whether in a pre-crisis or a post-crisis scenario, the ultimate question seems to pertain to political control in last resort. In fact, the Fed was never a deus ex machina:[14]

the Federal Reserve's freedom of action is constrained by political masters at both ends of Pennsylvania Avenue. Should all factions – the White House, and the Majority and Minority leaderships of the Congress – believe that the Federal Reserve's policies are destructive and desire them to be changed in the same direction, the Federal Reserve's policies will change – or possibly there might be a very different Federal Reserve.

(DeLong, 1995)

CENTRAL BANK ACCOUNTABILITY: A POST-CRISIS VIEW

On 26 May 2010, Ben Bernanke, Chairman of the Board of Governors of the Fed was invited to give a speech at the Bank of Japan in Tokyo. Referring to indispensable financial reforms, he insisted that they be conducted in respect of the central bank principles that had strengthened the effectiveness of monetary policy in times of crisis: 'chief among these aspects has been the ability of central banks to make monetary policy decisions based on what is good for the economy in the longer run, independent of short-term political considerations' (Bernanke, 2010, p. 2). Sound monetary policy thus continues to be linked to central bank independence after the crisis. Bernanke propounds this idea, and even refers to a

> *broad consensus*[15] [which] has emerged among policymakers, academics, and other informed observers around the world that the goals of monetary policy should be established by the political authorities, but that the conduct of monetary policy in pursuit of those goals should be free from political control.
>
> (ibid., emphasis added)

As for accountability, he added that central bankers must always be accountable to the public, but both theory and experience support the idea that insulating monetary policy from short-term political pressures leads to desirable macro-economic outcomes and financial stability (ibid., pp. 2–3). Bernanke seems to be aware of the tension between accountability and central bank independence, but he nevertheless leans in favour of the latter, and does so in a pre-crisis (NMC-like) fashion. Whereas the overarching theme of desirable macroeconomic outcomes brings us back to our discussion on the Great Moderation (Chapter 4), the linking of pre-crisis doctrine to financial stability appears as self-defeating. To hammer this point home, this is what a senior economist of the IMF wrote about the pre-vailing consensus view three years before the subprime crisis broke out: 'The International Monetary Fund (IMF) supports central bank autonomy and account-ability, since it facilitates price and *financial sector stability*, which are conducive to sustainable economic growth' (Lybek, 2004, p. 1, emphasis added). There is very little difference between Lybek's and Bernanke's quotes. One must note that Bernanke, three years into the crisis, was still endorsing core NMC precepts.

A critical assessment of mainstream monetary economics

What is mainstream monetary economics?

The legacy of the Barro–Gordon paper

We have already traced back the emergence of the so-called credibility liter-ature to the Barro–Gordon paper published in 1983. It has been argued by Forder (2004) that this landmark paper has conferred a new meaning to the term 'credibility' in central banking, to the extent that it is now common to talk about 'Barro–Gordon credibility'. It has also influenced mainstream monetary economics up until today. Barro and Gordon (1983) have defined credibility as the sustained ability of central banks to manage expectations of homogeneous private agents, endowed with rational expectations (character-ized by a single representative agent for firms and households altogether), in

order to convince the latter that the former are firmly committed to low inflation. The problem is clearly formulated in game-theoretic terms with two
players (the central bank and private agents) by Barro and Gordon, who demonstrate the existence of multiple reputational equilibria. The main result of
the paper is that a credible central bank is one that succeeds in convincing
market participants that it will not deviate from its low inflation objective.
Somehow, a central bank's reputational capital (in other words, its credibility)
is enhanced and comforted once it has convinced market participants that its
long-term commitment to credibility is substantiated by empirical evidence
(i.e. low inflation rates observed over a sustained period of time), and that
inflation will stay under control. Barro and Gardon have shown that transparency and credibility are vectors of monetary authority insofar as they help
strengthen the reputation of the central bank. Finally, they have affirmed the
superiority of rule-based policy making over discretionary policies,[16] for the
former has the decisive ability to act upon the expectations of the private
sector, when the latter merely take them as given.

Mainstream monetary economics

DEFINITION

Mainstream monetary economics is the dominant approach to quantitative policy
analysis in the field of central banking over the last twenty-five years. This
strand of thought can clearly be equated to the New Keynesian DSGE (Dynamic
Stochastic General Equilibrium) models tantamount to RBC models with price
stickiness. The Barro–Gordon paper has helped establish a mainstream research
programme compatible with rational expectations, the representative agent paradigm[17] and an aspiration of central banks to turn sustained low-inflation levels
into the *raison d'être* of monetary policy, thereby putting an end to the pessimism of the 1970s.

POST-CRISIS ASSESSMENT

Without going into the arcane and technicalities of the formal models that populated mainstream monetary economics in the last three decades, it is worthwhile investigating the nature of the intellectual posture adopted by the
mainstream during this period. The favoured critical perspective could be the
History of Economic Thought (hereafter HET), due to its ability to cast light on
present socio-economic conditions, in the light of the great contributions of past
thinkers. In an after-dinner speech given on 21 May 2011 at the annual conference of the European Society for the History of Economic Thought held in Ista-
mbul, Laidler (2011) criticizes the questionable attitude of mainstream
economists and their condescending epistemological outlook on scientific progress, viewed in an incremental fashion, merely incorporating past ideas in the
current body of knowledge, insofar as they are considered valid, and by

discarding the rest. In this view, HET is seen as being past-looking and unproductive at worst, and entertaining at best, whereas the mainstream is being viewed as far more progressive, thanks to its ability to absorb new knowledge in its relentless quest for truth:

> It is not news that today's mainstream believes economics to be a science,[18] which makes orderly progress, that old ideas which are still useful are in the current body of knowledge, and that those which are not there have disappeared because they are not useful.
>
> (ibid.)

However, in an implicit parallel with Fukuyama (1992) and his book *The End of History and the Last Man*, Laidler (2011, emphasis added) puts back mainstream monetary economics into a more critical HET perspective:

> today's mainstream monetary economics, with its reliance on clearing markets and rational expectations, has surely earned a permanent place in the subject's history of its on-going evolution, *not as an end-point* whose achievement has rendered what went before it irrelevant to understanding what is now happening.

Laidler, a former monetarist in dominion, goes on to launch a scathing attack against mainstream monetary economics, by claiming that the GFC that originated in the US subprime market in summer 2007 has had far-reaching consequences still reverberating around the world; the GFC has forced mainstream economists to reconsider their pre-crisis ideas, which had made them oblivious to the looming catastrophe, thereby helping create its preconditions.

The econometric standpoint and the questionable metric of credibility

How much does central bank credibility contribute to good monetary policy? Ferguson (2005) admits the limitations of central bankers' knowledge in this respect as he claims that the particular contribution of monetary credibility to central banks' objectives is hardly a measurable magnitude, in spite of academic evidence of the role of good policy and central bank independence for achieving price stability. Analysts tend to be much more comfortable with the measurement of the contribution of central bank policies, rather than with the measurement of their credibility. Blinder (2000) shares this point of view when arguing that: '[c]entral bank credibility plays a pivotal role in much of the modern literature on monetary policy, yet it is difficult to measure or even assess objectively'. The crucial issue of objectivity, and by extension measurability, raises the question of the commensurability with other economic magnitudes. In the same paper, Blinder conducted a landmark (questionnaire-based) survey. All in all, credibility was judged important by central banks and academics, although this appreciation was much more qualitative than quantitative. Yet, if credibility amounts to 'the quality of being believed or trusted' (*Collins English Dictionary: Complete & Unabridged*), one may wonder why and how credibility could *not* matter. What Blinder and Ferguson do is express their scepticism concerning the metric of credibility or, put differently, the ability of central bankers and academics to measure credibility within a thorough scientific process of inquiry. This issue is also at the heart of a paper written by Forder (2004), who argues that the word 'credibility' in ordinary English usage denotes effectiveness and competence. When referring to Bernanke's survey, Forder (ibid.) explains that its results are skewed towards Barro–Gordon credibility, thereby reflecting the cultural dominance of a specific approach to policy in a given period. As extensively argued since the beginning of the GFC, we have now entered a brave new world wherein old notions need to be revisited.

Reassessing central bank credibility in the eye of the storm

The ECB in July 2008

In order to broaden the scope of the discussion in a post-crisis context, one must necessarily take into account a recent and noteworthy episode of monetary policy, namely the decision made by the ECB to tighten monetary policy in July 2008,[19] in the face of a well-documented inflation scare caused by rising commodity prices in emerging markets. This decision was indeed justified in the light of the reigning consensus guiding the decisions of the ECB at the time. However, with hindsight, one cannot help asking a twofold question, whose answer will certainly determine the future sustainability of the NMC. How credible is a central bank trying to mitigate an inflation scare, by raising interest rates, so as to anchor medium- and long-term expectations? The answer to this question is straightforward and instinctive. By raising the short-term nominal interest rate in July 2008, the ECB adopted a credibility-building stance, which was justified in the light of the prevailing NMC. However, the aforementioned question was voluntarily incomplete. What if the European central bank made exactly the same decision two months before the unforeseen collapse of a major American financial institution, whose bankruptcy would create unprecedented ripple effects and unleash self-sustained contagion mechanisms that would drag down the global economy into the biggest financial crisis since the Great Depression? Of course, the question is purposefully thought-provoking, as what was a mere mind game in July 2008, resonates strikingly several years into the GFC. Yet, one cannot reasonably claim that a hypothetical visionary ECB endowed with perfect foresight in July 2008 would have changed the fate of the global economy, by merely leaving the short-term nominal interest rate unchanged. However, with all due precautions, it remains necessary to examine what was wrong with this decision. Therefore, we must now look at the transcript, and outline the most controversial statements therein.

What was wrong with the 3 July 2008 decision?

The 3 July 2008 monetary policy decision consisted of an interest-rate hike (+25 basis points). According to the ECB (2008), it was made 'on the basis of [its] regular economic monetary analyses'. The two reasons invoked by the ECB were respectively second-round effects and increasing risks to price stability in the medium term. The former concerns wage-setting behaviour and the price distortion that could result from rising commodity prices. The latter echoes the well-known mandate of the ECB, namely price stability. However, the medium-term perspective is adopted, which presupposes reasonable foresight: 'HICP inflation rates … are expected to remain well above the level consistent with price stability for a more protracted period than previously thought' (ibid.). However, neither the previously thought nor the newly assumed period of inflationary pressures was ever made explicit (or transparent) to the public. One could certainly argue that ECB inflation forecasts are based entirely on monetary analysis, such as 'continued very vigorous money and credit growth' (ibid.). However, financial conditions also come in the picture, with the stated 'absence thus far of significant constraints on bank loan supply in a context of ongoing financial market tension' (ibid.). Although the very possibility of financial distress is acknowledged, any rationing of credit is ruled out in the short run. However, at this moment in time, the subprime crisis had already broken out eleven months earlier, and the collapse of Lehman Brothers is around the corner. This turning point will trigger the amplification of the GFC, with largely unforeseen, albeit devastating, consequences for the world economy. It seems reasonable and legitimate not to blame the ECB for its lack of foresight two months before the collapse of Lehman Brothers. However, a few sentences below, the ECB reiterates its confidence that 'the economic fundamentals of the euro area are sound' (ibid.). So far, so good! Nobody at the ECB is willing to assume that the global economy will be looking into the abyss two months later. So, in line with the principles of the NMC, in the weeks prior to the most straining period for the world economy since the Great Depression, the ECB remained in oblivion and declared:

> [a]gainst this background and in full accordance with our mandate, we emphasise that maintaining price stability in the medium term *is our primary objective* and that it is our strong determination to keep medium and long-term inflation expectations firmly anchored in line with price stability.
>
> (ibid., emphasis added)

This statement probably captures the essence of the NMC. Price stability is the Holy Grail. It now resonates as both strikingly consistent and terribly misguided in the light of subsequent events. Relative optimism prevailed in July 2008, and so-called central bank transparency was reinforcing this outlook: 'the information available remains broadly in line with our expectation of moderate on-going growth'. Of course, there were no signs of a Great Recession in sight. Mainstream monetary economists would certainly have discarded the hypothesis as laughable at the time. Moreover, the European economy was depicted as being in very good shape: 'the fundamentals of the euro area economy remain sound and *the euro area does not suffer from major imbalances*' (ibid., emphasis added). Of course, the scenario of a wide-ranging devastating Euro-sovereign debt crisis was not credible, let alone the idea that countries such as Greece, Italy, Spain and Ireland could be causing some of the most spectacular imbalances the euro area ever suffered from since its inception. Yet, two sources of concern existed: excessive wage demands and rising public spending – '[t]he Governing Council is monitoring price-setting behaviour and wage negotiations in the euro area with particular attention. Furthermore, there are potential upside risks from unanticipated rises in indirect taxes and administered prices.' If only the ECB had known that a Minsky moment was about to occur, that plummeting purchasing power would soon be the primary concern of millions of Europeans and that massive bailout plans involving gigantic public spending would rapidly be put into place throughout the world, in order to prevent the collapse of the global financial system. If only the ECB had known this in July 2008, would it be more credible today?

Do past mistakes of central bankers matter in a post-crisis world?

To take up the credibility issue further in a post-crisis environment, one is tempted to broaden the scope of the debate. For instance, how credible are central bankers having made erroneous forecasts of asset price evolutions, with potentially damaging consequences on growth? Central banks need to be credible and accountable, NMC proponents say. One fundamental question raised by the GFC is the following: should central banks be accountable for past mistakes too? In 2006, for instance, as cracks in the housing bubble started to appear, Alan Greenspan declared:[20] '[t]here is a good chance of coming out of this in good shape, but average housing prices are likely to be down this year relative to 2005. I don't know, but I think the worst of this may well be over.' In the same vein, at a meeting of the Federal Open Market Committee held in the offices of the Board of Governors of the Federal Reserve System in Washington, DC, on 20 September 2006, a staff document claimed with assurance that Fed experts were 'not projecting large declines nationwide in house prices'. Last but not least, Bernanke said in response to a question after a speech in Washington in January 2008 that '[t]he Federal Reserve [was] not currently forecasting a recession'.

On more philosophical grounds, what do these spectacular forecasting errors tell about the state of economic knowledge in the twenty-first century? In this respect, it is worthwhile recalling how Keynes (1937, pp. 212–214) clarified his views on uncertainty:

> by 'uncertain' knowledge ... I do not mean merely to distinguish what is known for certain from what is only probable. The game of roulette is not

subject, in this sense, to uncertainty; nor is the prospect of a Victory bond being drawn. Or, again, the expectation of life is only slightly uncertain. Even the weather is only moderately uncertain. The sense in which I am using the term is that in which the prospect of a European war is uncertain, or the price of copper and the rate of interest twenty years hence, or the obsolescence of a new invention, or the position of private wealth owners in the social system in 1970. About these matters there is no scientific basis on which to form any calculable probability whatever. We simply do not know.

With hindsight, back in 2006, neither did the Maestro...

Conclusion

In this chapter, we have focused on an articulated presentation of the credibility concept with regard to the central bank's objective to maintain low inflation, spanning across several decades of monetary practices, under different paradigms and economic outlooks, up until its unconditional endorsement by proponents of the NMC.

Finally, central banking mistakes are human, even when made by the most powerful economic institutions on Earth. However, there are learning lessons for the central banking community. The hubris displayed by central bankers in the years prior to the GFC morphed into cracks in the NMC apparatus. Transparency about past mistakes should be on the agenda of all central bankers. Yet, where do we go from now?

6 Price stability and the influence of Wicksell on the NMC

Introduction

In this chapter, we address the single most important priority of central banks under the NMC, namely price stability. After presenting the concept itself, we investigate why monetary policy – rather than fiscal policy – has become the favoured policy option in the contemporary period. Then, we examine the oft-quoted filiation between the NMC and Wicksellian economics. We challenge the view that so-called neo-Wicksellianism is faithful to Wicksell's original ideas on monetary policy. Finally, we examine the ideological underpinnings of the NMC.

The primacy of price stability

Definition

For King (2005, p. 2), the fundamental objective of monetary policy is maintaining price stability. Under the new consensus, one of the policy advances is therefore the priority for price stability (Goodfriend, 2007, p. 60). The latter concept pertains to the optimal range for the inflation rate, and not to the absolute price level per se: '[t]he distinction between controlling the rate of inflation rather than the price index itself is crucial, as is the rule-based approach that is now generally followed by the world's major central banks'. Greenspan once defined price stability as follows: it is 'when economic agents no longer take account of the prospective change in the general price level in their economic decision-making'. The interesting aspect of this definition is the lack of a precise numerical target. However, inflation targets, whether explicit or implicit (see Chapter 8), are at the heart of the NMC. Averaging fourteen surveys on the US over twenty years, Edwin Le Heron (2003) finds an inflation rate of 2.96 per cent to be the implicit target of the Fed. Lavoie (2005) reports a 2 or 2.25 per cent target for the Bank of Canada in 2004. When made explicit, the inflation target is between 1 and 3 per cent (2.11 per cent on average). The accepted deviation from target is around 1 per cent (Le Heron, 2003). Le Heron (ibid.) concludes that there is no such thing as a consensus on price stability. Until recently, mainstream theory did not provide any explanation as to why a 0 per cent inflation rate was never a proposed target. However, the explanation is relatively simple to understand. Intuitively, substantial deflationary risks are palpable at such a tipping point. Hence, central banks unanimously reject this rigid 0 per cent objective. Galí (2010, p. 11) explains why, in practice, central banks always find a positive average level of inflation more desirable than zero inflation. *Inter alia*, Galí (ibid.) mentions the risk of hitting the zero bound on nominal interest rates (Chapter 11), the existence of downward nominal wage rigidities that may prevent further wage reductions and the existence of short-run trade-offs between inflation and output stabilization, which might be more easily accommodated with a positive rate of inflation. This argument is substantiated by the European Central Bank:

> an inflation rate at below, but close to 2% underlines the ECB's commitment to provide an adequate margin to avoid the risks of deflation. Having such a safety margin against deflation is important, because nominal interest rates cannot fall below zero. In a deflationary environment monetary policy may thus not be able to sufficiently stimulate aggregate demand by using its interest rate instrument. This makes it more difficult for monetary policy to fight deflation than to fight inflation.[1]

The ECB website features an explicit target, while admitting that the original framework was incomplete:

> While the Treaty clearly establishes the primary objective of the ECB, it does not give a precise definition of what is meant by price stability. The ECB's Governing Council has announced a quantitative definition of price stability. Price stability is defined as a year-on-year increase in the Harmonised Index of Consumer Prices (HICP) for the euro area of below 2%. The Governing Council has also clarified that, in the pursuit of price stability, it aims to maintain inflation rates below, but close to, 2% over the medium term.

Interestingly enough, the definition of price stability put forward by the ECB is circular: 'Reasons for aiming at below, but close to, 2%: inflation rates of below, but close to, 2% are low enough for the economy to fully reap the benefits of price stability.' Price stability is thus defined by the ECB as the ideal level of inflation at which the economy enjoys the full benefits thereof. To illustrate this ill-defined idea, let us have a look at the following Greek syllogism:[2]

- The economy enjoys advantages when prices are stable.
- Prices are stable when the economy is enjoying these advantages.
- Central banks must therefore aim for price stability!

This syllogism echoes the confidence of world monetary leaders that inflation was defeated during the 1990s. This view was unambiguously expressed by the Group of Seven in October 1995: '[t]he ministers and central bank governors agreed that

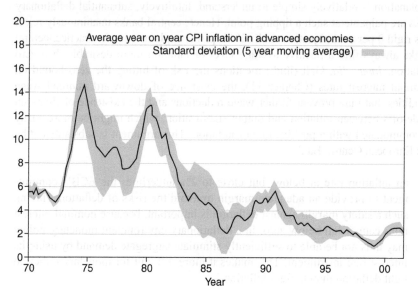

Figure 6.1 The triumph over inflation in advanced economies, 1970–2002 (source: C.A. Ullersma, available at http://repub.eur.nl/res/pub/811/rm0203.pdf).

in most countries the conditions for continued growth and employment gains are in place and inflation is well under control'. Regardless of the intricate logic or the validity of this syllogism, Woodford (2003, pp. 3–4) argues that price stability bears testimony to the intellectual triumph of the rule-based approach in monetary policy (Chapter 3). Although Woodford (ibid.) thinks that low and stable inflation are policy priorities emphasized in countries with explicit inflation targets (Chapter 8), although he acknowledges similarities with recent policy conducted in the US. Galí (2010, p. 11) argues that the NMC (that he calls New Keynesian framework) provides a justification for a monetary policy aiming at price stability and low inflation. In the absence of exogenous inflationary shocks, Galí thinks that the only inflationary pressures stem from the presence of nominal rigidities conducive to potential inefficiencies and sub-optimal output growth performance. Nominal rigidities can cause output to deviate from its long-term (or natural) trend; even when the central bank is not assigned a unique price stability objective and is primarily concerned with macroeconomic stabilization, it should nevertheless aim at maintaining a low inflation level, in order to close to the output gap.

Post-crisis assessment

What Jean Claude Trichet said on 3 July 2008[3]

The interest-rate policy decision made on 3 July 2008 by the ECB was commented in Chapter 5. The transcript was quoted several times. Jean Claude

Trichet restated therein some of the core principles of the NMC a few weeks before the dramatic collapse of Lehman Brothers.

One must also cite the profession of faith that was enunciated in favour of the price stability objective. In the light of the following (ECB, 2008), one might be tempted to redefine price stability as the ultimate objective of the NMC:

> [w]e are solemnly telling them that they can count on us to guarantee price stability in the medium term, to deliver price stability in the medium term and to solidly anchor inflation expectations. It is our mandate, it is our duty. This position is commanded by our mandate and by the decision of the people of Europe. We are doing what the Treaty calls upon us to do. It is also what the people of Europe are asking us to do today. If you look at the most recent surveys, you will see that inflation is now the number one concern of our 320 million fellow citizens.

Commenting on the failure of macroeconomic theory to predict the GFC, Stiglitz (2011, p. 592) stated that '[monetary authorities] focused on keeping inflation low, partly because the Standard Model suggested that low inflation was necessary and almost sufficient for efficiency and growth'. It seems that the above syllogism is an important feature (whether logical or rhetorical) of the Standard Model superstructure. In Stiglitz's terminology, the Standard Model refers to the DSGE[4] framework *à la* Kydland and Prescott that came to dominate central banking theory under the NMC. It is the outcome of the new classical revolution, emphasizing the micro-foundations of macroeconomics. It espouses the rhetoric of rational and utility-maximizing agents, with perfect foresight, interacting on perfectly competitive and clearing markets, in order to reach a state of equilibrium. Economic agents thus react to discrepancies between observed values and steady state solutions, with adjustment costs being the only obstacle to instantaneous market clearing. Along the lines described by RBC theory (Pilkington, 2011a), random supply-side shocks temporarily throw the economy into confusion. Business cycles are tantamount to random walks with drift, rather than cyclical fluctuations around a deterministic trend. However, in a multi-period and dynamic setting, market forces irrepressibly pull back the economy towards equilibrium, before a new random productivity shock unsettles this hard-fought configuration. Solow (2008, p. 245) offers a very interesting explanation of the success of the Standard Model in terms of its simplistic epistemological features, its clear ideological orientations and, finally, the historical circumstances in which it emerged. Solow (ibid.) argues that economics has long been dominated by a purist, and therefore uncompromising, streak, revolving around notions of greed, rationality and equilibrium. The Standard Model was perfectly suited to these aspirations; it extended the well-known microeconomic aspects to wide-ranging macroeconomic principles (ibid.). By the same token, mainstream economists achieved a remarkable epistemological feat, in the sense that they managed to impose a learnable, reasonably accessible and highly technical approach to the discipline in the ranks of academia, taking on the appearance of science (ibid.). The most striking feature was undoubtedly the

ideological underpinnings supporting this shift towards the global academic acceptance of the Standard Model, which coincided with the rise of neoliberalism in the
late 1970s and early 1980s under the political impulse of Thatcher and Reagan.

Are the NMC and neo-Wicksellian economics synonymous?

Wicksell's contribution to macroeconomics

Wicksell was a leading Swedish economist of the Stockholm school in the late
nineteenth and early twentieth century. His ideas in monetary theory have influenced modern macroeconomics, with wide-ranging theoretical contributions irri-
gating the Keynesian and the Austrian schools of economic thought. In his
description of monetary policy viewed as the 'study of the causes regulating the
value of money' (Wicksell, 1898), his reasoning runs as follows:

> [i]f prices rise, the rate of interest is to be raised; and the prices fall, the rate
> of interest is to be lowered; and the rate of interest is henceforth to be main-
> tained at its new level a further movement of prices calls for a further
> change in one direction or the other.
>
> (ibid., 1936 [1898], p. 189)

Wicksell (1936 [1898], pp. 70–76) described his pure credit system as a mere
cashless economy, in which all payments are made by bookkeeping transfers
between bank accounts, and in which interest-bearing deposits are created
when loans are granted to firms and households.[5] Loans make deposits, whose
volume is not limited by any predetermined reserve constraint. The supply of
money in the banking system is endogenously determined: 'No matter what
amount of money may be demanded from the banks, that is the amount which
they are in a position to lend ... The "supply of money" is thus furnished by
the demand itself' (ibid., pp. 110–111). Contrary to what Woodford (2003,
p. 46, fn 40) claims, Wicksell (1922, p. XII, n.1) had foreseen the existence of
endogenous inflation expectations and the role they played in the cumulative
process:

> As long as the change in prices ... is believed to be temporary, it will in fact
> remain permanent; as soon as it is considered to be permanent, it will
> become progressive, and when it is eventually seen as progressive, it will
> turn into an avalanche.

Neo-Wicksellian economics and the NMC

The monetarist economist David Laidler[6] (2004) reckons:

> There can be no doubt that the monetary systems of a number of advanced
> countries nowadays resemble Knut Wicksell's (1898) model of the 'pure

credit economy' much more closely than did any that actually existed in the world for which he wrote.

On the other side of the theoretical spectrum, the legacy of Wicksell was acknowledged by Lavoie and Seccareccia (2004):

> [m]onetarism is dead! Central bankers are all Wicksellians now! They target low inflation rates, with no regard to monetary aggregates whatsoever, by acting upon short-term real rates of interest. This is the New Consensus in monetary economics or simply the New Keynesian Synthesis.

In the same vein, Bliek and Parguez (2006, p. 99), leading proponents of monetary circuit theory, argue that the mission of the ECB is in line with the NMC, and is embedded in the early writings of Knut Wicksell, who is recognized as an influential thinker by proponents of the NMC (Woodford, 2003; McCallum, 2005; Tamborini, 2006). Woodford (2000) uses the qualifier 'neo-Wicksellian' to describe his own approach:

> We shall argue that inflation and output determination can be usefully explained in Wicksellian terms as depending upon the relation between a natural rate of interest *determined primarily by real factors* and the central bank's rule for adjusting the short-term nominal interest rate that serves as its operating target.

The emphasis on real factors in the determination of the natural rate of interest is crucial, as it reinforces the classical dichotomy between real outcomes, determined in a general equilibrium analytical setting, and monetary policy, the main instrument of the NMC, acting upon expectations[7] through the interest-rate setting policy.

The Wicksellian flavour of Woodford's Interest and Prices

The Wicksellian framework lent itself to the emergence of the New Keynesian approach such as Woodford's masterpiece *Interest and Prices* (2003),[8] with its emphasis on price stickiness, which prevailed under the NMC:

> It is only in an environment with sticky prices that we are able to introduce the crucial Wicksellian distinction between the actual and the natural rate of interest, as the discrepancy between the two arises only as a consequence of failure of prices to adjust sufficiently rapidly.

> (ibid.)

The neoclassical market-clearing mantra is evident here. The Panglossian claim that we live in the best of all possible worlds when markets clear, is nuanced by the existence of price stickiness at the heart of the New Keynesian research programme (market-clearing failures, due to information asymmetries and government-induced regulation). The reason why Woodford (2003, pp. 5–6) believed he had refined the

Wicksellian theoretical apparatus, in order to conform to 'the modern standards of conceptual rigour' is through the consistent use of a class of micro-founded models, incorporating nominal rigidities and including new classical inter-temporal optimization features. This methodology would naturally fall under the well-known DSGE umbrella term, and would dominate modern central banking theory in the 1990s up until the GFC. However, the true nature of the underlying theoretical model might have been overlooked by Woodford and his followers: 'much of the subsequent literature that Wicksell inspired, including Woodford's contribution, seems to me to accord rather more generality to the properties of the pure credit economy than they can really bear' (Laidler, 2004, p. 1).

Did Woodford betray Wicksell's key insights?

What are the central properties of the pure credit economy, and how could Woodford have accorded too much generality to them? To answer the first part of this question, Fontana (2006, p. 6) argues that there are at least two features that account for the intellectual filiation between Wicksell and Woodford. The first one is the substitution of monetary aggregates by the interest-rate setting procedure in the determination of the inflation rate (Chapter 7). The second one is the reversal of the sense of causality that underpins the quantity theory of money (ibid.), namely that changes in the prices cause changes in the supply of money. The second part is hence more complex, and creates an unresolved tension between the proponents of the quantity theoretic approach and the post-Keynesian endogenous money theorists (Moore, 1988; Lavoie, 1996). The alleged generality accorded by Woodford to the properties of the pure credit economy arguably comes down to a narrow interpretation of the interest-rate setting procedure and the subsequent determination of the price level. We will see in Chapter 13 that with the revival of quantitative easing in a post-crisis context, the proponents of the quantity theory of money have not yet conceded defeat to the neo-Wicksellian approach. Wicksell was critical of the applicability of his theories to the real world, because his pure credit economy was only an ideal type against which more robust and realistic analysis would need to be further developed. His description of the pure credit economy was conducted in mere pedagogical fashion, in order to characterize

> a state of affairs in which money does not circulate at all, neither in the form of coin (except perhaps as small change), nor in the form of notes, but where all domestic payments are effected by means of the Giro payment and book-keeping transfers.
>
> (Wicksell, 1936 [1898], pp. 70–71)

Needless to say that this gross simplification was not satisfactory, when used to draw conclusions on the way real-world economies operate. Therefore, it is all the more surprising that such an incomplete analytical framework, in the mind of its creator, would provide the theoretical premises, and pave the way for the New Monetary Consensus a century later. The emphasis on price stickiness and market imperfections in neo-Keynesian economics are well known to contemporary economists. These rigidities account for the divergence between the natural interest rate (that ensures the equality of investment and saving) and the monetary interest rate charged by the banking system, with real shock-induced misalignments triggering the business cycle. This is precisely how Wicksell came back in the picture, and why NMC policies are still considered neo-Wicksellian by most commentators to date. But while Wicksell was aware of the limitations of his pure credit model (following his didactic approach to monetary economics), Woodford (2003) seems to be overconfident that the class of models he uses, pertains to real-world phenomena in undifferentiated spatiotemporal conditions. In spite of its conceptual rigour and mathematical sophistication, one fundamental problem with the new consensus view, is the total omission of banks[9] in explaining the macroeconomic nexus of production and monetary processes that constitute the backbone of post-Keynesian and Circuitist literature. The pure credit system *à la* Wicksell was betrayed by Woodford's approach, which postulated a set of complete financial markets wherein bank intermediaries were relegated to theoretical artefacts (Goodhart, 2004, pp. 198–199). Woodford (2003, pp. 31, 35, 63 fn 1) occasionally alludes to the issue of the systemic capacity of banks to generate monetary expansion and contraction (Wicksell, 1898: ch. 6; Hayek, 1929, ch. IV), with feedback loop effects on monetary policy, but he seems to propound the view favouring an interest-rate rule facilitating the transmission mechanism of monetary policy (Woodford, 2003, pp. 24–37), without any consequential damage caused by the financial intermediaries, whether it be through credit rationing or excessive risk-taking practices.

The NMC ideology

The rampant ideological dimension of the NMC

The supply-side ideology

For Bliek and Parguez (2006, p. 99), the NMC is a supply-side ideology. Put differently, according to NMC proponents, long-term growth is necessarily supply-side determined. In the long run, growth follows a path determined by supply-side factors, such as labour productivity, demographic growth and the component of capital accumulation dependent on the saving rate. This framework is also a dynamic stochastic general-equilibrium model. The natural supply-side path of the economy is supposed to be characterized by price stability from which the economy only deviates, due to short-run demand shocks that may be caused by a temporary decline in the saving rate or an expansionary fiscal policy. The role of the central bank is then to neutralize these demand-pull inflationary pressures and adjust the short-term interest rate accordingly. Bliek and Parguez (ibid., p. 100) note that the NMC is intrinsically dualistic. Demand is determined in the short run by (mostly unanticipated) shocks affecting wages and fiscal policy, whereas supply-side factors (savings, demographics, productivity) are always determined in the long run within a neoclassical DSGE framework. The models evolved from efforts to add supply-side features to the IS/LM type framework, with the general equilibrium setting necessitating a set of equilibrium prices and quantities determined simultaneously on frictionless markets. DSGE models were also consistent with the hypothesized steady-state properties of the economic system that magnified the supply-side apparatus of New Keynesian economists under the NMC.

The DSGE models[10]

The starting point of the infamous DSGE class of models can be traced back to Kydland and Prescott's seminal paper 'Time to Build and Aggregate Fluctuations' published in 1982. These authors endeavoured to build calibrated models that explained business cycles, by accounting for exogenous supply-side technology and productivity shocks (Pilkington, 2011a). Albeit slow to translate into institutionally grounded orthodoxy, RBC theory progressively pervaded the realms of academia in top US economics departments, by introducing innovative and ground-breaking methodological techniques, such as recursive econometric models and equilibrium path computation. The result was the spectacular emergence of a new generation of ambitious graduate students and researchers acquainted with these powerful tools and accustomed to a new way of doing macroeconomics. However, the price to pay for this methodological breakthrough was an increasingly higher level of mathematical formalism that would eventually prove ontologically detrimental to the explanatory power of economic science (Lawson, 1997, 2006, 2009). Without going into the arcane of Lawson's ontological critique on mainstream economics, let us point out hereafter the limitations of the relevance of abstract models that omit certain features of reality. DSGE models often fail to capture key aspects of economic reality, but they compensate for this omission by elaborating sophisticated methods and calibration techniques that rely on fundamental parameter values at odds with empirical evidence. Yet, the subsequent replication of macroeconomic aggregates might well seem convincing from a scientific perspective.[11] However, blind reliance on the 'as if' principle pioneered by Milton Friedman (1953) misled 'the economics profession [who] went astray because economists, as a group, mistook beauty, clad in impressive-looking mathematics, for truth' (Krugman, 2009).

The neutrality of money

Woodford's framework (2003, p. 62) draws on neoclassical general equilibrium theory: 'markets are perfectly competitive, prices adjust continuously to clear markets, and there exist markets in which state contingent securities of any kind may be traded'. His conception of interest rates is also tainted with neoclassical concepts. The natural rate of interest is one that minimizes the output gap, in other words, that keeps aggregate demand in check with a so-called natural output, which corresponds to a theoretical situation characterized by frictionless and perfectly clearing markets. Natural real outcomes are therefore determined by this hypothetical general equilibrium, whereas observed (both real and monetary) magnitudes are the result of the divergence between the observed monetary interest rate and the natural (theoretical) interest rate that the central bank constantly needs to target. Money is neutral in the sense that the natural 'real' equilibrium is determined independently of monetary policy, the latter force only exerting its influence through the output gap. Although the NMC acknowledges that periods of equilibrium may be derailed by a number of different factors, it affirms that market forces will eventually pull back the economy towards equilibrium, provided that optimal[12] monetary policy is conducted by the central bank.

The role of fiscal policy

Commenting on a widely acclaimed textbook, Blanchard and Sheen (2007, p. 558) have questioned the relevance of fiscal policy in the real world. After arguing that an optimal policy mix between fiscal and monetary policy is the solution propounded by textbooks, in order to pull an economy out of a recession, resorb macroeconomic imbalances, keep inflation under control and stimulate investment, the authors call for a reality check of fiscal restriction. Drawing on the examples of the growth stability pact in the Eurozone, the 'Contract with America' devised by the Republican Party in 1994 and the fiscal surplus of the Howard–Costello government in Australia, they show how fiscal policy has been discarded by proponents of the NMC as a countercyclical policy option.

Alternative views: path dependence

So far, we evoked the idea that the NMC revolves around the existence of a long-run deterministic output trend from which the economy only deviates under the impact of nominal rigidities and short-term exogenous shocks that are conducive to price inefficiencies and sub-optimal output levels (or positive output gaps). In the NMC, monetary policy is therefore assigned a fundamental price stability objective, along with a short-run macro-stabilization objective, in order to close the output gap, and help realign the growth path of the economy on its long-term trend. Yet, too rarely are the intellectual premises of this beautiful theoretical construct questioned. At the heart of the matter, let us ask the following question: what if the long-run equilibrium is no longer predetermined? This would open the door for transitional dynamics that will condition the steady-state rate of accumulation. Concepts such as the New Normal (Chapter 11) or abnormal statistical breaks in economic growth after 2007 (Chapter 16) are discussed in this book. At this stage, let us underline that short-run events (such as the outbreak of the subprime crisis) have a qualitative impact on long-run equilibria. The assumption of a single long-term equilibrium is severely criticized by advocates of path dependence. Let us simply stress in this section the relevance of economic models that display hysteresis akin to permanent effects of a transitory shock.

In a literary fashion, the path dependency hypothesis in macrodynamics comes down to the idea that 'History matters' (Setterfield, 2008, p. 4). Contrariwise, the NMC revolves around path independent systems (ibid.) that can be described as merely a-historical. Long-run configurations, such as the one determined by the deterministic long-run trends in DSGE models, are unaffected by the past. Path-dependence amounts to a radical critique of systems organized around traditional equilibrium (ibid.) or determinate equilibria (Kaldor, 1934). The latter systems are defined in terms of temporary exogenous shocks imposed upon them from without, and display asymptotic convergence towards a deterministic long-run trend to which they automatically return following a random displacement (Setterfield, 2008 p. 4). Yet, any equilibrium should logically be defined with reference to the historical adjustment path taken towards it.[13] For instance, the GFC is a major historical event that probably modified the long-run adjustment path that was assumed by DSGE models in, say, 2005 or 2006.

Conclusion

In this chapter, the price stability mantra was defined as the ultimate objective of the NMC. After making the latter more explicit from the point of view of its proponents, we investigated the Wicksellian influence on the NMC, before addressing the most salient features of the rampant ideology embodied in the NMC. Finally, an alternative view embodied in the path-dependency hypothesis, was briefly discussed.

7 The interest-rate setting policy

The Taylor rule and beyond

Introduction

The filiation between monetarism and the NMC is best understood by pinpointing the change operated in the core assumptions of the underlying approaches. What the NMC did is replace the monetarist assumption of money-supply targeting by the assumption that the central bank follows an interest-rate setting procedure (Romer, 2000, p. 154), which is at the heart of the NMC. We consider this theoretical pillar in this chapter, by comparing two different perspectives: post-Keynesian and New Keynesian economics. This chapter continues the reflection initiated in Chapter 6. In Chapter 3, we presented a simple monetary policy rule. Generalizing this approach, we show in this chapter that interest-rate setting policies under the NMC are embedded in the well-known Taylor rule, developed with steadfast consistency by Stanford economist John Taylor and his followers. Meyer (2001, p. 3) argues that this precept of monetary policy 'has the advantage of more accurately capturing the prevailing operating procedures at central banks around the world'. However, one objective of this book is to show that a truthful characterization of the pre-GFC era may no longer be relevant in a post-crisis world.

The manipulation of the short-term interest rate

The interest-rate setting procedure is at the heart of the NMC. We examine this theoretical pillar in this chapter, by comparing two different perspectives: post-Keynesian and New Keynesian economics. Unfortunately, the latter distinction is not crystal clear either, as it also embodies sharp internal disagreements.

Post-Keynesian monetary theory: horizontalism vs structuralism

The once heated debate between horizontalism and structuralism is a well-known bone of contention within post-Keynesian economics, at least throughout the 1990s and up until the beginning of the following decade. The common ground between the two approaches was the sheer rejection of the old idea inspired by the quantity theory of money according to which the central bank sets policy by

resorting to 'quantitative constraints as a means to controlling the private creation of money' (Wray, 2007). We review hereafter the role of the central bank
in the two theories.

The central bank in horizontalist theory

Basil Moore (1988) is the author who has pioneered the horizontalist approach
to money creation within the post-Keynesian paradigm.[1] By reversing the traditional credit multiplier story, horizontalists (also known as accommodationists)
emphasize the decisions of private economic agents, who decide to borrow the
quantity of money[2] that they need, in order to finance their net flow of expenditure.[3] The supply of money is endogenously determined by the loan/deposit creation process. The central bank passively accommodates the demand for bank
reserves. Therefore, it cannot actively control the quantity of reserves that commercial banks hold at each moment in time, let alone the total quantity of money.
All the central bank can do, is set the short-term nominal interest rate, or, in
other words, set the *price* of reserves (and not the quantity thereof). The money
supply curve is horizontal in credit-interest space, the horizontal line stemming
from the perfect elasticity of the credit supply schedule. Wray (2007, p. 4) has
argued that the 'free to choose the target rate' interpretation of the horizontalist
position is ill-founded. After restating the principle of endogenous money,
emphasizing the horizontal accommodative stance of the central bank with
regard to the demand for reserves, Wray (ibid.) narrows down the freedom of
action to set the adequate short-term interest rate in the light of the impact and
the tolerance for the corresponding economic outcomes. The zero bound is
deemed inflationary by Wray, and an extreme 100 per cent interest rate level is
tantamount to a recipe for disaster on equity markets.

   The factors that determine the range within which the overnight rate can vary
are institutions, regulations, financial structures and central bank aversion for
economic and financial disruptions. For example, the Volcker episode in 1979 is
a classic example of an extreme policy stance, with policy makers willing to tolerate the adverse effects of interest rate decisions in terms of insolvency, bank-
ruptcies and unemployment.

The central bank in structuralist theory

Structuralists contended that central banks cannot control interest rates with
accuracy, given the diversity of market structures reflecting the existence of multiple risk premiums. They underlined the weight of financial innovation that
reduces the burden of capital requirements. Structuralists stress the active role of
bank behaviour. Wray (2007) argues that structuralists have drawn on earlier
arguments developed by authors, such as Schumpeter, Gurley and Shaw,
Minsky, and Rousseas, who had depicted banks as profit-seeking institutions,
whose propensity to innovate is driven by the desire to avoid regulatory constraints. Structuralists could not be satisfied with the horizontalist explanation of

bank behaviour that assumed its passivity in the face of a fluctuating demand for loans expressed by private sector agents. Instead, structuralists would argue that banks are actually very active, as shown by their innovation practices designed to economize on regulatory reserves (ibid.). Structuralists emphasize active asset liability management techniques, with the underlying idea that banks impose quantitative constraints on the money-creation process. Yet, Davidson (1992) argued that a non-zero elasticity of the credit supply schedule was enough to establish the endogenous nature of money, thereby rendering the horizontalist position a special case (in the more general case, the money supply curve is thus upward sloping in credit-interest space).

Setting the record straight now that the debate has faded away

'Horizontalism: Setting the record straight' is a contribution by Rochon (2001) in an edited book entitled *Credit, Interest Rate and the Open Economy: Essays on Horizontalism*. With regard to the heated debate between horizontalists and structuralists, Moore argues that post-Keynesians had better aim to establish a consensus, rather than emphasize their disagreements. Moore (ibid., p. 12) thus lists three consensual principles that should unite all post-Keynesian economists:

•   money is credit-driven and demand-determined (endogeneity principle);
•   causality runs from bank lending to deposits, then to the monetary base;
•   the short-term nominal interest rate is the main policy instrument of the central bank; it is exogenously determined.

All other considerations[4] amount to a 'storm in a teacup' (ibid., p. 13). However, prominent authors involved in this intellectual debate have been willing to vindicate their long-standing claims. This is precisely the case for Marc Lavoie: 'The original horizontalist depiction, that of Kaldor and Moore, is the most appropriate. Structuralists have helped to fill in some details.'[5] Lavoie also links strong empirical evidence in favour of horizontalism to enhanced central bank transparency (Chapter 4). Countries such as Canada, Australia and Sweden have more transparent central bank procedures that give support to the horizontalist position, while the operational logic of less transparent central banks fail to undermine horizontalism.[6]

Why the debate never interfered with the mainstream

This question is more fruitful than the internal one, whereby one tries to conclude in favour of one post-Keynesian subset of ideas or the other. Although some authors have argued that the mainstream is an ill-defined categorization (Colander, 2010), we use Woodford's masterpiece *Interest and Price* published in 2003 as a yardstick for the NMC in the first decade of the twenty-first century. Ironically, this is what Woodford (2003, p. 3, emphasis added) wrote about the state of monetary economics in the decades preceding his contribution:

> [i]t is true that the conceptual frameworks proposed by central banks to deal with their perceived need for a more systematic approach to policy were, until quite recently, largely developed *without much guidance from the academic literature on monetary economics.*

Woodford (ibid.) regrets that questions, such as the ideal level of the overnight interest rate and the optimal response to unexpected disturbances, had ceased to be suitable topics of study in the academic literature. A volume written on the centrality of monetary policy and the revival of the rule-based approach to the optimal interest-rate setting procedure in a post-monetarist world (that is, with no mention to money aggregates) could hardly leave post-Keynesians indifferent. In fact, it did not. A few years before Woodford's contribution, mainstream publications by Clarida *et al.* (1999), Romer (2000) and Walsh (2002) had already made theoretical claims that post-Keynesians economists had known all along (Howells, 2007). Even the endogenous nature of money, a core constituent to post-Keynesian economics, was later acknowledged by proponents of the NMC, but without attributing to post-Keynesians the paternity of the idea. In fact, New Keynesians all endorse the endogenous nature of money, which has been the bedrock of post-Keynesian monetary theory for several decades. Central bankers set the short-term nominal interest rate, and no longer keep track of money aggregates (Nersisyan, 2006–2007, p. 91). Unfortunately, the two types of economic discourse (New Keynesian and post-Keynesian) stemmed from distinct paradigms (one belonging to heterodoxy and the other akin to the NMC). In what may be viewed as a lack of tolerance of the mainstream (Lee, 2008), the two approaches were deemed incommensurable in the eyes of the economics profession (Pilkington, 2012b). As a consequence, the reigning paradigm was left unchallenged by endogenous money theorists in what can be regarded, with hindsight, as a massive failure of intra-disciplinary scientific dialogue.

New Keynesian economics: moving away from money supply control?

New Keynesian economics and the abandonment of money supply control

New Keynesian economics put forward the consensus view that monetary policy decisions would follow an interest-rate rule, also called the central bank reaction function, by adjusting the short-term nominal interest rate to unforeseen economic events (Taylor, 2000, p. 90). This evolution would mark the demise of the LM curve in the well-known IS/LM model, thereby replacing money supply control by interest-rate setting procedures as the favoured modus operandi of monetary policy: 'We shall show that the equilibrium evolution of these variables can be understood without reference to the implied path of the money supply, or to the determinants of money demand' (Woodford, 2000).

The schizophrenic Woodfordian rhetoric on money

On the one hand, the role of the money supply is explicitly undermined by Woodford, who nonetheless refuses to break away from monetarism, by offering a curious reinterpretation thereof. The absence of money in *Interest and Prices* may appear, at first glance, as a dividing line between monetarism and the NMC: 'It does not seem at all natural or useful to try to explain the predicted paths of inflation and output as consequences of the implied path of the money supply' (Woodford, 2003, p. 48). However, three years later, in a paper entitled 'How Important is Money in the Conduct of Monetary Policy?' Woodford seems to have departed from previously held views. Woodford (2006, p. 1) starts to note in the introduction that central banks seem to pay less and less attention to the quantity of money in their deliberations prior to their monetary policy decision, as shown by the very low frequency of the use of the term in the speeches given by the Governors of the Bank of England and the Fed (between 2000 and 2002, the term was used only once in twenty-nine speeches by the former, and once in seventeen speeches by the latter (King, 2002, p. 162)). Yet, in a rhetorical feat, Woodford (2006, p. 15, emphasis in the original) occults money without discarding the validity of the quantity theory of money:

> the model is not the one that requires the existence of a money-demand relation … but not one that is incompatible with such a relation. It is incorrect to claim […] that models such as the one set out above 'reject' the quantity of money, and can accordingly be dismissed in light of the empirical support for that approach.

This statement is precisely what we call the schizophrenic Woodfordian rhetoric on money, a phenomenon that has pervaded the whole NMC. Furthermore, Woodford seems to pledge allegiance to neoclassical economics: 'It is established that a non-monetarist analysis of the effects of monetary policy does not involve any theoretical inconsistency or departure from neoclassical orthodoxy' (ibid.). This quote seems to reinforce the neoclassical underpinnings of the NMC that remains embedded in mainstream economics.

The acceptance of the Taylor rule: the NMC and beyond

The Taylor rule

What is the Taylor rule?

Over the past two decades, policy rules developed by Stanford economist John Taylor have become the dominant metric for analysing and evaluating monetary policy. In Taylor's key paper published in 1993, a formula was presented to the economics profession, providing key recommendations for central banks that would be further elaborated upon in an abundant monetary economics literature that extends up until the recent period. The purpose of the Taylor rule is to provide a simple monetary rule (akin to the third equation of the three-equation simplified model of the NMC), in order to reconcile the short-run goal for stabilizing the economy and the long-run objective to keep inflation under control.[7] The Taylor rule was progressively endorsed by central bankers worldwide, and is still widely influential to date: '[t]he Taylor Rule became the most common way to model monetary policy' (Goodfriend, 2007, p. 59; see also Orphanides, 2007). In a neo-Wicksellian fashion, the Taylor rule states that the real (inflation-adjusted) short-term interest rate is determined by three factors:

1   the difference between actual and targeted inflation;
2   the output gap (the difference between actual output and the full-employment level);
3   the natural interest rate (that which is consistent with full employment).

The original Taylor rule stated that the Fed set the federal funds rate at one plus 1.5 times the inflation rate plus 0.5 times the output gap. Whereas Taylor's simple rule was primarily prescriptive, in Taylor (1999) the rule became explicitly normative, with large deviations from baseline rules identified as policy mistakes. Therefore, monetary policy tightening was recommended in times of overheating (when the economy is above its full-employment level).[8] Contrariwise, in the more recent period, the GFC has set the stage for monetary easing (i.e. lower interest rates). In case of conflicting macroeconomic goals, the Taylor rule provides guidance for setting an adequate level of the interest rate that supposedly balances the resulting tensions between the target inflation and output levels.[9] According to Quiggin (2010, p. 110), the Taylor rule is about keeping inflation and the growth rate of the economy as close as possible to their target values, with the help of a single policy instrument, namely the interest rate. The Tinbergen principle is not complied with (Chapter 2) under the Taylor rule, because two macroeconomic objectives (the inflation rate and the growth rate of GDP) are targeted by only one instrument (the short-term nominal interest rate). Therefore, the conduct of macroeconomic policy comes down to an econometric problem, whereby a single representative agent within a typical DSGE model aims at optimizing the trade-off between the two target variables (ibid., p. 110).

   Although the Fed never admitted to following the Taylor rule, some studies have shown that the latter accurately describes how monetary policy was conducted in the Greenspan era. However, alternative viewpoints have been expressed in the literature, most notably by John Taylor himself: '[the Taylor rule] worked well during the historical experience of the "Great Moderation" that began in the early 1980s' (Taylor, 2009a, p. 342). However, between 2000 and 2007, in the run up to the GFC, we witnessed the largest deviations from the Taylor rule since the inflationary chaos of the 1970s.[10] This observation leads Taylor (ibid., p. 343) to blame the housing boom mainly on pre-GFC monetary excesses.[11]

The Taylor rule as automatic stabilizer[12]

In an interview given in April 2011, Nobel Prize Laureate Robert Solow reinterpreted the Taylor rule as a policy strategy aimed at enforcing automatic stabilizers. Solow (2011) reiterates the primacy of the Taylor rule in the recent period, whether the later interest-rate setting procedure was deliberate or not. Solow describes the Taylor rule as one that determines the policy rate in terms of the deviations of the current inflation rate from a targeted rate and the deviations of current GDP from a targeted level of GDP. In other words, this type of central bank behaviour amounts to an automatic stabilizer (ibid.).[13] Taylor rules as automatic stabilizers in a stable world? That is precisely the configuration in which the NMC thrived prior to the GFC. It is unfortunate that a wide-ranging reflection was not conducted at the time, in order to assess the resistance and the robustness of the methodological apparatus endorsed by proponents of the NMC. As the saying goes, 'mend the roof before it rains'.

Post-crisis discussion of the Taylor rule: Senator Toomey and Ben Bernanke

On the occasion of the Federal Reserve's first monetary policy report for 2011, hearing before the committee on banking, housing and urban affairs[14] on 1 March 2011, an exchange took place between Senator Toomey and Chairman Bernanke[15] about the relevance of the Taylor rule in a post-crisis scenario, whether or not it provided a rationale behind quantitative easing (Chapter 13). Below is a summary of this exchange.

First, Senator Toomey briefly alluded to the ongoing Quantitative Easing 2 programme, and made a rather contrasted statement about the extent to which he agreed therewith. He then went on to describe the current situation in the USA, which is a 'subpar economic recovery' that does not call for a monetary solution.

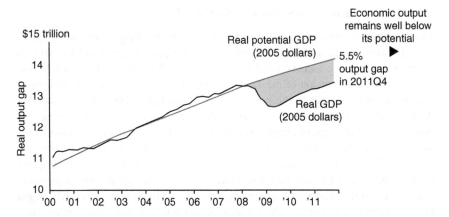

Figure 7.1 The output gap between 2000 and 2012.

Rather than a 'lack of money supply', it is a 'lack of liquidity' that is driving the economic problem experienced by the USA. In the light of a range of variables, such as money supply growth or commodity prices, Senator Toomey argued that the country is dangerously 'planting the seeds of serious inflation'. Money is deemed non-neutral, for monetary expansion creates 'the illusion of growth, not real growth'. Senator Toomey questioned Chairman Bernanke on the most appropriate definition of inflation, and whether asset price changes would affect future policy decisions. In his initial reply, Ben Bernanke made a stunning monetarist confession by admitting that below par growth rates of M1 and M2 money aggregates, along with Friedman's ideas on the appropriate level of nominal GDP growth, provided a rationale for more monetary stimulus, in other words, a new round of quantitative easing. Additionally, a Taylor rule used in a post-crisis context would suggest negative interest rates in the present economic circumstances. Ben Bernanke then alluded to a possible policy scheme going beyond the original Taylor rule. Senator Toomey wanted to know whether or not Ben Bernanke knew if John Taylor would have approved of this stance. Ben Bernanke was rather cryptic in his answer; he contended that there was no such thing as a single version of the Taylor rule. In this respect, the original version, dating back from 1993, reportedly came in sharp contrast with the one presented later in 1999. In spite of their efforts, Senator Toomey and Chairman Bernanke were unable to reach a compromise on the optimal interest rate derived from their respective understanding of the Taylor rule. Senator Toomey also asked Chairman Bernanke whether the sluggish growth experienced by the US economy would lead him to reconsider his policy stance on an inflation target of around 2 per cent in the medium term. Bernanke reiterated his commitment to low inflation, embedded in the Fed mandate, and discarded the surprise inflation policy option. He finally assured Senator Toomey that the Fed was monitoring the conjuncture with regard to inflationary pressures, and continued to be extremely vigilant in this respect.

John Taylor's incisive answer to Ben Bernanke[16]

Blogs written by prominent personalities can be particularly insightful at times. John Taylor responded to Ben Bernanke's statement on his personal blog, and his comments were very incisive (ibid.); Taylor rejects Bernanke's claim that he had put forward a new version of the Taylor rule by 1999. He is startled by this assertion, for he firmly sticks to the policy rule he presented in 1993. This means that there could not be any clearer substantive disagreement over post-crisis monetary policy between the current chairman of the Federal Reserve and the founder of the monetary rule the latter institution supposedly followed during the last two decades. Taylor refers to page 325 of his 1999 paper, by clearly distinguishing between his original policy rule put forward in 1993 and what other economists from the Federal Reserve later suggested. Taylor is willing to set the record straight for the distinction is not merely a matter of semantics, because the 'others have suggested' policy rule relies on a much larger coefficient on the GDP gap, which opens the door for negative interest rates that may provide a rationale behind quant-itative easing programmes (that Taylor precisely opposes). All in all, John Taylor claims that he never put forward any monetary rule that would remotely provide support to the Fed's post-crisis monetary policy, such as QE1 and QE2. Further, the following words by John Taylor are particularly instructive. It is crystal clear that not only Taylor questions the efficacy of the non-conventional policies imple-mented after 2008, but he also criticizes Ben Bernanke for being excessively ambiguous regarding the nature of the monetary policy rule that was being fol-lowed. On top of being sceptical in the face of low interest rates approaching the zero bound, John Taylor seems to remain faithful to core NMC precepts when he states that enhanced transparency about strategies would increase the predictability of policy actions, and would help stabilize market expectations with regard to the future of quantitative easing. Taylor goes on to teach a lesson of central banking to Bernanke as to which interest rate level would best correspond to a strict applica-tion of his own rule. The original Taylor rule states that the interest rate should be set, in a rather mechanical way, at about 1.5 times the inflation rate plus ½ GDP + 1. Relying on recent estimates for January and February 2011, Taylor shows that the inflation rate and the output gap lay respectively at 1.4 and 4.4 percent, which implies an interest rate of $1.5 \times 1.4 + 0.5 \times (-4.4) + 1 = 2.1 + -2.2 + 1 = 0.9$ per cent, or about 1 per cent. It is demonstrated that leaving the short-term interest rate within the 0–0.25 per cent range amounts to a policy mistake. The Fed should thus have raised the interest rate at the end of 2011. However, as shown by Figure 7.2, in early 2012 the Federal Funds Target Rate had not yet broken out of the 0–0.25 per cent range it has been engulfed in since January 2009. Sustained historically low interest rates therefore seem to indicate that the US economy might have entered a liquidity trap wherein the rather mechanical interest-rate setting procedure, one of the hallmarks of the NMC, has become obsolete for post-crisis monetary policy.

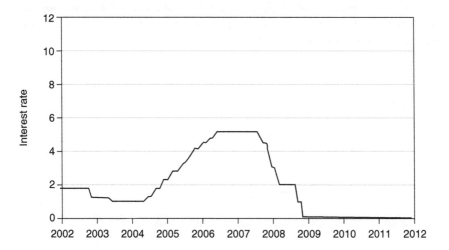

Figure 7.2 Federal Funds Target Rate, 2002–2012.

John Taylor (ibid.) was thus right when stating that Ben Bernanke was no longer following his eponymous monetary rule. In fact, the Fed fund rate finished the year 2011 unchanged, and there were no signs of an interest-rate hike in sight in the first quarter of 2012: '[b]ut if it is one of the other rules mentioned by the Chairman we might have to wait longer'.

Why Taylor believes governments misdiagnosed the credit market problems[17]

In his best-seller *Getting Off Track: How Government Actions and Interventions Caused, Prolonged, and Worsened the Financial Crisis*, John Taylor (2009) explains the worsening of the global economy after 2008. According to Taylor (p. 61), not only did government actions cause the financial crisis, but they also prolonged and worsened it. For Taylor, the root cause of the GFC is the deviation from historical precedents and principles for setting interest rates that had worked well since the inception of the NMC. Taylor goes on to argue that the crisis was prolonged, because the government merely misdiagnosed problems on the credit market. Instead of focusing on risk, they injected astronomical amounts of liquidity into the system, providing support for financial institutions and their creditors, thereby exacerbating moral hazard in times of financial fragility. Taylor (ibid.) emphasizes the lack of a proper framework at the time these actions were put in place. Policy was neither clear nor understandable, which comes in contradistinction with NMC core principles. Finally, Taylor (ibid.) does not dismiss the existence of other factors that account for the crisis; however, he is convinced that ill-advised government actions were on top of the list of most damaging policy mistakes.

Let us illustrate graphically Taylor's claim that substantial deviations from the Taylor rule caused the crisis. It is indeed true that in the aftermath of the bursting of the Internet bubble (immediately followed by the 2001 recession) up until 2006, the Federal Reserve set interest rates at low levels, in order to boost stock markets and economic growth.

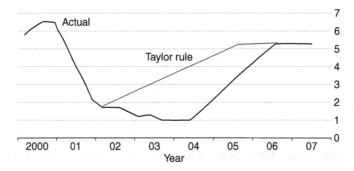

Figure 7.3 Federal funds rate, actual and counterfactual, US, 2000–2007 (%).

By the same token, low interest rates fed a credit bubble in the making, and amplified speculative trends characterized by the frenzy securitization of sub-prime mortgages, conducive to rising housing pricing, decoupled with the fundamentals of the real economy. However, in an ideological twist of fate, market failures were discarded by Taylor, who went as far as stating that the GFC was in fact a government-induced crisis.[18] However, in the same book, Taylor performs a rhetoric feat, by arguing that central banks helped prolong the recession with their near-zero interest rate policies. This stunning conclusion poses a burning question for central bankers: should central banks have ignored the GFC, and pursued pre-crisis NMC policies as if nothing had happened? In the next section, we take on a very different view. Along with Friedman and Wells, we see how Taylor's ideas cannot be left unchallenged in a post-crisis world.

Taylor's views under attack in a post-crisis world

Krugman and Wells (2010) are critical of Taylor's claims, and identify serious flaws in his conceptual apparatus and his idea that low interest rates and deviations from the Taylor rule triggered the GFC. Krugman and Wells (ibid.) defend the policy stance of the Fed after the short recession in 2001. The subsequent upturn was fragile, and interest rates had to be kept low, in order to sustain the nascent recovery. As far as employment was concerned, pre-recession levels were not attained until 2005. Back then, the Fed was concerned with inflation hitting a thirty-five year low (probably under the impact of NMC policies, but also of strong globalization and outsourcing trends, pushing the price of imported goods downwards). Low inflation meant that there was a non-zero deflationary risk. This is the tipping point for central bankers, when low inflation morphs into a deflationary trap whereby depressed wages and sluggish growth push prices downward in a self-reinforcing spiral. Why would the Fed have raised interest rates at this stage? It is well known that the institutional mandate of the Fed (Chapter 9) features an essential employment objective. High interest rates between 2002 and 2006 would have therefore contradicted its stated mission.

Krugman and Wells (ibid.) also argue that the real-estate bubble was a North-Atlantic phenomenon, and was not circumscribed to the USA. Any unilateral action of the Fed, in order to pre-empt asset price inflation, would have therefore affected the composition and the destination of international financial flows. This reallocation of international capital flows could have been highly detrimental to the United States. Hence, uncoordinated leaning-against-the-wind policies were never seriously envisaged by the Federal Reserve. Further, real estate bubbles in the UK and Spain were particularly pronounced. Yet, neither the Bank of England nor the ECB had adopted low interest-rate policies nearly as aggressive as the Fed's. Therefore, it is wrong to assume that low interest rates were to blame (exclusively) for the real-estate bubble. Financialization, securitization and deregulation trends (Pilkington, 2008) must also come in the picture; the impact of low interest rates should certainly not be disregarded, but it should not be overstated either. In a nutshell, it can be argued

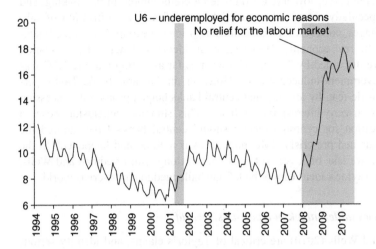

Figure 7.4 The underemployed US population for economic reasons.

that, in the light of employment figures between 2001 and 2005, low interest rates were justified for a prolonged period. Failure to do so would have entailed flawed policy decisions and a narrow conception of unemployment, viewed as a mere adjustment variable.[19]

Conclusion: the interest-rate setting procedure in a post-crisis world

A Goldilocks economy is one that is not too hot or cold,[20] sustaining moderate growth and low inflation within the framework of market-friendly monetary policy. The name is derived from the children's tale *Goldilocks and the Three Bears*. The phrase was first used by David Shulman of Salomon Brothers who wrote *The Goldilocks Economy: Keeping the Bears at Bay* in March 1992.

The shaded area marks the end of the goldilocks economy. In this new configuration, the Taylor rule loses its relevance. After the GFC, the number of Americans, who are underemployed for economic reasons rose sharply between 2008 (eight million) and 2010 (eighteen million people).[21]

8 Inflation targeting and the formation of a broad consensus

Introduction

In this chapter, we expose the main contention of the NMC, namely that monetary policy is totally effective as a means of inflation control. Therefore, it is the inflation rate, and not anything else, that must be strictly targeted. In a widely acclaimed article published in the *Journal of Economic Perspectives*, Bernanke and Mishkin (1997) had presented the salient features of inflation targeting regimes. Under the NMC, inflation targeting is the central policy implication of the price stability mandate of central banks. The NMC and inflation targeting policies have thus become synonymous in the literature. We investigate whether this identity is justified in the light of a wide range of central bank practices between 1989 and 2007.

Inflation targeting: what's in a name?

A non-Shakesperian view of IT

What's in a name? That which we call a rose
By any other name would smell as sweet.

These famous words uttered by Juliet in *Romeo and Juliet*, Shakespeare's masterpiece, are remembered as a timeless philosophical reflection on language-reality connections. The name given to an object or a phenomenon is often viewed as merely conventional, and does not alter the object's intrinsic qualities or properties. A rose is a rose as a matter of convention. However, if we look more deeply into the matter, is it really so? Aren't there any deeper connections between the name given to concepts and the conceptual entities themselves? This introductory digression is far from innocent. It can be argued that inflation-targeting central banks (hereafter ITers) are not merely given an extrinsic name, regardless of the real-world phenomena they endeavour to designate. Is not there a deeper connection between how self-defined ITers label themselves and actual central banking practices observed in IT countries? Is labelling oneself an ITer a very instance of inflation targeting? IT policies may indeed come in sharp contrast with the Shakespearean view of the relation between labels and their referents. The connection between what is labelled IT by the economics profession and actual experience of IT policies certainly deserves further enquiry.

IT and reflexivity

One may draw a parallel with the concept of reflexivity in social science (Soros, 2008). Reflexivity refers to circular relationships between cause and effect. Hence, a reflexive relationship is bidirectional with both the cause and the effect affecting one another. Reflexivity is therefore discordant with equilibrium theory, which stipulates that markets move towards equilibrium and that non-equilibrium fluctuations are merely random noise that will soon be corrected. In equilibrium theory, prices in the long run at equilibrium reflect the underlying fundamentals, which are unaffected by prices. Proponents of reflexivity assert that prices do, in fact, influence the fundamental values, and that these newly influenced set of fundamentals proceed to change expectations, thereby exerting feedback loop effects on so-called equilibrium prices; the process will then continue in a self-reinforcing pattern. As a consequence, markets inexorably tend towards disequilibrium (or permanently unstable equilibrium).

IT and equilibrium theory

The inflation target necessarily lies outside equilibrium theory. This means that there are fatal flaws in DSGE models assuming that low inflation is always the result of optimal and rational pricing decisions made by countless interacting utility-maximizing agents whose behaviour is shaped by expectations determined by policy decisions and present economic conditions. In fact, prices affect the perception of fundamentals by economic agents (money is said to be non-neutral). Newly modified fundamentals will have an impact on future price expectations in a complex feedback loop effect. Low inflation and price stability are best seen as disequilibrium macroeconomic phenomena in a world wherein price-influenced fundamentals constantly retroact on fundamentals-sensitive prices.

Textbook definition of IT

A textbook definition of inflation targeting was given by Bernanke *et al.* (1999, p. 4), where it was presented as a framework for monetary policy. A framework is a hypothetical description of a complex entity or process, and monetary policy encompasses all policy actions designed and implemented by central banks. This framework necessitates the public announcement of an official inflation target (or target ranges) for inflation over a specified time horizon. The central bank must be committed to low and stable inflation in the long run; this commitment must be explicitly acknowledged (ibid.). Amongst the features of inflation targeting, transparency – the effort to communicate the outlooks and objectives of the central bank to the public – is of paramount importance. Equally relevant are the mechanisms that reinforce the accountability of the central bank (ibid.). Wray (2007, p. 2) explains that the official range for an inflation target might be dictated by a political decision made by elected representatives. In turn, the central bank is given considerable discretion, in order to attain this ultimate objective. Central bankers will follow the standard NMC interest-rate setting procedure (embodied in the three-equation or six-equation model) akin to a Taylor type rule with a reaction function responding to deviations between actual inflation from the target and output gaps. The adjustment will be made towards a presumed neutral rate.[1] Wray (ibid.) therefore argues that inflation targeting practices under the NMC leave considerable discretionary scope to the central bank, in order to attain their ultimate goal (usually a low inflation rate). Discretionary monetary policy decisions include the celerity at which it must move towards the acknowledged neutral rate, the ideal response to exogenous inflationary pressures, or whether it should adopt a pre-emptive or reactive policy stance.

Unity of purpose, diversity of practices

Charles Bean (2007) draws a list of countries that consider themselves ITers. *Inter alia*, this list features Australia, Brazil, Canada, Mexico, New Zealand, Norway, Sweden and the United Kingdom. Policy strategies, tools and communication practices are not necessarily identical, as the latter might differ in the details. However, the common denominator of these central banks is that they all share a flexible interpretation of their mandate. In fact, an explicit inflation target over the medium term does not preclude the existence of an output and/or employment objective in the short run. So in the world of inflation targeting, there is assuredly a unity of purpose and a diversity of practices. However, there are a few prominent central banks, such as the European Central Bank (ECB) and the Swiss National Bank, that do not label themselves as ITers. Yet, these central banks are not alien to inflation-targeting practices, as they include key features of that framework for monetary policy. The latter include a 'numerical definition of price stability, a central role for communications about the economic outlook, and a willingness to accommodate short-run economic stabilization objectives so long as these objectives do not jeopardize the primary goal of price stability' (Bernanke, 2011b). Bean (2007) echoes our discussion on the (non)Shakespearean view of inflation-targeting, by explaining that the Fed and the ECB are not ITers although they behave as such. Bean (ibid.) therefore emphasizes the commonalities between self-proclaimed ITers and non-ITers. The differences between them amount to the rhetoric of communication. Pilkington (2012b) has raised the issue of the discursive nature of economics, in an ode to pluralism acknowledging the components of heterodoxy. In this respect, the words used by economists (or central bankers) are far from neutral. English for specific purposes and applied linguistics are therefore most relevant disciplinary fields, in order to reinterpret the Shakespearean debate on inflation targeting.

Inflation targeting and beyond: (re)shaping the NMC

The present book is entitled *The Global Financial Crisis and the New Monetary Consensus*. How does inflation targeting fit into the picture? Are the NMC and inflation targeting synonymous? Our answer is 'not quite'. However, the latter remains a central feature of the former. However, whilst the NMC is a wide-ranging intellectual edifice conducive to central banking wisdom, ITers' self-proclaimed flexibility makes inflation targeting a slippery field of critical enquiry.

The main contention of the NMC

For C. Taylor (2011, p. 51), the primary objective of macroeconomic policy, in what he calls the 1990s synthesis, is price stability, which should be enshrined in a legal framework (whether national, international or supranational). Price stability naturally leads to an explicit target for inflation (but implicit ones are also acceptable). One interesting feature is the idea that monetary policy (tantamount to the interest-rate setting policy exclusively conducted by an autonomous and independent central bank),[2] and monetary policy alone, can achieve its primary objective, namely price stability (ibid.). The idea that monetary policy is the sole determinant of inflation is in fact described by Arestis and Sawyer (2005, p. 10) as the backbone of the NMC:

> Monetary policy is the determinant of the rate of inflation through the effect of the interest rate on demand and on expectations, and in the long run the inflation rate is the only macroeconomic variable that monetary policy can affect.

We equate this affirmation to the expression of the main contention of the NMC. However, fiscal policy as a viable policy option is not explicitly discarded;[3] nor are multiple objectives for monetary policy ruled out (C. Taylor, 2011, p. 51).

Policy measures vs state of knowledge

The reason why IT cannot be equated to the NMC is that the scope of the latter is broader, while the former provides the policy features, which are the hallmark of the NMC, namely market discipline, central bank accountability, transparency and flexibility (Arestis and Sawyer, 2005, p. 10). The differences between IT practices and the NMC are expressed in terms of policy measures versus state of knowledge (in phase with the core principles sustaining the NMC). Inflation targeting is a pragmatic set of policy actions, that is, 'a robust way of achieving and maintaining price stability' (Orphanides, 2010, p. 13). In a nutshell, IT is a non-doctrinal guide for action (whose strengths are its flexibility and plurality of institutional incarnations), whereas the NMC is a powerful intellectual edifice, which morphed into monetary policy wisdom from the early 1990s onwards. In linguistic terms (Pilkington, 2012b), one wonders whether the main contention of the NMC can be made intelligible for IT practitioners? In the last instance, are IT and the NMC commensurate terms? The answer is affirmative, although the NMC must be understood in reference to a remarkable period of macroeconomic success. Ben Bernanke (2002a) reminds us that the conquest of inflation by the Fed took place in the 1980s. As a result, the US economy steadily converged towards a low inflation environment. The robustness of this prolonged period of prosperity was only mildly interrupted by two recessions, whose severity was low by historical standards. Output growth and inflation volatility declined sharply during this period, and the chaotic decade of the 1970s seemed to fade into a distant memory (ibid.). Yet, this remarkable pre-crisis optimism regarding the very idea that monetary policy is the fundamental determinant of inflation, was not shared by everyone: '[w]hile monetary policy may very well be a flexible instrument in terms of stabilization objectives, whether it is the most significant determinant of inflation is *a moot point*' (Arestis and Sawyer, 2005, p. 11, italics in original). Well before the GFC, noisy cracks in the consensus were not unheard of.

Reaching a consensus after decades of disagreements

Charles Bean (2007) acknowledges the idea that macroeconomics had been the least consensual branch of the dismal science until the emergence of the NMC. After being heatedly debated for decades; it is only in the decade (prior to 2007) that economists reached a consensus on the scope of monetary policy and the most adequate institutional framework for the conduct thereof. For Arestis (2009, pp. 2–3), the NMC is called New Consensus Macroeconomics (NCM), and was born following the demise of the Grand Neoclassical Synthesis in the 1970s. Macroeconomists had overlooked the revival of New Classical Macroeconomics augmented by rational expectations. In contrast, New Keynesian macroeconomics morphed into a consensual body of theory that incorporated early 1970s developments of macroeconomics, such as rational expectations, but without weakening the old neoclassical synthesis. When a New Keynesian paradigm arose in the 1980s (Galí and Gertler, 2007), it was given solid microfoundations alongside the RBC approach that featured an explicit optimizing approach (Pilkington, 2011a). Woodford (2008) argues that the NMC came into existence 'because progress in macroeconomic analysis has made it possible to see that the alternative which earlier generations felt it necessary to choose were not so thoroughly incompatible when understood more deeply'. In a paper entitled 'Convergence in Macroeconomics: Elements of the New Synthesis', prepared for the session 'Convergence in Macroeconomics?' at the annual meeting of the American Economics Association, New Orleans on 4 January 2008, Woodford (2008) asks the question whether there is a convergence of views in macroeconomics, which is the discipline 'concerned with understanding the determinants of national income, inflation, and the effects of monetary and fiscal policy'. Woodford (ibid.) acknowledges the persistence of a 'wide spectrum of opinions on many issues' and a substantial dispersion of opinions on the topics enjoying the best prospects for further research. In fact, Woodford argues that the hallmark of the consensus today is that there is 'less disagreement among macroeconomists about fundamental issues' (ibid.). In the two decades preceding the GFC, a 'substantial degree of consensus on the intellectual and institutional framework for monetary policy' within central banks and mainstream economics, was also acknowledged by Ben Bernanke in a presentation entitled 'The Effects of the Great Recession on Central Bank Doctrine and Practice' given at the Federal Reserve Bank of Boston 56th Economic Conference, Boston, Massachusetts on 18 October 2011.

Mishkin's top nine advances in the science of monetary policy

Frederic Mishkin, professor at the Columbia Business School, was a member of the Board of Governors of the Federal Reserve System from 2006 to 2008. He put forward nine advances in the Science of Monetary Policy that embody the NMC.[4]

1   As Friedman would put it, inflation is always and everywhere a monetary phenomenon. It is under the control of central bank policy.
    Comment: the first principle is inspired from monetarism; New Keynesian macroeconomists would certainly agree therewith in the long run.
2   Price stability improves economic welfare, because resources are employed more productively and efficiently in the economic system.
    Comment: this is tantamount to a postulate, rather than a scientific result.
3   There is no long-run trade-off between unemployment and inflation. Therefore, central banks cannot lower unemployment permanently (i.e. there exists a NAIRU), even by trying to generate surprise inflation.
    Comment: the old Phillips curve is thus discarded.
4   Market expectations play a key role in the transmission of monetary policy to the economy (Woodford, 2003).
    Comment: inflation is everywhere an 'expectational' phenomenon.
5   The Taylor rule is a good precept for sound monetary policy.
    Comment: an interest-rate rule is needed by the central bank. The Taylor rule is the most suitable tool in this regard.
6   The time-inconsistency problem applies to monetary policy; the latter states that discretionary policies lead to poor outcomes. Institutions that provide a form of commitment are strongly needed.
    Comment: rule-based policies are therefore preferred over discretionary ones. The institutional setting sustaining the NMC is made more explicit.
7   Central bank independence is a key element of optimal institutional design.
    Comment: monetary policy must be free from political inference.
8   Central banks must commit to a nominal anchor.
    Comment: this is the most effective way, in order for the central bank to anchor market expectations.
9   Financial frictions and financial instability are phenomena of utmost importance in explaining the business cycle.
    Comment: this is the most intriguing statement in the list, and deserves further inquiry. The Minskian financial instability hypothesis comes to

mind. Likewise, frictions and market imperfections are the hallmark of the New Keynesians, although business cycle theory is regarded as a wider branch of economic theory than the New Keynesian interpretation thereof.

The NMC epitomized by Michael Woodford

We list hereafter a list of fundamental questions, whose answers constitute an assessment of the NMC by Woodford himself.[5]

What is macroeconomics?

Modern macroeconomics requires the use of formalized models featuring inter-temporal general-equilibrium foundations. The neoclassical underpinnings of this approach are obvious; the models are designed to explain economic phenomena with a dual dimension: short-run fluctuations and long-run growth. As explained by Pilkington (2011a) in his review of dictionary entries devoted to real business cycle (RBC) theory in modern dictionaries, RBC theory is a wide-ranging framework that accounts for both short-run fluctuations and long-run economic growth. Hence, the methodological stance of both New Classical Macroeconomics and RBC should be regarded as the relevant mainstream approach to the explanation of economic phenomena. To put it bluntly, micro-economics is the stuff macroeconomic theory is made of. The two branches of economics involve the same sets of principles and merge into the well-known DSGE models that became widespread analytical tools under the NMC (Chapters 5, 6 and 7). Today, DSGE models are used by central bank research departments that compute the structural parameters of the economy, in order to analyze the short-run effects of alternative policies. The influence of New-Keynesian economics is evident; imperfect competition is the norm in both labour and product markets; money wages and prices are sticky for intervals of time.

How should quantitative policy analysis be conducted?

Woodford is convinced that policy analysis must rest on structural models subject to econometric testing and validation. This is the methodology inherited from Milton Friedman and RBC theory. A structural model will necessarily contain a data-generating process, whose nature is essential. The predictive power of the model (with regard to actual aggregate time series) will determine its explanatory power. However, unlike early equilibrium business cycle and RBC theories, DSGE models rely on estimated structural parameters with much higher pretence of quantitative realism. Yet, whether or not the economy really behaves as if DSGE models pertained to real-world economic phenomena, in ontological terms (Lawson, 1997, 2006, 2009), is a question that is not addressed. Empirical methods used by mainstream macroeconomists (e.g. calibration methods inspired by RBC theory or Bayesian estimates of DSGE models) merely reflect the diversity of their taste and methodological preferences. However, there is a broad consensus on the principles underlying quantitative modelling: first, the need for a valid data-generating process and, second, the econometric validation of the chosen structural models.

Are market expectations satisfactorily accounted for?

Market expectations are incorporated in economic models, and are considered endogenous. Expectations will differ according to the various scenarios envisaged and the alternative policy stances adopted. Economists can no longer omit these fundamental parameters in their models. The state of the economy is largely determined by these expectations, which play a crucial role.

Do exogenous shocks matter?

The answer to this question is affirmative. One may also refer to real economic disturbances (as in RBC theory) throwing the economy into confusion. Pilkington (2011a) shows that RBC shocks are not circumscribed to technology and productivity shocks. Disturbances are manifold, and apply to all aspects of economic phenomena (taxation, fiscal policy, financial markets, natural disasters, consumer preferences etc.). Unlike the traditional Keynesian story, business cycles are supply-side determined. The impact on aggregate demand is no longer the alpha and omega of economic theorizing. Exogenous shocks are best dealt with by stabilizing monetary policy. The Great Moderation itself can be explained by improvements in monetary policy. As argued by Pilkington (ibid.), there is nevertheless a contradiction inherent in using general-equilibrium macro-models, *à la* Taylor, that postulate the neutrality of money, while arguing at the same time that the Great Moderation is attributable to 'better' monetary policy (thereby effectively harnessing real forces in the economic system). Either money is neutral or it is not.

The Great Moderation and the quantity theory of money

One of the achievements of the Great Moderation is the indisputable victory over inflation following the failed monetarist experiment. We now know that monetary policy is effective as a means of inflation control by means of optimal interest-rate setting polices. It is a fundamental result of the NMC. The responsibility of central banks in this regard is now established. By no means does this major breakthrough (both empirical and theoretical) rehabilitate the old quantity theory of money. Thus, money supply targeting practices should not be reinstated by central banks.

The Deutsch Bank Prize in Financial Economics in 2007

The Deutsche Bank Prize in Financial Economics was created in 2005. The first laureate ever was Eugene Fama, who was awarded the Prize for his contribution to the efficient markets hypothesis.[6] As announced by the Deutsche Bank Prize Flyer:

> [t]he Deutsche Bank Prize in Financial Economics honours an internationally renowned researcher, who has excelled through influential contributions to research in the fields of finance and money and macroeconomics, and whose work has led to practice and policy-relevant results.[7]

Woodford received the 2007 prize[8] in recognition of his contributions to the theory and practical analysis of monetary policy:

> Woodford, with his monograph 'Interest and Prices: Foundations of a Theory of Monetary Policy', epitomizes the successful developments in monetary macroeconomics that have refined the New Keynesian research programme, and gained centre stage on the agenda of academic researchers, thanks to its class of rigorous micro-founded models. Michael Woodford must be given credit for analyzing the role played by transparency, and the need for central banks to incorporate expectations, in order to account for the transmission mechanism of monetary policy.

Lars E.O. Svensson, Professor of Economics at Princeton University[9] and notorious proponents of the NMC, in a self-congratulating moment of NMC brotherhood, paid a tribute to Woodford's intellectual contribution to the field of monetary economics. He insisted on the fact that the DB Prize Laureate should be given substantial credit for his outstanding contribution in finance, money and banking at the heart of modern economic policy making. Michael Woodford and his monumental monograph, *Interest and Prices: Foundations of a Theory of Monetary Policy* are the incarnation of the modern refinement of New Keynesian economics, with its improvement in building rigorous micro-foundations for monetary macroeconomics. Svensson explains that Woodford offered the first realistic quantitative estimates of the structural parameters that will be subject to econometric testing and validation. Woodford's works have provided strong support for the DSGE models developed by research departments within major central banks. Finally, he has uncovered the paradigmatic dimension of the NMC, with its emphasis on central bank transparency and the role of expectations in monetary policy implementation. Likewise, on Woodford's influential monograph *Interest and Prices*, Bennett McCallum (2010, p. 4),[10] another fervent NMC proponent, commented that it is 'the most important treatise on monetary economics in over 50 years; it seems likely to go down in intellectual history as one of the handful of great books on this topic'. McCallum (ibid.) criticizes the common use of the term 'New-Keynesian' as a faithful qualifier for describing the new mainstream approach. He also claims a filiation with the New Neoclassical Synthesis. In a stunning instant of candour, McCallum admits that the NMC is closer to monetarism than Keynesianism with which it crossed swords in the 1960s and the 1970s.

The success of the NMC: a post-crisis perspective

The list of speakers for the 2007 DB Prize in financial economics featured the most notorious advocates figures of the NMC, such as Bennett McCallum, Jordi Galí, Frederic Mishkin, Michael Woodford, Otmar Issing. Among these leading figures, the winner of the Prize seems to epitomize the NMC. The curriculum vitae of Michael Woodford, the John Bates Clark Professor of Political Economy at Columbia University (revised in March 2013) is most impressive.[11] Woodford wrote a *Handbook of Monetary Economics* in 2011, and published in the *American Economic Journal* and the *Journal of Monetary Economics*. In 2012, he contributed two long-awaited books entitled *The Taylor Rule and the Transformation of Monetary Policy* and *Rethinking Expectations: The Way Forward for Macroeconomics*; he also published in the *Journal of Economic Theory*, the *Journal of Monetary Economics*, and the *American Economic Review* that rank amongst some of the leading mainstream economics journals in the world. However, a 2013 publication in the *Annual Review of Economics* entitled "Macroeconomic Analysis without Rational Expectations Hypothesis" hints at a slight paradigmatic intellectual shift. The conclusion is that Woodford's aura has not been tarnished by the GFC, as the NMC continues to have the wind blowing in its sails six years into the crisis. However, can we sketch out a post-crisis perspective on the success of the NMC? Doing so would probably require the adoption of a novel perspective borrowed from the French Annales School.

The NMC: at the confluence of history and philosophy

As historian March Bloch, co-founder of the French Annales School, once argued, history's time is the plasma in which phenomena are immersed and the locus of their intelligibility. In this respect, the NMC may be reinterpreted as the spatiotemporal continuum (a period of fifteen years, starting from the early 1990s until the GFC) during which time its main theoretical propositions were empirically validated. Marc Bloch and Lucien Febvre founded the *Annales d'histoire économique et sociale* in the late 1920s. Rather than focusing on problem-oriented analytical history, the Annales School adopted a comprehensive multidisciplinary perspective on human activities, in order to single out the structural causes underlying social phenomena. The Annales School aimed to identify immobile stretches of time within which social phenomena could be rendered intelligible. The NMC may be an instance of such an immobile stretch of time that may be studied with the help of what Bloch calls collective illusions. By reading history backwards and proceeding from the known (e.g. the outbreak of the GFC in 2008) to the unknown (e.g. the structural causes behind the emergence of the NMC in the 1990s), it may be possible to cast light on recent monetary events. For members of the Annales School, conditions of possibility are always subject to philosophical investigation in the light of the unrepeatability of the past and the intervention of historical figures that shape our present reality. In this respect, the NMC, which shows a puzzling ignorance of the history of economic thought and economic history (Galbraith 2008), has long oscillated between scepticism at its inception, undisputed success throughout its existence and utter disillusion today: '[d]espite early scepticism, the 1990s settlement turned out to be effective for around 15 years in maintaining price stability and steady economic growth with (eventually) falling unemployment in economies' (C. Taylor, 2011, p. 50). Yet, the current reality of the history profession bears little resemblance to the professional practices experimented and developed by the Annales School. A modern and wide-ranging history of the NMC today would prove extremely ambitious, if not impossible. Indeed, intradisciplinary dialogue between historians has become increasingly difficult, due to the contemporary fragmentation of economic history, which is now divided into a multitude of sub-sets conducive to hyper-specialization.[12] A historiography of the NMC would hence amount to an academic tower of Babel. In spite of this radical evolution of the history profession, the need for a collective interdisciplinary effort, mirroring the all-encompassing scholarly ambition of the Annales School (Dosse, 1987), has never been as vivid as today. As argued by Michel Foucault, history and philosophy are inseparable. The ontology of the present entails a reflection on the emergence of modernity along a plurality of theoretical lines (McHoul and Grace, 2002, p.viii). This quest lies at the confluence of history and philosophy; it is really an 'interrogative practice rather than a search for essentials' (ibid.). Transposed to the theme of our book, the ontological arguments entailed by the NMC are inseparable from the history of the NMC itself. If 'by "crisis", we mean a gradual and uneven spitting of the complex network of ideas formed by [these] critical disciplines' (ibid.), the current crisis of the NMC is an instance of such a paradigmatic transformation. Why, then, does the mental reconstitution of the history of the NMC constitute a fruitful intellectual endeavour? The answer is instinctive, simply because the NMC is not a-historical. It is finite in the spatiotemporal continuum legitimizing its pervasive, albeit precarious, existence. The most evident features thereof are formed 'in the confluence of encounters and chances during the course of a precarious and fragile history' (ibid.). The NMC therefore emerged from a network of contingencies that can necessarily be traced back to its origins. What the NMC has done in the field of economic knowledge can be equally undone in a sudden epistemological twist of fate. Let us have a look at the etymology of the word 'consensus' that comes from Latin cōnsēnsus ('agreement, accordance, unanimity') and from cōnsentiō ('feel together; agree'). Is this the case that any perceived consensus could, in fact, be the by-product of a historical transformation propelled by radical events? Reforming imagination inspired by the inflation threats of the 1970s realized itself through a social magma that inexorably morphed into a new economic reality, which later dissolved into a river of significations drawn off as a 'representational flux', and that took the form of 'stable figures' constitutive of the 'necessary basis for all language' (Castoriadis, 1975, p. 251; Pilkington, 2012b) in the NMC. These stable figures are the building linguistic blocks of the NMC, and include central bank transparency, the Great Moderation, credibility, price stability, etc.

Hyman Minsky: the great missing figure in the NMC

The absolute emphasis on price stability at the expense of prudent macro-financial management (financial stability mechanisms and macro-prudential rules) might have been extreme under the NMC. Minsky's works and his emphasis put on the de-stabilizing forces of the market might have been overlooked (Wray, 2011). Likewise, Jeanne (2011) argues that central banks in a post-crisis world need to reconcile price stability with a broader financial stability objective. As argued by Cagliarini *et al.* (2010, p. 23), it was hoped in the 1990s and early 2000s that an environment characterized by macroeconomic stability would obviate financial instability. The Great Moderation was never what it seemed. In many respects, it laid the ground for risk-taking behaviour by complacent investors, who propelled the extreme instability of the world economy during the GFC. Cagliarini *et al.* (ibid.) seems to depict a rather pessimistic scenario for the future in which 'it may be unrealistic to think that the financial system will ever settle into a steady state, since innovations, including new types of financial institutions and new ways to take on risks, will probably continue to be the norm'. This constitutes a rather pessimistic interpretation of the financial instability hypothesis. In financialized economies, apparent macroeconomic stability does not preclude recurring financial crises. Sadly enough, the Great Moderation, if this term ever conveyed any meaningful specialized knowledge (Pilkington, 2012b), seemed, with hindsight, to have contained the germs of its own disintegration.

The NMC after 2007: ill-founded optimism?

The annual meeting of the America Economics Association was held in New Orleans in January 2008. Michael Woodford gave a paper with a resolutely optimistic tone:

> the current moment is one in which prospects are unusually bright for the sort of progress that has lasting consequences, due to the increased possibility of productive dialogue between theory and empirical work, on the one hand, and between theory and practice on the other.[13]

What did Woodford actually mean? Not only would the link between empirical facts and theory soon be weakened, but with the advent of the GFC a few months later, central bankers would find themselves in uncharted territory, without any proper framework to rely upon.

Is the consensus still consensual after 2007?

For Wray (2011), economic policy in the NMC only works indirectly through its ability to shape market expectations. The word 'consensus' is therefore ambivalent. Either it refers to an increasing level of agreement amongst monetary macroeconomists on monetary policy, or it means that central banks aim at achieving a consensus of all market participants (notably, regarding policy decisions and strategies outlook). Another possibility is that the consensus principally exists at the paradigmatic level. In the NMC, an environment characterized by low and stable inflation is believed to be growth enhancing. Yet, the latter statement is hardly verifiable; it is therefore tantamount to a questionable postulate in a post-crisis world (ibid.). In both cases, one must agree on the problematic substantive reality surrounding the term 'consensus'. Whether we refer to a legitimized community of macroeconomists or to an ill-defined set of market participants, it seems that the very idea of an indefectible consensus has lost most of its appeal since 2007.

The narrow conception of monetary policy under the NMC

Woodford's definition of monetary policy's raison d'être

In his conclusion of *Interest and Prices*, Woodford (2003, p. 623) declared that

> It is hoped that the present study will help to stimulate further work in this sphere and, in so doing, reveal as a practical possibility the sort of rational management of national standards of value that could only be dreamed of by the monetary reforms of a century ago.

The rational management of national standards of value merely confines monetary policy to the price stability objective (unsurprisingly, the essence of the NMC) at the expense of alternative macroeconomic goals such as employment, growth or exchange rate management. It can be objected that Woodford's very conception of monetary policy's *raison d'être* is excessively narrow, and no longer pertains to a post-crisis world, whose new challenges are discussed in the second part of this volume.

The explanatory power of Woodfordian economics

Laidler (2004) is critical of the relevance of the class of micro-founded models used by Woodford, in order to describe modern economies, and the difficulties faced by the theorists when confronted with situations that his models are unable to account for: 'Woodford's treatment is disconcerting, because monetary economies still pose more problems than can be analyzed by the class of models that he elaborates' (ibid., p. 1). More difficulties arise from the uncritical application of Woodford's models to complex international monetary issues for which it has very little explanatory power. Woodford also seems to be powerless in the face of the zero lower bound occurring in recessionary conditions (ibid.). A parallel may be drawn between the US economy in the 1930s and the Japanese economy in 1990s. In both set of historical circumstances, the NMC seems to be unable to provide a satisfactory interpretation or guideline for the future. Laidler had foresight, because these are precisely the burning questions posed by the macroeconomic evolutions in the aftermath of the GFC. Another problem is the lack of reflection on the international monetary system and the problematic issue of the US dollar, for instance in a world-system perspective (Pilkington, 2010). The macro-effects of US policy are not confined to the domestic monetary system of the United States (Laidler, 2004, p. 1), as shown by the mixed reactions spurred by QE1 and QE2 programmes after 2009. It strikes us as evident that these burning issues have been occulted by proponents of the NMC (in spite of an embryonic reflection by Woodford on the effectiveness of monetary policy when approaching the zero bound). The obvious weakness of Woodford's theoretical framework is that it necessitates a relatively stable system, such as a low-inflation environment and a very credible central bank, in order for his theoretical reasoning to be validated, while these are precisely the results that he is trying to establish (Walsh, 2005). Woodford has very little to offer to audiences willing to understand the most acute phases in the unveiling crisis of capitalism that is shaking the epistemological foundations of his models. Economists have drawn on Woodford's theory of monetary policy for elaborating and codifying the models used by central banks, in order to keep inflation under control; they undoubtedly gained tremendous benefits from his approach. However, the downside is that the elegance and the mathematical rigour of his framework have diverted attention away from the legitimate concerns on the real-world relevance and the explanatory power that Michael Woodford could possibly claim on scientific grounds (Laidler, 2004, pp. 8–9). Another problem with Woodford's approach is his epistemological treatment of uncertainty. Uncertainty cannot be circumscribed to mere external shocks (that may or may not be translated into stochastic calculus). This is a huge misconception of probabilistic theory. Fundamental or radical uncertainty might be systemic in essence. This systemic uncertainty constitutes a very serious attack on the class of models that form the bedrock of the NMC. Again, Woodford has very little to say on the subject.[14]

Conclusion

Three years before the GFC, Laidler (ibid., p. 8) expressed his scepticism about Woodford's framework; his assessment nevertheless proved visionary. Laidler recognized that Woodford's theory of monetary policy, epitomized by his masterpiece *Interest and Prices*, amounts to an elegant theoretical construct that proves extremely useful in teaching how monetary authorities ought to conduct policy in calm conditions during fair fiscal weather (i.e. before the GFC) preferably in a closed economy. In a calm macroeconomic course defined by low inflation and stable prices, the NMC simply teaches us how *not* to deviate from this idealized path. The NMC was an extremely valuable theoretical benchmark for select low-inflation countries, unthreatened by fiscal crises or major foreign disturbances (ibid.). The philosophy of science has testified that the decline of consensual frameworks is inevitable; economic theory and the NMC seem to be no exception: 'Goodhart's meta-law dictates that as soon as a consensus has been arrived at, something will come along to blow that consensus apart' (Bean, 2007).

Part III
Monetary policy after the GFC

9 The statutory missions of the Fed and the ECB and the issue of the US dollar

Introduction

A vast literature is devoted to the institutional differences between the Fed and the ECB (Guttmann, 2008). It is not our intention to reignite this long-standing debate. However, the GFC is a unique time to examine the extent to which actual central banking practices have deviated from statutory missions since 2007–2008. In this chapter, the pragmatism of the Federal Reserve is examined against the policy stance of the ECB. We attempt to single out the NMC principles that have suffered the most since the outbreak of the GFC. Furthermore, the sheer magnitude of the first global crisis of financial capitalism in the twenty-first century inevitably calls for a re-examination of the problematic issue of the US dollar.

The objectives of the Federal Reserve and the ECB

The Federal Reserve System

The creation of the Fed

Economic historians have presented detailed historical accounts of the emergence of the Federal Reserve System, which was the third attempt ever to establish a central bank in US history. We evoke hereafter the six years preceding the establishment of the Fed. Wall Street was already known for being a temple of speculation back in 1907, when frenzy speculative trends resulted in a massive failure marked by a banking panic (with the famous intervention of J.P Morgan, in order to prevent a total collapse of the banking system). In spite of widening political divisions in the country between conservatives and progressives, a growing consensus slowly emerged as regards the institutional need for a central banking authority supervising the whole American banking system, providing an elastic supply of currency and helping maintain a smooth functioning of the economy. The Aldrich–Vreeland Act of 1908 was an emergency institutional response to the banking panic of 1907, with the establishment of a national Monetary Commission, which was designed to monitor financial and banking developments in the country. The debate raged from late 1912 to late 1913 between proponents of a central bank controlled by bankers and those who thought it ought to be controlled by the public. The Federal Reserve Act was signed into law by President Wilson in 1913, giving rise to a decentralized system of regional banks functioning under the supervision of a federal entity. It still stands as a classic example of a compromise between the professional interests of financial institutions and the public at large. The Federal Reserve was founded with the aim to furnish an elastic currency. Its role was strengthened in the aftermath of the Great Depression, with a broader mission to help stabilize the economy, through the enlightened conduct of monetary policy. To date, none of the numerous amendments to the original Federal Reserve Act have supplanted the fundamental role to act as a lender of last resort or central supervisor of the US system of payments.

The fundamental objectives of the Fed

Section 2A of the amended Federal Reserve Act[1] contains a puzzling multiplicity of objectives for monetary policy in the United States:

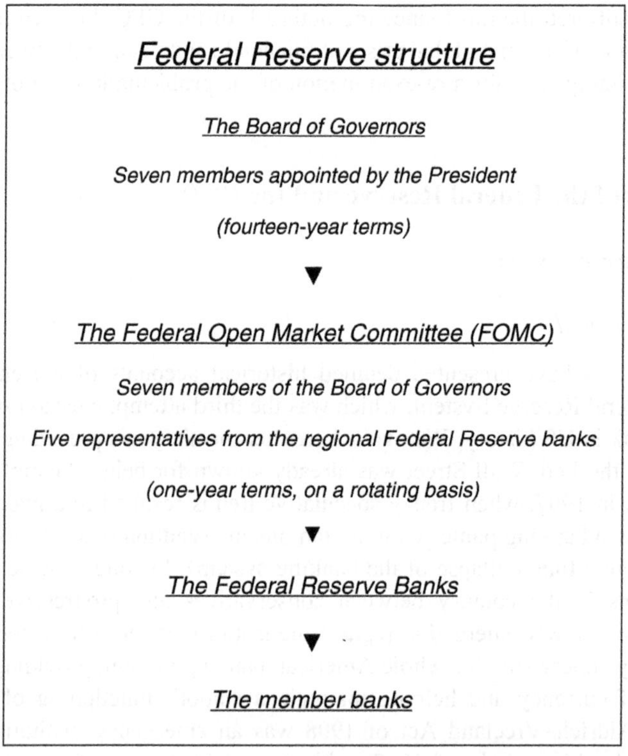

> ## *Federal Reserve structure*
>
> ### *The Board of Governors*
>
> *Seven members appointed by the President*
>
> *(fourteen-year terms)*
>
> ▼
>
> ### *The Federal Open Market Committee (FOMC)*
>
> *Seven members of the Board of Governors*
>
> *Five representatives from the regional Federal Reserve banks*
>
> *(one-year terms, on a rotating basis)*
>
> ▼
>
> ### *The Federal Reserve Banks*
>
> ▼
>
> ### *The member banks*

Figure 9.1 The structure of the Federal Reserve system.

The Board of Governors ... and the Federal Open Market Committee shall maintain long-run growth of the monetary and credit aggregates commensurate with the economy's long-run potential to increase production, so as to promote effectively the goals of maximum employment, stable prices, and moderate long-term interest rates.

In his *remarks before the New York Chapter of the National Association for Business Economics*, New York, on 15 October 2002, Bernanke (2002a) clarified the major objectives of the Federal Reserve. The first set of responsibilities of the Fed pertains to the safeguarding of a healthy US economy, through the following macroeconomic objectives: maximum sustainable employment, stable prices and moderate long-term interest rates. The second set of responsibilities pertains to the supervisory powers with respect to the financial system, which includes regulatory oversight, the lender-of-last resort function and the refinancing of banks through the discount window. The primacy of price stability over other objectives is not inscribed in the statutes of the Federal Reserve. However, in his July 2000 'Monetary Report to the Congress' Greenspan hinted at the low-inflation core strategy of the Fed by stating that, irrespective of the complexities of the changing economic environment, the primary goal of the Fed was to enact policies contributing to a non-inflationary environment and growth. It is well known that the Fed does not pursue an explicit inflation targeting strategy. Yet, in times of financial distress, the need for projections can be particularly acute. How do projections of unemployment and inflation rates fit into the mandatory statutes of the Federal Reserve? Ben Bernanke held a news conference following the 24–25 January 2012 Federal Open Market Committee (FOMC) meeting to present its projections.[2] It is worthwhile stressing that, unlike the ECB, maximum employment is given equal importance in the monetary policy of the Fed. However, Ben Bernanke seems to rest his case that inflation is a monetary phenomenon (and controllable by the central bank), while the unemployment rate depends on a wide range of real factors. As far as explicit targets are concerned, Woodford (2010, p. 29) recently distinguished between the prominence that should be given to inflation, for which monetary policy can always achieve its desired long-run average rate, and the role conferred to output for which 'a fixed long-run target could be futile and in any event unnecessary'. Bernanke (2012) endorses Woodford's claim, by stating that the maximum level of employment is determined by non-monetary factors affecting labour-market dynamics; Bernanke therefore denies any realism to quantitative targets assigned to long-term employment levels.

The European Central Bank

The legal basis for monetary policy in the euro area is laid down in the Treaty on the European Union (TEU), the Treaty on the Functioning of the European Union (TFEU) and the Statute of the European Central Banks and of the EBC (ECB, 2011).[3] As laid out in Article 127(1) of the TFEU, the primary objective

of the ESCB is to maintain price stability without prejudice to the general economic policies in the euro area. Unlike that of the Federal Reserve, the mandate
of the European Central Bank is clearly to maintain price stability, as laid out in
Article 105 in the original Treaty establishing the European Community. The
ECB has hence defined price stability as a year-on-year increase in the Harmonized Index of Consumer Prices (HICP) for the euro area of below, but close to,
2 per cent over the medium term. In private conversations, Jean Claude Trichet,
former Governor of the EBC used to refer to the price stability objective as the
'magnetic North' (Trichet, 2004). A significant evolution was the addition of the
'below, but close to, 2%' quantification of the desired range for inflation. This
clarification was introduced by the Governing Council's evaluation of the
monetary policy strategy in May 2003, thereby providing a quantitative definition of price stability. Yet, it was made clear at the same time that a safety
margin (a non-zero inflation rate) was required for the euro area as a whole, in
order to guard against deflationary risks (Chapter 6). Can the ECB therefore be
viewed as a self-labelled ITer (Chapter 8)? Notwithstanding the spread of direct
IT practices observed worldwide since the early 1990s, it is worthwhile stressing
that the latter policies were born out of repeated policy failures throughout the
1970s and 1980s (Chapter 2). In many ways, IT was a pragmatic response to the
demise of monetarism, whose credibility had been tarnished by the dire macroeconomic outcomes of the 1980s. Inflation targeting later morphed into the
dominant benchmark for discussions of monetary policy throughout the world,
both among practitioners and academics.

Yet, the EMU constitutes a unique experiment in world economic history,
facing a much deeper set of uncertainties than previously existing central banks.
The complex institutional set-up of the euro area is characterized by a common
monetary policy delegated to an independent central bank for the member countries of the currency area. At the same time, sovereign states retain a number of
prerogatives such as responsibility for fiscal policy, labour market reforms and,
more generally, all the structural policies that will determine the long-term competitiveness of member states (e.g. research, innovation, education). The track
record of the EMU ought to be cautiously assessed by economists, especially when
conducting comparative analysis with the policy actions of their counterparts in
sovereign countries. We now know that the creation of a new currency area devoid
of a Treasury and without fiscal integration[4] has given rise to a number of difficulties that have become all the more apparent following the outbreak of the Euro
sovereign debt crisis in 2010 (Chapter 15). The ECB's two-pillar approach, with
the analysis of economic dynamics and shocks, on the one hand, and the analysis
of monetary trends, on the other hand (with the announcement of a reference value
for monetary growth) is central to understanding the modus operandi of the ECB in
the euro area, that is the way that it organizes, evaluates and cross-checks the
information relevant for assessing the risks to price stability.[5]

The existence of the two-pillar approach to monetary policy is precisely the
reason why the ECB does not fall into the narrowly defined category of inflation
targeters in the academic literature. The assessment of macroeconomic conditions

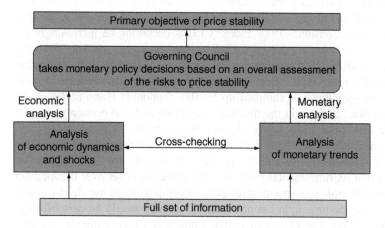

Figure 9.2 The monetary policy strategy of the ECB (source: ECB website).

by the ECB, and the relationship with the decision-making process of the Governing Council, are far more complex than what can ever be encapsulated into formal econometric models and sophisticated forecasting techniques (ECB, 2011).

Another set of complementary objectives pursued by the ECB pertains to the complex relationship between price stability and financial stability. The central question is whether there exists a relationship between the two concepts. At first glance, price stability constitutes a necessary (albeit not sufficient) condition for financial stability. However, the reverse relationship should not be overlooked. The ECB (2008) published its own definition of financial stability in the *Financial Stability Review* in June 2008: financial stability refers to a condition in which the financial system – comprising financial intermediaries, markets and market infrastructures – is capable of withstanding shocks and the unravelling of financial imbalances, thereby mitigating the likelihood of disruptions in the financial intermediation process which are severe enough to significantly impair the allocation of savings to profitable investment opportunities.

In 'Essays on Financial Stability',[6] Chant *et al.* (2003, p. 3) have put forward a definition, starting from the opposite concept, namely financial instability, referring to

> [t]he conditions in financial markets that harm, or threaten to harm, an economy's performance through their impact on the working of the financial system. It can arise from shocks that originate within the financial system being transmitted throughout the system, or from the transmission of shocks that originate elsewhere by way of the financial system.

Yet, under the aegis of the Bank for International Settlements (BIS), a new hypothesis was recently put forward in the literature (slightly before the GFC), in order to conceptualize anew the relationship between price stability and financial stability. The thrust of the so-called 'New Environment' Hypothesis is the idea that the standard Consumer Price Index (CPI) is becoming an increasingly ill-suited device, in order to account for inflationary pressures resulting from the unwinding of financial imbalances on international capital markets, triggering sequences of erratic asset price movements delinked with economic fundamentals. This hypothesis is summed up by BIS economist Borio (2006, p. 3), who argues that 'changes in the financial, monetary and real economy regimes worldwide may have been subtly altering the dynamics of the economy and hence the challenges that monetary and prudential authorities face'. It seems that the 'New Environment' hypothesis has been endorsed by the ECB, which has announced that its fundamental price stability objective is set over the medium term: 'monetary policy cannot control price developments in the short run and ... attempts to fine-tune inflation or economic activity would be destabilising' (ECB, Stark, 2007). The ECB's two-pillar strategy is a good example of a procedural monetary policy framework (ECB, 2001) that hardly fits in any epistemological category within the wide spectrum of debates spanning across the monetary economics literature (Bernanke, 2004b), thereby puzzling commentators in academia, who aim to characterize the ECB policy actions in a way that enhances the predictability of phenomena explained by scientific models (Friedman, 1953).

Post-crisis differences between the Fed and the ECB

In this section, we focus on differences between the ECB and the US Federal Reserve, most notably after 2007–2008. Guttmann (2008) has presented a detailed account of the two central banks during a debt-deflation crisis. Before addressing the institutional differences between the two institutions, let us outline a few similarities. The ECB and the Fed are both politically independent (ibid., p. 1).[7] They both have a decentralized structure, organized around a nexus of regional or national banks coordinated by a board of governors enjoying strong authority (ibid., p. 2). They both monitor the term structure of interest rates, with varying degrees of inclination towards explicit targets (ibid.). Finally, they both employ the same monetary policy tools: reserve requirements, the financing of banks through the discount window and open-market operations (ibid.).

At first glance, the Fed and the ECB followed similar (albeit not identical) patterns in their interest-rate setting procedure between 2005 and 2011. However, it must be noted that the policy rate of the Fed was lowered much more aggressively (i.e. faster and lower) after summer 2007. The Federal funds rate stood at 2 per cent when Lehman Brothers collapsed (compared to 4.25 per cent for the ECB). This margin probably gave the ECB more scope for manoeuvre in the course of subsequent policy actions. Section 2A of the amended Federal Reserve Act contains a multiplicity of objectives for monetary policy in the United States:

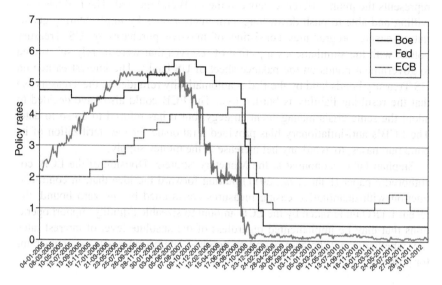

Figure 9.3 Policy rates of the Fed, the BoE and the ECB, 2005–2012 (sources: Fed, BoE, ECB).

> The Board of Governors and the Federal Open Market Committee shall maintain long-run growth of the monetary and credit aggregates commensurate with the economy's long-run potential to increase production, so as to promote effectively the goals of maximum employment, stable prices, and moderate long-term interest rates.

Regardless of their effectiveness, the variety of non-conventional policies put in place by the Fed since the outbreak of the GFC, shows that these policies have been consistent with the dual mandate of the Fed for inflation and output stabilization. Contrariwise, the mandate of the ECB is clearly to maintain price stability, as laid out in Article 105 in the Treaty establishing the European Community. The ECB has hence defined price stability as a year-on-year increase in the Harmonized Index of Consumer Prices (HICP) for the euro area of below, but close, to 2 per cent over the medium term. Whether the ECB has substantially deviated from this institutional line of conduct is still an open question. What can be stated with confidence is that the ECB contrasts sharply with the Fed, insofar as there is no meta-European state enabling the supranational coordination of fiscal and monetary policies in the Eurozone. While this coordination is enacted in the USA by the Humphrey–Hawkins Full Employment and Balanced Growth Act of 1978, it is still, at best, a remote prospect in the Eurozone and, at worst, a political conundrum.[8] The faulty coordination of fiscal and monetary policies in the Eurozone has far-reaching consequences as far as the prerogatives of the central bank are concerned. Weisbrot (2012) argues that this represents the main difference between the ECB and the Fed. The Fed has been willing and able to push down long-term interest rates by implementing quantitative easing programmes consisting of massive purchases of US Treasury bonds, with the simultaneous injection of reserves that were merely substituted to government bonds on the balance sheet of US banks. The interest earned on US Treasury bonds held by the Fed is automatically refunded to the Treasury, so that the resulting liability is burden free. The ECB could also have decided to adopt the same crisis management strategy, but it has refused to do so to date. The ECB's anti-inflationary bias provided a rationale for the sterilization of its bond purchases, to avoid any net increase in the money supply.

Stephan Fahr, economist at the Monetary Strategy Division of the ECB, co-authored a paper (Fahr *et al.*, 2011) putting forward the idea that, in contradistinction with quantitative easing measures constrained by the zero bound, the recent LTRO undertaken by the ECB amount to sizeable liquidity support operations that may be implemented regardless of the absolute level of interest rates (i.e. whether or not the zero bound on nominal interest rates acts as a constraint for policy):

> quantitative easing can be seen as a substitute for conventional policy easing, to be exploited only once there is no more room for manoeuvre in policy interest rates.... The enhanced credit support programme [of the ECB] was independent of the level of the MRO rate: it could have been adopted, thus generating a large expansion of the ECB's balance sheet, at any interest rate level.
>
> (ibid.)

Weisbrot (2012) also puts forward a thought-provoking explanation to account for these differences, by arguing that both the ECB and the monetary union were created to promote the neoliberal agenda. From the onset, the mandate of the ECB was circumscribed to price stability with disregard for any full-employment objective. The idea that the ECB could be involved one day in a lender-of-last-resort scheme aimed at rescuing the countries of the Eurozone was alien to the EMU. However, as Weisbrot notes, when Mario Draghi told the European Parliament that the ECB's monetary policy was aimed at maintaining price stability in the euro area over the medium term, he added the following words '[a]nd when I say this, I mean price stability in either direction'. How, then, should we interpret Draghi's statement? In case of compelling deflationary fears, the ECB would certainly start doing what the Fed has been doing all along. The existing institutional and ideological obstacles to the implementation of ECB-style quantitative easing would quickly vanish in case of worrying financial stress and macroeconomic emergency.

The NMC and the new normal

This section addresses the recent discussions surrounding the new normal narrative in a post-crisis scenario. In the light of a novel terminological device, we propose hereafter three different versions of the new normal in a tentative comparative perspective, respectively from a member of the ECB executive board in 2010, the ECB Chairman in 2012 and finally from the consulting firm Pricewaterhouse Coopers in 2012.

Jürgen Stark's vision of the new normal (November 2010)

Let us examine in this respect the intervention by Jürgen Stark, Member of the Executive Board of the ECB, at the 13th Euro Finance Week in Frankfurt on 16 November. Stark (2010) argues that the sovereign debt crisis requires a new sense of direction at odds with the pre-crisis world. After restating that times of crisis are intrinsically periods of transition, marked by uncertainty and rapid changes eventually shifting economic reality from one stable situation to another, Stark asks whether the new normal constitutes an appropriate terminological choice. First and foremost, let us recall the weight of rhetoric in shaping the discourses at the heart of economic theorizing (McCloskey, 1985; Pilkington, 2011b, pp. 377–382). A new normal implies the existence of an old or past state of normality. Stark (2010) is certainly spot on when he asks whether pre-August 2007 were in fact normal times. In many ways, they were not (Pilkington, 2011b, p. 373). Stark (2010) sums up the stunning (and potentially misleading) characteristics of the pre-crisis years: *circa* 5 per cent growth rates of the world economy, vast accumulation of foreign exchange reserves, huge macroeconomic imbalances (e.g. the US current account deficit), housing bubbles in advanced economies, reduced volatility of output and steady upward growth, massive financialization trends and vastly underestimated probabilities of default of large financial institutions, low measures of credit risk and absence of liquidity risk in the price of financial contracts. For Stark, the idea of a new normal may emerge naturally given the sheer magnitude of the GFC. Yet, what does it mean? Hereafter are some of the characteristics of the new normal for Stark (ibid.): the unsustainability of deficits paths, the business models in financial markets coming under increased scrutiny, the increased valuation of liquidity, and the better regulated and more costly nature of financial intermediation. Practically speaking, Stark depicts a gloomy scenario, predicting that pre-crisis growth rates are unlikely to be reached again in the foreseeable future, risk premiums will continue to exceed pre-crisis levels for a sustained period of time, more and more market players will be forced to exit financial markets due to their unsustainable business models. All in all the GFC has marked the end of the Great Moderation, as macroeconomic variables will become increasingly volatile. Furthermore, lean against the wind (LATW) policies will be more prevalent in case of large and erratic asset price movements. The European Systemic Risk Board (ESRB), which consists of an independent EU body responsible for the macroprudential oversight of the European financial system, is a timely initiative in a post-crisis scenario. Yet, in the same intervention (and it is unclear whether this is also part of his vision of the new normal), Stark (ibid.) reiterates his beliefs in the validity of NMC core principles, such as the enduring primacy of price stability, exemplified by the following sentences: 'The mandate of the ECB to deliver price stability is clear and will remain unchanged. It is anchored in the Maastricht Treaty.' Referring to the works of Tinbergen and Theil, who advocated the use of an equal number of policy instruments and objectives, in order not to overburden monetary policy, Stark is admittedly satisfied that the ECB has a single mandate geared at maintaining price stability, instead of a dual mandate, such as the Fed's, with more objectives. Stark (ibid.) stresses the paramount importance of central bank credibility in anchoring long-term inflation expectations. The strength of the central bank commitment is therefore measured against its determination to pursue the price stability objective. Stark does not break away with the central bank independence mantra, and reaffirms the need for monetary policy to stay free of political influence, as inscribed in the European treaties, and argued at length by proponents of the NMC. For Stark, the acknowledgement of this central NMC mantra entails the rejection of the monetization of budget deficits (and therefore of quantitative easing programmes). Stark (ibid.) reiterates the medium-term orientation of monetary policy (and therefore the theoretical foundations upon which DSGE models are built), and also discards short-term demand management policies. On top of credibility commitments, the intricate link between the overriding price stability objective and the transparency/accountability mantras are restated. Stark puts forward the idea that the banking industry needs to be reshaped, so as to create the incentives that will help the financial sector assume its own responsibilities. In a subtle dialectic between the need for regulatory reforms placing banks at the service of the real economy, and the self-regulation argument that has pervaded economic thinking for two-and-half centuries. Although he reckons that the crisis is far from over, Stark (ibid.) is convinced that there is indeed a new normal unfolding before our eyes, although this new landscape remains difficult to characterize properly, owing to the deep economic and financial changes undergone in the global economy. In spite of ongoing recessionary fears, Stark (ibid.) predicts that the new normal will be conducive to more stability, more sustainable growth, better priced risks and bank regulation, as exemplified by the Basel III recommendations and the latest G20 summits.

Mario Draghi's vision of the new normal (February 2012)

In a interview given to the Wall Street Journal on 24 February 2012, ECB Chairman Mario Draghi (2012c) bluntly announced that 'Europe's vaunted social model – which places a premium on job security and generous safety nets – is "already gone", citing high youth unemployment; in Spain, it tops 50%.' Does it mean that the new normal is synonymous with the death of the European social model? This is indeed the proposition put forward by Mario Draghi, the new flagship advocate of austerity measures in Europe (Chapter 12). In this interview, Mario Draghi (ibid.) emphasizes the centrality of so-called structural reforms that mostly consists of reforming product and services markets, although Draghi does not make the latter structural reforms explicit.[9] Then, Draghi (ibid.)

pushes in favour of enhanced labour market flexibility. He criticizes the fundamentally unfair nature of the prevalent dual labour market in European countries, with the youngest fraction of the workforce being offered renewable, albeit very precarious, short-term job contracts, whilst a protected part of the workforce enjoys relatively secure career paths following seniority, rather than productivity. All in all, Draghi argues that the burden of economic adjustment should not be put on the youngest part of the population, as it is the case today. Moreover, the hypothesis of the death of the European social model is already corroborated by the astonishingly high unemployment rates observed in some European countries such as Spain (Chapter 12). This leads Draghi to conclude by ironizing on Dornbush's famous quotation on Europe, that life-time job security is now a feature of the past.[10]

Pricewaterhouse Coopers: discussion led by Andrew Sentance (21 February 2012)

In February 2012, a discussion supervised by British economics professor Andrew Sentance, took place at Pricewaterhouse Coopers UK. The New Normal was described therein as 'something of a buzzword, a sort of shorthand for communicating a sense that the world is in the midst of changes so fundamental that people need to reorder their thinking about what is going on around them' (Pricewaterhouse Coopers, 2012a). The term was discussed by chief executives, senior officials, PwC experts in a very specific context, namely the outworking of the GFC and the subsequent emergence of a new world economic order. In a report devoted to the management of British charities published by Pricewaterhouse UK in April 2012,[11] the new normal is referred to as a new era characterized by weak growth (Pricewaterhouse Coopers, 2012b, p. 5). The report evokes the sentiment of a respondent to a 2011 survey, who pointed to 'the sense of the unknown in the economic and political environment and lack of coherence in the [UK] Government's plans – [the problem] is not just the downturn, but the lack of certainty around how far the decline might be' (ibid.). This condenses the prevailing atmosphere in the early stages of the new normal.

The problematic issue of the US dollar

Following the crisis of 1997–2000, many Asian countries decided to adopt a proactive export-led growth strategy, in order to build high foreign reserves and reduce their macroeconomic vulnerability to rapid capital inflows. Undervalued exchange rates and high domestic saving rates enabled the formation of massive current account surpluses that found their counterpart with the sky-rocketing current account deficit of the United States. Along with unprecedented US household debt levels, paving the way for the frenzy securitization of mortgages by under-regulated financial institutions, these global macroeconomic imbalances were conducive to an ever-increasing demand for Treasury bonds, and led to an over-accumulation of liquidity on financial markets. By the same token, they depressed long-term US interest rates, thereby encouraging excessive leverage and risk-taking behaviour. Yet, new problems (e.g. banking and financial regulation) should not drive out existing ones, such as the reform of (the non-system of) international payments (Benassy-Queré and Pisani-Ferry, 2011) The outbreak of the GFC has indeed reflected the vulnerabilities and systemic risks inherent in the present international monetary system.

The role of the US dollar in enabling this situation has been explicitly criticized by the People's Bank of China, who has argued that the use of a national currency as the global reserve currency is an ill-suited approach to the management of the international monetary system (Hongcai, 2012). The issuing country of the reserve currency is confronted with the major dilemma of whether to achieve domestic policy goals or meet the demand for reserve currencies of other countries (ibid.). Zhou Xiaochuan, the central bank's governor, released this statement on 23 March 2009. He argued in favour of

> a super-sovereign reserve currency managed by a global institution [that] could be used to both create and control the global liquidity. And when a country's currency is no longer used as the yardstick for global trade and as the benchmark for other currencies, the exchange rate policy of the country would be far more effective in adjusting economic imbalances. This will significantly reduce the risks of a future crisis and enhance crisis management capability.

One wonders if the success of monetary policy in a post-crisis scenario will not be contingent on the adoption by the international community of a new reserve currency:

> [t]he desirable goal of reforming the international monetary system, therefore, is to create an international reserve currency that is disconnected from individual nations and is able to remain stable in the long run, thus removing the inherent deficiencies caused by using credit-based national currencies.

In this respect, special drawing rights have recently received renewed attention (Aiyar, 2009), in spite of significant objections to the extension of their role, notably in terms of the new global governance mission, and the massive currency risks that would be transferred to the IMF. The transition could be facilitated by the diversification of international reserve currencies, which would enable the US dollar to continue to play a major role in the long run, while elevating other currencies such as the euro, the pound sterling, the yen and the renminbi to the international reserve currency status. Ideally, the composition of this basket of currencies should reflect the geopolitical forces at work in the twenty-first century, characterized by the rising weight of emergent economies. As argued by Hongcai (2012), such an evolution would certainly require a larger degree of involvement of the G20, which would set up a permanent secretariat within the IMF to improve world governance mechanisms. A reform agenda could then be put together by the G20 in coordination with the IMF (ibid.). A new consensus could be pushed forward on the guiding ideology, the basic principles, a viable roadmap for reform objectives, and finally the respective responsibilities of each nation (ibid.). This consensus would encompass international monetary matters (which the NMC failed to address, with the notable exception of the six-equation model presented in Chapter 3, although the latter analytical tool was largely centred on domestic monetary management in an open-economy framework). The prerogatives of the IMF could be extended, so as to include a new international financial mandate that would focus on systemic risk, global financial stability and the issuance of diversified international reserve currencies.

10 Exchange rate movements and global derivatives markets

Introduction

With a $4 trillion average daily turnover, the foreign exchange market is one of the largest financial markets in the world.[1] Its scope is truly global, as it is a vast decentralized interbank market, whose main participants are central banks, commercial and investment banks, hedge funds, corporations and private economic agents (such as households and self-employed traders). From a historical perspective, the foreign exchange market experienced exponential growth with the advent of the free-floating currency system, which arose from the collapse of the Bretton Woods agreement in 1971. Another milestone in the historical evolution of this global technology-driven market was the emergence of online trading in the mid 1990s. Yet, ever since the seminal papers by Meese and Rogoff (1983a, 1983b),[2] exchange rate prediction based on empirical models has become a difficult art. The matter became even more complex with the advent of the GFC. Foreign exchange markets[3] are more and more unpredictable today; this constitutes one of the rare emerging truths that economists seem to agree upon in a post-crisis scenario.

The unpredictability of the foreign exchange market

Why exchange rate predictability is a useful objective

Currency trading is essential in a globalized world wherein individuals, banks, corporations and governments constantly engage in cross-border transactions spurred by the astonishing functional integration of the global economy (Dicken, 1998). Global markets exist for goods and services, financial assets and hedging instruments (whose speculative dimension cannot be understated). These market forces, broken down into supply and demand schedules, constantly drive exchange rates up and down in uninterrupted trading flows[4] across the globe. The international business environment is therefore shaped by these global market forces. Business actors (consumers, corporations, institutional investors) would greatly benefit from enhanced short-term visibility and predictability. The same could be said from policy makers designing economic policy in an increasingly interdependent and globalized world.

Has the GFC slowed down global foreign exchange market activity?

The answer to this fundamental question is clearly negative. Between the 2007 and 2010 BIS triennial surveys, global foreign market activity experienced another significant increase (+20 per cent from $3.3 trillion in April 2007 to $4 trillion in April 2010). This came after the huge rise between 2004 and 2007 (the biggest increase ever recorded between two triennial surveys), most notably on the foreign exchange swap market. The foreign exchange market was unable to keep up with this rapid pace of expansion after 2007, mainly due to the impact of the GFC on international trade and cross-border investment flows (Nightingale *et al.*, 2010). However, the turnover of the spot market experienced strong and continued market growth, which constitutes an exception overall. This can be explained by the dynamism of new technology-driven segments, such as high frequency trading (ibid.). A report from Aite Group has examined the presence of high frequency trading in the global foreign exchange (FX) market. The report analyzes the changing market dynamics between 2007 and 2010.

After a small decline between 1998 and 2001, the global foreign exchange market turnover has experienced rapid growth since 2001, with an unprecedented pace of expansion between 2004 and 2007. Interestingly enough, the GFC has barely affected the growth pattern of this crucial financial market in the global economy. The global foreign exchange market is headed for even higher levels of turnover in years to come, notably under the impulse of high-frequency trading.

The most spectacular figure for average daily turnover is the one experienced by foreign exchange swaps (FX swaps).[5] An FX swap agreement is a financial contract whereby one party borrows one currency from another to whom it simultaneously lends another currency. Each party uses the repayment obligation to its counterparty as collateral. The contact stipulates the amount to be repaid, which is fixed at the FX forward rate. To a certain extent, FX swaps amount to FX risk-free collateralized borrowing/lending. FX swaps are used to raise foreign currencies.

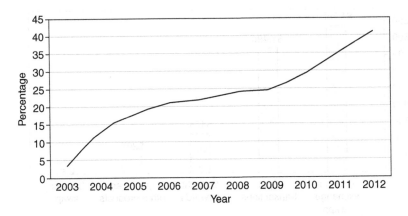

Figure 10.1 High frequency trading on the Forex, 2003–2012 (% orders) (source: Aite Group).

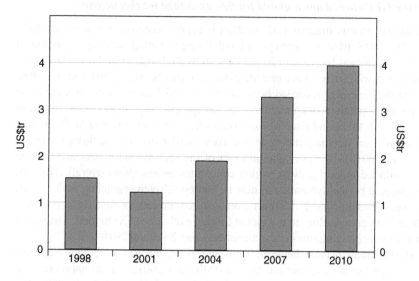

Figure 10.2 Global foreign exchange market turnover, 1998–2010.

Typical buyers include financial institutions, such as institutional investors, companies engaging in international trade (exporters and importers) and all actors of the international business environment, who wish to hedge their positions. They are frequently used for speculative purposes. A typical strategy consists of combining two offsetting positions with different maturities.

In the foreign exchange market, bilateral counter-party risk mitigation practices are common,[6] and market participants now have access to some of the post-trade services typically offered by a central counterparty. However, collateral agreements are increasingly supplementing bilateral netting agreements to

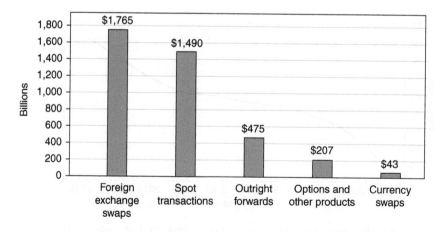

Figure 10.3 Daily turnover by instrument, 2007–2010 (source: BIS, 2010).

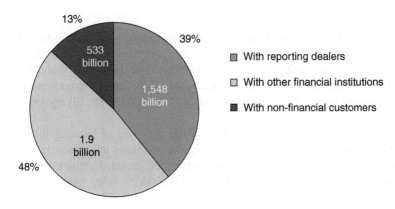

Average daily turnover by counterparty

■ With reporting dealers

□ With other financial institutions

■ With non-financial customers

Figure 10.4 Average daily turnover by counterparty (source: BIS, 2010).

countervail mark-to-market losses on bilaterally netted exposures, as shown by an international survey (ISDA, 2010) of collateralization practices assessing the use of collateral as a credit risk mitigating factor on the OTC market (ISDA Collateral Steering Committee, 2010), almost half of exposures by value across foreign exchange derivative products were collateralized in 2009. What is more, the scope of risk management tools has widened with the introduction of new OTC derivatives designed for non-financial end-users, in order to hedge exchange rate risks.

Comment

Geopolitical and linguistic considerations should not be overlooked; the Anglo-Saxon world still generates close to 60 per cent of the average daily turnover on the OTC derivatives market. This might be explained by the dominance of the English language as the lingua franca in international business and financial circles, and also the oligopolistic structure of the global derivatives market,[7] which constitutes a growing source of concern for the OECD (Blundell-Wignall

Table 10.1 Average daily turnover by geographic location

Country	Share (%)
UK	37
US	18
Japan	6
Switzerland	5
Singapore	5
Hong Kong	5
Australia	4
Other	20
Total	100

Source: BIS, 2010.

et al., 2011). Global financial conglomerates have turned into too-big-to-fail (TBTF) institutions with increased market shares in key derivative markets. In a groundbreaking report entitled 'Bank Competition and Financial Stability' (ibid.), OECD experts have raised deep concerns about the excessive concentration in the banking sector, before and after the GFC. The OECD (p. 19) argues:

> [o]n competition grounds ... the oligopolistic structure of banking likely contributed to the financial crisis. That structure meant that many banks were perceived as systematically important, which impeded market discipline and led to moral hazard, with excessive risk taking being underwritten by perceived guarantees.

Comment
The global derivatives markets remain decentralized, with the OTC segment accounting for 95 per cent of the global daily turnover in 2010, whereas only 5 per

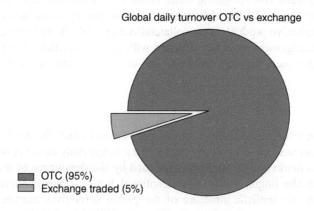

Global daily turnover OTC vs exchange

OTC (95%)
Exchange traded (5%)

Figure 10.5 A decentralized and unregulated global market (source: BIS, 2010).

cent were exchange traded. Yet, this abnormal market structure (high concentration of market operators and huge discrepancy between exchange-traded and OTC derivatives) poses a number of problems that have been identified by Zingales (2011). OTC trading is accentuating the opacity of the derivatives market, thereby undermining competition (that market fundamentalists are generally so keen on defending). Profits margins enjoyed by traders are artificially kept at very high levels. Prices are consequently severely distorted with end-users of derivatives (such as industrial firms) carrying the burden of the adjustment. The system works as if the key players of the banking sector, with a market total $80 billion, were imposing a colossal tax upon the real economy, by means of market price distortion practices.[8] Zingales (ibid.) suggests that this huge opacity problem could be solved by moving OTC derivative trading on to organized exchanges where operations are more transparent. Along the lines suggested by the Dodd–Frank Act in the US, this would work as a stepping stone for enhanced central bank transparency (Chapter 4), reduce profit margins on derivatives markets, which would hamper moral hazard, and promote financial stability. These actions would effectively supplement the price stability objective at the heart of the NMC.

The increased volatility of the foreign exchange market

The post-crisis context

Foreign exchange volatility grew dramatically between 2007 and 2010. Exchange rate risk management, already high on the agenda of hedging strategists since the collapse of the Bretton Woods exchange rate system in 1971, became a central matter of concern for banks, non-banking financial institutions (Pilkington, 2008) and corporations. When the economy is not stable, FX risk is amplified by companies whose operations are internationalized with substantial exposure to foreign markets. Foreign exchange markets have witnessed sharp swings since the outbreak of the GFC, and exchange rate volatility has reached historical levels. Forecasting has become increasingly challenging, adding to the uncertainty surrounding the global business environment, given that most international transactions are settled in the near future. Even the pricing of hedging instruments is affected by uncertainty on global markets.

The NMC and exchange-rate management strategies

The proponents of the NMC were never alien to exchange rate considerations. Authors such as Clarida *et al.* (1998) have suggested that a Taylor rule could incorporate the difference between the actual exchange rate and the target exchange rate defined by PPP (purchasing power parity), giving rise to an asymmetric model of interest-rate determination using the real exchange rate. However, authors that embraced the NMC never wanted to go as far as an explicit exchange rate commitment in the Taylor rule. This would have reduced the scope for constrained discretion discussed in Chapter 3.

The lost appeal of Taylor-rule fundamentals

Pre-crisis views

The Taylor rule as a domestic treatment of the interest rate

Arestis and Sawyer (2003) have criticized the use of the Taylor rule as a central guide to monetary policy, as it treats the setting of interest rates as a purely domestic matter, with disregard for international considerations such as interest-rate differentials between countries and exchange-rate dynamics. For Arestis and Sawyer (ibid.), this is not just a criticism of closed-economy analysis, as it applies to the general case. An all-encompassing interest-rate rule is thus an ill-suited policy strategy in a globalized world.

Taylor rules extended to the international arena

Even before the GFC, Arestis and Sawyer's criticism of the domestic applicability of the Taylor rule was not shared by all economists. For instance, it can be empirically observed that interest-rate differentials between the US and the Eurozone were correlated to exchange rate movements until the GFC (Brender *et al.*, 2009). It was thought that interest rate differentials might have been a function of output and inflation gaps. In short, Taylor-rule fundamentals (Chapter 7) were sometimes used as empirical determinants of exchange rates, with a rather good forecasting ability (Molodtsova *et al.*, 2008). It can be argued that, as early as 2005, exchange rate models of the 1990s had been invalidated by empirical facts. However, the unpredictable behaviour of the foreign exchange market after 2007–2008 means that Taylor-rule fundamentals are no longer considered as safe explanatory variables for exchange rate movements in a post-crisis context. Given the size and the unpredictability of global foreign exchange market forces, can monetary policy (conducted on a mere domestic scale with the exception of the Eurozone) reasonably incorporate any exchange-rate commitment? The rising actors of the Forex now belong to the *haute finance* sector (Pilkington, 2009):

> [t]he higher global foreign exchange market turnover in 2010 is largely due to the increased trading activity of 'other financial institutions' – a category that includes non-reporting banks, hedge funds, pension funds, mutual funds, insurance companies and central banks, among others. Turnover by this category grew by 42%, increasing to $1.9 trillion in April 2010 from $1.3 trillion in April 2007.
>
> (BIS, 2010)

Therefore, wouldn't it be a more fruitful research strategy to incorporate these global market dynamics into a stock-flow consistent framework *à la* Lavoie–Godley? Simulations could hence be conducted on exchange rate movements with their subsequent impact on the output gap, considering the scope for monetary policy (with relevant parameters such as fiscal space, the objectives enshrined in the central bank reaction function and the employment objectives of the central bank).

Fiscal discipline as exchange rate determinants in a post-crisis world

Linking fiscal policy to exchange rates before the crisis

US journalist Thomas Friedman (2000) wrote an influential book entitled *The Lexus and the Olive Tree*, wherein he coined the term 'golden straightjacket' (pp. 101–111), to condense the central idea whereby access by countries to long-term financial funds on international capital markets is subordinated to strict compliance with a set of rules akin to the outward expression of the Washington consensus (i.e. the straightjacket). In the case of a country that deliberately decides to break these rules, the consequences are limpid and inevitable. It will inevitably be disciplined by the international financial community (ibid., p. 110), with powerful institutional investors refusing to lend to this country or suddenly withdrawing their funds, thereby creating a credit crunch and a recession as experienced by a number of Asian countries in the late 1990s.

The NMC and the fiscal theory of the price level (FTPL)

CRITICAL VIEWS ON THE FTPL

In a BIS working paper, Leeper and Walker (2011) argue that 'not so long ago, macroeconomists interested in understanding inflation and its determinants were comfortable sweeping fiscal policy under the carpet, implicitly assuming that the fiscal adjustments required to allow monetary policy to control inflation would always be forthcoming'. Leeper and Walker are certainly right to pinpoint the fact that the GFC has brought back fiscal policy in the spotlight in what may be termed a Keynesian revival. However, it is an entirely erroneous assertion to claim that the impact of fiscal policy on price determination had previously been neglected in the monetary economics literature. Hence, the FTPL is a controversial rule-based approach that arose in the 1990s, and aimed to explain the price level in accordance with government debt, present and future tax, and spending plans. While the price level is defined in quantity-theoretic terms in conventional monetary theory by the following identity: $P = 1/M$ (i.e. how much money is needed to buy a standard basket of goods), the FTPL focuses instead on the inverse relationship between money and the value of government debt (Cochrane, 2005). As Buiter (2002) argues, stocks of government debt and money do not necessarily coincide in the real world (and probably have very little chance to do so). Further, in case of a rising probability of government default, the resulting market-driven discount on government bonds will take place without distorting the value of money, thereby leaving the price level

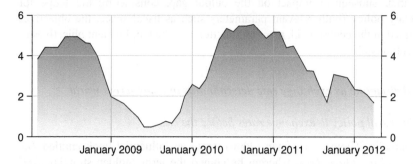

Figure 10.6 Evolution of Greece's inflation rate since the beginning of the GFC (sources: www.tradingeconomics.com and the Hellenic Statistical Authority).

unaffected by the higher stock of government debt. In order to illustrate this criticism of the FTPL, let us examine below the evolution of Greece's inflation rate since the outbreak of the GFC.

Comment

After a steep decline in the price index in 2010 (foreshadowing deflationary fears), inflation started to pick up again in early 2010, peaking above 5 per cent in the middle of the year. In 2011, the inflation rate resumed a downward trend up until March 2012. It must be noted that inflation is no longer a major source of concern in Greece's faltering economy, as it was reported at 1.7 per cent in March of 2012 (the optimal level for proponents of the NMC).[11]

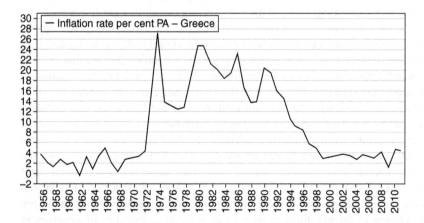

Figure 10.7 Evolution of the Greek inflation rate in the long run (since 1956) (source: www.aboutinflation.com).

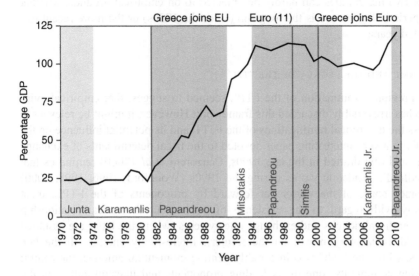

Figure 10.8 Greek public debt, 1970–2010 (% GDP) (source: data compiled by
'ΕΠΙΛΟΓΗ' (February 2010 issue, p. 7), available at www.allmedia.gr/All-
media/_gr/digitalpublications/epilogi/2010-02/EPILOGI_02-2010.html).

Comment

Of course, as elsewhere in the world economy, the 1970s was a decade marked
by inflationary chaos in Greece, with the inflation rate peaking at a staggering 27
per cent in 1974. The 1980s were barely more successful, as inflation rates com-
prised a two-digit danger zone throughout that tormented decade. However,
1990 seems to be the turning point with the introduction of policies that will
later inspire the NMC.

Comment

The Greek government debt seems to have been spiralling out of control ever
since the 1980s after the election of Papandreou Sr. However, 1998 marked
the beginning of a new period of stabilization for government debt level that
continued up until 2007–2008 and the advent of the GFC. In fact, government
debt was on a downward trend between 1998 and 2007. It is yet unclear
whether the deliberate manipulation of official statistics by the Greek Treasury
prior to the GFC with the help of notorious investment banks (Pilkington,
2011b) might have blurred the real evolution of the government debt in
Greece, and whether this apparent fiscal consolidation during that period was
a mere mirage.

Conclusion: by all means, it appears that the FTPL has been unambiguously
discarded by the observation of the parallel evolution of government debt levels
and the inflation rate in Greece over the long period. The total delinking between

these two magnitudes can hardly be objected to on empirical grounds, whether the period of reference is the long run (since the 1950s) or the more recent tormented years.

Our previous examination of the FTPL seemed to suggest that empirical evidence has irreversibly discarded this framework. However, it might be relevant to assess the theoretical ramifications of the FTPL and its potential influence on the NMC. In a very interesting paper devoted to the fiscal determinants of exchange rates, and first drafted in the late 1990s, Canzoreni *et al.* (2000) remind us that Woodford's academic works during the 1990s (Woodford, 1996, 1998, 2000) endorsed some of the views put forward by proponents of the FTPL, most notably with regard to the existence of a clear-cut theoretical relationship between fiscal deficits and exchange rate systems (where the latter are assumed to hold explanatory power on the former). Interestingly enough, in the late 1990s, while the NMC was inexorably gaining momentum amongst the central banking community, one of its leading proponents and flagship author in the making, namely Michael Woodford, emphasized the necessary distinction between Ricardian[9] and non-Ricardian regimes in economic theorizing. Indeed, in a non-Ricardian regime, primary government surpluses are assumed to be exogenous; price determination and exchange rates can therefore be influenced by fiscal policies, which is nothing less than the central proposition put forward by the FTPL. Likewise, Woodford (1998, 2001) has clearly adopted the view that a central bank whose primary purpose is price stability cannot and should not be indifferent to fiscal policy. Woodford (1995) also argued that in a hypothetical Ricardian world, the price level and exchange rates are mechanically determined by market forces[10] (i.e. the confrontation between the supply and the demand for money). Of course, such a conception of economic reality runs counter to Woodford's, who believes that the impact of fiscal policy on monetary conditions and economic performance does matter.[12]

International monetary coordination: where do we stand?

Exchange rate targeting strategies are nowhere to be found in the NMC. Somehow, this amounts to a negation of the underlying prioritization of policy objectives entailed by the inflation-targeting philosophy (Chapter 8). Can it be argued that countries having embraced the NMC are alien to exchange rate considerations? We have seen that NMC proponents such as Clarida, Galí and Gertler had already incorporated real exchange rates in their Taylor rules as early as 1998. We have also outlined the intellectual influence of the FTPL on Woodford's ideas and, by extension, on the NMC. Yet, having a mere intermediary objective for monetary policy, formulated in terms of more or less explicit exchange rate targets, does not warrant the existence of a consistent exchange rate policy under the NMC. Bini Smaghi (2009) disagrees with this scepticism, and endorses the existence of an active exchange rate policy for the euro area since its inception. He also defends the idea of monetary cooperation between the 'authorities in charge' before, during and after the peak of the crisis, even though he fails to explain the nature of the latter arrangements. Bini Smaghi's optimism acknowledges 'a level of trust and cooperation within central banking community that some would have considered unthinkable a couple years ago', arguing that 'global cooperation by central banks is now mirroring the globalisation of finance' (ibid.). This note of optimism, however, comes in contradistinction with the road map set by the NMC, as the modalities of an advanced framework for international monetary cooperation remain undefined to date. The mild willingness to promote a new system of international monetary cooperation might be attributable to a powerful strand of literature called new open economy macroeconomics that aims to provide the micro-foundations of the international transmission analysis of monetary shocks. For instance, renowned economists Obstfeld and Rogoff (2002) established the important analytical result that welfare gains from monetary coordination were quite small, and that optimal policies pursued by individual countries had the potential to maximize global welfare, even in the absence of any international monetary coordination. One never really witnessed any cross-fertilization of ideas between the new open economy macroeconomics and the NMC. It was certainly the outcome of a hyper-specialization tendency within the economics profession that Pilkington (2011b) has equated to a prejudicial epistemological drift. Nonetheless, the propositions of the new open economy macroeconomics and the NMC complement each other. The common denominator between the two strands of literature seem to be the need to develop and refine the micro-foundations of macroeconomic analysis (a methodological stance shared by New Keynesian economics and new open economy macroeconomics). It was probably enough for NMC proponents that there existed so little enthusiasm for international monetary coordination solutions. This lack of enthusiasm paved the way for the strengthening of interest-rate rules that nicely fitted into the optimizing strategies of individual countries willing to maximize their welfare by providing a low-inflation environment, and by abstracting from serious international considerations.

All in all, little progress has been made since the 1990s in the field of international monetary coordination. The advent of the euro area was not sufficient to create more effective mechanisms of exchange rate stabilization, notably between the members of the Triad (Europe, the USA and Japan). The Chinese exchange rate has been a major source of concern for policy makers worldwide. Considering the new stature of China as the biggest world exporter, the competitive prices of Chinese exports should certainly have triggered a reflection on the non-negligible impact of the value of the Chinese currency on the Consumer Price Index of its trading partners. China has been a key player in shaping the new global business environment characterized by deep integration of product and labour markets, alongside new global commodity chains. Increased global competition propelled by China's trading power has undoubtedly reduced the pricing power of Western firms, thereby weakening inflationary pressures in IT countries. The stabilization of market expectations around low inflation levels might have as much to do with the newly acquired credibility of IT central banks as with the integration by market participants of the new rules of the game in the world trade arena. Yet, international monetary coordination has played a minor role in anchoring expectations, which are still subject to great uncertainty surrounding exchange rate movements amongst the countries of the Triad.

11 The zero bound on nominal interest rates and deflationary fears

Introduction

Following the bankruptcy of LB in 2008, unprecedented worldwide panic on global financial markets prompted central banks to make aggressive interest-rate cuts to mitigate the collapse of aggregate demand, and prevent a deflationary spiral. The interest-rate cutting pace surprised most observers although central banks quickly hit the zero nominal interest bound that restricted their scope for manoeuvre. How do monetary policy committees conduct and communicate their policies when the short-term nominal interest rate is approaching the zero bound (Bernanke *et al.*, 2004, p. 84)? This dark scenario precisely matches the situation encountered by central banks in the aftermath of the GFC. Indeed, the interest rate is the single most important policy instrument to achieve the objectives of the NMC. When it reaches zero, one thus refers to the zero bound on nominal interest rates.

Historical trends

The zero bound on nominal interest rates is best apprehended in a historical perspective that captures the long-term evolution of interest rates in the major industrialized countries since the late 1970s and the early 1980s.

Comment

Obviously, the zero bound was not paramount in the economics literature when interest rates were kept at high levels in the 1980s due to worrying inflationary pressures. Figure 11.1 shows the historical trend towards a low inflation environment throughout the world; interestingly enough, the triumph over inflation coincides with the emergence of the NMC in the early 1990s. Krugman (1998, 1999) warned in the late 1990s that this structural decline in nominal interest rates since the 1980s could foreshadow a situation similar to Japan's lost decade in the 1990s, when the country hit the zero bound for a sustained period of time after the explosion of the real estate bubble.

The zero bound and the liquidity trap: two distinct concepts?

We choose to distinguish hereafter between two notions, which are often intertwined in the literature,[1] namely the zero bound on nominal interest rates and the liquidity trap.

The zero bound on nominal interest rates

The paternity of the zero lower bound on nominal rates is sometimes attributed to Irving Fisher, who argued that the zero bound arises when economic agents store the currency themselves, rather than lend it at a loss (Fisher, 1896). In an almost-visionary speech, Bernanke (2002b) had clearly foreseen that:

> the zero bound on the nominal interest rate raises another concern–the limitation that it places on conventional monetary policy. When the short-term interest rate hits zero, the central bank can no longer ease policy by lowering its usual interest-rate target.

For Bernanke *et al.* (2004, p. 84), the technical impossibility to conduct further monetary easing (i.e. lower interest rates) is also the biggest problem with the zero bound on nominal short-term interest rates.[2] Eggertsson and Woodford (2003) claim that real interest rates below zero, amount to a failure of the 'divine coincidence', the simultaneous attainment of low inflation and a zero output gap.

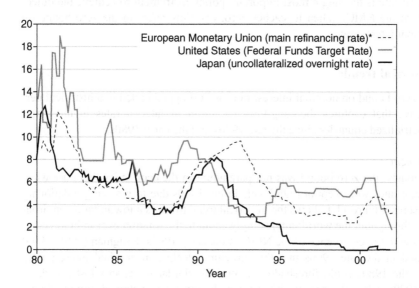

Figure 11.1 The evolution of interest rates in the countries of the Triad (source: C.A. Ullersma, available at http://repub.eur.nl/res/pub/811/rm0203.pdf).

Note
* German rates for the period until 1999. Thereafter: Eurosystem rates.

A recent strand of literature in phase with the NMC views the zero bound on nominal interest rate as an essentially short-term concern for policy makers. NMC proponents have therefore analysed the problem in a DSGE framework (Orphanides and Wieland, 1998; Svensson, 2000, 2001; Smets, 2000; Viñals, 2001). The stochastic nature of the approach has led them to assess the likelihood of hitting the zero bound, by conducting complex stochastic simulations on a small structural rational expectations model. Generally speaking, these authors have concluded that the risk of hitting the zero bound is very limited (Orphanides and Wieland, 1998; Viñals, 2001), due to the structural characteristics of the US and the European economies.

The liquidity trap

Keynes and the liquidity trap

Keynes (1936) argued that zero interest rates have the negative aspect of producing a liquidity trap, whereby a further increase in the money supply has no expansionary effects. For Keynes (ibid., p. 252) the interest rate is simply the price to pay to compensate for the renunciation of liquidity. In times of crisis, liquidity is well sought after because 'people want the moon', that is the object of their desire (money liquidity) cannot be produced. Keynes elaborated upon this problem in the *General Theory* (Chapters 15 and 17). He emphasized liquidity preference in an environment characterized by nominal price stickiness. The uncertainty about the future (*General Theory*, Chapter 12) and the speculative motive account for the existence of liquidity preference. When economic agents perceive the low level of interest rates, they expect the long-term nominal interest rate to rise in the future, and they decide to hold liquid assets (money) in the hope that they will benefit from it. The liquidity trap was equated by Keynes to 'a bottomless sink for purchasing power'. This opens the door for a grim scenario of an absolute preference for liquidity (ibid., p. 207):

> [t]here is the possibility [that], after the rate of interest has fallen to a certain level, liquidity preference may become virtually absolute in the sense that almost everyone prefers cash to holding a debt which yields so low a rate of interest. In this event, the monetary authority would have lost effective control over the rate of interest.

Alternative view: the Pigou effect

A liquidity trap is a situation wherein monetary stimulus becomes powerless, because consumption no longer bears any meaningful relationship with money demand. Pigou (1943) offered a critique of Keynesianism called the real balance effect, by arguing that there exists an inbuilt mechanism to restore equilibrium, and avoid the pitfalls of the liquidity trap. Rising unemployment causes downward pressures on prices and raises real balances, which in return stimulates consumption. The subsequent shift of the IS curve (within the well-known IS-LM model) defines a new equilibrium level (i.e. the intersection with the LM curve) above the threshold of the liquidity trap. Finally, the economy moves back to full equilibrium.

A global liquidity trap?

When the liquidity trap is caused by a collapse in aggregate demand in a major country, natural real interest rates in other countries can become aligned on the epicentre of the crisis. The liquidity trap phenomenon is no longer circumscribed to closed economy analysis, and might spill over to the rest of the world.[3] Cook and Devereux (2011) have emphasized trade and financial integration, which explains how the zero bound becomes the common denominator of a global liquidity trap. The authors (ibid.) analyzed the complex interaction between fiscal and monetary policy in order to devise the most effective policy response, and maximize joint welfare of all countries. The merit of the paper is to provide a solid analytical framework, which undermines the mechanical nature of the liquidity trap in the sense that it is the outcome of a deliberate policy decision that may reflect a falling natural real interest rate and rather perplexing Taylor-rule fundamentals.[4] It is important to be aware of the 'intriguing complications' entailed by the international dimension to macroeconomic policy at the zero lower bound (ibid.). In such a complex environment, the standard NMC remedies based on the omnipotence of monetary policy no longer apply (ibid.). This is largely so because exchange rate dynamics reflecting advanced trade and financial integration have the potential to exacerbate negative demand shocks. Escaping a global liquidity trap is a matter of utmost complexity[5] that calls for enhanced coordination of monetary and fiscal policies in mutually supportive ways (ibid.). This issue is particularly acute in the context of the euro crisis (Chapter 15).

Emerging strategies after the GFC

For Bernanke *et al.* (2004, p. 84), there are three strategies that central bankers may resort to, when faced with the zero bound on nominal short-term interest rates, which cannot be equated to monetary policy impotency.

Providing assurance to markets that interest rates will be kept lower and for a longer period than what they expected

This is reminiscent of the forward-guidance policies (Chapter 4). An illustration is the move made by the US Federal Reserve chairman in early 2012, as part of the enhanced communication strategy of the Fed in favour of more central bank transparency (Chapter 4). Bernanke said at a news conference following the 24–25 January 2012 FOMC meeting in Washington, DC, that full recovery was years away, and that it was therefore likely to keep interest rates low until late 2014, an extension by eighteen months of the period that it planned to hold down interest rates, compared to previous Fed announcements. In what was described in the *New York Times* by Appelbaum (2012) as a six-year campaign to increase spending by rewarding borrowers and punishing savers that started in the Winter 2008, the Fed is using this communication plan as an unconventional monetary strategy, in order to boost US economic growth, which was initially thought to pick up in early 2012, but was drastically revised downwards a few month later.[6] How confident really was Ben Bernanke in early 2012 that this unconventional communication strategy would eventually prove effective? Did the Fed really believe it could shape expectations through mere announcements in a NMC fashion? Bernanke (ibid.) was realistic that Fed monetary policy actions were not a panacea: 'I wouldn't overstate the Fed's ability to massively change expectations through its statements.' However, he reiterated his conviction that central bank transparency is of utmost importance in times of uncertainty, with an output gap exceeding its desired value. Bernanke (ibid.) explained that the Fed had to provide the right amount of monetary stimulus, in order to help mobilize the economy's underutilized resources.

Altering the composition of the central bank balance sheet

The Fed holds a variety of assets on its balance sheet, whose composition offers a lever for monetary policy, even when interest rates are near zero (Bernanke *et al.*, 2004, p. 86).

Comment

In Table 11.1, the variation of daily figures in the composition of the balance sheet shows that the Fed has engaged in so-called open-market operations i.e. supplied securities to (and withdrawn securities from) financial markets. Open-market operations are designed to control the supply of liquidity made available to the banking system as a whole.[7] The result is presented in Table 11.1 as the factors affecting reserve balances of depository institutions at Federal Reserve banks. By shifting the composition of its holdings, the central bank can affect financial variables, such as term premiums and overall yields (ibid.). The central bank is thus a major market participant, whose supply and demand schedules have the potential for 'altering relative security prices' (ibid.). How effective is this unconventional approach to monetary policy? For Bernanke *et al.* (ibid., p. 87), empirical evidence in the early 2000s was at best inconclusive, and, at worst, very disappointing. But this took place in a pre-GFC world that might have very little to do with today's. The pre-crisis composition of the asset side of central bank balance sheets reflected the operational framework of monetary policy (Borio and Nelson, 2008) based on the control of the short-term nominal interest rate. The liability side mainly consisted of currency and bank reserves.

Although the balance sheet of all central banks expanded massively after October 2008, the ECB's was kept at reasonable levels, expressed in percentage of 2007 GDP, until mid 2011. During a very tormented summer, marked by renewed fears of an aggravation of the Euro sovereign debt crisis (and a

Table 11.1 Alteration of the balance sheet structure of the Federal Reserve Banks (between 20 May 2009 and 27–28 May 2009)

H.4.1
Factors Affecting Reserve Balances of Depository Institutions and Condition Statement of Federal Reserve Banks
28 May 2009
1. Factors Affecting Reserve Balances of Depository Institutions
Million of dollars

Reserve Bank credit, related items, and reserve balances of depository institutions at Federal Reserve Banks — *Averages of daily figures*

	Week ended 27 May 2009	Change from week ended 20 May 2009	Change from week ended 28 May 2008	Wednesday 27 May 2009
Reserve Bank credit	2,074,457	+ 90,672	+ 1,197,013	1,063,747
Securities held outright	1,108,234	+ 22,634	+ 617,170	1,107,447
U.S. Treasury securities (1)	597,579	+ 17,013	+ 106,515	600,142
Bills (2)	18,423	− 0	− 15,873	18,423
Notes and bonds, nominal (2)	532965	+ 16,737	+ 120,573	534,022
Notes and bonds, inflation-indexed (2)	41,475	+ 222	+ 2,304	42,803
Inflation compensation (3)	4,716	− 55	− 490	4,894
Federal agency debt securities (2)	79,753	+ 5,204	+ 79,753	79,753
Mortgage-backed securities (4)	430,902	+ 417	+ 430,902	427552
Repurchase agreements (5)	0	− 0	− 105,036	0
Term auction credit	372,541	− 56,294	+ 222,541	372,540
Other loans	124,232	+ 3,699	+ 95,897	123,572
Primary credit	38,153	− 2	+ 22,203	38,047
Secondary credit	29	+ 9	+ 28	0

Seasonal credit	15	+	4	—	39	14
Primary dealer and other broker-dealer credit (6)	0		0		12,329	0
Asset-Backed Commercial Paper Money Market Mutual Fund Liquidity Facility	26,423	—	1,698	+	26,423	25,944
Credit extended to American International Group, Inc. (7)	44,157	—	1,551	+	44,157	44,116
Term Asset-Backed Securities Loan Facility	15,454	—	461	+	15,454	15,451
Other credit extensions	0		0		0	0
Net portfolio holdings of Commercial Paper Funding Facility LLC (8)	154,694	—	6,087	+	154,694	149,389
Net portfolio holdings of LLCs funded through the Money Market	0		0		0	0
Investor Funding Facility (9)						
Net portfolio holdings of Maiden Lane LLC (10)	25,688	—	4	+	25,688	25,717
Net portfolio holdings of Maiden Lane II LLC (11)	16,175	+	23	+	16,175	16,252
Net portfolio holdings of Maiden Lane III (12)	20,367	+	54	+	20,367	20,379
Float	−1,975	+	18	—	857	−2,861
Central bank liquidity swaps (13)	184,932	—	51,527	+	122,932	181,647
Other Federal Reserve assets (14)	69,568	+	4,208	+	27,441	69,666
Gold stock	11,041		0		0	11,041
Special drawing rights certificate account	2,200		0		0	2,200
Treasury currency outstanding (15)	42,373	+	14	+	3,582	42,373
Total factors supplying reserve funds	2,130,071	—	90,658	+	1,200,595	2,119,361

Source: www.federalreserve.gov/releases/h41/20090528/.

Table 11.2 Typology of balance sheet policies

		Impact on private sector balance sheets		
		Change in net FX exposures	Change in the composition of claims on the public sector	Change in profile of claims on private sector and/or composition of claims on public vs private sector
Market targeted	Foreign exchange	★		
	Public debt/securities		■	
	Private credit/securities			◆
	Bank reserves			

Source: Borio and Disyatat (2009).

Notes
★ Exchange rate policy; ■ Quasi-debt management policy; ◆ Credit policy. Shaded area Bank reserves policy.

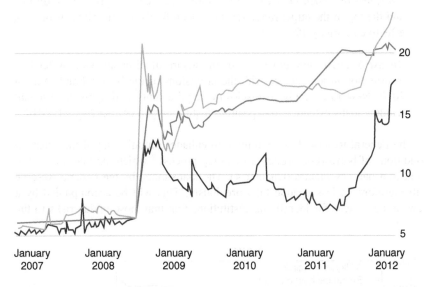

Figure 11.2 Balance sheets of the Fed, the BoE and the ECB, between 2007 and 2012 (in % of 2007 GDP) (sources: Fed, BoE, ECB).

hypothetical Greek default), the balance sheet of the ECB started to increase sharply, almost catching up with levels observed with the Fed and the BoE.

Post-crisis assessment

By adding new instruments to those traditionally used by before the GFC, central banks have (sometimes drastically) altered the composition of their balance sheet. The Board of Governors of the Federal Reserve System (2011) have analyzed the new lending procedures put in place after the GFC. Recent developments in lending facilities to support overall market liquidity have been thoroughly described in the 'Monthly Report on Credit and Liquidity Programs and the Balance Sheet' in February 2011.

We mention hereafter a few significant dates in this report:

August 17, 2007: narrowing of the spread between the Fed discount rate and the FOMC's target federal funds rate (to 50 basis points)

March 16, 2008: narrowing of the spread between the primary credit rate and the target federal funds rate (to 25 basis points); increase in the maximum maturity of primary credit loans to 90 days.

November 17, 2009: reduction of the maximum maturity on primary credit loans to 28 days (effective January 14, 2010)

February 18, 2010: increased in the spread between the primary credit rate and the top of the target range for the federal funds rate (to 50 basis points), effective February 19, 2010.

August 6, 2010: new practices for disclosure of discount window lending information in accordance with the provisions of the 'Dodd–Frank Act' of 2010. New rules apply to disclosure requirements will apply to discount window loans extended to depository institutions on or after July 21, 2010.

The Federal Reserve has committed to enhanced monitoring of the financial conditions of borrowers through a four-step process,[8] which fits into the central bank transparency mantra (Chapter 4). The loans made by the Federal Reserve will therefore be less opaque than previously. This will be accompanied by a new rating system for identifying institutions that may pose undue risks to the

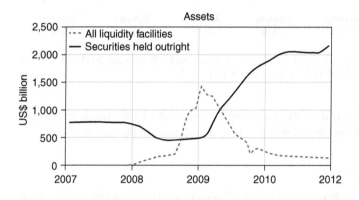

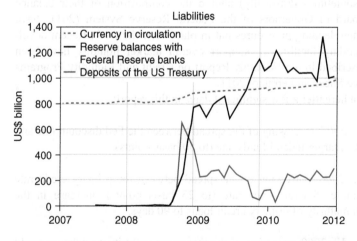

Figure 11.3 Selected assets and liabilities of the Fed, 2007–2011 (source: Federal Reserve Board of Governors).

Fed. The core idea is to put in place a new risk management system to identify key institutions that may compromise the banking sector at the system-wide level.[9] After the outbreak of the GFC, new lending procedures (or unconventional open-market operations) were put in place by the Fed, such as the Term Auction Facility (TAF), a type of funding for commercial banks through an anonymous auction facility and the Primary Dealer Credit Facility, a new type of lending rights extended to primary dealers with whom the Federal Reserve conducts its daily open market operations. Finally, a new set of tools was developed (such as the Commercial Paper Funding Facility, CPFF, or the Asset-Backed Commercial Money Market Mutual Funds Liquidity Facility, AMLF), in order to provide liquidity directly to key credit markets, and avoid a repeat of the turmoil experienced in August 2007 on the money market

Increasing the size of the balance sheet by buying up bonds from banks

The fact that the Federal Reserve almost tripled the size of its balance sheet between December 2006 and December 2010 cannot go unnoticed. The total assets of the Fed as percentage of GDP rose from 6.7 to 17.1 per cent over the same period. In Switzerland, this percentage reached slightly less than 50 per cent in 2010, which signals an unprecedented weight of the central bank's balance sheet in relation to the size of the Swiss economy. In most advanced countries and in the Eurozone, economies have entered uncharted territory. Central banks could only expand their balance sheets as a result of massive purchases of securities from banks and NBFIs. Bernanke *et al.* (2004, p. 87) argue that in the standard textbook presentation of monetary policy, the central bank sets the short-term interest rate, and actively engages in open market operations by buying and selling securities in order to modify the quantity of reserves and therefore the money supply:

> Most central banks choose to calibrate the degree of policy ease or tightness by targeting the price of reserves ... However, nothing prevents a central bank from switching its focus from the price of reserves to the quantity or growth of reserves.

This assertion would certainly be contested by post-Keynesian economists, notably the proponents of horizontalism, such as Basil Moore or Marc Lavoie, who have long argued that money is endogenous (i.e. credit-driven and demand-determined), and the control of the short-term nominal interest is the only tool available to the central bank. We agree with the horizontalist position, and endorse the view that open-market operations, regardless of their volume, do not have any clear-cut and interpretable quantitative effect on the money supply (provided that the latter term is relevant, and conveys any meaning). The needs of the economy, the forward-looking expectations of entrepreneurs and the allocation of credit by the banking system satisfactorily explain the money-creation process.

Along the lines developed by post-Keynesian theory, the central bank passively accommodates the demand for reserves by granting short-term loans to depository institutions through the discount window. However, the injection of reserves into the banking system (and not directly into the economy at large) is not ruled out in the post-Keynesian story. The massive injection of reserves is better known as quantitative easing (QE)[10] discussed in Chapter 13.

Let us illustrate the inconclusive impact of the expansion of the supply of aggregate reserves to the banking system, when the central bank buys government bonds (or other securities) from financial markets in the attempt to promote increased lending and liquidity. On 25 April 2012, ECB Head Mario Draghi expressed his concerns that commercial bank lending to companies[11] is likely to remain subdued for some time because of a slow Eurozone economy. This admission was made in spite of the astonishing €1 trillion loans made to the financial system in December 2011 and February 2012.[12] But why is not this massive injection of liquidities making it to the wider economy, thereby materializing in an equivalent increase in the money supply? First of all, as previously explained in the post-Keynesian tradition, money is not exogenous. It is not (and never was) dropped from a helicopter.[13] When growth is sluggish, entrepreneurs form expectations that preclude optimism for a number of investment projects that would be deemed viable in more euphoric times. Therefore, the non-systematic translation of the ECB policy actions (i.e. the massive injection of liquidities into the financial system) into an equivalent increase of cash circulating in the real economy is due to the reluctance of firms to borrow, that is, to increase their indebtedness towards the banking sector, in order to generate sales that will subsequently help pay off company debt in the reflux phase of the monetary circuit (Parguez, 1986). As Mario Draghi stated on 25 April 2012, before the European Parliament's committee on economic and monetary affairs (in the pure and non-admitted post-Keynesian theoretical spirit of endogenous money), '[w]e cannot replace the lack of demand. In the real world, money does not reach businesses and consumers until the latter economic agents see a reason to ask for it.' Again, there could not be any clearer statement of the post-Keynesian money endogeneity principle.

Exceptional credit facilities granted to banks by the ECB in December 2011

In late 2011, the ECB balance sheet increased to a record €2.73 trillion after it lent exceptional amounts to euro-area banks (lending skyrocketed from €214 billions to €879 billion in the week ended 23 December 2011). The balance sheet increased by a stunning €239 billion during that week, and was €553 billion higher than three months earlier. In the midst of renewed concerns on a possible aggravation of the Euro sovereign debt crisis in late 2011, a total of €489 billion was awarded to 523 banks in the form of three-year loans, in order to prevent a new credit crunch. Finally, the increase in the money supply was estimated at €193 billion by Barclays Capital.

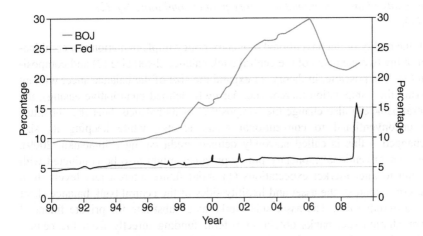

Figure 11.4 Central Bank assets, Bank of Japan and Fed, 1990–2009 (% GDP) (sources: Bank of Japan and Board of Governors of the Federal Reserve System).

Comment

The outbreak of the GFC with the collapse of Lehman Brothers in September 2008 marked the steepest increase ever in ECB liabilities. The upward trend continued throughout the fourth quarter of 2008, and a peak slightly above €2 billion was reached at the end of the year. Then the size of the ECB balance sheet oscillated between €1.7 and €2.2 billion until the end of 2011, just before the massive pro- gramme of three-month loans to the euro-area banks were put in place. Within a few weeks, the liability side of the ECB balance sheet experienced a new sharp increase, and was steadily converging in early 2012 towards €3 billion.

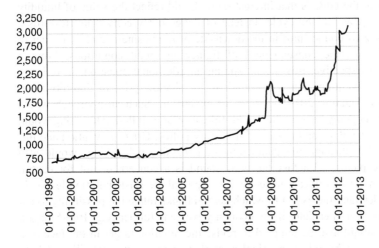

Figure 11.5 Evolution of the ECB balance sheet during the GFC (source: http:// en.wikipedia.org/wiki/File:ECB_balance_sheet.png).

*The reality of unconventional monetary policy: combining (1), (2)
and (3)*

Yet, the reality of unconventional monetary policy implementation is a combination of the two elements of the central bank balance sheet: size (2) and composition (3). It is possible, in theory, to expand the size of the balance sheet without
altering the composition thereof (i.e. narrowly defined quantitative easing); the
central bank can also change the composition of its balance sheet (by substitut-
ing unconventional to conventional credit assets), while keeping its size
unchanged – this is called narrowly defined credit easing (Shitatsuka, 2009).
These unconventional monetary policy practices might also be conducted with
the aim to alter market expectations (1) about future interest rate levels. In a
post-crisis context, the asset and liability sides of the central bank balance sheet
play different roles. The asset side works as a substitute for private financial
intermediation (i.e. banks obtain short-term funding directly from the central
bank), whereas the expansion of the liquidity side of the balance sheet works as
a buffer for liquidity risk in the financial markets. It is therefore a financial
stability tool (more than a monetary policy one). However, Shitatsuka (2009)
shows that the separation is not clear cut. Malfunctioning in private financial
intermediation and the funding of liquidity risk on financial markets are in fact
interconnected. Hence, as the central bank balance sheet expands and its composition is modified, a complex web of interrelations unfolds between the asset and
liability components; these interrelations may reflect rather complex and
dynamic financial phenomena within the very financial institutions seeking refinancing and protection from the central bank.

The incompleteness of the NMC

One lesson of the GFC is that interest rates should reflect the value of liquidity
in the boom phase of the cycle, instead of dangerously converging towards a
deflationary zero bound limit in the downside of the business cycle, in order to
mitigate the adverse consequences of tightening credit conditions. From a
Taylor-rule perspective, this means adding an additional equation, in order to
account for a premium that corresponds to the shadow price of liquidity (Giavazzi and Giovannini, 2010) in times of expansion. Such an approach would
probably mean going beyond the Taylor rule, insofar as inflation targeting would
no longer be the alpha and omega of monetary policy. Crisis prevention and financial stability (through the dampening of excessive risk taking) would also
come in the picture. Whether the zero bound is a concern or not for central
bankers, it might be relevant to re-examine optimal pre-crisis inflation levels, in
order to understand the extent to which central banks retain the possibility to cut
interest rates at a later date, if the economy worsens further (e.g. Bini-Smaghi,
2008). One might also be tempted to revise the inflation target in the face of a
constraining zero bound on nominal rates that increases the volatility of both
output and inflation as in the old stop–go policies. Other solutions might also be

substituted to the standard interest-rate channel. This includes the rather contro-versial monetization of deficits. Until recently, the ECB could not buy up sover-eign bonds in order to finance member states' deficits. This situation changed dramatically with the advent of the 2010 Greek crisis when unprecedented pur-chases of some €16.5 billion of Eurozone bonds were decided in May by the ECB in the secondary market, in order to enhance market liquidity (Wilson and Oakley, 2010). Although the ECB is still reluctant to resort to quantitative easing, the latter option is no longer ruled out (Mackintosh, 2010) in the face of a global liquidity trap that accounts for 70 per cent of world GDP. All in all, a viable substitute to the interest-rate channel is yet to be designed under a new narrowly defined monetary consensus.

12 Austerity measures versus growth

A post-crisis conundrum?

Introduction

As King *et al.* (2012, editorial, p. 1) argued in the *Cambridge Journal of Economics*, present conditions are painfully synonymous with an unprecedented global economic crisis. Yet, the policy responses do not lack for precedent. States and international organizations (such as the IMF or the World Bank) have looked to crises of the past. Austerity has therefore become an all-too-familiar theme all over the world (ibid.). Austerity is indeed high on the agenda of political leaders five years into the global crisis. The trade-off between growth and fiscal consolidation has become a burning issue in Europe and elsewhere. The situation is unprecedented, as policy leaders are now facing a post-crisis conundrum. We analyse the NMC stance towards fiscal policy, and the reasons why the latter framework has become conceptually inadequate in the present extraordinary context. In the light of the painful experience of the Great Depression, we evoke new initiatives, such as the Roosevelt 2012 citizen manifesto in France, and we browse through various institutional sources, such as a report on the economic performance of the UK or the 'World of Work Report 2012', published by the International Institute for Labour Studies, an emanation of the International Labour Organization.[1] We try to understand the extent of the macroeconomic problems experienced by Spain, and we briefly address issues that were never brought up by proponents of the NMC, such as massive youth unemployment, despair and suicides incurred by job instability, the rise of right-ring populist movements in Europe. We also allude to the shifting views emanating from temples of orthodoxy, such as the IMF. The idea for this chapter is to go beyond the mere (mainstream) economic perspective, that has monopolized the debate over the growth vs austerity debate for too long. By the same token, we hope that this discussion will help go beyond the confines of the NMC. It is a personal essay that would deserve to be elaborated upon, notably with the help of the cross-fertilization of ideas from a multitude of perspectives.

The NMC stance towards fiscal policy

The downgrading of fiscal policy by the NMC

Fiscal policy was never high on the agenda of proponents of the NMC. A clear statement of the NMC stance as regards fiscal policy was presented by Mishkin (2000, p. 2, emphasis added): 'Restraining the fiscal authorities from engaging in excessive deficits financing thus *aligns fiscal policy with monetary policy* and makes it easier for the monetary authorities to keep inflation under control.' This quotation has two important implications. First, deficit spending takes on a negative connotation, although Mishkin's rhetoric merely lashes out at excessive deficits financing. Second, the primacy of the price stability objective is clearly reaffirmed, and fiscal policy, through its necessary alignment with monetary policy, appears, at best, as the junior partner, and, at worst, as the subordinate instrument in the policy mix. Yet, some post-Keynesian authors go even further by stating that 'one of the most controversial assumptions of the NMC model is the absence of any essential role for the public sector and fiscal policy' (Fontana, 2009, p. 6). Fontana (ibid.) quotes Charles Goodhart (2005b), who believes that this omission might be part of a broader ideological hidden agenda, as shown by this very acid criticism aimed at the NMC:

> This is symptomatic of a deeper reluctance among macro-economists to conceive of any essential role for government. They seem intellectually happier to imagine an economy which is only inhabited by private sector agents and an 'independent' Central Bank with its own loss function (and no mandate from, or acceptability to, a democratically elected government).

Fiscal austerity: the consequence of monetary dominance in the NMC

Although he does not explicitly refer to the NMC, but to the consensus model of monetary policy, Jeanne (2011, p. 4) makes a very important point about an oft-neglected feature underpinning the pre-crisis consensus shared by central banks, namely the monetary dominance hypothesis. Jeanne argues that monetary dominance amounts to the unambiguous refusal by central banks to monetize fiscal deficits. Put differently, monetary policy is never driven by the needs of fiscal policy. Jeanne (ibid.) adds that the monetary dominance hypothesis is such a basic and implicit tenet in the consensus model that its proponents have seldom taken the time to surface it out. This is most unfortunate for the monetary dominance vs fiscal dominance debate is of utmost interest, in order to comprehend the ongoing reflection of central banks on crisis management strategies. Yet, the primacy of monetary dominance in the consensus model (that we equate here to the NMC) has a clear-cut implication on the role given to fiscal policy. Any insolvent state (and the Greek example hovers here in the background of our reflection) must either respond promptly by a fiscal adjustment or default. Hence, austerity can be interpreted anew as the logical consequence of the monetary dominance principle in the NMC in situations of state insolvency. Monetary dominance is in fact enshrined in the Maastricht Treaty, which is unlikely to be renegotiated in the absence of any major institutional transformation of the European project. However, the outbreak of the Euro sovereign debt crisis (Chapter 15), with its skyrocketing debt levels, is increasingly challenging the primacy of monetary dominance.

Austerity in the present extraordinary context

Austerity: what's in a name?

Etymology and contemporary meaning

The same way we reflected on the semantics of inflation targeting in Chapter 8, we now venture into a lexical analysis of the term austerity. The word 'austere' comes from the Latin *austerus* (dry, harsh), which is a transliteration of the Greek *austeros* (bitter, harsh; Gr.: αυστηρός). Today, austerity has become synonymous with a set of painful economic conditions imposed upon a country by a political authority capable of obtaining the consent of the population. If the latter condition is not fully satisfied, the country is exposed to political turmoil and possibly civil unrest (Misir, 2011, p. 8). The Greek scenario immediately springs to mind:

> The continuing civil unrest in both countries suggests that there is a significant body of opinion opposed to the summary imposition of unelected 'technocrats' to push through packages of austerity measures and, unsurprisingly, there is much suspicion of these former bankers, who are seen to have contributed significantly to the development of the crisis in the first place.
>
> (King *et al.*, 2012, p. 3)

The recent European context

Rising public debt and the dire state of public finances in a certain number of European countries have caught the attention of political leaders, commentators and ordinary citizens alike since 2010. Rating agencies have been quick to integrate a new type of danger, namely the default risk, into the valuation of sovereign bonds issued by these countries, by downgrading some of them. In what may be termed as a vicious circle, these downgrades have inexorably exacerbated the crisis, by raising sovereign risk premiums, synonymous with higher interest payments, thereby weakening the credibility and aggravating the default risk. The fear of contagion has turned into a systemic threat that could spread to all of Europe and beyond. Debates have intensified in the media and political circles concerning the necessity of deficit reduction. Profligate governments have been under serious attack, and several administrations have toppled down since the second wave of the Euro sovereign debt crisis in the summer 2011. These issues will be further discussed in Chapter 15.

When is it time for austerity?

Austerity or the unwanted risk of killing the sick patient

Austerity is never a popular policy choice, as the welfare losses are often supported by populations already seriously weakened by deteriorating economic conditions. As the saying goes, the risk is that the cure may kill the patient, if austerity is pushed too far. Given the potentially harmful effects of these waves of austerity on the economy, the question of their timing occurs. In this regard, the current Spanish situation is both instructive and alarming. Spain is experiencing somewhat of a depression-like conjuncture with one-quarter of the workforce and more than half of the youth population out of work in 2012. Spain was not fiscally profligate in the run-up to the crisis. It was enjoying relatively low debt levels and running a budget surplus of 2 per cent of GDP. It had a large capital account surplus matched by a substantial private sector deficit. Its economy was healthy, if it were not for a housing bubble carrying the seeds of destruction. These would have been the perfect times for austerity measures that would have countervailed the sizeable private sector deficit, and prevented some of the excesses that characterized the pre-crisis era. Contrariwise, today's austerity measures are nothing short of a heresy: massive spending cuts in a depressed economy have a self-reinforcing effect with further risks of depression; a healthy economy, or a strong recovery under way, are therefore a sine qua non to ensure the effectiveness of austerity programmes. It is most unfortunate that austerity was the ill-suited cure for a misdiagnosed disease: with faltering tax revenues, the Spanish fiscal deficits were a consequence of its depression, not its cause (Krugman, 2011).

Since the outbreak of the Euro sovereign debt crisis, European policy makers and American politicians have promoted a destructive economic doctrine in sharp contrast with (Keynesian) textbook wisdom. Instead of using fiscal policy to offset ailing private sector demand, they have advocated austerity measures, spending cuts and balanced budgets (Krugman, 2012b). In Europe's periphery, from Spain to Latvia, austerity has generated depression-like unemployment levels (ibid.).

Lessons from the 1937–1938 recession in the US

The recession within the Depression is an oft-overlooked episode that commentators of the current crisis could fruitfully draw upon and reflect on in a proactive manner. The 1937–1938 recession occurred at a time of nascent recovery following the Great Depression of the 1930s, with the US economy experiencing stubbornly high unemployment rates. With real GDP falling 11 per cent and industrial production plummeting by 32 per cent, it remains the third worst recession after 1929–1932 and 1920–1921, an utterly disastrous episode in twentieth century economic history.

THE MONETARIST INTERPRETATION

Orthodox (or monetarist) economists explain the 1937–1938 recession as a direct consequence of a severe monetary shock that stemmed from the decision to sterilize gold inflows starting in December 1936. Monetary authorities were still relying on a quantity-theoretic framework under a gold standard,[2] and they feared that the sudden afflux of gold in the mid 1930s would prove inflationary, and could jeopardize the fragile recovery. So the sterilization of gold was merely a pre-emptive monetary policy tightening measure set against the backdrop of a very hypothetical inflation scare. Gold reserves constituted 85 per cent of the monetary base; the weight of gold on the money supply was therefore decisive. As Figure 12.1 shows, the money supply (M2) grew at a consistent rate of about 12 per cent a year from 1934 to 1936. Expansionary monetary policy was the primary reason for the recovery (Romer, 1992). Under the impact of sterilization, money growth came to halt in early 1937, and M2 declined later in the year.

THE KEYNESIAN INTERPRETATION: ROOSEVELT'S LEGACY

In 1937, Keynes proclaimed that '[t]he boom, not the slump, is the right time for austerity at the Treasury'. Against the odds, the *New Deal* did not borrow much from the yet unborn Keynesian project that would later be embodied in the *General Theory*,[3] at least when using an indicator called the cyclically adjusted deficit. Throughout the Great Depression, fiscal policy was slightly expansionary (and even contractionary in 1937–1938) as regards the colossal 42 per cent output gap that characterized the US economy, in spite of the self-proclaimed very responsible stance adopted by F.D. Roosevelt.

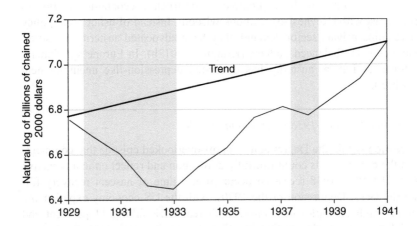

Figure 12.1 US real GDP, 1929–1941 (source: U.S. Department of Commerce: Bureau of Economic Analysis).

Note
Shaded areas indicate US recessions as determined by the NBER.

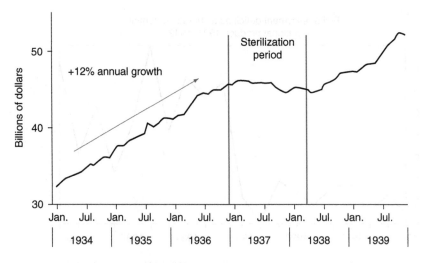

Figure 12.2 US money supply (M2), 1934–1939.

Is FDR's legacy living on?

Roosevelt 2012: a timely French initiative

The Roosevelt 2012 Collective[4] is the name of an action group composed of French economists, politicians, artists, athletes, etc., who put out in early 2012 an online manifesto calling for a Roosevelt-type solution to the GFC. Among the main founders, let us mention French ex-Prime Minister Michel Rocard, Pierre

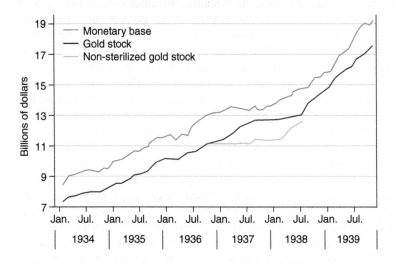

Figure 12.3 US monetary base and gold stock, 1934–1939.

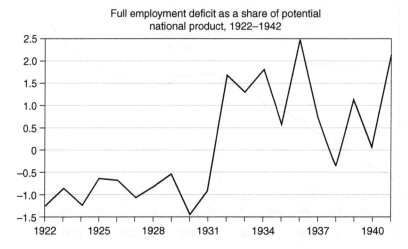

Full employment deficit as a share of potential
national product, 1922–1942

Figure 12.4 The fiscal stance of the United States, 1922–1941 (source: Brad DeLong).

Larrouturou[5] and Stéphane Hassel. The manifesto starts with an invocation. Can we remain voiceless and powerless in the face of current events? In the aftermath of an increasingly threatening social, financial, ecological, democratic crisis, contemporary societies are dangerously approaching a breaking point, from which there is no turning back. After thirty years of neoliberalism and five years into the GFC, the present times are indeed crucial for the future of the world. The question posed to our societies is a clear-cut choice ahead of us: death or metamorphosis? Michel Rocard[6] had warned us in 2007 that capitalism was living an unprecedented crisis, the magnitude of which could prove suicidal for mankind. Meanwhile, a massive transfusion of private debt has been merely replaced by an equally massive transfusion of public debt, but the world economy, as we know it, is still living on drips. On 6 October 2011, Bank of England governor, Mervyn King[7] warned that 'this is the most serious financial crisis at least since the 1930s, if not ever' (Elliott and Allen, 2011). Roosevelt succeeded Hoover as president in 1933. These were times of utter despair for the American population, with fourteen million unemployed and crashing industrial production (–45 per cent in three years). The unparalleled determination of Roosevelt was the driving factor behind the enormous boost in confidence and the wave of reforms passed during the first three months of his mandate (i.e. fifteen fundamental reforms were voted during that period): '[t]he process is extraordinarily swift: some laws are introduced, discussed, voted and promulgated in the same day' (Roosevelt 2012 Collective, 2012). In a statement casting light on political discursive practices in 2012,[8] the Roosevelt Manifesto reminds us that 'Roosevelt's purpose was *not to reassure the markets but to bring them to heel*' (ibid., emphasis added). Financial markets, represented by groups of shareholders, were quick to express their anger at a law separating deposit banks and investment banks. There was utter discontent with new taxes on the highest incomes, and with a new federal tax on profits decided by the Roosevelt administration. As the manifesto points out, the catastrophes announced by financial experts did not occur. Moreover, the US economy performed well under these rules for almost half a century. The manifesto also makes reference to Vaclav Havel, who wrote several weeks after the fall of the Berlin wall that each one of us had the power to change the world. This extraordinary conviction was later reported by US President George Bush Sr, who had met Vaclav Havel:

> President Havel never stopped believing in what he called this unbelievable thought: that any one of us can shake the Earth. Shake the Earth, Mr. President, and part the Iron Curtain. Shake the Earth and knock down the Berlin Wall. Shake the Earth and set in motion a process of change from Budapest to Bucharest, from Warsaw to Wenceslas Square.[9]

The third proposal of the Roosevelt 2012 manifesto

Out of the fifteen proposals put forward in Roosevelt 2012, the third one, 'putting an end to the fiscal abandonment of the nation' pertains to the current debate on austerity and growth. The manifesto clearly proposes a way out of the dependency on markets, currently strangling public policies, in order to balance future budgets. The groundbreaking proposal consists of cancelling the bulk of tax cuts granted to big corporations and wealthy citizens over the last decade (Roosevelt 2012, Proposition 3). Quoting Gilles Carrez, a French conservative and general rapporteur to the Parliament for the budget, who presented a report on 5 July 2010 on French public finances, the Roosevelt 2012 manifesto argues that the immediate cancellation of all tax cuts voted since 2000 would generate €100 billion of tax revenues.[10] Further, switching back to the taxation system in place in 2000 in France (at a time when nobody thought it amounted to a confiscatory Sovietized system), would have the stunning effect of turning the budget deficit into a surplus! When Roosevelt was first elected, the tax rate applicable to wealthiest citizens was around 25 per cent. It was immediately raised to 63 per cent, and, soon after, it reached 79 per cent. Quoting French economist Thomas Piketty, international specialist of inequalities and comparative taxation systems, the manifesto reminds us that the aforementioned tax rate (on wealthy citizens) was kept above 70 per cent until the election of Ronald Reagan. This means that the USA enjoyed a sustained period of expansion and unprecedented economic growth (barely interrupted by the Second Worl War) without relying on a debt-financed growth model. However, the American economy (along with many others) will switch to the latter regime of accumulation from the 1980s onwards. The Roosevelt 2012 manifesto puts forward a transformative proposal for a new European tax that would reduce the extent to which the previously tax cuts voted since 2000 have to be cancelled. Merely cancelling 50 per cent of these contentious tax cuts would mechanically bring the budget deficit back into the Maastricht Treaty range, that is, to a very reasonable level of 1.2 per cent of the GDP.

And if, at the same of time, the cost of servicing the French debt is reduced[11] (an expected €45 billion in 2012), a balance budget would soon be in sight.

The fifth proposal of the Roosevelt 2012 manifesto

The fifth proposal is devoted to the boycott of tax havens, and clearly pertains to austerity measures. Skyrocketing public debts worldwide can be attributed to excessive public spending. They are also explained by recession-induced faltering tax revenues. The latter component of the budget is sometimes overlooked due to the required expertise to engage in informed discussions on taxation. A vast literature exists on comparative taxation systems, jurisdictional competition and tax strategies of multinational firms.[12] At first glance, the fifth proposal of the Roosevelt 2012 manifesto is rather simplistic, and merely sketches out a boycott of tax havens, in order to counteract tax evasion trends. Yet, the concern appears legitimate in the light of the increasingly sophisticated tax-liability management of global firms specializing in the production and the distribution of knowledge-based and intangible assets. On 28 April 2012, the *New York Times* published a controversial paper entitled 'How Apple Sidesteps Billions in Taxes' by Charles Duhigg and David Kocieniewski. The paper shows how the most profitable company on Earth manages to minimize its tax liabilities both at the domestic level, thanks to jurisdictional competition with regard to differences in corporation tax levels between states, and at the international level, by shifting profits from high-taxation to low-taxation countries. This is facilitated by a set of wide-ranging international business trends towards specialization in intangible and knowledge-based assets:

> an international financial engine kicks into gear, moving money across continents in the blink of an eye ... [Apple's] international subsidiaries – particularly the company's assignment of sales and patent royalties to other nations – help reduce taxes owed to the American *and other governments*.
>
> (Duhigg and Kocieniewski, 2012, emphasis added)

The rationale behind austerity: opposing views

The pure economic approach: austerity measures are justified

In a Voxeu column, Daniel Gros (2011) presented a pedagogical case in favour of austerity programmes, with a very simple calculation, in order to single out a self-defeating mechanism for fiscal deficits. Let us assume a country with a debt/GDP ratio of 120 per cent that reduces its deficit by 1 per cent of GDP by cutting public expenditure. We assume the existence of a fiscal multiplier (elasticity of GDP to the public deficit) equal to 1.5. A 1 per cent deficit reduction therefore reduces GDP by 1.5 per cent. The GDP drop thus increased the debt/GDP ratio by 1.8 percentage points (>1.5 per cent). Gros (ibid.) assumes path dependence and the automatic recovery of the economy following a cut in expenditure after a certain period of time. In other words, the debt/GDP is lower in the long run since GDP returns to path, but debt does not – it remains lower than it would have been in the absence of austerity. Gros (ibid.) argues that a short-run increase in debt/GDP due to the short-run fall in demand is fully compensated in the long run. Finally, the long-run impact of a lower deficit on the debt/GDP ratio is equal to the reduction in the deficit itself. Gros (ibid.) assumes both a permanent cut in public expenditure and a permanent impact on GDP; debt/GDP must therefore decrease in the long run. Surprisingly enough, on grounds of realism, Gros (ibid.) discards the hypothesis of a permanent deficit cut reducing the long-run growth rate. Gros also argues that the central question in the Euro sovereign debt crisis is the adopted time horizon. If the long-term time horizon is favoured over short-termism, it is likely that debt reduction will have a positive impact on growth. Yet, this result is invalidated, if financial markets are irrational or subject to erratic short-term movements affecting their long-term trajectory. Therefore, the key question seems to come down to the shortsightedness of financial markets. Can governments abandon fiscal consolidation on the altar of financial market shortsightedness, or should they attempt to harness debt accumulation patterns?

In a *New York Times* article entitled 'The Calming Effect of Central Banks', Jeff Somer (28 April 2012) analyzes the shortsightedness of financial markets. Quoting an HSBC strategist in London, world markets in 2011 were seen as trading in unison to an astonishing extent. The risk of a European meltdown drove markets for months. The latter were tightly synchronized, and were merely moving up and down in reaction to changing risk assessments in the short run. Gros (2011) thinks that this kind of turmoil can only produce negative effects on a country, whose heightened risk aversion necessarily leads to bad choices. Yet, Gros (ibid.) concluded that, in spite of the potential aggravation of the cyclical downturn, the effective implementation of credible austerity measures is the lesser evil. This pure economic argumentation would probably be endorsed by a majority of orthodox economists, who have been advocating austerity since the beginning of the Euro sovereign debt crisis. Yet, this is not the only approach that may be adopted. Austerity has indeed become a heated topic in contemporary debates about society and the economy.

Austerity measures: an absurdity in the current economic and social climate

In a *New York Times* column entitled 'Keynes was right' on 29 December 2011, Paul Krugman lamented over the erroneous beliefs held by politicians and policy makers throughout the Western world in late 2010 and early 2011. It was widely believed that the focus should be on deficit reduction, and not on job creation. In this respect, we shall examine the eye-opening findings of the ILO and the International Institute for Labour Studies in the next section. A year later, Krugman (2012b) hammered his point home, by bringing even more discredit on the 'austerians', who held firm to the myth that more austerity would result in enhanced confidence, notwithstanding the pain inflicted on the peoples of Europe. Jean Claude Trichet, former ECB Chairman was one of those believers in the confidence building power of austerity (ibid.). Drawing a bottom line under the year 2011, Krugman (ibid.) regrets the utter obsession of the political elite to promote a deficit reduction agenda on highly indebted countries, as a result of the socialization of private debts in the aftermath of the 2007–2008 crisis, thereby aggravating the real problem of a depressed economy and mass unemployment.

In the *World Economic Outlook*, the IMF (2012b) argues in favour of slowing down austerity, notably for countries enjoying low borrowing costs. Pushing fiscal consolidation too far will necessarily be counterproductive; short-term adjustments to countercyclical revenue losses being detrimental to economic activity and unpopular, for the public and the market (IMF, 2012a, 2012c). The IMF calls for a sound targeting of priorities for austerity alone cannot cure the ills of major advanced economies. Fundamental problems must be targeted to sustain weak US households and vulnerable sovereigns in the euro area. Resources from stronger peers must also be effectively drawn on (IMF, 2012b, p. xvii). In a column entitled 'Has Austerity Gone too Far?' (Corsetti, 2012), the platform of debates Voxeu, puts forward the idea that fiscal consolidation has become a watchword in Europe. The measures adopted by EU leaders have not yet convinced financial markets that debt dynamics are actually sustainable. These renewed doubts coincide with a recent slowdown and even contraction, thereby posing the question of the desirability of austerity policies. By arguing that monetary policy alone cannot bring back the output gap to pre-crisis levels, contrary to NMC policy insights, DeLong and Summers (2012) provide a tentative mathematical proof of the controversial proposition according to which austerity policies are necessarily self-defeating and expansionary policies self-financing in a depressed economy wherein future potential output has been hampered by underutilized productive capacities caused by the recession (ibid.). This result is derived from the exceptional borrowing conditions enjoyed by the US Treasury for years. The two authors are manifestly confident that a cost–benefit analysis would give support to expansionary fiscal polices, and *not* to austerity policies.

A mathematical argument against austerity (DeLong and Summers, 2012)

A shadow cast in a downturn creates uncertainty on the labour market, due to discouraged workers, outdated skills, organizational anxiety and missing investment on future productivity. Yet, if output rises above expectations, the uncertainty will be reduced, and this will raise potential output in the future by a fraction η. $\eta\mu$.

Additional government expenditure with a Keynesian multiplier μ, boosts future real GDP by the multiplier times a hysteresis coefficient η. With a tax rate τ, the flow of future total tax collections will be multiplied by $\tau\eta\mu$.

$(1-\mu\tau)$ is the additional debt incurred by the additional flow of government debt expenditure ΔG. With a stable debt-to-GDP ratio, the cost of amortizing this additional debt equals $(r-g)(1-\mu\tau)$, where r is the real interest rate at which the Treasury borrows, and g is the long-term growth rate of the economy.

If $r<g+\tau\eta\mu/(1-\mu\tau)$, then a benefit–cost calculation for expansionary fiscal policy becomes obsolete. Expansionary fiscal policy is self-financing, because there are no costs. No future tax increases are needed to amortize the extra debt, because economic growth, in itself, is revenue generating!

It is, rather, *austerity that requires future tax increases.*

For a multiplier $\mu=1.0$, a hysteresis shadow-cast-by-the-recession coefficient $\eta=0.1$, a growth rate $g=2.5\%$/year, and a tax share $\tau=1/3$, the critical value of r becomes $r<7.5\%$.

Long-run Treasury borrowing rate must exceed 7.5%/year in real terms – above 9.5%/year in nominal terms – for fiscal expansion to be a negative policy option.

For multiplier $\mu=0.5$, hysteresis shadow-cast-by-the-recession coefficient $\eta=0.05$, growth rate $g=2.5\%$/year, and tax share $\tau=1/3$, the condition becomes $r<3.75\%$.

Long-run Treasury borrowing rate needs to be above 3.75%/year in real terms – above 5.75%/year in nominal terms – for fiscal expansion to be a bad deal.

WHAT IS THE SIZE OF THE FISCAL MULTIPLIER IN AUSTERITY TIMES?

While fiscal policy was seemingly discarded in the core tenets of the NMC, the magnitude of the global downturn, and the spectacular nature of the stimulus programmes put in place in the aftermath of the GFC, have reignited interest in fiscal policy, which is now in the forefront of research agendas in economics departments worldwide. A key lesson arising from this line of research is that there is no unique answer to the question of the actual size of the fiscal multiplier. Structural parameters, such as the specificities of fiscal and taxation policies, features of the economic and geographic environment, government purchases and transfers, modes of financing of public investment and its implementation, yield a great variety of answers (Wilson, 2012). Auerbach and Gorodnichenko (2010) make a case for fiscal policy and stimulus programmes in times of recession. They argue that the adverse impact of austerity measures is much higher in a depressed economy than during the expansionary phase of the business cycle. The fiscal multiplier differs in recessions and expansions. The long-run effect is found to be positive in recessions (2.5), but negative in expansions (–1.0). Finally, adverse hysteresis effects should not be overlooked (Chapter 6) by macroeconomists, as a prolonged period of slow growth cannot be ruled out (Chapters 9 and 16). Human capital losses can have a major impact on productivity levels for the long-term unemployed population. For a country as whole, innovation capabilities may be seriously affected, through credit constraints on innovative firms (Aghion *et al.*, 2009; Aghion *et al.*, 2012). The link between innovation and unemployment is crucial to the understanding of the transformation of growth patterns in a post-crisis context, but this fascinating theme remains beyond the scope of the present book.

The Spanish example was evoked in this chapter. In late April, the government projected that the planned budget tightening, by itself would reduce economic growth by 2.6 percentage points. A mapping of demonstrations in Europe resulting from austerity measures shows that social discontent is spreading to the richer Northern countries.[13]

For instance, in the Netherlands,[14] the toppling of Prime Minister Mark Rutte's government (ironically, one of the most pro-austerity European administrations) occurred on 23 April 2012, after it failed to get its austerity package through parliament.

Yet, in Greece, arguments in favour of more austerity measures are dressed in mere rhetorical clothes (Pilkington, 2011b), as exemplified by the

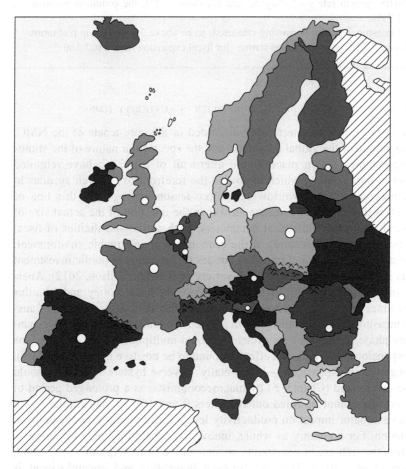

Map 12.1 European industrial federations called on their members to support the European day of action (29 February 2012).

Note
White dots = demonstrations on 29 February 2012.

Photograph 12.1 Scene of desolation after an anti-austerity protest (source: Angelos Tzortzinis).

declaration of the leader of Greece's Pasok party Evangelos Venizelos ahead of crucial elections on 6 May 2012, stating that the country is 'on a course that is difficult but safe, after having covered most of the distance, to finally emerge from the crisis'.[15] Failing to stay on this (austere) path to recovery means that Greece would 'embark on an adventure, sliding back many decades and taking the country to default, to leave Greeks facing mass poverty' (ibid.).

Wyplosz (2012b) agrees that the advocates of austerity are undoubtedly suffering from an enormous credibility deficit. Yet, two fundamental macroeconomic objectives namely, long-term growth and fiscal discipline, are often associated in the media and the literature, although there ought to be clearly distinguished. Wyplosz confirms that austerity measures in the midst of a double-dip recession are indeed absurd. Economic and social pain experienced by the Greek people bears testimony to the invalidation of austerity measures. Other Mediterranean countries have grown disillusioned, with the burden of sacrifices far outweighing their fragile and imperceptible benefits. Wyplosz (ibid.) underlines a striking paradox characterizing financial markets in 2012. Growth is unanimously recognized by market participants as sine qua non to ensure deficit reduction. Yet, while the ECB is lending enormous amounts of short-term liquidities to the European banking system at very low interest rates,[16] a growing number of European countries are facing unbearable borrowing costs on the sovereign bond market.

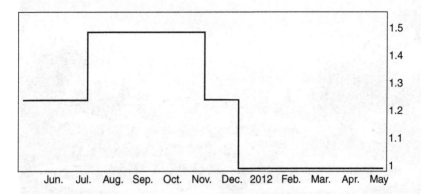

Figure 12.5 ECB key interest rates, May 2011 to May 2012.

Comment
The refinancing costs of banks in the Eurozone are incredibly lower than the borrowing costs imposed upon the weakest European countries.

Comment
The spread of Italian and Spanish sovereign bond yields against German bonds is a good measure of the risk premium of the corresponding government bonds, given that Germany is usually regarded as the benchmark country against which the solvency of other countries is checked. The spreads kept rising throughout the GFC until they reached a peak until the end of 2011. The exceptional credit facilities granted in December 2011 by the ECB to European banks, under the form of three-year loans, have helped reverse the trend and diminish the spreads, although the decline was far less pronounced in Spain, due to the uncertainty about the macroeconomic environment. All in

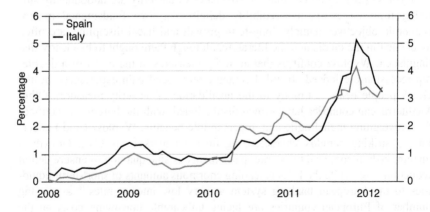

Figure 12.6 Spread of Italian and Spanish government bond yields, 2008–2012.

all, the Euro sovereign debt crisis that started in early 2010 was conducive to a rise in borrowing costs for Mediterranean countries with doubtful public finances. The surprise refinancing operation of the banking system decided by the ECB in December 2011 seems to have been a positive strategic move that provided some relief to financial markets and sovereigns. Yet, much uncertainty remains in 2013 around future political, economic and social conditions in countries of the Eurozone.

Finding a compromise between these seemingly antithetic objectives

Wyplosz (ibid.) has listed five principles designed to find a way out of the growth vs fiscal consolidation conundrum.

Principle 1: long-term growth and fiscal discipline are distinct objectives

Empirically, there is no evidence that fiscal discipline affects the long-term growth trajectory of the economy. The two objectives should therefore be kept separated. There is a need for a fiscal compact with decentralized rules, whose implementation lies at the national level. Unlike arguments put forward by certain European politicians, growth objectives should not interfere with the fiscal compact (which is mostly about keeping the European house in order).

Principle 2: the Lisbon Strategy is a failed experiment

The Lisbon Strategy to turn Europe into the most competitive and dynamic knowledge-based economy in the world has proved disappointing so far. Its job creation potential needs to be fully reevaluated.

Principle 3: a framework for fiscal policy cooperation is needed

The lack of international coordination between countries of the Eurozone accounts for the grave institutional shortcomings of the Stability and Growth Pact. The underlying cause is probably the lack of fiscal integration, whose importance was once underlined by Mundell (Chapter 14). Without any federal budget, counter-cyclical policies cannot be effective in the face of an asymmetric macroeconomic shock of the magnitude of the GFC. Yet, the emergence of a full-fledged fiscal union is probably not a realistic hypothesis (at least not before the year 2050). Meanwhile, the role of the European Stability Fund System could be strengthened.

Principle 4: imminent debt restructuring is needed

Debt restructuring should precede all market-led contagion effects. The debt burdens of Portugal, Italy, Greece and Spain have made debt restructuring inevitable. Other countries are on the same path (France and Germany). Waiting for the implosion of the system would amount to economic suicide. Banks holding large amounts of these quasi-toxic sovereign bonds need to be urgently recapitalized. In this respect, the measures agreed upon on 28–29 June 2012 by EU leaders,[17] in order to restore confidence in the economy, invest more in growth and establish a stronger union, mark a step in the right direction. Although debt restructuring was not part of the final package, the Eurozone's bailout fund is now allowed to directly recapitalize troubled banks. Before the 28–29 June EU summit, governments had to apply for prior funding to the bailout fund, before subsequently lending the money to their banks.

Principle 5: adopting the Swiss debt-brake arrangement in the long run

With public debts in the 90–100 per cent GDP range in many European countries, the only way for governments to bring debt down is to generate primary surpluses. At projected growth rates, it will take years, if not decades, to curb down debt. A way out of the current fiscal impasse would be the Swiss debt-brake arrangement approved by 85 per cent of Swiss voters in 2001, and implemented in 2003. Its main requirement is to maintain government spending on par with, or slightly below, trendline revenues over a multiyear period. Since the reform came into effect, Swiss government spending has increased by only 2.6 per cent annually (against 4.3 per cent per year prior to the reform).

The Swiss experience shows that this type of institutional reform is effective insofar as it clearly shows that fiscal discipline is a 'long-term characteristic, which may allow for significant temporary slippages along with offsetting surpluses' (Wyplosz, 2012a). As shown by the Spanish and Irish examples, good tracks of record and bad equilibria are not incompatible.[18]

Recent evidence against austerity

The poor economic performance of the UK[19]

In a report published by the UK Office for National Statistics in April 2012, Malindi Myers provides an assessment of the recent economic performance of the UK. With a 0.2 per cent contraction in the first quarter of 2012, the verdict is severe. The UK showed no growth in 2011, and has recovered less than half the output lost during the Great Recession. Employment figures, slightly improving at first glance, mask broad differences between part-time and full-time workers, the former accounting for the bulk of employment gains at the expense of the latter. This structural shift in the composition of employment bears testimony to the increased precariousness of the UK workforce.

Table 12.1 Budget and public debt in Switzerland (% GDP)

Swiss budget	Swiss public debt
Surplus: 0.8% of GDP (2011 est.)	52.4% of GDP (2011 est.), 54.5% GDP (2010)
34th best performance in the world	49th best performance in the world

Source: CIA World Factbook, updated on 26 April 2012.

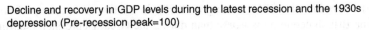

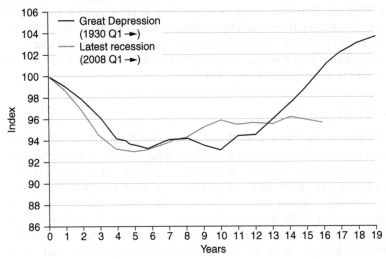

Figure 12.7 Recovery in GDP levels after 1930 and after 2008 (source: Office for National Statistics).

Table 12.2 Performance of the UK economy after 1930 and 2008

	Great Depression (1930 Q1→)	Latest recession (2008 Q1→)
0	100	100
1	99.1	98.7
2	97.9	96.8
3	96.3	94.6
4	94.2	93.1
5	93.6	92.9
6	93.3	93.2
7	94	93.8
8	94.1	94.2
9	93.5	95.3
10	93.1	95.9
11	94.6	95.5
12	94.6	95.7
13	96	95.6
14	97.6	96.2
15	99.1	95.9
16	101	95.7
17	102.4	–
18	103.3	–
19	103.8	–

Comment

Sixteen quarters into the GFC (starting in 2008), in relative terms, the performance of the British economy is *worse* than during the Great Depression (starting
in 1930). While the British economy had come back to pre-recession levels after
sixteen quarters during the Great Depression, it was still below the 2008/Q1
level in early 2012. The conclusion is straightforward for the present analysis.
Pro-growth policies have not been the primary concern of British political and
economic leaders since the beginning of the GFC.

'World of Work Report 2012'

In the editorial of the 'World of Work Report 2012' (International Labour
Organization (International Institute for Labour Studies), 2012), the Director of
the International Institute for Labour Studies, Raymond Torres (2012, p. vii)
portrays a gloomy and even alarming situation on the job front worldwide four
years into the GFC: 'labour markets had not fully recovered from the global
crisis that erupted in 2008: there is still a deficit of around 50 million jobs in
comparison to the pre-crisis situation'. Two-thirds of all European countries
experienced an increase in their unemployment rate between 2010 and 2012.
Torres (ibid.) stresses the very unusual pattern of the economic slowdown and
the worrying structural evolution of labour market imbalances. He warns against
the weakening of certain populations, such as the long-term unemployed and the
precarious part-time workers; whole segments of the labour force are now on the
verge of being excluded from the job market (thus falling into poverty); and this
trend is likely to continue even when recovery is more firmly under way (ibid.).
Sadly so, women and youth are the most vulnerable population groups.[20]

Job instability is described by Torres (ibid., p. viii) as a human tragedy for
workers and their families with disastrous consequences spurring a

> waste of productive capacity, as skills tend to be lost as a result of excessive
> rotation between jobs and long periods of unemployment and inactivity.
> More job instability therefore means weaker productivity gains in the future
> and less room for prospering and moving up the career ladder.

Along with fiscal consolidation, a number of countries have further deregulated
their labour markets, in order to calm financial markets. However, these reforms
have proved disappointing to date (ibid.). From a policy perspective, the refusal
to give priority to economic growth and job creation in the name of fiscal discipline amounts to sowing the seeds of socio-economic destruction (ibid.).

*Illiberal Politics in Neoliberal Times: Culture, Security and Populism
in the New Europe (Berezin, 2009)*

Misir (2011, p. 8) casts light on the painful period of adjustment undergone by
many European countries as a result of the implementation of austerity policies.

The progressive elimination of basic social services, wage depression and reduced investments in infrastructure have been conducive to higher levels of insecurity and rising inequalities, thereby undermining the essence of the social contract.[21] Austerity measures disproportionately affect individuals belonging to low-income groups, who have been already weakened by deteriorating macro-economic conditions in the aftermath of the GFC. The main characteristic of austerity measures is that they are usually presented to the population in a TINA fashion.[22] The appalling intellectual state of the political debate surrounding austerity measures is exacerbated by the impressive rise in right-wing populist movements throughout Europe:

> A strong case can be made that the turn to austerity only makes sense if it is considered as part of the evolution of capitalism and the balance of class power within it – towards wealthy households, economically dominant firms (chief among them being financial firms), conservative politicians and right-wing populists.
>
> (King *et al.*, 2012, editorial, p. 3)

Although they have become widespread, the magnitude of these socio-political phenomena have surprised observers over the last two decades. Mabel Berezin (2009) takes issue with the commonly held view blaming the rise of European right-wing populism on the successive waves of immigration from non-Western countries. Instead, she points to

> [t]he accelerated process of Europeanisation that includes political, economic, and cultural integration in the core trans-European context ... within which the rightwing populist movement emerged ... and the transformation, if not outright disappearance, of the postwar 'world of security'.
>
> (Ibid., p. 8)

The historical evolution of capitalism, the shifting balance of class power, the disappearance of the post-war Welfare State, those seem to be new relevant analytical grids that need to be relied upon and further developed, in order to go beyond the confines of the NMC, which has very little to say about current events in an extraordinary context marked by the ongoing debate over the growth versus austerity post-crisis conundrum.

Avoiding economic suicide: the painful Spanish example[23]

Austerity and suicide rates: a socio-epidemiological approach[24]

Sadly enough, suicide rates come in the picture of our analytical framework for understanding the rationale behind austerity. The economic crisis in Europe has inflicted woes on nations such as Greece, Ireland, Spain and Italy, and a sharp increase in suicide rates among entrepreneurs and small-business owners have been observed in a novel phenomenon coined suicide by economic crisis. Researchers investigating the causes of suicide have found that they are complex and manifold. Among them, severe economic stress levels are generally corre-lated to higher suicide rates. David Stuckler, a sociologist at the University of Cambridge led a very instructive study published in the *Lancet* (Stuckler *et al.*, 2011). He singled out a sharp rise in suicides across Europe from 2007 to 2009, more particularly in countries afflicted by the GFC, such as Greece and Ireland: 'financial crisis puts the lives of ordinary people at risk, but much more danger-ous is when there are radical cuts to social protection'. Stuckler *et al.* (ibid.) epit-omize the phenomenon by stating that austerity can turn a crisis into an epidemic. The conclusion of the paper bears testimony to the idea that the pure economic approach to the Euro sovereign debt crisis (Pilkington, 2011b) is irrel-evant, if not dangerous. The gravity of the Greek situation demonstrates that the burden of debt-financing for ordinary people can lead them to sacrifice basic health care and preventive services. These microeconomic choices may increase the risks and transmission probabilities of HIV and sexually transmitted diseases. In the most desperate cases, for very sick patients, life might be the ultimate price to pay. Beyond deficit reduction strategies extending to austerity policies, access to health care remains an absolute priority, so that the 'crisis does not undermine the ultimate source of the country's wealth – its people' (Stuckler *et al.*, 2011).

The macro-picture: the economic suicide of Europe

In an acid *New York Times* column entitled 'Europe's Economic Suicide', on 15 April 2012, Krugman (2012a) broadens the scope of the reflection on suicide rates, by polemically arguing that the macro-picture is one of a whole continent on its way to committing economic suicide under the impulse of European leaders. Krugman insists on the Spanish case which he calls the new epicentre of the crisis. In what amounts to a depression-like economy, with almost one-quarter of the labour force and more than half of the youth out of work in April 2012, Spain now resembles the USA at the depths of the Great Depression.

What on earth is going on in Spain?

Much attention has been given to the Greek situation since the outbreak of the Euro sovereign debt crisis. Yet, three years into the crisis, although the cure of austerity is an increasingly worrying source of concern for European leaders, the epicentre of the crisis seems to have shifted to a country whose GDP is five times the size of the Greek one, namely Spain. The rationale behind austerity since the beginning of the crisis has been quite simple. Weak economies severely hurt by the GFC can still be rewarded by investors and financial markets pro-vided that their leaders agree to pursue austerity policies. Collapsing growth, job losses and other social costs will be immediately painful, but these ills are supposed to be the price for economic redemption. That day will come when investors start buying massively their sovereign bonds again with much less pressuring risk premiums and therefore lower interest rates. Yet, risk premiums, as the barometer of the fragile economic health of Mediterranean countries, have proved, at best, an unreliable guide for action and, at worst, a recipe for disaster. The latter dark scenario materializes when escalating government promises of fiscal consolidation become correlated with the unloading of sovereign bond holdings, thereby signalling utter distrust in the policies pursued in the name of fiscal austerity. The illustration was Standard & Poor's decision to downgrade Spanish bonds by two notches on 28 April 2012. With an alarming 24 per cent unemployment rate,[25] the highest level since the early 1990s and one of the worst jobless figures in the world, this evolution prompted Foreign Minister Jose Manuel Garcia-Margallo to admit in a radio interview that the figures are terrible for Spaniards and for the government, Spain now being in a crisis of huge proportions.

The shifting stance of economic orthodoxy: the example of the IMF

At the Davos summit in Switzerland in 2012, IMF managing director Christine Lagarde issued an austerity warning, suggesting that inappropriate spending cuts could strangle growth prospects. In a reversal of priorities, from the perspective of the IMF, she added that austerity measures should not be blindly applied across the board, and should be tailored to each economy. This concern was echoed by US Treasury Secretary Tim Geithner: '[t]here is a risk that every disappointment in growth will be met with an austerity that will feed the decline, and that is a cycle you have to arrest to solve financial crises'.[26]

Conclusion

Fiscal policy was never high on the agenda of the NMC. The latter policy option was, at best, the junior partner of monetary policy, and, at worst, its mere subordinate function. It was also argued (Goodhart, 2005b; Wray, 2007) that the NMC probably purported a hidden intellectual agenda that denied any active role for the government in the conduct of economic policy. The marginal role granted to fiscal policy might be explained by the prevailing monetary dominance hypothesis that consistently rules out the possibility of monetizing fiscal deficits. The implication is clear cut, as insolvent countries having endorsed the monetary dominance hypothesis need to choose between austerity and default. There is no middle ground. Yet, the Euro sovereign debt crisis has uncovered the first cracks in the supremacy of the monetary dominance hypothesis, thereby weakening the superstructure of the NMC. An etymological analysis of the word 'austerity' shows that the latter can only be imposed upon a country by a political authority with the consent of the population. In other words, there is no such thing as a natural order from which austerity measures automatically stem. Somehow, austerity is necessarily the result of a political decision, whether the forces at work belong to the national, international or supranational domain. The recent Greek and Spanish examples show how austerity amounts to a brutal medicine with the unintended risk of killing the patient. Austerity measures blindly imposed upon a depressed economy undoubtedly have self-reinforcing effects that can potentially aggravate the depression. In contradistinction with the latter policy approach, the legacy of F.D. Roosevelt is living on today with the Roosevelt 2012 collective that originated in France. Finding a compromise between fiscal consolidation and austerity is no easy task. We have proposed elements for further reflection in this chapter, although we emphasized the need to be wary of purely economic solutions to the crisis. In times of social distress marked by rising suicide rates amongst the most fragile segments of the population, new interdisciplinary studies combining the insights of economics, sociology, psychology and medical science are urgently needed, in order to shed light on the crucial decisions made by our political leaders. The last noteworthy observation about the growth versus austerity debate is that the first cracks in the doctrine of established temples of orthodoxy have recently surfaced over proposals to impose further strains on economies already weakened by the GFC and, more particularly, by the sovereign debt crisis.

13 Quantitative easing

Sound policy making or an admission of defeat?

Introduction

Quantitative easing has become one of the buzzwords of the GFC; it is an unconventional monetary policy that 'increases the money supply by flooding financial institutions with capital, in an effort to promote increased lending and liquidity'.[1] Yet, this conception is reminiscent of the monetarist conception of monetary policy that is criticized in this chapter. For the Bank of England (Wolf, 2012), 'asset purchases work by restoring confidence, signaling future policy, forcing rebalancing of portfolios, improving liquidity and increasing the money supply when the standard mechanism – lending by banks – has frozen'. Quantitative easing is thus a confidence building and liquidity enhancing policy. Contrariwise, critics often argue that quantitative easing puts the economy on a path to hyperinflation. In this chapter, we try to answer the question whether quantitative easing amounts to sound policy making, or an admission of defeat by monetary authorities. We briefly review the Japanese quantitative experiment between 2001 and 2006, before addressing the programmes implemented by the Fed in 2009 and 2010. Finally, we adopt a critical approach of quantitative easing, whose monetary underpinnings and effects on international macroeconomic balances are singled out.

The Japanese quantitative easing experiment

Quantitative easing in Japan

In his widely acclaimed book entitled *The Holy Grail of Macroeconomics: Lessons from Japan's Great Recession*, Koo (2008, pp. 73–76) begins his presentation of the Japanese quantitative easing (hereafter QE) experiment, by making a preliminary assessment of the state of mainstream macroeconomic theory since the late 1980s: 'For the past twenty years ... the economics profession has been dominated by the view that monetary policy is all-powerful.' Although the term is alien to Koo's terminology, this brief description echoes our presentation of the NMC. This intellectual climate helps explain how influential academics managed to convince Japanese leaders that monetary policy was the only suitable cure capable of putting an end to the difficulties of the economy (Ryan-Collins *et al.*, 2012, p. 80), namely a decade-long recession along with interest-rates hitting the zero bound. Koo (2008, pp. 73–76) explains that, as early as the late 1990s, orthodox economists were strongly urging the Bank of Japan to engage in QE. These recommendations did not go without resistance. Yet, in the light of Japan's ills and under the pressure of orthodox monetary thinking, Governor Masaru decided to implement QE programmes in 2001.

What really happened in Japan between March 2001 and March 2006?

Koo (2008, p. 73) explains that the Bank of Japan pumped ¥25 trillion of reserves into the system between March 2001 and March 2006. Money pumping might not necessarily be the most accurate description of what QE actually is about. Figure 13.1 shows the evolution of base money, broad money and bank loans throughout the QE experiment in Japan.

It is obvious that the increase in base money during that period did not translate into an expansion of bank lending and, by extension, of broad

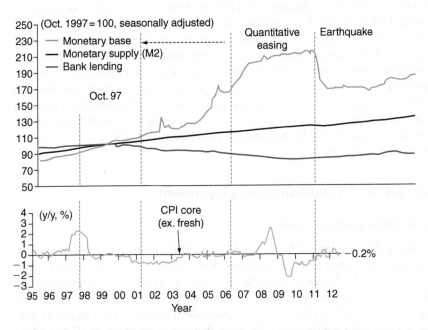

Figure 13.1 Monetary aggregates and bank lending in Japan, 1995–2011 (source: Bank of Japan).

Note
Bank lending figures are seasonally adjusted by Nomura Research Institute.

money. Koo (ibid., p. 75) explains this apparent paradox by stressing the reluctance of borrowers to go into debt.[2] Koo seems to endorse the post-Keynesian tenet of endogenous money when he argues that, in the absence of willing borrowers, the injection of central bank money is deemed to be a failure. It is way more accurate to refer to expansions in excess reserve balances during the QE phase.[3] This view is also shared by Ryan-Collins *et al.* (2012, pp. 80–81).

Can the expansion of excess bank reserves induce additional bank lending to the real economy?

This fundamental question is at the heart of the post-Keynesian reflection on endogenous money developed by major theoreticians, such as Nicholas Kaldor, Basil Moore, Marc Lavoie, Paul Davidson, since the late 1970s or the early 1980s.[4] Post-Keynesians have long combatted the idea of exogenous money that rests on the erroneous credit multiplier story propounded by mainstream economics. The credit multiplier was first explicitly dismissed by great French economist Jacques Le Bourva (1962), and replaced by the credit divider, by reversing the direction of causation between the monetary base and the quantity of money. Indeed, stating that money creation is conditional on a pre-existing monetary base amounts to the recognition of the validity of the money exogeneity postulate. Where do leading and well-respected supranational institutions, such as the Bank of International Settlements, stand in this important debate that is not circumscribed to internal dissensions between heterodox Keynesians? In a working paper entitled 'Unconventional Monetary Policies: An Appraisal' published by the BIS in November 2009, Brio and Disyatat clarified their views[5] on the relationship between the excess of bank reserves and bank lending. The authors (Borio and Disyatat, 2009, p. 19, fn 30) begin with this important reminder: 'The money multiplier view of credit creation is still pervasive in standard macroeconomic textbooks including, for example, Walsh (2003), Mishkin (2004), and Abel and Bernanke (2005).' Yet, Brio and Disyatat adopt the opposite view,[6] by stating that the level of bank reserves play little role to none in shaping banks' lending behaviour. As explained by Moore (1988), money creation is credit-driven and demand-determined: 'The amount of credit outstanding is determined by banks' *willingness to supply loans*, based on perceived risk-return trade-offs, and by *the demand for these loans*' (Borio and Disyatat, 2009, p. 19, emphasis added). This quote is particularly instructive, and fits simultaneously into post-Keynesian and neo-Keynesian traditions, as it leaves the door open for both the theory of endogenous money (money is credit-driven and demand-determined) and credit rationing (the supply of loans may be constrained by the risk assessment of the banker). However, it clearly departs from the quantity theoretic premises of the credit multiplier.

If credit expansion is constrained by banks' lending behaviour, as in a credit crunch, the insufficient aggregate level of bank reserves cannot be the culprit.

The role of the central bank is mainly accommodative and defensive (i.e. the horizontalist approach in post-Keynesian theory). It cannot afford to disrupt the banking system by imposing quantitative restrictions upon the refinancing of banks. The only instrument it controls is the short-term nominal interest rate. Raising the level of reserve requirements might raise the cost of intermediation. Provided that the mark-up is flexible, credit conditions might even be left unchanged. If the mark-up is rigid in the short term, the increase in the cost of intermediation will result in higher lending rates for end-borrowers. Yet, credit expansion will not be directly affected. Of course, the elasticity of the supply of credit with respect to the interest rate provides a well-known transmission channel for monetary policy that monetary economists are familiar with. However, what matters here is that the ball is clearly in the borrowers' court, which echoes the argumentation put forward by Koo (2008) in his criticism of the Japanese QE experiment. In the absence of willing borrowers, shifting reserve requirements and massive injections of base money will not necessarily influence the lending behaviour of banks. Likewise, an increase in the money supply does not necessarily make it to the real economy, let alone foster economic growth. To be complete, there is nonetheless a fundamental type of regulatory requirements capable of influencing bank lending (Borio and Disyatat, 2009, p. 19): 'the main exogenous constraint on the expansion of credit is minimum capital requirements'.[7] This theoretical question is of utmost importance, and must be analyzed in the light of the fantastic rise in credit derivatives (such as credit default swaps) and securitized credit assets over the last decade (before and during the GFC).

Bernanke's assessment of Japanese QE experiment in 2003[8]

We briefly review hereafter the 'Remarks by Governor Ben S. Bernanke before the Japan Society of Monetary Economics, Tokyo, Japan: Some Thoughts on Monetary Policy in Japan' on 31 May 2003. Ben Bernanke begins to emphasize the sheer complexity of the Japanese economic situation in the early 2000s, which involves structural, monetary and fiscal dimensions interwoven with political and social forces, thereby impairing the room for manoeuvre of policy makers. Price-level targeting bears similarities to inflation targeting insofar as they both establish targets for the Consumer Price Index. Whereas inflation targeting is a forward-looking policy, price targeting relies on the price level of past years to maintain the base at the beginning of the period, say 100, constant. Price-level targeting is usually not at the heart of policy recommendations made by the NMC. Yet, interesting exceptions exist, such as in Eggertson and Woodford (2003), who have advocated such a policy stance for Japan when the nominal interest rate approaches the zero bound. At this tipping point, the central bank can only lower the real interest rate by generating inflation expectations. Eggertsson and Woodford (ibid.) argue that, near the zero bound, the creation of inflation expectations is more effective with a price-level target than with an inflation target. For Bernanke (2003), price-level targeting is more suited to the Japanese deflationary environment of the 1990s. The price-level target must comply with key principles of the NMC, such as transparency (i.e. the price target must be clearly announced) and credibility (i.e. it should be gradually rising, so as to anchor the inflation expectations of financial markets and the public at large). One of the most significant contributions of this speech by Bernanke, given five years before the GFC, is his positive assessment of quantitative easing, in order to fight deflation. Bernanke argues that the solution is 'greater cooperation, for a limited time, between the fiscal and the monetary authorities', which is by no means inconsistent with central bank independence. Bernanke (ibid.) therefore argues that the Bank of Japan should increase its purchases of government debt in conjunction with tax cuts or fiscal stimulus. Furthermore, the central bank should not fear the effects of an increase in the money supply in the face of deflationary pressures on the economy.

Influencing inflation expectations: the true objective of quantitative easing

Treasury Inflation-Protected Securities and inflation expectations

Bernanke (2004b) stated that 'Although clues about inflation expectations abound in financial markets, inflation-indexed securities would appear to be the most direct source of information about inflation expectations and real interest rates.'

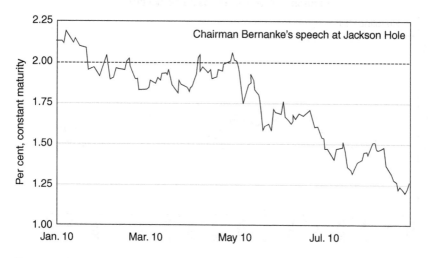

Figure 13.2 Five-year TIPS[a] breakeven inflation rate (source: James Bullard, Federal Reserve Board).

Note

Treasury Inflation-Protected Securities are indexed to inflation in order to protect investors from the negative effects of inflation.

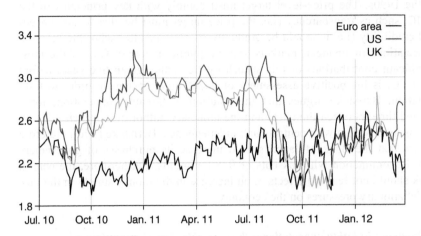

Figure 13.3 Inflation expectations in an international comparison (source: ECB calculations).

Note
Five-year forward 5-years ahead break-even inflation rates.

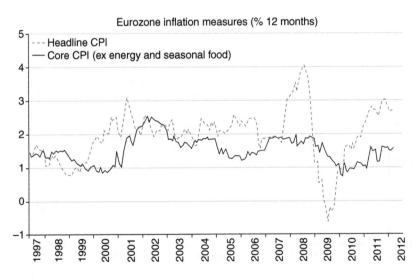

Figure 13.4 Headline CPI and core CPI in the Eurozone, 1997–2012 (% 12 months) (source: ECB).

QE1 and QE2: timeline and assessment

Quantitative easing 1

24 November 2008: the Fed announced a quantitative easing programme to buy $500 billion in mortgage bonds beginning 1 January 2009. The thirty-year fixed interest rates are at 6.09 per cent.

December 2008: the Federal Open Market Committee (FOMC) lowered the target for the federal funds rate to a [0–25] basis points range, thereby entering uncharted territory near the zero-bound on nominal interest rates (see Chapter 11).

1 January 2009: before the Fed started its massive purchases of mortgage-bonds, thirty-year fixed rates drop to 5.05 per cent. This 1 per cent rate drop can be explained by self-fulfilling market expectations, yields on mortgage bond being driven downwards ahead of the Fed purchases.

18 March 2009: the Fed increases mortgage bond buying programme to $1.25 trillion two weeks later (and again in November 2009), thirty-year fixed interest rates drop to 4.78 per cent: their lowest level since official records started in 1971.

31 March 2010: the end of the Fed mortgage bond buying programme. Thirty-year fixed rates rise at 5.125 per cent. The rise can be explained from investors' exit strategy ahead of the possible termination of quantitative easing.

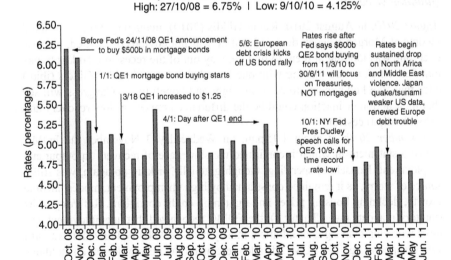

Figure 13.5 Impact of quantitative easing on 30-year rates,[a] October 2008 to June 2011 (source: © Copyright 2011, The Basis Point, Inc. ®).

Note
$0 to $417,000 is called a conforming loan.

6 May 2010: the climax of the Greek crisis with the creation of the EFSF and the subsequent bailout plan drive global investors into US mortgage and Treasury bonds most of summer. Thirty-year fixed rates drop to 4.78 per cent.

30 September 2010: thirty-year fixed rates set a new record low of 4.27 per cent.

According to Brian P. Sack (2009), Executive Vice President of the Federal Reserve Bank of New York, the Large Scale Asset Purchases (LSAP) implemented in December 2009 aimed at pulling the US economy out of the Great Recession and supporting activity by lowering long-term interest rates. Massive purchases drove asset prices upwards, and lowered security yields. Adjustments normally take place as a restructuring of public and private asset holdings.[9] Yet, asset classes purchased under QE1 were predominantly agency securities and mortgage-backed securities, rather than Treasury securities. As an unconventional monetary policy, QE1 fell on to the credit easing asset side of the Fed balance sheet expansion. One central objective of QE1 was also to provide more liquidity to the financial system, and was therefore a major lender of last resort operation. During QE1, the Fed purchased $175 billion of agency debt securities and $1.25 trillion of mortgage-backed securities in addition to purchases of Treasuries. In effect, in a spectacular crisis management move designed to separate deposit banks and investment banks, just as they fought taxes on the highest incomes or the creation of a federal tax on profits avoided a replay of the Great Depression, the Federal Reserve swiftly morphed into the main market maker, while the shadow banking system (Pilkington, 2008) imploded.

Quantitative easing 2

August 2010: in August 2010, Kevin Giddis (2010), managing director of fixed income at Morgan Keegan declared that he was not envious of the Fed, because everyone was looking at them to find the way out of the recession. Giddis thinks that Fed officials 'are playing with one hand behind their back'.[10] Giddis (ibid.) adds that 'the Fed appears to be in the fight and hopefully … Congress will see that their action or inaction could be the difference between a slow recovery and a double-dip recession'.

3 November 2010: at about 1:15 p.m. on Wednesday 3 November the FOMC issued a statement in which it confirmed the slow pace of recovery in output and employment. Household spending, though gradually picking up again, was still a source of worry, as it remained constrained by high unemployment, modest income growth, declining housing prices and tightening credit conditions. Referring to its statutory mandate (see Chapter 9), the FOMC recognized that unemployment was more worrying than signs of inflation, mostly because resource utilization was still very disappointing. The FOMC decided to expand the Federal Reserve's holdings of securities in the System Open Market Account (SOMA) to promote a stronger pace of economic recovery, and to help ensure that inflation remains at levels consistent with its mandate. The FOMC directed the Open Market Trading Desk (the Desk) at the Federal Reserve Bank of New York to purchase an additional $600 billion of longer-term Treasury securities by the end of the second quarter of 2011.

The focus this time was on Treasury bonds, and not on mortgage bonds. The FOMC also directed the Desk to keep reinvesting principal payments from agency debt and agency mortgage-backed securities into longer-term Treasury securities. At the time, the Desk was anticipating $850 billion to $900 billion of purchases of longer-term Treasury securities through the end of the second quarter, a pace of about $75 billion per month.[11]

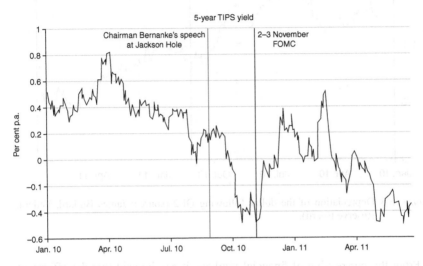

Figure 13.6 The decline in real interest rates following the announcement of QE2 (source: James Bullard, Federal Reserve Board).

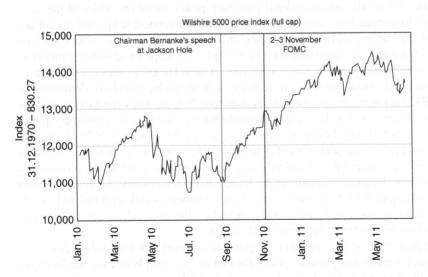

Figure 13.7 The increase in equity prices following the announcement of QE2 (source: James Bullard, Federal Reserve Board).

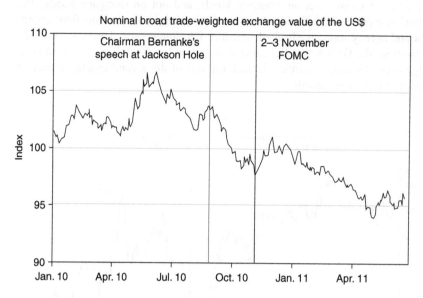

Figure 13.8 Depreciation of the dollar following QE2 (source: James Bullard, Federal Reserve Board).

From the perspective of financial markets, it can be said that the effects of QE2 looked the same as if the Fed had reduced the policy rate substantially. In particular, real interest rates declined, the dollar depreciated and equity prices rose. All in all, unconventional monetary policy measures achieved the same results as monetary easing through the standard interest-rate channel in ordinary times. The experience sheds lights on our discussion on the zero bound for nominal interest rates (Chapter 11). There is still scope for aggressive monetary easing when the policy rate is near zero. A time lag exists between policy decisions and effects on the real economy (six to twelve months). Therefore, the GFC has not made monetary policy impotent. Yet, the assessment of QE remains extremely complex. Economists must disentangle the effects of monetary policy and other shocks hitting the economy. In the first quarter of 2011, the US economy was beset by a number of shocks: *inter alia*, let us mention the strong winter storms in January and February, bringing many construction projects to a halt, the Japanese tsunami on 11 March 2011, temporarily disrupting imports from Japan for US industries reliant on components and semi-finished goods, and finally the rise in uncertainty caused by the political uprisings (the Arab spring) in the Middle East and North Africa.

30 June 2011: The second round of quantitative easing ended on 30 June 2011. Financial markets had probably priced the end of QE2 well before the deadline; yet, stocks performed much better during periods of QE support as compared to periods following the termination of QE support (grey shaded areas on Figure 13.10).[12]

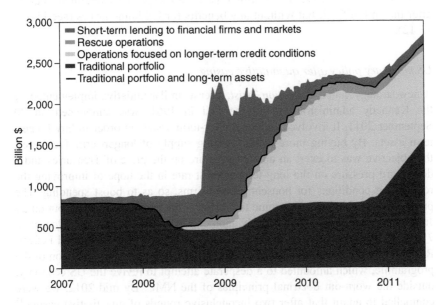

Figure 13.9 Composition of the Federal Reserve's balance sheet assets, January 2007 to June 2011 (source: James Bullard, Federal Reserve Board).

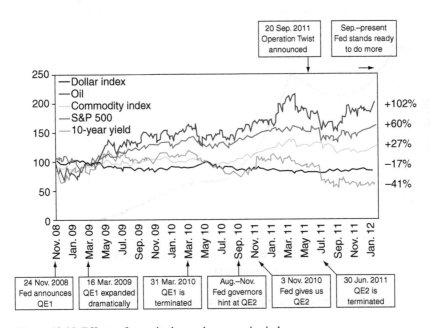

Figure 13.10 Effects of quantitative easing on major indexes.

As shown on Figure 13.11, thirty-year mortgage rates declined sharply after the end of QE2, but without any benefits for US home prices (see Figure 13.12).

US monetary policy after quantitative easing

A new strategy called *Operation Twist*, after a similar initiative implemented by the Kennedy administration and the Fed in 1961, was announced on 20 September 2011. It involved selling shorter-term assets, in order to buy longer-term assets. By buying more of the existing supply of longer-term Treasuries, the objective was to exert an upward pressure on the price of Treasuries and a downward pressure on the long-term interest rate in the hope of improving the refinancing conditions for households and firms, so as to boost spending. The programme was supposed to come to a close at the end of June 2012, but on 29 June 2012, the FOMC voted to apply another $267 billion to continue *Operation Twist* until the end of 2012. Jeffrey Lacker, president of the Richmond Federal Reserve Bank, was the only FOMC member to vote against the extension of the programme, which amounted to a desperate attempt to revive the US economy, outside the worn-out doctrinal principles of the NMC. By mid 2012, we were compelled to admit that after two inconclusive rounds of quantitative easing,[13] with the Federal Funds rate near zero, the Federal Reserve had already exhausted its policy tools.

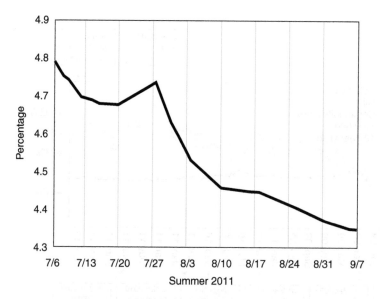

Figure 13.11 How mortgage rates reacted to the end of QE2.

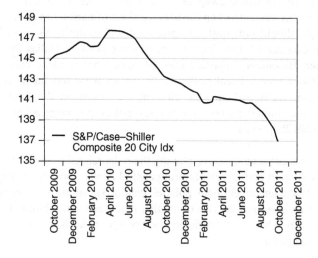

Figure 13.12 S&P/Case-Shiller Composite 20 City Index, October 2009 to December 2011 (source: S&P Dow Jones Indices).

Conclusion: quantitative easing and bank lending – a critical view

Professor Bernanke once promoted quantitative easing, before joining the Fed. This unconventional policy response to recessionary fears consists of massive asset purchases by the central bank, to create excess reserves in the banking system. Yet too much of these idle reserves on bank balance sheets should encourage banks to increase lending, in order to earn more interest on their assets. Increased lending therefore generates more spending, economic growth and job creation. In post-Keynesian monetary theory, money is said to be credit-driven and demand-determined (i.e. the money stock is endogenously determined). As the story goes, money cannot be supplied to the real economy unless there are creditworthy borrowers willing to increase their indebtedness level towards the banking sector. Do the reserves or the bank deposits created by quantitative easing programmes artificially increase the money supply, in contradistinction with the theory of endogenous money? Does quantitative easing increase the ability of banks to create loans *ex nihilo* (with the help of a helicopter printing press, to paraphrase Bernanke), to spend money that did not exist before?

Of course the answer to these seemingly innocent questions is negative. The effect of quantitative easing is to replace longer-dated treasuries with low-yield bank reserves on bank balance sheets, thereby forcing the private sector out of treasuries and into cash. Therefore, the money-printing metaphor, akin to the exogenous money thesis long-combatted by Post-Keynesian economists, is particularly misleading. Double-entry bookkeeping is what quantitative easing amounts to, namely, an electronic swap of bank deposits (i.e. reserves) with interest-bearing assets (i.e. treasuries) on the balance sheet of banks. Discussions revolving around QE should not mask the broader fiscal austerity vs growth debate discussed in Chapter 12. Quoting Federal Reserve Bank of Dallas President Richard Fisher, Bloomberg reported that 'Monetary policy alone cannot solve problems without proper fiscal policy ... If we let it go too far as the Greeks obviously did, we'll end up with riots in the streets in the United States.'[14] Likewise, the limited power of monetary policy has been acknowledged by the IMF (2012b, p.xvii):

> Policymakers must guard against overplaying the risks related to unconventional monetary support and thereby limiting central banks' room for policy maneuvering. While unconventional policies cannot substitute for fundamental reform, they can limit the risk of another major economy falling into a debt-deflation trap, which could seriously hurt prospects for better policies and higher global growth.

14 Revisiting the theory of optimum currency areas

Introduction: Robert Mundell and optimum currency areas (1961)

The article published by Robert Mundell in the *American Economic Review* in 1961 is one of the post-war masterpieces in international economics, and has been widely cited in the economics literature to date.[1] In the real-business cycle tradition (Pilkington, 2011a), Mundell argues that the economy is constantly bombarded by asymmetric shocks with the potential to undermine its performance. An introduction to the Optimal Currency Area (OCA) theory thus consists of a cost–benefit analysis of the adoption of a single currency, with, on the upside, lower transactions costs and the elimination of currency risks and, on the downside, the inability of states abandoning their currency to pursue independent monetary policies (Eichengreen, 1997, pp. 1–2). In a nutshell, the costs of the adhesion to a single currency area are the loss of monetary sovereignty with regard to monetary and exchange rate policy. Contrariwise, the benefits of a single currency area stem from the conditions, which need to be fulfilled, in order to mitigate the adverse effects of asymmetric shocks. Yet, it has been argued in this book that, although exchange rates matter in the NMC, as in the six-equation model presented in Chapter 3, the NMC does not feature any exchange rate commitment. Mundell (1968, p. 177) predicted that balance-of-payments crises would continue to afflict the world economy in the absence of floating exchange rates that help prices adjust between countries, thereby fulfilling a 'natural role' (ibid.).[2] Mundell characterized the pre-1971 era as an international disequilibrium system (ibid.), and was therefore a fierce opponent thereof. The roots of Mundell's framework were clearly Keynesian, with a predominant role given to fine-tuning macroeconomic policy, understood as the adequate combination of monetary and fiscal policy, in order to manage aggregate demand and offset supply-side shocks (McKinnon, 2000). Yet, in 1968, he was unaware of the soon-to-come collapse of the Bretton Woods exchange rate system that would occur from 1971 onwards. With hindsight, his belief in the natural adjusting powers of the international price system was too optimistic in the light of the suboptimal outcomes experienced under the post-1971 floating exchange rate system wherein 'the main currencies float and crush against each other like continental plates' (Soros, 1997, p. 15). Yet, Mundell's interrogations on future monetary arrangements, including the possibility of a single currency area, were already very relevant at the time: 'supposing that the Common Market countries proceed with their plans for economic union, should these countries allow each national currency to fluctuate, or would a single currency area be preferable?' (Mundell, 1961, p. 657). His reflection on exchange rates was rather healthy, and his foresight acute, because the rising forces of economic integration and disintegration had begun to shape the international economy in the 1960s: '[c]ertain parts of the world are undergoing processes of economic integration and disintegration, new experiments are being made, and a conception of what constitutes an optimum currency area can clarify the meaning of these experiments' (ibid.).

It would be unwise to neglect Mundell's insights for casting light on the ongoing Euro sovereign debt crisis. Today, macroeconomic imbalances between Mediterranean and core countries of the Eurozone are indeed as relevant as the current size of their fiscal deficits:[3] 'The deeper balance of payments problems in the eurozone remain unresolved, and cannot be resolved by liquidity assistance alone', noted Brevan Howard, Europe's biggest global macro hedge fund in its last letter to investors (Jones, 2012). Phrasing the question in Mundellian terms therefore requires using his definition of a currency area: 'The problem can be posed in a general and more revealing way by defining a currency area as a domain within which exchange rates are fixed and asking: What is the appropriate domain of a currency area?' (Mundell, 1968, p. 177). Mundell proposes a threefold answer to this question.

Characteristics of an Optimal Currency Area

An OCA is one in which capital is mobile and wages/prices are flexible (1), and/ or labour is a highly mobile factor of production across the OCA (2), and/or there exists an effective system of budgetary transfers between the subsets of the OCA (3). Following Eichengreen *et al.* (1997), we try to assess whether Europe is an OCA.

Labour mobility across the OCA

Can workers easily travel from one region to another? This is dependent on the quality of infrastructures and availability of transportation services (roads, trains, airlines...). Are there cultural barriers that impede the free movement of workers? One may refer to the linguistic diversity of Europe that may be successfully dealt with by the expansion of student exchange programmes, such as the Erasmus scheme (Pilkington, 2012a). Superannuation schemes are retirement benefits given to employees by companies. Are the latter schemes transferable from one region to the other? The answer is not straightforward, for they are regulated under national law, companies being linked to public or private employment agencies, where their contributions are paid. The superannuation contribution of firms is measured as a percentage of basic wages, which varies from one region to the other. The superannuation contribution might be invested under different forms with varying investment patterns, with the interest on contributions being credited to the member's account. The retirement age and the taxation rates applicable to the balance available in the employee's account might differ from one region to another. From a labour law perspective, the tax treatment of resignations might also be regarded differently from one region to the other. Moreover, institutionalized categories of employees (and the corresponding tax rules) might differ from one country to the other.

Openness with capital mobility and price and wage flexibility across the region

Long-term debt and equity finance are provided by capital markets, whose function is to allocate financial funds and capital goods for the government or the corporate sector. The rationale behind capital mobility is to ensure that market forces ensure the automatic distribution of money and capital goods to the sectors of the economy where they are most needed. Price flexibility across the region is ensured by trade integration, which is greatly facilitated by the reduction in trade costs, which may be caused by the end of exchange rate volatility, the elimination of currency risk, enhanced market transparency and macroeconomic stability. Empirical research (Cafiso, 2008) on European trade integration since the introduction of the euro suggests conflicting evidence between the so-called Rose and border effects, the former indicator suggesting higher trade integration due to reduced trade costs, while the latter indicator seems to rule out any positive impact of trade-cost reductions. Wage flexibility has been an accelerating trend in the Eurozone under the growing pressure of decentralization within multi-employer bargaining systems (i.e. wage determination at company level). In this respect the slow erosion of sectoral and inter-sectoral agreements has been an element of downward wage flexibility. One must also mention the growth of variable payments systems (VPS), which are regulated at intersectoral, sectoral and/or company level. The latter schemes are key in reinforcing the link between wages and productivity growth, performance and profit levels. It comes as no surprise that VPS are being promoted by employer organizations across the Eurozone. Overall, competitive pressures for wage flexibility in the Eurozone are a widespread reality, in spite of enduring country-level and sector-level differences. A multi-employer scheme is a pension scheme that has more than one employer, while a single-employer pension plan is designed by an organization to help provide for employees in retirement. As argued by Arrowsmith and Marginson (2008), the extent to which VPS fall under the aegis of collective bargaining agreements under these schemes is determined by the mode of governance of wage-setting practices in Europe, that is whether the emphasis is on the involvement of multiple stakeholders, or is shifting towards unilateral employer regulation. To date, the joint cooperation of the social partners is still regarded as a defining feature of the European social model.[4]

An automatic fiscal transfer mechanism to redistribute money between the areas and the sectors of the OCA

The perfect illustration of this institutional architecture is the United States, 'a transfer and fiscal union where Massachusetts supports Mississippi in so many ways. These are known as "automatic stabilizers": Social Security, federal unemployment benefits, Medicaid, etc' (Joffe, 2011). This architecture entails effective taxation redistribution processes from prosperous into less developed areas of the OCA. Although it seems quite simple in theory, it is politically difficult to implement, as better-off countries are reluctant to give up a share of their revenue and/or welfare.[5] In the Eurozone, the situation has been rendered extremely complex with the advent of the European sovereign debt crisis. In his trans-disciplinary analysis, Pilkington (2011b) has discussed the irrelevance of the no-bail out clause in the Stability and Growth Pact, at the confluence between political discourse analysis and rhetoric.

The ambivalence of Mundell's legacy

The striking feature of Mundell's framework is that it has been used both by advocates and opponents of the single European currency project as a decisive argument in the debate. Yet, the confusion might be removed by distinguishing between two Mundell models. First, a standard model directly inspired by the OCA framework of 1961 that we will call *OCA with stationary expectations*. Second, a model that was presented in the early 1970s (first published in 1973), and that is not as widely known as the first one. We shall call this second approach *OCA with international risk sharing*. Whether economists are referring to the first or second model leads to dramatically opposite conclusions as regards the desirability of the single European currency.

OCA with stationary expectations

The model features two countries A and B in a state of neoclassical equilibrium (full employment and no external imbalance). An asymmetric shock (such as a

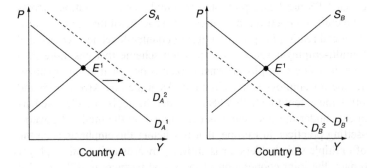

Figure 14.1 Aggregate supply and demand curves for two countries (A and B).

natural disaster) shifts the aggregate demand curve downward in B and upward in A. Price stickiness prevents short-term market-clearing mechanisms from taking place. Inflation is not tolerated by the central bank. Because of the very existence of more than one OCA in the world, a system of variable exchange rates prevails. The only solution to counteract external imbalances arising out of the asymmetric shock is the depreciation of B's currency (artificial stimulation of its competitiveness, followed by a decrease in unemployment) or the appreciation of A's currency (the opposite phenomenon with a resulting reduction in inflation).

Mundell (1961, pp. 510–511), who was yet unaware of the high exchange rate volatility in the post-1971 world, argued that the aforementioned example was the most favourable case for flexible exchange rates.

OCA with international risk sharing

Following a significant, albeit little known, publication (Mundell, 1973a), the objective of the study of OCA morphed into the modelling of interrelations between exchange rate uncertainty and macroeconomic outcomes. A large OCA is desirable insofar as the currency union is well managed by the political authorities. In this second model, asymmetric shocks are not equated to systematic threats to the performance of the currency union. Within an OCA, regions share claims on each other, with the potential to mitigate the adverse impact of asymmetric shocks. A country of the OCA might be hit by an asymmetric shock, such as a bad harvest, a banking panic or social unrest. In this case, the country will suffer a loss of real income, whose impact might nonetheless be effectively cushioned by drawing on the resources of the other countries of the OCA, thereby allowing for an efficient spread of the adjustment costs in the future. Flexible exchange rates for countries using separate monies do not yield the same macroeconomic outcomes, for the country impacted by the asymmetric shock will have to bear the costs alone. By all means, '*the common currency cannot serve as a shock absorber* for the nation as a whole except insofar as the dumping of inconvertible currencies on foreign markets attracts a speculative capital inflow in favor of the depreciating currency' (ibid., p. 115, emphasis added). Mundell (1973b, pp. 147, 150) therefore advocates further integration of capital markets in the European Union, and opposes competitive devaluations that are necessarily harmful in the long run. Instead, he favours closer integration of capital markets with the creation of a common currency, rather than a regime with flexible exchange rates. Mundell's arguments combine social and economic perspectives. In the event of social unrest generating inflationary pressures, through higher wage claims delinked with current productivity levels, flexible exchange rates may cause a de facto devaluation, thereby threatening the international standing of the domestic currency. The long-run costs are neglected, as governments prefer to derive short-term political benefits from the devaluation of the currency. This situation can nevertheless be avoided with the creation of an OCA, by binding currencies together, which will soften the impact of exogenous shocks, through higher capital mobility (ibid.).

Conclusion: asymmetric shocks or behaviour – a cultural explanation?

Contrary to the teachings of the theory of optimal currency areas, Boltho and Carlin (2012) argue that the experience of the Eurozone over the last decade is not one of dealing with asymmetric shocks. In fact, the Great Recession was surprisingly symmetric, insofar as all countries simultaneously experienced postwar record negative growth rates. It was not so much asymmetric shocks that mattered, but behaviour. More particularly, fiscal behaviour was the decisive factor in explaining what went wrong in the Eurozone. Whilst North-European countries embraced austerity along with export-led growth strategies, Mediterranean countries, such as Greece, Italy and Spain, were more profligate and less focused on maintaining their competitiveness levels. Boltho and Carlin (ibid.) illustrate this contrast by pointing to the sharp decline in long-term interest rates from the early 1990s (i.e. the emergence of the NMC), which created favourable macroeconomic conditions, and a unique opportunity for painless government debt reductions. Boltho and Carlin use the example of Italy and Belgium, which had similar public debt-to-GDP ratios when the euro came into existence in 1999 (i.e. 121 per cent in Belgium and 128 per cent in Italy). Nine years later, this ratio was still at 113 per cent in Italy, but had fallen to 91 per cent in Belgium (in spite of a steeper decline in long-term rates in the former country). This ratio rose during the same period in Greece and Portugal, while low interest rates set the stage for the formation of a massive housing bubble in Spain, along with sky-rocketing private debt levels, which proved largely detrimental to the economy (and Spanish public finances) once the bubble went bust, giving rise to a situation of extreme bank fragility. Unfinished projects, such as the (privately financed) €1.1 billion airport in Ciudad Real (intended to serve Madrid and the Andalusia coast, each accessible by train in less than an hour) that shut down in April 2012 after three years of operation.

How can we account for the determinants of asymmetric behaviour in Europe? To answer this question, Pilkington (2011b, p. 374) has proposed a transdisciplinary approach to the Euro sovereign debt crisis, in order to move away from the pure economic interpretation of the fiscal problems plaguing countries of the Eurozone: 'the economic substrata cannot be artificially (or experimentally) isolated from the societal context, the political conflicts or the cultural, linguistic and religious diversity, which characterize human communities'.

15 Lessons from the Euro sovereign debt crisis

Introduction

At the time of writing, the Euro sovereign debt crisis is far from over. This is precisely the conclusion reached by Martin Wolf (2013) in a *Financial Times* column entitled 'Why the Euro Crisis is Not Yet Over': 'Those who believe the Eurozone's trials are now behind it must assume either an extraordinary economic turnaround or a willingness of those trapped in deep recessions to soldier on, year after grim year. Neither assumption seems at all plausible.'

However, a few lessons may be drawn at this advanced stage. After briefly summarizing how the crisis has unfolded since early 2010, and subsequently turned into a major source of concern for the world economy, we try to decide whether the crisis is the outcome of a systemic failure in the design of the euro or, more broadly speaking, of failed European integration, viewed as a unique long-term political and economic project. We also assess how the NMC may fit into this complex discussion. We therefore outline its weakened explanatory power; we propose a tentative diagnosis and thus put forward a new methodological approach for solving the crisis.

The legacy of the Bundesbank

In an article entitled 'Fifty Years of Monetary Policy: What Have We Learned?' Cagliarini *et al.* (2010, p. 22) argue that, for historical and cultural reasons, Europe has long been prone to rule-like behaviour in its central banking practices. Prior to the EMU, the long-established credibility of the Bundesbank, with its quasi-monetarist ideology that translated into an anti-inflationary bias and a strong political independence, led several European countries to give up a share of their monetary sovereignty, through their commitment to a wide-ranging European exchange rate mechanism. European integration (with the notable exception of the UK and a handful of other countries) reached its climax with the creation of the euro and the ECB in 1999. The legacy of the Bundesbank[1] and its impact on the ECB has been emphasized ever since. The Bundesbank was created in 1957, and replaced the *Bank deutcher Länder* (Bank of the German States) founded on 1 March 1948. The Basic Law for the Federal

Republic of Germany (*Grundgesetz*, GG) was promulgated on 23 May 1949 (first issue of the *Federal Law Gazette*, dated 23 May 1949); it was amended up to 20 December 1993. On 3 October 1990, Germany moved towards reunification; the Basic Law achieved constitutional status. Article 88 [The Federal Bank] of the Basic Law states that

> [t]he Federation shall establish a note-issuing and currency bank as the Federal Bank. Within the framework of the European Union, its responsibilities and powers may be transferred to the European Central Bank that is independent and committed to the overriding goal of assuring price stability.

As far as political control is concerned, it is worthwhile drawing a parallel between the management of the Deutschmark after the Second World War and the management of the euro since 1999. Under the impact of significant political and economic forces, the Deutschmark became a hard and strong currency in post-war Europe. The Bundesbank was characterized by strong independence from the Bundestag. Likewise, political independence is a central institutional characteristic of the ECB, arguably inherited from the Bundesbank. Price stability remains the overriding goal of monetary policy as laid out in the statutes of the ECB (Art. 105, EC). Yet, the ECB also acknowledges another more general objective: 'without prejudice to the objective of price stability [the ECB] support[s] the general economic policies in the Community with a view to contributing to the achievement of the objectives of the Community' (Art. 105, EC).[2] However, it remains unclear how the two pillar strategy of the ECB could constitute a deviation from the philosophy of the Bundesbank.

The Euro sovereign debt crisis as it happened

Ever since the Maastricht Treaty was ratified in 1992, the single currency has been progressively taking shape in the political, institutional, economic and social arenas of the EU. The Treaty had set forth a number of constraining macroeconomic criteria, in order to qualify for the new currency. These euro convergence criteria pertained to budget deficits, inflation, long-term interest rates and exchange rates. The United Kingdom, Sweden and Denmark decided not to join the euro. The currency officially came into existence on 1 January 1999.[3] Two years later, Greece, which had been left out at the inception of the euro in 1999, became the twelfth member of the euro area, after drastic cuts in inflation and interest rates. The then president of the European Central Bank, Wim Duisenberg had nevertheless sent explicit warnings to the Greek leaders, asking them to consolidate macroeconomic fundamentals. Yet, on 15 November 2004, Greece openly admitted fudging entry in the euro area. Indeed, close scrutiny of the country's budget showed that it failed to meet the Maastricht criteria (for instance, its deficit-to-GDP ratio was never below 3 per cent after 1999). In 2007, Slovenia joins the euro, followed by Malta and Cyprus in 2008 (and Slovakia in 2009). In December 2008, three months after the collapse of

Lehman Brothers, a €200 billion stimulus plan was agreed upon by EU leaders to boost growth, as part of an unprecedented coordinated response to the GFC. On 27 April 2009, the EU set deadlines for France, Spain, Britain, Ireland and Greece to reduce their deficit-to-GDP ratio below the 3 per cent limit of the Maastricht treaty. In October and November 2009, the Dubai sovereign debt crisis was raging. Concerns of a potential contagion to the euro area started to grow. In December 2009, Greek public debt officially reached the €300 billion threshold, while the debt-to-GDP ratio reached 113 per cent. The Prime Minister insisted that Greece was not about to default. In January 2010, severe irregularities in Greek public accounting were condemned by the European Union. On 12 January 2010, Eurostat, the EU's statistics arm, stated that Greece's budget figures were unreliable and were likely to have been falsified to downplay the gravity of the crisis. The budget deficit was revised upwards from a slightly excessive 3.7 per cent to an alarming 12.7 per cent. The first austerity measures for Greece were announced in February 2009. On 11 February, the EU's injunction calling for more spending cuts sparks riots in the streets of Athens. In March, a €22 billion safety net was agreed upon by the IMF and the Eurozone. One month later, €30 billion of emergency loans were announced by European leaders. A new budget figure was put forward: 13.6 per cent of GDP! On 2 May 2010, a €110 billion bailout package was agreed upon by Eurozone countries and the IMF. In November 2010, an €85 billion bailout package was announced for the Republic of Ireland. In April 2011, a permanent bailout fund called the European Stability Mechanism was set up by Eurozone finance ministers. Portugal was the first country to benefit therefrom in May with the approval of a €78 billion bailout plan. In June, new austerity measures for Greece were advocated by Eurozone ministers. Talks of a Greek default were no longer a rare occurrence in the media. In July, the Greek parliament voted in favour of further austerity measures and more drastic spending cuts. A new bailout by Eurozone leaders was announced, with a comprehensive €109 billion package. In August, European Commission President Jose Manuel Barroso warned that the sovereign debt crisis was spreading beyond the periphery of the Eurozone. On 7 August 2011, the European Central Bank made a groundbreaking announcement, with a plan to buy Italian and Spanish sovereign bonds, in order to bring down the borrowing costs of these countries. In September, the 'golden rule' was added to the Spanish constitution to keep future budget deficits under control. Likewise, Italy passed a €50 billion austerity budget to balance the budget by 2013, thereby sparking fierce public opposition. In its *World Economic Outlook*, the IMF revised growth forecasts downwards, and warned that countries in the Eurozone were entering a 'dangerous new phase', as new data showed that growth in the private sector shrank for the first time in two years. Stock markets started to plummet across European financial markets. A meeting of finance ministers and central bankers in Washington on 24 September 2011 fell short of any concrete proposal. On 28 September, president of the European Commission, European Union's top official Jose Manuel Barroso warned that the EU faced its greatest challenge. UK Foreign Secretary William Hague, who once ran the 'Keep the

Pound' campaign as a Conservative Party leader, said that Europe was now dealing with the fallout from the decision to create the single currency. Hague compared the euro to a burning building with no exits, an expression he had already used in 1998. On 14 October, G20 finance ministers convened in Paris in what resonated as the latest repetition of an endless chain of last-chance summits to solve the European sovereign debt crisis. Aware of the gravity of the situation, on 23 October 2011, IMF head Christine Lagarde urged countries to act now and act together, in order to preserve the sustainability of economic recovery. After marathon talks in Brussels, on 26 October 2011, European leaders reached a three-pronged agreement. Banks holding Greek debt accepted a 50 per cent loss; the Eurozone bailout fund was strengthened, and banks were required to raise more capital, to prevent bankruptcy, because of rising government default risks in the Eurozone. On 9 December 2011, European leaders unveiled a yet unsigned inter-governmental treaty enshrining new budgetary rules to tackle the crisis, the so-called fiscal pact. At this advanced stage, austerity had undoubtedly become the central idea in the unfolding European sovereign debt crisis. The transition to 2012 offered little more hope for optimism. Credit rating agency Standard & Poor's downgraded France on 13 January 2012, along with eight other Eurozone countries. On 16 January 2012, the European Financial Stability Facility itself was downgraded by S&P. The fiscal pact was eventually signed by twenty-five countries at the end of January (although two notable countries, the United Kingdom and the Czech Republic, decided to abstain): these twenty-five countries agreed to keep their GDP-to-deficit ratio below 3 per cent, and debt-to-GDP ratio should not exceed 60 per cent. Countries refusing to sign the fiscal compact would not be eligible for funding from the European Stability Mechanism, the permanent bailout fund replacing the European Financial Stability Facility. It became increasingly apparent that the new governance of the euro area was firmly structured around the so-called Troika composed of the European Commission, the European Central

Table 15.1 Estimated impact of the fiscal measures in Spain on 13 July 2012

	2012	*2013*	*2014*	*Total*
VAT	2.30	10.13	9.67	22.10
Corporate income tax	2.59	2.45	2.45	7.49
Excise duties	−0.06	0.39	0.39	0.73
Personal income tax	0.15	1.93	2.04	4.11
Additional expenditure cuts	1.00	0.00	0.00	1.00
Public services	5.43	1.92	1.87	9.22
Employment	1.90	5.81	6.05	13.76
Social security	0.07	−1.15	−3.89	−4.98
Dependency law	0.16	1.39	1.47	3.02
Total	13.53	22.86	20.05	56.44

Source: Ministry of Economy and Competitiveness in Spain, available at http://cdrtse.meh.es/Site CollectionDocuments/en-gb/Public%20Finances%20and%20Public%20Debt/Public%20Finances/ 120713%20Additional%20Fiscal%20Measures.pdf.

Photograph 15.1 Protests in Greece (source: Angelos Tzortzinis).

Bank and the International Monetary Fund. On 10 February 2012, a drastic austerity bill was passed in the Greek parliament. Furor began to mount in the streets of Athens and beyond. On 9 June 2012, after a reportedly heated two-and-a-half-hour conference call of the seventeen Eurozone finance ministers, the Eurogroup agreed to lend Spain up to €100 billion to shore up its ailing banking system. IMF Managing Director Christine Lagarde immediately called this move a credible backstop. Yet, this new bailout plan was still conditional on the results of an independent audit report expected in mid June. Spain's new austerity plan will claw back €56 billion for the state until 2014, according to figures published on 13 July 2012 by the Spanish ministry of economy and competitiveness.

Five years into the GFC, the overall picture for the European economy is grim. Eurostat's flash estimates reported in February 2013 that the Eurozone recession had deepened. In the fourth quarter of 2012, GDP fell by 0.6 per cent in the Eurozone, and by 0.5 per cent in the European Union. In 2012, GDP fell 0.5 per cent in the Eurozone and declined 0.3 per cent in the EU27. It was the third consecutive quarter of contraction (after a 0.2 per cent decline in GDP in the second quarter and a 0.1 per cent contraction in the third quarter) in the Eurozone. The EU27 narrowly escaped a technical recession thanks to a 0.1 per cent expansion in the third quarter of 2012.[5]

Comment
One of the most striking features of the European debt crisis is the sky-rocketing long-term interest rates of debt-laden and deficit-spending Mediterranean

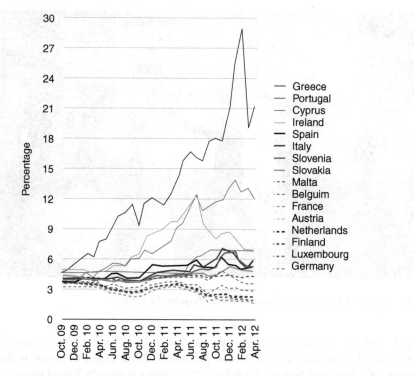

Figure 15.1 Long-term interest rates in the Eurozone, October 2009 to April 2012 (source: ECB).

countries, Greece being the most dramatic example. Contrariwise, the core of countries in Northern Europe (Germany, Luxembourg, Finland, Netherlands and Austria) have kept their borrowing costs at moderate levels, or even reduced them in the case of Germany, thereby exacerbating macroeconomic imbalances within the Eurozone. However, the European Economic Forecast (European Commission, 2013, p. ix) published on 22 February 2013, points to decreasing risk premia for sovereigns in early 2013. At the same time, the report hints at a slow transition towards a period of moderate growth after a difficult economic contraction in 2012, although the labour market and its shrinking employment figures will continue to remain a major source of concern for several more quarters.

The NMC in Europe: a weakened explanatory power after the crisis

Three years before the GFC, Laidler (2004, p. 8) critically assessed the validity of the NMC (that he more or less equated to Woodfordian economics). His comments would later prove visionary:

In short, my verdict on the theory of monetary policy that Woodford has so elegantly and thoroughly elaborated in his *Interest and Prices* is that it is well adapted to teaching us how to sail in already calm monetary conditions, in fair fiscal weather and in the confined waters of a closed economy. It teaches us how to stay on a course defined by low and stable inflation in such an environment, and therefore is going to be of great value to the practitioners of monetary policy in a few select economies where inflation is already behaving itself and monetary stability is not threatened by fiscal policy or foreign disturbances.

Pre-crisis conditions in the Eurozone were indeed akin to the fair fiscal weather conditions described by Laidler. Taking the argument further, it is possible to state that the NMC has currently nothing to say about the Euro sovereign debt crisis. This stems from the very narrow conception of monetary policy put forward by proponents of the NMC. The monetary policy framework developed by Woodford has codified the set of models that central banks rely upon in many advanced economies. It is a key theory in explaining how to keep inflation under control; it is therefore very valuable as long as it performs this function. There are yet pitfalls that threaten to distract the attention of economists. The elegance and the mathematical rigour displayed by Woodford can lead us to forget how narrow the scope of his theory really is. There are also broader issues that monetary policy must sometimes deal with, but for which Woodfordian economics is ill-suited (ibid., pp. 8–9). Walsh (2005) criticizes Woodford for relying on a method that is only applicable to a central bank already enjoying high credibility in a low inflation environment. Woodfordian economics is valid in times of macroeconomic stability when the amplitude of exogenous shocks is weak or moderate. Yet, uncertainty cannot be equated to the possibility of exogenous shocks assessed in probabilistic terms. This echoes the long-standing critique of ergodicity in mainstream economics by post-Keynesian economists, such as Davidson (1986, 1992). Woodfordian economics and, by extension, the NMC are ill-suited in situations of radical (non probabilistic) uncertainty that have the potential to undermine the foundations of the models relied upon, when intended to inform policy decisions.

The Euro sovereign debt crisis: a tentative diagnosis

A flawed institutional setting?

Why did the Euro sovereign debt crisis occur in spite of the complex design and architecture of European institutions, which had seemed to function rather well since the inception of the EMU? First, concerns over macroeconomic imbalance across the Eurozone were never seriously addressed by EU leaders. Except for inflation, the Eurozone was never set up with strict surveillance prerogatives over macroeconomic magnitudes. Pragmatic crisis management strategy was integrated rather abruptly into the institutional apparatus, in a global context of emergency that had not been anticipated by the founding European treaties. Prior to the GFC, there was no institutional framework prepared to deal with insolvent countries. Neither was the prospect of a massive liquidity crisis seriously dealt with. The consequence of a monetary union is to delegate monetary sovereignty to a supranational authority, which means that individual countries can no longer issue debt in their own currency. Individual countries lose a share of sovereignty, and thus become subordinated to market forces that can potentially force default on them.

Another hurdle is the lack of a proper banking union with adequate supervisory powers. Against the odds, more than three-and-a-half years after the demise of Lehman Brothers, the European Commission called for the first time on 30 May 2012 for a supranational banking union with the power to oversee and bail out banks, thereby breaking away with the domestic scale of European banking regulation[4] (Pilkington, 2009). The current architecture of the European banking system is still centred on national supervision that omits to take into account the impact of the fragility of other European countries (e.g. Greece, Spain, Italy). In times when bank balance sheets are crippled with increasingly risky government bonds issued by other euro area countries, this regulatory feature is most problematic. It would also be part of the transparency agenda of central banks (in the case at hand of the European System of Central Banks) to provide updated cross-country analysis of the structure of bank balance sheets across the euro area, along with new tools to assess contagion risks. Of course, a lot of the abovementioned shortcomings come down to the absence of a proper European fiscal union and the sub-optimal nature of the euro area (Chapter 14). Moreover, concerns over labour and product market institutions should be addressed by the European Union insofar as their implications on the functioning of a monetary union can be tremendous. On 25 April 2012, the President of the ECB Mario Draghi (2012b) gave a speech at the Committee on Economic and Monetary Affairs of the European Parliament. Draghi stressed the large imbalances that accumulated in Europe over the last few years. He blamed these imbalances on a number of factors, such as fiscal profligacy, the lack of implementation of structural reforms, most notably in labour and product markets and, more generally speaking, faltering competitiveness across the Eurozone. Draghi admits that these imbalances lie beyond the mandate of the ECB, which cannot address these macroeconomic ills. He therefore calls for enhanced governmental responsibility 'to address major weaknesses in the fiscal, financial and structural domains' (ibid.). In a rather ambiguous statement, Draghi also made a plea for 'growth-enhancing structural reforms to facilitate entrepreneurial activities, the start-up of new firms and job creation' (ibid.). Yet, this is reminiscent of the rhetoric of the new economy that was the landmark of the US economy in the 1990s.[6] Hence, the Information Technology and Innovation Foundation and the Kauffman Foundation states that: 'The New Economy is a global, entrepreneurial, and knowledge-based economy in which the keys to success lie in the extent to which knowledge, technology, and innovation are embedded in products and services.'[7]

On 31 May 2012, Mario Draghi (2012a) went further, and admitted that the ECB could not fill the vacuum left by member states' lack of action as it was claimed the zone is on the point of disintegration. The president of the ECB seemed to concede defeat, and rejected responsibility on national governments: 'It's not our duty, it's not in our mandate to fill the vacuum left by the lack of action by national governments on the fiscal front.' Draghi hammered this point home, and warned that the euro 'is being shown now to be unsustainable unless further steps are being undertaken' (ibid.).

Competence, mindset and leadership

Without understating the gravity of the problems of specific Mediterranean countries, Veron (2011) argues that the central problem at the heart of the Euro sovereign debt crisis is that of decision making at the European level. Since early 2010, Europe's leaders have been powerless to contain contagion from the periphery to the core of the euro area. In other words, the roots of the problem are largely institutional. Therefore, it would be unfair to blame the situation on individuals or on the incompetence of Europe's leaders (ibid.). Veron (ibid.) thinks that 'from a historic or international perspective, most are reasonably competent, dedicated and honest'. Yet, this opinion is not shared by Marc Weisbrot (2012, emphasis added), who blames the European crisis on some 'some combination of ideology, politics, *incompetence*, and of course powerful interests who want certain things'. Veron (2011) argues that European leaders must take drastic steps, with some actions requiring a Treaty change, while others only a new mindset. National deposit insurance schemes must be guaranteed at the supranational level, in order to mitigate the systematic risk of sudden and massive retail bank runs. This progressive acceptance of the legitimacy of a supranational regulatory level calls for a new European mindset. In this respect, the call by Jose Manuel Barroso in the *Financial Times* on 12 June 2012 for a single cross-border banking supervisor to regulate banks from all twenty-seven European Union states is illustrative of this long-awaited evolution (Spiegel, 2012). On 8 June 2012, President Obama speaking at a news conference said that strong European leadership would be key to resolving the European debt crisis, and avoiding a new recession: '[t]hese decisions are fundamentally in the hands of Europe's leaders, and, fortunately, they understand the seriousness of the situation and the urgent need to act'.

Can the Euro be saved?

The Long-Term Refinancing Operations (LTRO)

Mark Weisbrot (2012) explains how, in spite of the highly criticized governance of the Eurozone throughout the Euro sovereign debt crisis, European and political leaders had indeed put together an action plan, in order to avoid a repeat of a

Photograph 15.2 A rioter against austerity in Europe (source: Angelos Tzortzinis).

Lehman Brothers type of crisis. In this regard, it would useful to assess the ECB's decision to loan $638 billion to European banks in December 2011, thereby easing a liquidity crisis, which was threatening the banking system. The success (or the failure) of the operation may be measured against the immediate avoidance of a systemic crisis, or the reduction in sovereign debt yields enabled by the reinvestment of the proceeds of these loans in further purchases of government bonds. In a report entitled 'Non-Standard Policy Measures: A First Assessment', the Policy Department (Economic and Scientific Policy) of the European Parliament (2012) provided a preliminary assessment of LTRO. The executive summary (ibid., p. 6) contains the following words: 'the overall assessment of the LTRO is therefore a mixed one. It has stabilized financial conditions and the interbank market. At the same time, it has not fundamentally altered credit conditions in Southern Europe.'

All in all, at the time of writing, we do not know whether LTRO have actually benefited the European economy at all. This lack of diagnosis is attributable to an incomplete methodological approach, as we shall argue. Yet, in 2012, there were still a handful of reputable experts who expressed doubt about the very survival of the euro. In this respect, George Soros's views are briefly described below.

George Soros's predicament on 2 June 2012: an early assessment

At a conference in Trento, Italy, George Soros declared on 2 June 2012 that Germany and its central bank were unlikely to provide the momentum in order to find a solution to the Euro sovereign debt crisis. After a period of three months, Soros said it would be too late to save the euro. The Eurozone countries would then be threatened by a lost decade reminiscent of Latin America in the 1980s or Japan in the 1990s. Soros also described the unfolding crisis as an interlinked sovereign debt crisis (Greece being the emblematic symbol thereof) and a banking crisis (Spain being the perfect illustration). Soros believed that the Greek crisis would reach its climax before the end of 2012. With worrying signs of fragility in Germany, the strongest European economy so far, the political equation would become insoluble. Soros (ibid.) thought that without the quick implementation of a European deposit scheme to stem the capital flight, the crisis would threaten to destroy the European Union.

Was Soros's pessimism founded? The answer is most certainly negative in the short run. As the European Commission (2013, p. 1) points out, 'since the summer of 2012, financial market conditions in the EU have improved substantially as perceived tail risks of EMU break-up receded'. The quality of the economic recovery in the EU was believed to depend mostly on external demand in 2013 while 'by 2014 domestic demand is expected to take over as the main driver of further strengthening GDP growth' (ibid.). Yet the European Commission (ibid., p. 27) is fully aware of persisting risks that reflect the potential damage caused by a re-escalation of the Euro sovereign debt crisis. In what could be interpreted as a pro-austerity bias (see Chapter 12), the European Commission (ibid.) then warns against policy uncertainty, which could result from 'waning support for necessary fiscal consolidation and structural reforms'.

The European sovereign debt crisis: what methodological framework?

In the history of capitalism, sovereign debt crises are a rather ancient phenomenon. Yet, it is unclear how particular responses have been conducive to an accepted doctrine that would provide guidelines to help solve the current one. For Dickerson (2004, p. 997), 'The failure to enact a statutory system to restructure sovereign debt suggests that the international community is still unwilling to adopt a unified global response to insolvency issues.' As Krueger (2002) stated, 'the objective of an SDRM[7] is to facilitate the orderly, predictable, and rapid restructuring of unsustainable sovereign debt, while protecting asset values and creditor's rights'.[8] Such an SDRM would provide a framework for resolving sovereign debt crises. We propose hereafter another type of framework for dealing with this burning issue in Europe, by drawing on the productive thinking model (also know as Thinkx) developed by Tim Hurson, a Canadian creativity theorist. Hurson, the founding partner of Thinkx intellectual capital, an adviser to some of the biggest corporations in the world and the author of the 2008 best-seller *Think Better: An Innovator's Guide to Productive Thinking*, is a faculty member of the Creative Education Foundation (US) and a member of several international creativity associations. This iconoclastic figure in the business world is well known for his extraordinary problem-solving abilities, notably by relying upon the famous piece of advice attributed to Albert Einstein: 'The significant problems we face today cannot be solved at the same level of thinking we were at when we created them.' The importance of creativity[9] in designing an effective solution to the crisis should not be understated. We thus venture into an unprecedented methodological 'out of the box' thought experiment by trying to address the ongoing Euro sovereign debt crisis with the help of Hurson's innovative approach.

First step: understanding what is going on
This is the first question that needs to be formulated, in order to contextualize the problem. Can the latter be stated in several distinct ways? Are there any opportunities arising out of the Euro sovereign debt crisis? What are the specific factors (e.g. the banking system, the international financial architecture), the global circumstances (e.g. the GFC, the Great Recession) and the entities (e.g. banks, states, the European Union, the IMF) involved? Sketching out the skeleton of what a solution might look like is *not* a premature initiative at this stage. Further, in the Thinkx methodology, there are five sub-steps within this first phase.

- *'What is the Itch?'*
  A number of entangled and interrelated problems are symptomatic of the Euro sovereign debt crisis. It might be useful to try and generate a detailed list thereof, with the corresponding opportunities, in order to single out novel patterns and clusters of ideas. The ensuing selection of the key problem will be greatly facilitated.
- *'What is the Impact?'*
  How does the aforementioned key problem currently affect the world economy?
- *'What is the Information?'*
  How well can we describe the various aspects of the problem in detail, notably with the mass of economic and financial information and all the databases available?
- *'Who is Involved?'*
  Who are the other stakeholders in this crisis? Identifying them is of paramount importance. Given the interconnectedness of the global economy, one might suspect that the list is rather long. This idea was confirmed by the European Commission (2013, p. 28) that pointed to significant downside risks resulting from the external environment whether it be the political deadlock in the United States (where a fiscal crisis of huge proportions is also raging) or the sheer interconnectedness between Eurozone countries and emergent economies through the well-known trade channel (ibid.). In this respect, the ongoing debate on the appreciation of the euro (and whether the ECB should pursue a more explicit and easy-to-track foreign exchange policy) is not circumscribed to member states. This burning international macroeconomic issue, which affects the competitiveness of euro-area exports (thus the health of the European economy), is one that involves the major stakeholders of the world monetary system (see Chapter 10).

- '*What is the Vision?*'
  This is an important sub-step in the creative process of enquiry. One must identify what would be different if the euro debt crisis was resolved (i.e. debt levels moving back to their pre-crisis levels or credible growth prospects ensuring rapid and sustainable public debt reduction). One might resort to 'wish' statements here (e.g. 'if only Germany could break away with monetary orthodoxy or the IMF with austerity measures').

Second step: defining success

This second step requires *a vision* for the future in a hypothetical scenario wherein the Euro sovereign debt crisis has been solved or the corresponding opportunities exploited (e.g. the emergence of new modes of global governance). How would the world look without a Euro sovereign debt crisis? Active imagination is of paramount importance here. We seek to explore and describe new paths that would emerge in the absence of the problem under scrutiny. For instance, without a Euro sovereign debt crisis, peoples of Europe would feel less inclined towards populist and nationalistic ideas that best prosper in times of economic distress. An insightful way to define success here is to posit that if member states were given the chance to reconsider their decision to join this unprecedented political and economic project, they would not turn away from the euro. Yet, in his 19 February 2013 *Financial Times* column, Martin Wolf draws on the following metaphor: '[a] good marriage is one spouses would re-enter even if they had the choice to start all over again'. Against this backdrop, Wolf (2013) admits that we are currently light years away from this ideal configuration: '[i]f all members of the Eurozone would rejoin happily today, they would be extreme masochists'. Wolf further argues that the likely refusal to join the euro, were this fundamental decision to be made today, would be justified, because many countries of the Eurozone currently 'find themselves inside a nightmare of misery and ill will'. Another reason is the comparison between current and pre-crisis GDP levels for the Eurozone and the United States: 'In the fourth quarter of [2012], Eurozone aggregate gross domestic product was still 3 per cent below its pre-crisis peak, while US GDP was 2.4 per cent above it.'

So, it is well understood that a definition of success is absolutely essential, if we want to overcome the enormous problems caused by the euro crisis. Once this vision has been established, a heuristic tool designed by Hurson called DRIVE may be implemented.

Drive is short for:

- **D**o: what should the solution do?
- **R**estrictions: what should the solution *not* do?
- **I**nvestment: what resources can be invested for the future?
- **V**alues: what are the values that this crisis has strengthened?
- **E**ssential outcomes: in a nutshell, what are the essential outcomes?

Third step: phrasing a question

The third step is about turning the Euro sovereign debt crisis into a single question. From a methodological point of view, brainstorming sessions can be a fruitful activity. If several quality questions are competing with one another, clusters and original combinations thereof might help single out the most stimulating one.

Fourth Step: generating answers

The fourth step is about using idea-generating techniques, so as to generate a long list of possible solutions to the problem, which has previously been identified. One must select one or several (combined) solutions for further consideration. The abundant literature devoted to the European sovereign debt crisis shall help us select a meaningful set of possible solutions at this stage.

Somehow, this enlightened selection process is tantamount to shortlisting the best candidates for a specific position, before the final round of job interviews takes place.

Fifth Step: forging the solution

The fifth step is about the development and the consolidation of the selected solution(s) thanks to another heuristic tool called POWER, which is short for:

- **P**ositives: what is positive about the selected solution(s)?
- **O**bjections: what is not desirable about the selected solution(s)?
- **W**hat else? What does the solution remind us of?
- **E**nhancements: how can the positive aspects of the solution be improved?
- **R**emedies: how can the negative aspects be corrected?

A good example of solution to the euro crisis using the problem-solving approach emphasized here was sketched out by Marcus Miller and Robert Skidelsky (2012) in an article entitled 'How Keynes would Solve the Eurozone Crisis', in the *Financial Times*. Drawing on insightful elements borrowed from economic history, and a rather unknown period of Keynes's career when he was employed as a young official in the UK Treasury as well as an adviser on external debt matters to European policy makers, the authors methodically address the current crisis plaguing the Eurozone. The argumentation unveiled by Miller and Skidelsky is of particular interest, as it astutely bridges the gaps between several fundamental issues discussed in the present book. For instance, Keynes's solution to the Eurozone crisis (or what it would have been using his chosen methodological approach) is contrasted with the economics austerity that is equated to the German counsel (ibid.) and summarized by Angela Merkel's words: 'in the long run you can't live beyond your means'. Yet this issue must be put back in the broader context of the functioning of the international payments system. In the Merkel view (which is a modern incarnation of the White view at the end of the Second World War that eventually helped shape the postwar world monetary system), the economics of austerity is justified, because the burden of adjustment always lies on debtor countries. However, as Pilkington (2010, p. 249) argues: 'Keynes had a very different understanding of the nexus of debtor/creditor relations between countries in the international political economy.' Likewise, Miller and Skidelsky (2013) state: 'Keynes, by contrast, held that both creditors and debtors should share the task of getting economies out of holes they had jointly dug.'

Hence, using the abovementioned POWER heuristic tool, it is possible to shed light on these oft-overlooked Keynesian views on international payments, in order to work towards an acceptable solution for all the stakeholders of the euro crisis.

Sixth Step: putting together an action plan
The sixth and final step consists of an action plan that results from the previously selected solution. This action plan will include timelines and milestones, a list of political, business and economic leaders who will be involved in the process, and finally a list of issues that will have to be further dealt with.

We argue here that such an action plan is what is presently needed for the Eurozone. Yet, from a methodological viewpoint, skipping some or all of the five previously described steps would not only lead to sub-optimal macro-economic outcomes, from a historical standpoint, it would potentially have some destructive consequences for the European project as a whole too. As American historian Samuel Eliot Morison once put it, historical methodology is a product of common sense applied to circumstances.

Conclusion

In spite of a burgeoning post-crisis reflection, the communication of the ECB has not been supplemented by a reliable meta-methodological framework, transcending the compliance of policy actions with the institutional mandate of the ECB. Interestingly enough, in 'Non-Standard Policy Measures: A First Assessment' (European Parliament, 2012), the authors write:

> [m]onetary policy cannot solve the underlying structural problems in the banking system, the structural reform needs as well as the shortcomings of the euro area governance set-up. *Monetary policy is made difficult and less effective by the existing economic and institutional heterogeneity.*
>
> (emphasis added)

The latter sentence, coupled with our reflection on the impact of cultural heterogeneity on currency area optimality (Chapter 14), shall give us a clear idea on how to best redefine the academic debate on the future of the euro. In the context of our critical reflection on the NMC in a post-crisis era, this is indeed a most pressing task.

16 Post-crisis methodological considerations in central banking theory

Introduction

In this final chapter, we critically address the NMC from a methodological standpoint. Although the mantras of the consensus are hardly questionable in their own right, we argue that the methodological underpinnings of the NMC account for its paradigmatic failure both to predict the GFC, and to be a reliable source of inspiration for post-crisis policies. We particularly insist on the problematic pre-crisis DSGE models, and we sketch out new methodological directions for the future. Finally, we conclude.

Macro-financial interaction and issues with DSGE modelling

As argued by Smith (2009, p. 2), standard DSGE models do not account for interactions between macroeconomic and financial variables, which were often overlooked in NMC models. In a post-crisis scenario, there is a fundamental need to re-examine our understanding of macro-financial interactions, in the light of the widely discussed DSGE models.

The need for a renewed macro-financial understanding

The GFC has shown that macro-financial interactions ought to be the object of further research in macroeconomics, as our pre-crisis frameworks have proved to be largely inadequate. What Scott Rogers (2010) calls the workhouse macroeconomic models for policy analysis and forecasting (namely the New Keynesian DSGE models) lacked a sound representation of the financial sector. Asset prices were often left aside, although progress has been made in the recent period, with DSGE models incorporating an active banking sector (Gerali *et al.*, 2008; DeWalque *et al.*, 2010; Dib, 2009). Rogers (2010) also criticizes our poor pre-crisis understanding of macro-financial interaction between the financial sector, households and firms. Jeanne (2011) argues in favour of the theoretical recognition of the financial sector as an economic force in its own right, characterized by powerful vested interests, in order to apprehend the macro-interactions with the rest of the economic system (deposit-taking institutions, firms, households). In this regard, it might be useful to incorporate the financial sector in a stock-flow consistent framework (Pilkington, 2009). The need for better macro-financial understanding has been endorsed with the Bank for International Settlements, and is exemplified by Andrew Crockett (2002), who explains that inflation-targeting central banks are ill-prepared to deal with the build-up of financial imbalances at the heart of contemporary financial instability. In these monetary regimes, central banks are generally not inclined to tighten monetary policy by making pre-emptive moves in order to lean against credit bubbles and erratic asset price movements. A number of writers have argued for an activist response to asset price booms. *Inter alia*, let us mention Claudio Borio and Philip Lowe (2002), Stephen Cecchetti, Hans Genberg and Sushil Wadhwani (2002) and Michael Bordo and Olivier Jeanne (2002). Wadhwani (2008) discards the idea that assets prices should be directly targeted by monetary policy, whether it be through the objective function of the central bank, or through their inclusion in an extended inflation measure by the monetary authorities. Rather, Cecchetti *et al.* (2002) believe that macroeconomic outcomes can be enhanced by responding to asset price misalignments in a systematic fashion, over and above what inflation forecasts and output gaps would lead them to react. For Bernanke (2011b), one of the most important legacies of the GFC is that price stability should be on par with the financial stability objective. Asset price bubbles are now at the heart of central banks' concerns, with new regulations being seriously considered, in order to fight unjustified increases. Wadhwani (2008, p. 5) hammers this point home, when he states that central banks willing to tame the business cycle can improve macroeconomic outcomes by keeping an eye on misalignments in asset prices, in order to mitigate potential distortions in investment and consumption that could amplify the business cycles and generate inflationary pressures at unwarranted levels. This is so because during an emerging financial bubble, there is an increase in the price of collateral against which investors can borrow. Increased investment will therefore stimulate aggregate demand and output in the short run, which might result in overcapacity that may accelerate the occurrence of a downturn (ibid., p. 6). All in all, it appears that macroeconomic stability can be enhanced by pre-emptively lowering interest rates, to offset the impact of asset movements on output and inflation volatility. Yet, alternative views against LATW policies abound in the literature. For instance, Bernanke and Gertler (1999, p. 74) oppose the idea that inflation-targeting central banks should respond to asset price movements unless the latter signal changes in expected inflation. Bernanke and Gertler (2001) also warn against a sharp increase in short-term rates that are certain to slow down the economy, but are unlikely to kill the bubble in the making. The authors use the example of the late 1990s Internet bubble that was not a phenomenon that could have ever been prevented through mere monetary tightening. Bernanke and Gertler (ibid.) offer a rather fatalistic view of asset bubbles that policy makers should only be concerned with, once the bubble has gone bust, in order to mitigate the fallout.[1] This has certainly been a recurrent view in the literature before the GFC amongst proponents of the NMC. For instance, Bernanke (2002b) was adamant that leaning against bubbles would be counter-productive, because monetary policy is an ill-conceived tool for fighting off asset price bubbles. However, Bernanke (ibid.) is not short of solutions to improve financial stability, such as

> supervisory action to ensure capital adequacy in the banking system, stress-testing of portfolios, increased transparency in accounting and disclosure practices, improved financial literacy, greater care in the process of financial liberalization, and a willingness to play the role of lender of last resort when needed.

Another question is whether inflation-targeting regimes will outlive the GFC. Bernanke's answer is affirmative: 'the current framework for monetary policy – with innovations, no doubt, to further improve the ability of central banks to communicate with the public – will remain the standard approach, as its benefits in terms of macroeconomic stabilization have been demonstrated' (Bernanke, 2011b, p. 5). Although the world witnessed an extraordinary period of macro-economic stability prior to the GFC, namely the Great Moderation, the flexible inflation targeting framework was not sufficient to ensure financial stability. Yet, Bernanke (ibid.) still questions the likelihood of a revolution in the field of central banking in the aftermath of the GFC.

The standard macroeconomic tools and the DSGE financial accelerator model

As Cagliarini *et al.* (2010, p. 26, nbp) argue, standard macroeconomic analysis operates within a Phillips curve/IS-LM setting. Yet, these well-known tools offer very little explanatory power as far as the financial sector is concerned. Cagliarini *et al.* refute the idea that finance is a passive component of the economic system that merely accommodates the needs of the real economy (the so-called needs of trade). Rather, macroeconomic shocks often originate from the financial sector itself, as with the recent crisis propelled by the subprime meltdown in the United States. The other key dimension, which is utterly neglected by standard macro-economic tools, is the impact of small variations in the level of the short-term nominal rate on the risk-taking behaviour of financial actors (ibid.). As argued by Cagliarini *et al.*, 'the financial sector's propensity to be a source of shocks is a function of, among other things, the setting of monetary policy'.

The failure of the DSGE models to explain the GFC

Background

DSGE (Dynamic Stochastic General Equilibrium) modelling is a branch of applied general equilibrium theory, which has been extremely influential in shaping the macro-policies of the NMC. DSGE models aim to explain aggregate business cycles and macroeconomic magnitudes, such as GDP, consumption, investment, prices, wages and employment. DSGE models can help assess monetary and fiscal policies. DSGE has thus become the emblematic acronym in modern macroeconomics. 'Dynamic' refers to the forward-looking behaviour of economic agents. 'Stochastic' refers to exogenous shocks *à la* Real Business Cycle theory. 'General' refers to the standpoint of the whole economy. Finally, 'equilibrium' refers to explicit constraints and objectives, expressed in mathematical terms, for households and firms. DSGE models are micro-founded, which is one of their fundamental theoretical features, in direct lineage with New Classical Macroeconomics. It is worthwhile stressing the legacy of Real Business Cycle (hereafter RBC) theory that may be traced back to Kydland and Prescott's seminal article in 1982. RBC theory thrived in the 1980s with the design of fully articulated artificial economies (Lucas, 1980), inspired by advances in neoclassical growth models. In his entry on Real Business Cycles in the *International Encyclopedia of the Social Sciences*, Neville (2008, p. 407) explains that

> Kydland and Prescott convincingly[2] argued that a DGSE model driven by technology shocks can mimic the main statistical features of the US macro time series when calibrated using means and variances of macro data using reasonable[3] parameter values to fit the real world.

Yet, RBC theory only constitutes a starting point of the DSGE methodology. Today, the mainstream economists, who have most deliberately placed DSGE models at the heart of their research programme, are the New Keynesians. While RBC theory was rooted in neoclassical microeconomic theory (Plosser, 1989, p. 53), which assumed instantaneous market-clearing mechanisms, prices in the New Keynesian models are set by monopolistically competitive firms, and feature real frictions (e.g. habit formation in consumption and adjustment costs in investment). Markets no longer clear automatically in the New Keynesian DGSE models featuring nominal price and wage stickiness, in order to account for stylized facts.

Theoretical principles

The DSGE approach bears a connection to empirical macroeconomic research, with its objectives to identify key parameters underlying the structural apparatus of the economy, and test substantive hypotheses by using modern statistical techniques (Summers, 1991, p. 129). One reason why DSGE models became the dominant methodology in modern macroeconomics is their robustness to the Lucas critique formulated in 1976. Lucas argued that individual economic agents were bound to modify their optimal decision rules in the face of a policy change; thus, econometric models could not be assumed to be constant over shifting policy and historical configurations. Parameters that are not policy invariant are therefore misleading in macroeconomic modelling. The Lucas critique subsequently called for a dual disciplinary evolution of the discipline, one that emphasized the micro-foundations of macroeconomics, with the search for the deep structural (i.e. policy invariant) parameters of the economy describing household preferences and technological or institutional constraints, and one that focused on the long-term economic fundamentals, whose changes could affect the time path of the economy. In New Keynesian models, realized future inflation rates are often used as a proxy, and utility-maximizing economic agents are endowed with rational expectations; DSGE modellers resort to advanced econometric techniques, such as the Generalized Method of Moments, to determine the most appropriate functional forms of their models.

Kocherlakota (2010), President of the Federal Reserve Bank of Minneapolis, draws a list of five ingredients characterizing the DSGE approach. First, all economic agents in the model must be resource and budget-constrained. Firms use costly inputs to increase production, while all economic agents must satisfy a budget condition, which means they cannot increase their spending without an equivalent increase in revenue. Second, in order to avoid the Lucas critique, preferences and objectives must be described in the most accurate fashion (at the individual and firm levels). Third, macroeconomic outcomes are dependent on expectations, whose formation must be explained by the model. Economic agents are said to be forward-looking; positive macroeconomic outlooks shape households' decisions to consume, work and borrow more; the same can be said of firms' decisions to hire workers and invest, and banks' decisions to increase lending. Fourth, all economic agents are assumed to be rational. The market behaviour of utility-maximizing households and profit-maximizing firms can only be understood though the lenses of rationality, although elements of bounded rationality have long been introduced in the literature in the tradition of Herbert Simon. Notorious examples thereof are the rational inattention framework of Christopher Sims (2006) and the robustness ideas of Thomas Sargent (Hansen and Sargent, 2008). Sims and Sargent have provided constructive attempts to improve the realism of the rational expectations hypothesis; the latter merely assumes that all economic agents are omniscient and endowed with supernatural computational abilities, allowing them to continuously optimize their satisfaction in response to all relevant information that might affect their utility functions. Of course, Sims and Sargent understood that this pure *homo oeconomicus* fiction contrasts with empirical evidence.

Fifth, all DSGE models are mathematical formalizations.[4]

Core assumptions in New Keynesian DSGE models

We list hereafter four core assumptions of DSGE models (Chatelain and Ralf, 2012):

- First, in DSGE models, credit rationing is assumed, and depends on a collateral constraint. The collateral is owned by borrowers, and its value is given by its expected price in the next period and by a cyclical maximal loan-to-value ratio. All in all, in the bulk of the DSGE literature, the valuation of the collateral is made at its long-term fundamental value, which requires that the efficient-market hypothesis be valid.[5]

- Second, the interest rate on credit includes a default premium. This premium mirrors the Loss Given Default (or LGD),[6] which is a common parameter in risk models used under the Basel II framework.
- Third, a flow of fund accounting identity is required, as it determines a dynamic relation for the asset-liability financial structure of the economy. Indeed, a consistent set of economic accounts is a prerequisite for any DSGE modelling endeavour.
- Fourth, there exists an arbitrage condition between lending and stock buyback opportunities, implying steady state price dynamics for the lender's assets. Again, the steady path can only be followed by economic agents, in spite of multiple equilibria for financial asset prices and unstable (and potentially explosive) paths, if the efficient market hypothesis is valid.

Review of literature

The RBC approach usually begins with the seminal article by Kydland and Prescott (1982). An overview of this theoretical approach to macroeconomic phenomena is provided by Pilkington (2011a), through the lenses of economic dictionaries and encyclopedias. On the Neo-Keynesian side, Rotenberg and Woodford (1997) and Galí and Gertler (1999) have initiated this new research framework under the name of the New Keynesian Phillips Curve (NKPC) approach, by focusing on the optimal price setting behaviour of firms, notably with a reflection on marginal costs borne by firms. The financial accelerator mechanism is put forward by Bernanke *et al.* (1999). Christiano *et al.* (2001) presented a model featuring frictions reflecting the empirical persistence of sticky prices and wages in the euro area. Other landmark papers include Bernanke and Gertler (1999, 2001), Smets and Wouters (2003) and Iacoviello (2005). DSGE models have continued to abound in the economics literature well after the beginning of the GFC, as shown by the success of www.dsge. net, which claims to be an 'international research network for DSGE modeling, monetary and fiscal policy'. The website (ibid.) states that 'in recent years, development of dynamic stochastic general equilibrium modeling made it an important tool for analysis of economic policy'. It must be noted that DSGE models have been at the heart of central banks' policy analysis since the late 1990s. For instance, in its presentation of the 2003 Smets–Wouters[7] model, the ECB is full of praise for these micro-founded models deemed more suitable for policy analysis than previous central bank models, because the utility of agents are equated to the measure of their welfare. The 2007 Smets and Wouters model, endorsed by the ECB for purposes of policy analysis, is considered as a state-of-the-art New Keynesian model, and arguably captures some of the key features of the NMC presented in this book.

Representative agents models

This is a long-standing controversy, which has been widely debated to date in the economics literature. Representative agent models appeared for the first time with Lucas and Rapping (1969). There has always been immense and unquestionable evidence that the real word is populated by heterogeneous agents. In this respect, the use of representative agents in economic models represents at best a fallacy, and, at worst, an absurd methodology. In a paper entitled 'Representative Agents and the Micro-Foundations of Macroeconomics', Grabner (2002) convincingly shows that representative agent models are not robust to the Lucas critique, in the sense that their claimed deep structural and policy-invariant parameters are determined on flawed analytical grounds wherein the use of the term 'deep' amounts to a mere rhetorical device (Pilkington, 2011b, 2012b). The criticism of representative agent models is not new in the economics literature. At the time of the emergence of the NMC, one may mention the significant contributions of Kirman (1992) and Hartley (1997). Kirman (1992) points to the well-known fallacy of composition in macroeconomic theory. Kirman even provides an example wherein the representative agent can possibly disagree with every single individual economic agent, which raises huge problems of democratic accountability and political legitimacy.[8] Therefore, the reduction of a group of heterogeneous agents to a representative agent is 'both unjustified and leads to conclusions which are usually misleading and often wrong' (ibid.). Kirman (ibid.) launches a fierce attack against the representative agent, who 'deserves a decent burial, as an approach to economic analysis that is not only primitive, but fundamentally erroneous'. Likewise, Chang *et al.* (2011) develop a controversial DSGE model with uninsured labour income risk. The estimated representative-agent DSGE model, on the basis of the aggregate data implied by the authors' heterogeneous-agent economy, gives literally inconsistent results for the estimated coefficients, when compared to the true parameters of the heterogeneous economy. They argue that '[s]ince it is not always feasible to account for heterogeneity explicitly, it is important to recognize the possibility that the parameters of a highly-aggregated model may not be invariant with respect to policy changes'. In another scathing attack launched against representative agent models, Hartley (1997, p. 199) very ironically argues that 'perhaps, someday, we will find a planet populated by clones where these models will be useful, but until then to be of much use in studying economies about which we know'.

Other criticisms of DGSE models

In a *Financial Times* column, Wilhem Buiter (2009) of the London School of Economics lamented over the so-called advances in macroeconomics since the 1970s, which he considers useless. Buiter blames this situation on the self-referential and inward-looking nature of most macroeconomic models that amount to mere distractions. Buiter's critique is quite similar to what Krugman (2009) wrote in his notorious *New York Times* editorial. The obsession with self-generated mathematical puzzles and the inner logic of intellectual games arguably prevented economists from addressing real-world concerns. Of course, DSGE models naturally fall into the type of models severely criticized by Buiter, who wholeheartedly agrees with Charles Goodhart, who once said of DGSE models that they excluded everything he was interested in,[9] such as money, financial intermediation and stability. More surprisingly, Mankiw (2006), one of the founders of New Keynesian DSGE modelling, argued before the crisis in an article entitled 'The Macroeconomist as Scientist and Engineer' published by the *Journal of Economic Perspectives* that both New Classical and new Keynesian economists had failed to make any significant impact on practical policy. In contradistinction with Keynes's (1931) oft-quoted aspiration to see the field of economics evolve one day towards a humble and competent professional practice, such as dentistry, Mankiw (ibid.) describes the evolution of modern macroeconomic research as 'an unfortunate wrong turn' from the point of view of macroeconomic engineering. And, then, why did the majority of economists utterly fail to foresee the GFC? The US Congress should be given credit for taking the initiative to host a series of hearings on macroeconomic modelling methods on 20 July 2010. On this occasion, Robert Solow, Nobel Prize recipient in 1987 'for his contributions to the theory of economic growth', literally thrashed DSGE models accused of failing 'to pass the smell test'. Solow criticized the implicit view in all DSGE models that there exists a rationally designed, long-term trajectory for the economy, devised by an omniscient planner endowed with supernatural Walrasian abilities. Although this dream-like economic construct can be occasionally perturbed by exogenous shocks, the latter events do not cause the economy to deviate from its long-term deterministic trend. All in all, the phantasmagoric claims of DSGE models are justified on the basis of the alleged micro-foundations of macroeconomic analysis (ibid.). It seems that DSGE models convey the message that, first and foremost, macroeconomists must know the micro-foundations of macroeconomics. Micro-foundations quickly gained prominence in mainstream and, more surprisingly, in post-Keynesian economics (King, 2008) from the 1970s onwards. Few mainstream dissenters (Laidler, 1982) and post-Keynesian (Chick, 2002) economists refused to turn the quest for micro-foundations into a sine qua non for good macroeconomic theory; this dissenting choice was made either in the name of 'technical details, which can safely be left for later' (Bryant, 1985, pp. 122–123, reviewing Laidler, 1982), or because 'impeccably logical micro-foundations' are necessarily made at the expense of the 'logic of the whole' (Chick, 2002, p. 55). Yet, this frequent focus on micro-foundations is somewhat surprising, as it never really occurred to DSGE modellers that macroeconomic variables themselves (along with the so-called 'deep' structural parameters of the economy) could also be capable of shaping microeconomic behavior (see King, 2008). This is precisely the view endorsed by Colander (1996, p. 61, emphasis in original): 'before there is any hope in undertaking meaningful micro analysis, *one must first determine the macro context within which that micro decision is made*'. The conclusion is powerful: post-crisis microeconomic analysis must rest on a sound understanding of GFC macroeconomics. In other words, the macro-foundations of microeconomics must come to the fore of the economics profession.

DGSE models and the GFC

In spite of specific proposals devised to improve (or salvage) DSGE models' explanatory power in the aftermath of the GFC,[10] notably by adding a full-fledged banking sector and introducing heterogeneous agents, it will come as no surprise that these models came under criticism in the last few years. Chatelain and Ralf (2012) has identified a number of stylized facts observed throughout the GFC that contrast with the prediction of pre-crisis models.

- The welfare cost of the GFC was largely underestimated by pre-crisis DSGE models. Following a large exogenous shock, recovery is normally forecasted to take place gradually, with output smoothly converging back towards a deterministic trend. Yet, the observed recovery was much slower than predicted; the GFC led to hysteresis effects and a persistent loss of output. One explanation is that DSGE models were designed to explain only certain restrictive frequencies of economic time-series, by removing stochastic trends from the data and filtering high and low frequencies. These models can explain relatively small fluctuations around a fixed long-term steady-state, but remain alien to so-called black swan events, and are incapable of predicting breaks or trends in economic growth.

- In the US, four years into the crisis, the persistence of unemployment was still much higher than the persistence of the loss of output, which hints at a jobless recovery. This worrying trend is evidenced by Jaimovich and Siu (2012), who show that the US economic recovery since the thwart of the Great Recession has been conducive to job polarization and sustained high unemployment levels. The American middle class is clearly afflicted by this recent socio-economic evolution. Yet, this trend has been going on for the last three decades: 'since the mid-1980s, 92 percent of job loss in routine, middle-skill occupations has happened within 12 months of a recession' (Freeland, 2012). This evolution calls for a renewed reflection on the interrelatedness between recent recessions and long-term growth patterns: '[w]e think of recessions as temporary, but they lead to these permanent changes' (ibid.). Unfortunately, most DSGE models, with their emphasis on temporary shocks, have been unable to account for the permanent effects of these structural evolutions on the US labour market.

- Most observers expressed their surprise in 2007–2008 when a housing crisis originating in the subprime segment of the US real estate market rapidly morphed into a global crisis resulting in substantial output losses way above the most pessimistic forecasts of pre-crisis models. The reason is that the massive securitization of dubious subprime loans, coupled with overwhelming financialization trends, resulted in dangerously high levels of interconnectivity between banks and other financial institutions, which should, in principle, have led DSGE modellers to revise the covariance between housing prices and output upwards well before 2007 (unless a break in the covariance occurred after 2007), and propose more realistic open-economy models of macro-financial interaction at the global level.

• The link between the volatility of asset prices and the variation of output after 2007 is still poorly understood. One cannot help think that the covariance between asset prices and output was not well specified in pre-crisis models. Furthermore, the volatility of asset prices increased after 2007–2008 in comparison with the previous period of expansion. This asymmetry between negative and positive shocks is not satisfactorily explained by the linearized DSGE models.

• The previous observations cast doubt on the relevance of the Taylor rules used by central banks before the GFC. In these previously well-accepted monetary policy rules, the observed fluctuations of asset prices were not sufficient to justify swift interest rate movements.

• The effectiveness of non-conventional monetary policies implemented by the Fed after the beginning GFC (Chapter 13) has been very limited, and their impact on employment very disappointing. When approaching the zero bound, the Taylor rule has become a less reliable guide to monetary policy. Yet, in order to salvage his framework, John Taylor (2011b) himself argued that short-term nominal rates should not have been kept low for so long, although his stance comes in sharp contrast with actual decisions and forward guidance policies implemented by the Fed during the GFC.

• Fiscal policy has been utterly neglected by most DSGE models. Yet, the latter gained prominence over monetary policy during the GFC. All these shortcomings of standard DSGE models thus question the validity of the efficient market hypothesis in weakly regulated international financial markets, where opacity, rather than transparency, is the norm. Chatelain and Ralf (2012) think that deviations of the expected price of collateral from its fundamental value (provided that the latter can be determined in such a complex and crisis-prone environment) change the rules of the game for the banking industry in terms of exit options. Whether consciously or not, financial institutions surf from one bubble to the other (the Asian bubble to the Internet bubble to the housing bubble to the next bubble in the making, whether in emergent economies or in commodity markets, etc.). International capital is the driving factor of financial expansion and overabundant liquidity (Arrighi, 1999, p. 223), before the bubbles finally burst, and international capital, in mere predator-style, starts to seek new profit opportunities elsewhere.

Of the good use of mathematical models: back to reality!

Monetary theory and the true nature of the economy

A consensus such as the NMC refers to a general agreement on the current state of knowledge reached by a vast group of scholars, who hold a dominant position in the field. It may be argued that for its proponents, a consensus should capture the true nature of its object of inquiry. In the case at hand, the NMC is a leading monetary framework, from the early 1990s up until the GFC, which would accurately describe the true[11] nature of the economy and its workings during that period. Yet, an interpretation of the world, which seemingly gets its right for two decades, is necessarily subject to caution, simply because there is no unique way to get at the essential nature of things. A relevant metaphor would be to evoke the diversity of languages that have existed since the emergence of human communities; this linguistic diversity has always been compatible with a plurality of discursive approaches that do not exhaust the potential for explaining phenomenological reality in its entirety. It is a much more reasonable epistemological stance to deny theories the possibility of making absolutely true knowledge claims. Reality is always the object of a plurality of interpretations (Pilkington, 2012b), none of which are capable of claiming any sense of superiority on others.

Realism has long been a recurrent theme in the philosophy of sciences; the debate has very naturally shifted to economic theory with oft-heard heated discussions concerning the validity and the realism of assumptions employed in mainstream models. The wide-ranging criticism has become all the more acute in times of dissatisfaction over the current state of economic theory (Krugman, 2009; Kay, 2011; Pilkington, 2012b). A position that has long dominated the field is that of Milton Friedman (1953, pp. 14–15), who once circumscribed the importance of a hypothesis to its explanatory and predictive power, and not to its ability to account for the 'mass of complex and detailed circumstances surrounding the phenomena to be explained' (ibid.). Friedman equated an important hypothesis to a 'descriptively false' one. Abstraction is of paramount importance, and presupposes an underlying and uncovered equivalence between formal mathematical propositions and substantive reality (Pilkington, 2012b). Real-world circumstances surrounding the hypothesis are irrelevant for the phenomena to be explained. In a sweeping statement, Friedman hence denies any scientific validity to epistemological concerns over the realism of assumptions with regard to the ultimate *raison d'être* of economy theory, namely its explanatory and predictive power. Yet, this long-standing epistemological belief of the philosophy of science is no longer shared by the majority of economists today. John Kay (2011) wrote a paper published by the Institute for New Economic Thinking entitled 'The Map is Not the Territory: An Essay on the State of Economics' about the relationship between economics and real-world phenomena (in Lawson's terminology, this amounts to the ontology of economics). Kay offers a powerful methodological critique of mainstream economic theory and DSGE models. The pivotal role played by DSGE models in the NMC have been emphasized in this book (Chapter 6). We have presented critical views that question the ability of these models to capture key aspects of reality, although they do display sophisticated methods and calibration techniques reminiscent of the real business cycle approach (Pilkington, 2011a). Kay's paper echoes the criticism of DSGE models insofar as their salient characteristics (e.g. the role of micro-foundations and their reliance on hypothetico-deductive reasoning), their intrinsic weaknesses (e.g. their unrealistic simplifying assumptions) and their analytical strengths (e.g. their rigour and consistency) are singled out. Kay goes as far as comparing the artificial worlds constructed by DSGE models to Tolkien's famous fictional setting *Middle Earth*, or even to the famous computer game *Grand Theft Auto*. Yet, these grandiose constructs hardly resist the epistemological test of open-systems ontology popularized by Lawson (2006, 2009). The deductive kind of logic in DSGE models requires the ontological assumption of pre-existing closed systems, a kind of closure imposed upon real phenomena, which is objectionable on theoretical grounds. Yet, rigour and consistency (that Kay, very interestingly, equates to mathematics and ideology) are undeniable qual-ities of DSGE models. But is skilful mathematical modelling sufficient to ensure scientific validity? For Hennig (2010, p. 46), the answer to this ques-tion is negative.[12] The interpretation of various elements taken from the formal mathematical domain in terms of real-world phenomena (i.e. within the social realms) must be subject to caution. Pilkington (2012b) discusses the corres-pondence between mathematical propositions and economic reality by drawing on the insights of German philosopher Ludwig Wittgenstein. He concludes in favour of a renewed discursive approach to economics that would effectively promote pluralistic approaches. To elaborate upon this idea, let us use an inter-disciplinary digression borrowed from contemporary analytic philosophy, with Donald Davidson's works on Richard Rorty. The benefits of such an approach is underlined by Rorty (1987, p. 125) himself who argues that Donaldson's 'non-reductive physicalism gives us ... all the respect for science we need, combined with more respect for poetry than the Western philosophical tradi-tion has usually allowed itself'. Kay (2011) reminds us of the commonly held view, which is implicitly endorsed by DSGE modellers, that the hallmark of science is hypothetico-deductive reasoning, which contrasts sharply with inductive methods that would be best suited to the humanities. Kay is critical of Chicago-based economist John Cochrane's response to Krugman's famous *New York Times* editorial in 2009. Krugman had begun his argumentation by stating that 'the economics profession went astray because economists, as a group, mistook beauty, clad in impressive-looking mathematics, for truth'. In defence of mathematical hypothetico-deductive reasoning, Cochrane (2011, p. 37) later responded by contending that 'the first siren of beauty is simple logical consistency'.[13] Kay seems to take sides with Krugman, by arguing that it is impossible that some of the greatest works ever in Arts, Humanities and Science produced by immortal figures such as Shakespeare, Mozart or Picasso, Newton or Darwin were driven by the mere pursuit of logical consistency. Kay (2011) puts forward the idea that the whole issue should *not* come down to mathematics versus poetry. Yet, the tension that has existed since Plato between poetry and art, on the one hand, and scientific research, on the other hand, is also emphasized by Rorty (1987). Another bone of contention is what we actually mean by referring to 'truth' and 'reality' in economic discourse. For Rorty (2000a, p. 184), ' "truths" and "facts" are nearly equivalent notions'.

If we follow this thought-provoking line of reasoning, the bankruptcy of Lehman Brothers in September 2008 was a fact *and* a truth. Hence, trying to uncover the truth behind the global financial crisis,[14] an endeavour that has preoccupied some of the greatest minds in the fields of economics and finance since 2008, can only lead to epistemological confusion. Why cannot we grasp the inner nature of the GFC, the ultimate reality that economists and other social scientists seek to explain? To this essential, ontological and metaphysical question, Rorty (2000b, p. 375) would certainly answer as follows: 'Because there are no norms for talking about it.' The crucial problem raised by Rorty is therefore a linguistic (and discursive) one. As early as 1981, Karl Brunner wrote a seminal piece entitled 'The Art of Central Banking':

> Central banking thrives on a pervasive impression that it is an esoteric art. Access to this art and its proper execution is confined to the initiated elite. The esoteric nature of the art is moreover revealed by an inherent impossibility to articulate its insights in explicit and intelligible words and sentences.

Understanding how central banking was conducted throughout the GFC would thus mean accurately grasping all GFC-related phenomena from a linguistic point of view. Yet, following Rorty, there is no such one-way correspondence between the discourse on and the actual reality of the GFC. In other words, what economists have failed to understand in the aftermath of the GFC, mostly because they have failed to resort to Philosophy is that there is no 'true' and unique discourse on the GFC, only particular propositions formulated within specific knowledge frames, subject to further scientific inquiry. Transposed to the theme of this book, it seems that the central question becomes: does the NMC, an established body of knowledge, have anything to say about the GFC? Does it bear any relevant discursive dimension with regard to related empirical facts? To answer this fundamental question, let us quote James K. Galbraith (2008, pp. 5–6, emphasis added) hereafter:

> What in monetarism, and what in the 'new monetary consensus,' led to a correct or even remotely relevant anticipation of the extraordinary financial crisis that broke over the housing sector, the banking system, and the world economy in August 2007 and that has continued to preoccupy central bankers ever since? Absolutely nothing [...] [t]hat consensus, *having nothing to say* about abusive mortgage loans, speculative securitization, and corporate fraud, is simply irrelevant to the problems faced by monetary policy today.

In the light of this alleged failure of the NMC, it is perfectly relevant to ask what constitutes a theory with *something to say about reality*. This takes us to the examination of the discursive nature of economic theory and the so-called story-telling view of economics.

The storytelling view in economics

Since the early 1990s, proponents of the NMC have been telling a very particular story about the way the economic system operates, one that is structured around the mantras presented in the first part of this book, namely transparency, credibility and price stability, and one in which the central bankers as managers of expectations provide both the thread and the punch line of the story. But why, then, were they unable, in their immense majority, to foresee the GFC? McCloskey (1990) provides a thought-provoking answer to this interrogation: '[e]conomists cannot predict much, and certainly cannot predict profitably. If they were so smart, they would be rich ... Mainly, economists are tellers of stories.' Economists lost track of what economic theory is about, namely 'a set of discourses that provide the economic concepts, modes of analysis, statistical estimates, econometric methods and policy debates that constitute the different analytical understandings of the economy' (Brown, 1993, p. 70). As argued by Pilkington (2012b), economics is a polymorphic discursive construct. Economists merely tell stories, whilst the economy is the actual content of these narratives. The storytelling view can help us cast light on modern central banking practices. As argued by Barbaroux (2008, p. 167), 'If monetary policy became an art, it is without any doubt the art of managing expectations. ... Eichengreen ... said that "monetary policy is not doing something, but it is telling something."' Though these words were uttered shortly before the outbreak of the crisis, they still resonate today. Central banks are still storytellers today; their stories are increasingly marred with the crisis phraseology (Fiedler, 2010), but their chief storytelling *raison d'être* has been left untouched.

Assessing the discredit on mathematical models

Pre-crisis mainstream models

Michael Woodford (2008) lists a few DSGE models reflecting the pre-crisis methodology, such as the International Monetary Fund's Global Economy Model, the Swedish Riksbank's RAMSES, the European Central Bank's New Area-Wide Model and the Norges Bank's Norwegian Economic Model (NEMO). These models were said to be matched to data either through calibration or Bayesian estimation. Yet, 'it is obvious, even to the casual observer that these models fail to account for the actual evolution of the real-world economy' (Colander *et al.*, 2009b, p. 2). After the crash, the economics profession found itself in a state of disarray wherein it could no longer rely on 'macroeconomic models of stable stated that are perturbed by limited external shocks and that neglect the intrinsic recurrent boom-and-bust dynamics of our economic system' (ibid.). Modern finance was built upon premises that financial economists themselves saw as highly unrealistic, such as the restrictions imposed to assure stability. Yet, financial economists failed to issue warnings to the public with regard to the underlying fragility of the financial structure they had helped generate (ibid., p. 3).

Post-crisis models: a need for a rethink

Has there been a serious rethink within the academic community on how economics ought to be conducted in a post-crisis scenario? For James Galbraith the answer is negative as far as the mainstream is concerned:

> So far as I know, no 'mainstream' department has redesigned its approach since the crisis. This is remarkable. In fact, so far as I know, no mainstream department has hired a single senior figure from any dissident tradition. You have to ask, what does this tell you?[15]

THE EQUITY PREMIUM: ADMITTING OUR LIMITATIONS

The GFC compels economists to admit their limited understanding of fluctuations in equity prices. Why do investors buy stocks rather than bonds? This question is almost as old as financial markets themselves. Roughly speaking, the equity premium corresponds to the extra return on investment that investors require, in order to hold equities rather than bonds in their portfolio of assets. As early as 2002, Bernanke had underlined the poor understanding of economists of this equity premium, which can drastically alter their assessment of fundamental values. Subsequently, our imperfect knowledge of fundamental values will run against our ability to monitor financial stability effectively.

THE LOST APPEAL OF MATHEMATICAL MODELS

Chick (1998, p. 161) has identified a symmetry between the axiomatic approach and mathematic models in the process of scientific inquiry. While the former rests on self-evident axioms and hypothetico-deductive reasoning, in order to reach demonstrable truths, on condition of the proper use of logic, the latter is far more flexible as to the initial choice of assumptions. Mathematical modelling does leave scope for judgement to the theorist. Agreed rules of logic are the common denominator of these approaches conducive to a procedural homology in the ordering of the scientist's thoughts with regard to the starting point of the analysis, its precision and the biases inherent in modelling techniques. But the picture is not yet satisfactory, notably for the critics of mathematical models, who direct their fierce criticism, and even caricature, towards these sophisticated tools unable to inform policy in a sensible fashion (Lucas, 2009). John Kay (2011) argues that the GFC set the stage for a renewed criticism of economists, who confidently manipulate supposedly useless models with an illusory universal dimension. Following Krugman (2009), Kay thinks that these models blinded their designers to real-world issues staring them in the face. Kay (ibid.) argues that this blindness to the pitfalls of mathematical models was the strongest factor in spurring the GFC, and might account for the ineffectual policy responses put into place to date. Ten years before Krugman's notorious *New York Times* editorial, Blinder (1999, pp. 146–147) had already criticized the role of mathematics, viewed as an end in itself. He dated back the shift to the mathematization in economics to the works of 'intellectual giants', such as Samuelson and Arrow. This evolution attracted considerable scholarly work geared at quantitative and mathematical methods, and marginalized others working in the more literary tradition. The problem is that this increasing reliance on mathematics progressively turned into infatuation and even obsession. Blinder (ibid.) does praise the rigour and the difficulty of mathematics, as a demanding school of reasoning, which is an integral part of contemporary science. Yet, taken alone, mathematics is an excessively self-referential, deductive and pure discipline. These three characteristics are the reason why modern economics has slowly drifted away from truth and wisdom. Economists have pushed too far what Dow (1990) calls the 'Cartesian mode of thought' and Lawson (1997, pp. 17–18) 'deductivism'. So the pressing question thus becomes the following. In the aftermath of the GFC, should economists cease to entrust models with the ability to account for real-world phenomena? This is certainly *not* the stance adopted by Woodford (2011) in his reply to Kay (2011). Woodford refuses the idea that modelling should be abandoned in economic theory. He therefore praises the merits of models, which allow for a better and more precise assessment of the internal consistency of proposed arguments in economics. Alternative hypotheses can be more easily differentiated with models. Formal chains of reasoning warrant a higher degree of objectivity, thanks to the limited involvement of the reader and the author. Woodford (ibid.) also rejects the idea that formal mathematical analysis leads to more dogmatic conclusions than analyses expressed in a more literary fashion. Formalism allows economists to see how the strength of a particular assumption conditions the validity of an argument. It also shows how different conclusions might be derived from small changes in the initial assumptions. A modeller must display intellectual honesty, and be ready to face the criticism of those challenging the choice of his assumptions. Woodford (ibid.) claims that models are of paramount importance in the process of scientific inquiry and the quest for truth:

> Modelers should be modest in their claims for what they have found – carefully spelling out a model's limit, and pointing out inappropriate uses of the model by others. If someone draws implications from a model that cannot be legitimately drawn, the modeler should publicly point out.
>
> (Colander *et al.*, 2009a, p. 118)

As Strachman and Fucidji (2010) put it, 'the problem with formalism, in economics or elsewhere, is misunderstanding that precision and consistency are completely different from validity, let alone practical implications – and giving to the formers ultimate worth.' Let us also cite Chick (1998, p. 1868):

> I hope that I have argued persuasively that the role of formalism is to be precise and rigorous where that is possible, and that other modes of analysis exist as valid and valuable complements. Formalism is fine, but it must know its place.

Regarding the alleged dogmatism of models, it is important to underline the question of the numerical dimension of the analysis, and recall Keynes's insights in the *Treatise on Probability* (*TP*). In Chapter 15 of *TP*, Keynes (1921) had pointed out the role of non-numerical probabilities in the theory of rational choice. Yet, this distinction was a rather subtle one, and was not meant to refer to the use of mere numbers in probabilistic theory. While it has been argued that non-numerical probabilities referred in fact to intervals within which probabilities were placed, in other words, probabilities between certain numerical limits (Keynes, 1973[1921], pp. 176–180), Brady and Arthmar (2010) put forward the idea that the end of Chapter 15 of the *TP* proposes an original solution to Boole's Challenge Problem first formulated in 1851. Without going into the mathematical arcane of Keynes's demonstration, it can be shown that Keynes had assigned Greek letters to constituent probabilities, called non-numerical probabilities, that are subsequently eliminated by means of algebraic techniques. These non-numerical probabilities played a pivotal role in Keynes's analysis, although they were strongly, and almost irremediably, criticized by F.P. Ramsey (1922, 1926), who had overlooked Chapter 15 of the *TP*. This reflection casts light on the suitability of models aimed at proposing complete descriptions of artificial worlds. Woodford (2011) argues that the latter constructs, whether they are given a numerical dimension or not, cannot be given any explanatory power, simply on the basis of the rigour and the formalism displayed in the underlying reasoning. Therefore, Woodford insists that mathematical rigour does not warrant scientific truth.

Rejecting models or imaginary worlds?

The previously discussed storytelling view of economics suggested that economists are in fact tellers of stories. In this respect, Sugden (2002, p. 133) thinks that models are useless, if they do not tell us anything about the real world, that is, if they merely describe self-contained imaginary worlds. Unfortunately, this is what theoretical models amount to. What is a model? It is 'a schematic description of a system, theory, or phenomenon that accounts for its known or inferred properties and may be used for further study of its characteristics'.[16] It is self-evident that models are simplified representations of economic reality that abstract from details, in order to single out key features of the real world:

> The object of a model is to segregate the semi-permanent or relatively constant factors from those which are transitory or fluctuating so as to develop a logical way of thinking about the latter, and of understanding the time sequences to which they give rise in particular cases.
>
> (Dahlem Group on Economic Modeling, 2009, p. 118)

Yet, Sugden (2002, p. 133) argues that most theoretical models in mainstream economics are not derived from the observation of the real world. Instead, macro-models (and we decide to focus on the macro-level here) are generally constructed from scratch, and are the outcome of the imagination of the modellers, with a thin veneer of reality taking the form of parameters derived from observations made at the microeconomic level.

Addressing shortcomings of pre-crisis models by designing better models?

Tony Lawson (2009, pp. 774–775) argues that the GFC is not something that must be modelled. In a line of reasoning reminiscent of the Rortyan interpretation of language-reality connections, Lawson would probably subscribe to the view that there is no one-way correspondence between the models and the reality of the GFC. Bouleau (2011, p. 104) explains that the mathematization of economics is well understood when 'one assigns a value of absolute truth to the interpretative framework we work in, so that syntactic developments will be seen as revealing reality'. Bouleau (ibid., emphasis added) adds that it is so, because modellers often believe that 'their models *are* reality'. Yet, 'maths does not need to be the framework for a grand and unique building of knowledge' (ibid.). In fact, viewing mathematics as a language following Wittgenstein (Pilkington, 2012b), is misleading; more accurately, mathematics is the sum of many languages (Dahlem Group on Economic Modeling, 2009, p. 118). So, can we follow Lawson (2009, pp. 774–775), who rejects the idea that what is needed in the aftermath of the GFC is an internal theoretical evolution of mathematics like a mere emphasis on heterogeneous (as opposed to atomistic) agents or on the formation of independent expectations. Economists would be mistaken to expect too much from the development of models with multiple or dynamic equilibria (ibid.), or from sophisticated cointegrated vector autoregression (VAR) models. For Lawson (ibid.),

> the legitimate and feasible goal of economic analysis is not to attempt to mathematically model and perhaps thereby predict crises and such like, but to understand the ever emerging relational structures and mechanisms that render them more or less feasible or likely.

The discursive nature of mathematics (Pilkington, 2012b) is an oft-neglected concern in modern economics. Perhaps, we would be well-inspired to recall the following words by Maurice Allais (1997):

> [a]ny author who uses mathematics should always express in ordinary language the meaning of the assumptions he admits, as well as the significance of the results obtained. The more abstract his theory, the more imperative this obligation. In fact, mathematics is and can only be a tool to explore reality. In this exploration, mathematics does not constitute an end in itself; it is, and can only be a means.

Critical realism in mathematical modelling

In his reply to John Kay, Woodford (2011) reminds us of the importance of assessing the realism of the assumptions made in the model. Woodford is well aware that models are simplified representations of reality, and can never fully describe all aspects of the world. This would be utopian, if not absurd. More reasonably, modellers must assess the realism of their assumptions with regard to the aspects of reality the latter pretend to represent (ibid.). Woodford insists on assessing the 'robustness of the model's conclusions to variations in the precise assumptions that are made'. He postulates a range of possible assumptions subject to empirical scrutiny so as to ensure their relevance. He also acknowledges the fact that '[these kinds of critical scrutiny] make the sound use of model-based reasoning harder', but 'hardly represent an abandonment of model-based deductive reasoning' (ibid.) However, this concern with the empirical relevance of assumptions in models must be distinguished from critical realism in economics. Unfortunately, mainstream empirical methods are solely concerned with singling out empirical regularities, thereby failing to reflect reality (Lawson, 1997, 2006, 2009), because these observations merely take place at the level of the experienced. Instead, economic theory should aim to uncover hidden generative structures with the underlying presupposition that there exist several layers of reality that traditional empirical methods of investigation cannot exhaust. Sugden (2002, p. 121) stresses the role of thought experiments that can only convey knowledge about reality if 'our reasoning ... replicate[s] the workings of the world'. He uses the analogy with structural engineers, who use theoretical models when testing the strength of a new design. The established validity of the underlying theory describing the general properties of a predetermined set of structures, allows them to conduct a thought experiment on a new structure that will lead to valid conclusions, although the real experiment was not conducted in reality. Engineers often rely on this type of prediction derived from sophisticated models, well before real-world experiments are carried out.

Robert Sugden (2000) authored a very interesting paper entitled 'Credible Worlds: The Status of Theoretical Models in Economics' in the *Journal of Economic Methodology*. Sugden (ibid., p. 3) admits he does not feel part of the community of economists merely 'playing games with other theorists'. He claims that his 'starting point is that model building in economics has serious intent only if it is ultimately directed towards telling us something about the real world'. Economic theorists (ibid.) have long used the term 'real world' to name everything that lies outside the model. In a clever analogy with the game of chess described as a model of warfare, Sugden (ibid.) regrets that an economic model is often reduced to 'a self-contained world with no reference to anything outside itself'. By building on two examples, Akerlof's market for 'lemons' and Schelling's checkboard model of racial sorting, Sugden (ibid., p. 33) concludes that most economic models fail to make the connection with the real world explicit. All too often, inductive inferences from models to the real world are left in the air. The existence of gaps in the explicit reasoning of economists is problematic, and might account for the frequent use of rhetorical devices (McCloskey, 1990, Pilkington, 2011b, 2012b). Strachman and Fucidji (2010) thus argue that explanatory frameworks need to be subject to discussion, given that models are 'inherently interpretative, semantical, such that their elements are debatable, and their assumptions can be questioned'.

Future directions in economic modelling

We present hereafter a few research directions with the potential to overcome some of the shortcomings of pre-crisis mathematical models; we consider respectively ensemble modelling (derived from weather forecasting techniques) and agent-based modelling.

Ensemble modelling

Ensemble forecasting is a numerical prediction method used to generate a representative sample of the possible future states of a dynamical system. Tantamount to Monte Carlo analysis, ensemble forecasting is conducted using different initial conditions that might differ slightly. All these initial conditions are deemed plausible by the modeller in the light of past and present observations, data sets and measurements. Multiple simulations help remove the uncertainty inherent in traditional forecast models, such as the errors caused by erroneous initial conditions and path-dependent chaotic dynamics. Ensemble forecasting is also a way to mitigate the imperfections in model formulation and algebraic techniques. The modeller determines an ensemble spread (the size of which is linked to the uncertainty in the environment) within which the dynamical system falls. These recent modelling advances are particularly useful in times of radical uncertainty spurred by the GFC. As explained by Leutbecher and Palmer (2008, p. 3515), 'Numerical weather prediction models as well as the atmosphere itself can be viewed as nonlinear dynamical systems in which the evolution depends sensitively on the initial conditions.' Knowing how sensitive on initial conditions pre-crisis mathematical models were, it is worthwhile adopting a new forecasting technique capable of generating a representative sample of the possible future states of a dynamical system. Ensemble modelling helps collect a vast set of observations on past and current conditions, so as to retain only the most plausible values for initial conditions. The latter might only differ slightly, but given the complexity of the models employed, multiple numerical predictions might yield a range of results forming a spectrum of possible future configurations. This approach is based on multiple computer simulations; and aims at a better understanding of uncertainty (and the resulting forecast errors).

Revisiting Polanyi's insights on man as a social being

For Polanyi (1957, p. 46), the main conclusion derived from the study of early societies is the timelessness of the conception of man as a social being.

Research in history and anthropology has provided us with rich insights on the embeddedness of the economy in social structures. Man does not merely act as a utility-maximizing rational agent driven by self-interest. Rather, he is concerned with preserving and improving his social standing. The possession of material goods acts as a catalyst of the latter aspiration, rather than the former. His claims and assets, whether tangible or not, are primarily social in essence. Material goods serve an intrinsically social end, detached from any economic interest attached to individual ownership. All in all, the economy is run on non-economic motives (ibid.). Modern market-oriented economies give rise to an idiosyncratic type of social structure wherein self-interest behaviour is superimposed on more natural social patterns, such as reciprocity, redistribution, shared values, traditions and various communitarian forms of organizations that determine social motivations and transcend individualities (ibid.). The insights of behavioural economics shed light on social framing and the impact of social norms on choice. Yet, how do social norms arise? It is all the more surprising here to acknowledge the fact that sociologists are so poorly cited by mainstream economists. This paradox might be explained by the axiomatic focus on representative agents and an atomistic view of society wherein the introduction of norms is merely viewed as an exogenous constraint on individual rational behaviour. The reasons why social norms actually emerge, and are accepted by so-called rational individual agents, are not given any consideration (Dow, 2008, p. 19).

Further, for Strachman and Fucidji (2010), uncertainty is an intrinsic feature of social reality, with its relations that are both internal (constitutive) and external (contingent). Positions in society (i.e. hierarchy) and social rules (norms, laws, conventions, etc.) are vectors of social mediation (ibid.). But what is society? It is an unbroken net of relations, whose totality is not reducible to the sum of its parts (i.e. individual actions), with mechanisms and power relations that do not necessarily require micro-foundations (King, 2008). Society constrains the alternative courses of action at the decision-making-level, without being deterministic as to which course of action is eventually followed. Finally, individual action simultaneously performs a transformative and a social reproduction function (Strachman and Fucidji, 2010).

Agent-based modelling

ABM in a nutshell

Agent-based modelling (ABM) is a style of computational modelling focusing on individuals, viewed as heterogeneous parts of a complex system. The innovativeness and the complexity of ABM, also known as agent-based computational modelling and generative social sciences, requires both mathematical and experimental approaches for its development and application. Models with artificial adaptive agents have been discussed by Holland and Miller (1991). For a good introduction to agent-based modelling, valuable references abound in the literature. *Inter alia*, let us mention Axelrod (1997), Klosa and Nooteboom (2001), Tesfatsion (2002, 2003, 2006), Epstein (2006), Judd (2006), Fagiolo *et al.* (2007), Colander *et al.* (2009a), Farmer and Foley (2009) and for dictionary entries, Hommes (2008) and Page (2008). For a good post-crisis perspective, let us mention Buchanan (2009), Oeffner (2009, PhD thesis), Seppecher (2012, PhD thesis). Economists must single out emergent macro-properties arising out of complex interactions between countless economic agents that are assigned specific rules of behaviour.[17]

ABM: a vector of empowerment of economic agents?

On his reflection on post-crisis models, Woodford (2011) states that models are not only meant to be correct representations of reality designed for policy purposes, but must also 'be assumed to be self-evidently valid to everyone in the economy as well'. Economic outcomes are dependent on people's beliefs about the economy. Yet, it is people themselves who arguably have the most privileged access to these beliefs. For Woodford (ibid.), the shift in perspective will have wide-ranging consequences for economists, notably for the validation and parameterization of their models, and also in terms of policy proposal assessment programmes. The key idea is that mathematical models constructed by economists have long been hermetic to the non-expert process of enquiry. Therefore, empowering people in the task of interpreting the correct model of the economy naturally constitutes the next step in economic modelling. We believe that agent-based modelling is a very fruitful endeavour in this respect. Non-experts could be taught to run their own computer simulations on downloadable freeware, by using relevant parameters derived from publicly available information on the state of the economy, and compare their results with actual decisions made by policy makers.

The JAMEL software

A perfect illustration of the empowerment of non-experts in the process of inquiry about the economy is the Java agent-based macroeconomic simulator (JAMEL) developed by the French economist Pascal Seppecher. The free software is distributed under the terms of the General Public Licence (GPL), and can be downloaded, installed and enabled on any personal computer without any technical knowledge. The merit of Seppecher is to have offered an innovative and powerful agent-based computational macroeconomic model entirely compatible with endogenous money in post-Keynesian monetary theory. JAMEL is a free java computer program that can help generate a wide variety of simulations easily usable by non-experts. This powerful software rigorously combines Keynesian thinking and the well-known agent-based computational approach. The JAMEL-user is immediately empowered with an operational virtual laboratory wherein full macroeconomic experiments may be effectively conducted without any prior technical knowledge of econometric techniques.

The empowered user will define the initial conditions of the artificial economy he has created, with the number of agents and the various parameters needed to provide applicable rules of economic behaviour. He can be tempted to replicate disturbances with the introduction of exogenous shocks at various dates; he will be able to monitor the real-time and system-wide effects of these shocks, so as to grasp their consequences on the principal macroeconomic indicators under scrutiny (income distribution, unemployment and inflation levels, money velocity, inventory levels, capacity utilization, bankruptcy rate...). Seppecher has made a number of simulations available online, in order to replicate some of the stylized facts in contemporary economies; one may mention productivity and expenditure shocks, deregulation (flexibilization) of the labour market, the introduction of a minimum wage in a deflationist context and, finally, credit bubbles.

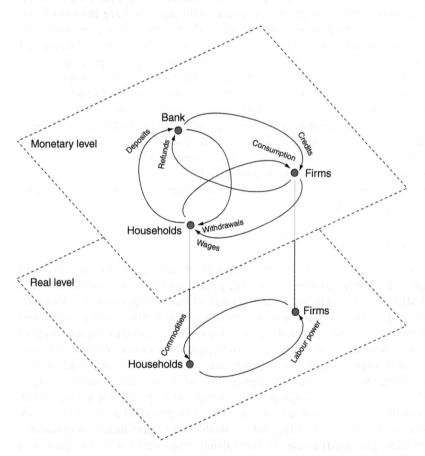

Figure 16.1 Interaction diagram – monetary and real flows with endogenous money
(source: http://p.seppecher.free.fr/jamel/javadoc/index.html).

Conclusion of the book

Let us acknowledge that there is little monetary policy can do *alone* at this juncture in History to support today's global economy. The omnipotence of monetary policy was the main message conveyed by proponents of the NMC (*1989–2007†). Regrettably enough, its real-world relevance arguably lies in tatters today. To quote Tony Lawson (2012, p. 17, emphasis in original), 'The scandal of modern economics is *not* that it gets so many things *wrong*, but that it is so largely *irrelevant*.' The NMC will live on in economic history books, and will remain an extraordinary scholarly object of study in the history of economic thought. At the time of writing, uncertainty still prevails in the world economy. Nobody knows yet what emerging consensus will be capable of replacing the theoretical supremacy of the NMC in the foreseeable future. Perhaps, the real question that economics is facing today is not doctrinal, but essentially discursive in nature. There are times in history when political, economic and social structures seem to experience a vast transformative process conducive of hastening change. The last six years have been a stunning example of such an uninterrupted whirlpool of strains and instability in the world economy. This should be interpreted as a signal to reconsider our most firmly established knowledge frameworks, for history teaches us that old and new consensuses alike are often bound together by the same inexorable doctrinal fate. In the aftermath of the biggest crisis since the 1930s, the first global crisis of the twenty-first century, we would like to conclude this essay by some friendly advice for the economics profession which, we believe, has yet a pivotal role to play in the social sciences.[18]

In a post-crisis world, economists of all persuasion would be well inspired to make theirs the following words by French critic, essayist and novelist André Gide.

Believe those who are seeking the truth. Doubt those who find it.

Notes

1 The Global Financial Crisis: an unprecedented configuration for monetary policy

1 These reflections will often take the form of sub-sections entitled 'post-crisis assessment'.

2 Introduction: monetary policy prior to the NMC

1 If, for some reason, the number of policy targets exceeds the number of instruments, the effectiveness of policy is hampered, that is, some objectives are less likely to be met.

2   The measure compares the actual GDP (output) of an economy and the potential GDP (efficient output). When the economy is running an output gap, either positive or negative, it is thought to be running at an inefficient rate as the economy is either overworking or underworking its resources. Economic theory suggests that positive output gap will lead to inflation as production and labour costs rise.

            (www.investopedia.com/terms/o/outputgap.asp#ixzz1iCGdvJUG)

3 Ironically, it is precisely at the same time that mainstream economics in the making (the rational expectations schools, real business cycle theory etc.) set out to establish the microeconomic foundations of macroeconomics (King, 2008).
4 'Monetarism' by Bennett T. McCallum, retrieved from www.econlib.org/library/Enc/Monetarism.html.
5 C. Taylor (2011, pp. 67–75), however, devotes a section to new consensus macroeconomics, a neo-Keynesian presentation of the NCM in a three- or six-equation model (see also Chapter 3).
6 The qualifier 'undemocratic' might sound like inflammatory language to refer to the ECB, as the Maastricht treaty was adopted with the consent of European peoples. However, voices of dissent are more frequently heard today in the midst of the Eurozone crisis:

    [b]y any objective measure the euro is a failure. And who exactly is responsible, who is in charge out of all you lot? The answer is none of you because none of you have been elected; none of you have any democratic legitimacy for the roles you currently hold within this crisis.

        (UKIP MEP Nigel Farage at the European Parliament, November 2011)

7 www.treasury.gov/resource-center/data-chart-center/Documents/20120413_Financial-CrisisResponse.pdf.
8 In fact, it will be argued that New Keynesians have pursued the agenda of New Classical Macroeconomics, by making only slight adjustments such as incorporating price stickiness and information asymmetries, but without altering the market-fundamentalist nature of the paradigm based on rational expectations and market clearing.

9 This is very much the viewpoint expressed by Solow (2008: 243): 'I think the last phrase is a little too self-congratulatory, and the last three decades have produced rather a mixed bag.'

3 A simple macroeconomic model of the NMC

1 See also 'Teaching Intermediate Macroeconomics using the 3-Equation Model', by Wendy Carlin and David Soskice, available at www.ucl.ac.uk/~uctpa36/3equation_book_chapter.pdf.
2 See www.ecb.int/mopo/strategy/princ/html/orientation.en.html.
3 Put differently, why blowing on our soup does not necessarily make it cool faster than simply letting it sit on the kitchen table for a few minutes.
4 See www.guardian.co.uk/business/2010/sep/28/world-in-international-currency-war-warns-brazil.

4 Transparency: an essential feature of the NMC

1 A landmark survey of ninety-four central banks was conducted by Fry *et al.* (2000) and revealed that three-quarters of central banks under scrutiny considered transparency as a vital or very important component of monetary policy.
2 See www.ecb.int/ecb/orga/transparency/html/index.en.html
3 Jeanne omits exchange rate stabilization in the first part of his presentation.
4 See www.ecb.int/ecb/orga/transparency/html/index.en.html.
5 See www.federalreserve.gov/newsevents/press/monetary/20120125c.htm
6 Forward-guidance policies were used again by the Fed in 2009, but this time as a response to recessionary fears and a tool for crisis management.
7 See www.thefreedictionary.com/mantra.
8 This conception of central banks as a government agency runs counter to the theoretical strands structured around central bank independence upon which the NMC has thrived (see Chapter 5). However, 'monetary policy has always presented something of a challenge in this regard. Even such dedicated free-market advocates as Milton Friedman have strongly defended the central bank's role as a necessary deus ex machina, exogenously fixing some economic magnitude' (B. Friedman, 2005). It is therefore correct, whether the central bank is truly independent or not, to state that market outcomes and central bank decisions are logically distinct phenomena.
9 In August 2007 and September 2008, it is, of course, uncertain how much retention of information had been secretly agreed upon by central bankers as part of their crisis management strategy as well as their unprecedented emergency policy response to the dramatic events unfolding in world financial markets.
10 To be precise, B. Friedman and C. Sims do not refer explicitly to the NMC. Instead, they state: 'it is important not to claim for any policymaking regime, *even inflation targeting*, virtues it does not possess' (2005, p. 51).
11 There are notable exceptions, such as the Bank of Sweden. The Riksbank's 'Monetary Policy Report' was previously published under the name 'Inflation Report'. This constitutes a rather healthy evolution.

12 The standard deviation of the rate of economic growth was 2.0 percentage points in the 1960s, as compared to 1.5 percentage points in the 1990s. This seems to support the usual story suggesting a decline in the volatility of output growth. But average rate of output growth was 2.0 percentage points in the 1960s, as compared to 1.5 percentage points in the 1990s.

(Quiggin, 2010, p. 24)

13 If Fukuyama had been right, the idea for the present book would never have germinated in the author's mind…

14 See www.politico.com/arena/perm/Peter_Fenn_149A409A-FDA2–41EA-ACA1-41133DF86F66.html.

15 The book also contains an interesting psychological dimension, with a surprise appearance of Sigmund Freud, in the final chapter entitled 'The Power of Money'. The author's line of reasoning is not alien to Keynes's famous quotation:

> The love of money as a possession – as distinguished from the love of money as a means to the enjoyments and realities of life – will be recognised for what it is, a somewhat disgusting morbidity, one of those semi-criminal, semi-pathological propensities which one hands over with a shudder to the specialists in mental disease.
>
> (Keynes, 1930b)

16 The term 'haute finance sector' is used by Pilkington (2009), in order to characterize the financial sector, viewed as a full-fledged macroeconomic building block in a stock-consistent framework *à la* Lavoie Godley.

17 See www.imf.org/external/np/mae/mft/code/index.htm.

18 Wishful thinking is usually not the tone the IMF wishes to set, when it issues such wide-ranging statements.

19 See www.ecb.int/ecb/legal/pdf/c_10420100423en00080009.pdf?90bb484f207f5b43b d0d53a2c7bf7c37.

20 See www.ecb.int/ecb/html/mission.en.html.

21 In defence of the IMF, one may nonetheless mention that the failings of the institution were acknowledged and thoroughly exposed in a background paper entitled 'IMF performance in the Run-Up to the Financial and Economic Crisis: Multilateral Surveillance' by Angana Banerji, Independent Evaluation Office of the International Monetary Fund on 9 December 2010, available at www.ieo-imf.org/ieo/files/complete devaluations/01102011Crisis_BP2_Multilateral_Surveillance.pdf.

5 Credibility in the NMC

1 This will also be the strategy of the NMC proponents two decades later.

2 In Pepper and Oliver's classification (2001), a political monetarist is someone who does not share the views of genuine monetarists (i.e. advocates of strict money supply targeting), but who endorses the same conclusions, because monetary authorities ought to manage inflationary expectations formed on financial markets.

3 Therefore, it is undoubtedly a forerunner of the NMC.

4 His words could have been uttered two decades later, and would certainly have resonated with striking vigour in the aftermath of the GFC.

5 Although the monetarist experiment only lasted a few years, the MTFS featured in the presentation of Britain's economic policy until it was abandoned by Tony Blair in 1997 (C. Taylor, 2011, p. 38).

6 The world-systems change foreseen by Margaret Thatcher in 1977 was nothing short of the birth of neoliberalism (Harvey, 2005). See Wallerstein (2008).

7 Credibility and transparency thus amount to the two sides of the same coin in the NMC.

8 Various reasons have been put forward in the literature, such as the inability to define unequivocally a controllable monetary aggregate or the instability of the demand for money.

9 The literature contains various appellations such as 'the 1990s synthesis' (C. Taylor, 2011) or 'New Consensus Macroeconomics' (Arestis, 2007; Arestis and Sawyer, 2005).

10 The New Neoclassical Synthesis is not alien to the NMC. It emerged from a symposium at the 1997 Annual Meeting of the American Economic Association (published

in the *American Economic Review* 87(2)), where notorious economists such as Blanchard, Blinder, Eichenbaum, Solow and Taylor were asked to discuss a core of practical and consensual macroeconomic principles underpinning macroeconomic policy.
11 Blinder (Forder, 2004) says that the idea of generating surprise inflation never crossed his mind once as a central banker.
12 Unless this commitment is given a legislative mandate, as advocated by NMC proponents.
13 Another controversial aspect of this articulation concerns the treatment of voting behaviour (as a necessary element of transparency and accountability).
14 A deus ex machina is a god introduced by means of a crane in ancient Greek and Roman drama to decide the final outcome of a narrative or a theatre play.
15 McCallum (1999) has emphasized that official views within the central banking and academic communities converged throughout the 1990s, which is a landmark of the NMC.
16 Although we noted in Chapter 3 that this type of dichotomy leads to misleading simplifications on the very nature of monetary policy.
17 The model is micro-founded, although homogeneity is postulated to bridge the gap between the micro- and the macro-level.
18 A good illustration of this sense of superiority of mainstream monetary economics is the title of a book published in 2010, bringing together research contributions of leading proponents of the NMC on the occasion of the Deutsche Bank Prize in Financial Economics. This edited book arguably epitomizes the spirit of the NMC, and is entitled *The Science and Practice of Monetary Policy Today* edited by Volker Wieland. One could perhaps have thought of a more humble title in the light of the failure of the contributors to predict the GFC.
19 Introductory statement with Q&A, Jean-Claude Trichet, President of the ECB, Lucas Papademos, Vice President of the ECB, Frankfurt am Main, 3 July 2008.
20 At an event in Calgary, Canada, sponsored by BMO Financial Group.

6 Price stability and the influence of Wicksell on the NMC

1 See www.ecb.int/mopo/strategy/pricestab/html/index.en.html.
2 A syllogism (Greek: συλλογισμός – syllogismos – 'conclusion', 'inference') is a kind of logical argument in which one proposition (the conclusion) is inferred from two or more others (the premises) of a certain form (Wikipedia).
3 Introductory statement with Q&A, Jean-Claude Trichet, President of the ECB, Lucas Papademos, Vice President of the ECB, Frankfurt am Main, 3 July 2008.
4 DSGE models have contributed to NMC policies in several ways (Galí, 2010).
5 Wicksell restates the quantity theory in credit theoretical terms (Boianovsky and Trautwein, 2001, p. 500).
6 'Woodford and Wicksell on Interest and Prices: The Place of the Pure Credit Economy in the Theory of Monetary Policy' by David Laidler, Notes for a panel discussion held at the History of Economics Society Meeting in Toronto, 25–28 June 2004.
7 The emphasis put on market expectations has been criticized by Wray (2011):

> Returning to the obsession with control over expectations, out in the real world, expectations alone cannot govern any economic phenomena: inflation expectations will determine actual inflation only if those with ability to influence prices act on those expectations. And inflation below the high double digits has never proven to be a barrier to economic growth.

8 Starting with the title, [*Interest and Prices*] contains many references to *Geldzins und Güterpreise* (1898), Wicksell's landmark contribution to monetary theory which was translated as Interest and Prices in 1936. Woodford relates his concept

of a 'monetary policy without money' to Wicksell's concept of the pure credit system.

See 'Wicksell after Woodford' by Mauro Boianovsky and Hans-Michael Trautwein, Paper presented at the History of Economics Society meeting at Toronto in June 2004.

9 In Woodford's index (2003), there is simply no entry for 'banks'.
10 For a good introduction to DSGE models, see Sbordone *et al.* (2010).
11 The scientific appeal of these models is one reason why central bank economists have been extremely active in developing DSGE models (Smets and Wouters, 2003).
12 The word 'optimal' is understood in a Woodfordian sense that is, within a general equilibrium theoretical framework that incorporates nominal price stickiness and information asymmetries.
13 As Setterfield (2008, p. 7, italics in original) argues,

> 'path-dependent' equilibrium configurations are influenced by the specific (historical) sequence of adjustments that a system undertakes in the process of reaching or attaining them, as a consequence of which the system's dynamics are of *primary* importance, since they are intrinsic to the very creation of any configuration ... that the system experiences.

In this regard, the global economy having experienced the first global crisis of financial capitalism since 2007–2008, the set of macroeconomic equilibria attained in the post-crisis period define a new path-dependent configuration that pre-crisis models, let alone the NMC, had *not* integrated.

7 The interest-rate setting policy: the Taylor rule and beyond

1 Let us mention the contributions of Kaldor and Trevithick (1981) and Lavoie (1985, 2007).
2 Provided that these borrowers meet the creditworthiness criteria decided upon by lenders.
3 There exists an intellectual filiation between Moore's ideas and the 'needs of trade' that were the hallmark of authors of the Banking School in the nineteenth century.
4 One may also add the following principle: 'Fed actions with regards to quantities of reserves are necessarily defensive. The only discretion the Fed has is in interest rate determination' (Wray, 1998, p. 115). It will be an important argument in our chapter on quantitative easing.
5 See 'Money, Credit and Finance' (Marc Lavoie, Powerpoint presentation), available at http://aix1.uottawa.ca/~robinson/Lavoie/Presentations/en/E22%20PK%20%20Money,%20Credit%20and%20Finance.ppt.
6 Ibid.
7 These two objectives must be understood within the ideological climate of the Great Moderation.
8 Although, under neoliberalism, that kind of configuration has been illusory in most countries.
9 This view is reminiscent of the Phillips curve.
10 Although speaking of deviations from the Taylor rule in the 1970s constitutes an anachronism.
11 It does not occur to Taylor that unsustainable household debt levels, securitized mortgages granted to subprime borrowers or bank balance sheets crippled with toxic assets might have played a significant role too.
12 Robert Solow, interviewed by Viv Davies, 1 April 2011, available at www.voxeu.org/index.php?q=node/6310.
13 Many economic variables are contingent on economic conditions and have a stabilizing

effect on activity. For instance, increased unemployment benefits in times of recession will offset the decline in economic activity, feeding through to consumer spending and eventually helping to boost employment. Fine-tuning the overnight interest rate can also be viewed as an instance of using automatic stabilizers.

14 United States Senate one-hundred-twelfth congress – First session on oversight on monetary policy – Report to the full employment and balance growth act of 1978.
15 Ben Bernanke, testimony before the Senate Banking Committee, 1 March 2011. See www.federalreserve.gov/newsevents/testimony/bernanke20110301a.htm and www.gpo.gov/fdsys/pkg/CHRG-112shrg65824/html/CHRG-112shrg65824.htm.
16 See http://johnbtaylorsblog.blogspot.fr/2011/03/lessons-learned-from-ben-bernankes.html, 'They say they're using the Taylor Rule, but they're not'. John Taylor, interview with Bloomberg News, 28 July 2009 (Mckee, 2009).
17 John B. Taylor (Hoover Institution Press, 2009).
18 cogent, thorough and compelling … Taylor sums up his argument in his subtitle: How Government Actions and Interventions Caused, Prolonged and Worsened the Financial Crisis. Take a moment to absorb that. Although we're told every day that the crisis arose from failures in the free markets – that it represents a crisis of capitalism itself – an eminent economist has now stepped forward to say, in effect, 'Nonsense.' The markets didn't fail, Taylor argues, the government did.'
(Peter Robinson, 'What Caused the Crisis?' Forbes.com)
19 The relevance of this thought-provoking accusation nevertheless deserves to be examined in a rigorous assessment of the socio-economic philosophy of the NMC.
20 Goldilock economy is therefore a metaphorical term used to describe the US economy. It prevailed during the 1990s, period during which the NMC emerged. Its proponents considered this state as an optimal policy stance, and in such situations the central bank considered other macroeconomic indicators as residual variables.
21 The concept of underemployment discards the extreme stance inherited from New Classical Macroeconomics stating that unemployment is always voluntary. The underemployed population (whether this term denotes the unemployed population or all the part-time workers, who do not work as much as they wish to) calls for a reinterpretation of the Phillips curve.

8 Inflation targeting and the formation of a broad consensus

1 Regarding the natural rate, one famous quote is the following: 'You can tell whether you're below or above, but until you're there, you are not quite sure you are here' (Greenspan, 2004).
2 The interest-rate setting procedure at the heart of the NMC is best described by Woodford (2003), who put forward a framework enabling policy makers to track down the variations in the natural rate, in order to put in place the most appropriate policy response through the fine-tuning of the short-term interest rates. In Woodford's framework, the adoption of a neo-Wicksellian perspective helps us understand how price stability is achieved, by scrutinizing the reaction function of the central bank that targets the nominal short-term rate in response to variations in the natural rate.
3 However, it might well be an implicit consequence of the NMC. This is at the heart of another central debate tackled in this book.
4 In the same vein, see also Taylor, 2000, p. 90.
5 See www.columbia.edu/~mw2230/Convergence_AEJ.pdf.
6 Three major versions of the hypothesis: weak, semi-strong and strong are often distinguished in the literature. However, the EMH is one that propounds the informational efficiency of markets. It is rightly viewed as a research programme that provides

support to market-friendly policies. The EMH has become even more controversial and disputed since the outbreak of the GFC.

7 See www.ifk-cfs.de/fileadmin/downloads/dbprize/DB_Prize_Flyer.pdf.

8 'In 2005 the first Deutsche Bank Prize was awarded to Eugene F. Fama, Professor of Finance at the University of Chicago, who was honored for his theory of efficient markets.'

9 It is worthwhile stressing that the leading figures of the NMC teach at some of the most prestigious universities in the world (Columbia for Woodford and Princeton for Svensson).

10 *The Science and Practice of Monetary Policy Today: The Deutsche Bank Prize in Financial Economics*, edited by Volker Wieland, Springer (2010).

11 See www.columbia.edu/~mw2230/WebCV03-12.pdf.

12 The secular trend toward hyper-specialization in academia was criticized by Pilkington (2011b) in his trans-disciplinary analysis of the sovereign debt crisis.

13 'Convergence in Macroeconomics: Elements of the New Synthesis', Michael Woodford, Prepared for the session 'Convergence in Macroeconomics?' at the annual meeting of the American Economics Association, New Orleans, 4 January 2008. To be totally fair, the following book chapter authored by Woodford in 2013 bears testimony to the almost imperceptible paradigmatic shift in his latest writings: Woodford, M. (2013), 'Principled Policymaking in an Uncertain World,' In Rethinking Expectations The Way Forward for Macroeconomics, Edited by Roman Frydman, Edmund S. Phelps, Princeton: Princeton University, Press, pp. 389-414

9 The statutory missions of the Fed and the ECB and the issue of the US dollar

1 As added by act of 16 November 1977 (91 Stat. 1387) and amended by acts of 27 October 1978 (92 Stat.1897); 23 August 1988 (102 Stat. 1375); 27 December 2000 (114 Stat. 3028).

2 On Wednesday 25 January 2012, Federal Reserve Chairman Ben Bernanke held a news conference in Washington, DC, to present the Federal Open Market Committee's (FOMC) current economic projections. The FOMC also announced its plans to keep interest rates near zero until at least late 2014.

3 See www.ecb.int/pub/pdf/other/monetarypolicy2011en.pdf?2d615d9c6471bb547f6 ac933d40d3c80.

4 'But the crisis does reveal that the European monetary union can move forward only if it really moves toward a fiscal – and thus, inescapably, political – union. Germany is central to this', 'Showing a need for deeper ties', Yannis Ionnides, *New York Times*, 12 September 2011, available at www.nytimes.com/roomfordebate/2011/09/12/will-culture-clash-splinter-the-european-union/euro-crisis-shows-need-for-deeper-ties.

5 See www.ecb.int/mopo/strategy/html/index.en.html.

6 See http://publications.gc.ca/collections/collection_2008/bank-banque-canada/FB3-1-95E.pdf.

7 We evoked in Chapter 5 some of the limitations associated with this idea (Buiter, 2005, C1).

8 The Euro sovereign debt crisis will be discussed in Chapter 15. Let us note at this stage that, by mid 2012, the appointment of a finance minister endowed with fiscal powers for the Eurozone (a so-called 'Mr Euro') was high on the agenda of European leaders.

9 In a controversial interview with the New Left Project, Mark Weisbrot goes as far as arguing that the so-called Troika (the ECB, the European Commission and the IMF) are deliberately abstaining from putting an end to the crisis, in order to have enough leverage to enforce the structural reforms part of the neoliberal agenda:

the ECB's strategy was clear: they weren't going to end the crisis because if they did, they wouldn't have the leverage to force Italy, Spain, and other countries to adopt 'reforms' – like raising the retirement age, shrinking the size of government, privatizations and other unpleasant things that people would never vote for.

(Weisbrot, 2012)

10 'Rudi Dornbusch used to say that the Europeans are so rich they can afford to pay everybody for not working. That's gone', Mr Draghi said.

11 See www.cfg.org.uk/news/press-releases/2012/april/~/media/Files/News/27547%20 -%20A4%20Portrait%20-%20FINAL.ashx.

10 Exchange rate movements and global derivatives markets

1 Some interesting equivalences hereafter:

- more than twelve times the average daily turnover of global equity markets (about $320 billion – source: World Federation of Exchanges Aggregate, 2009);
- more than fifty times the average daily turnover of the NYSE (about $70 billion – source: World Federation of Exchanges, 2009);
- more than $500 a day for every man, woman and child on Earth (based on world population of 6.9 billion – source US Census Bureau);
- an annual turnover more than ten times world GDP (about $58 trillion – see World Bank, 2009).

2 These authors examined the out-of-sample performance of several exchange rate models, using data from March 1973 and November 1980, they found that the random walk model outperformed all the empirical exchange rate models on the basis of the root mean squared error comparison.

3 For a good overview of the Forex, see www.goforex.net/forex-market-snapshot.htm.

4 Twenty-four hour market. Sunday 5 p.m. EST through Friday 4 p.m. EST. Trading begins in the Asia-Pacific region followed by the Middle East, Europe and the US.

5 See www.bis.org/publ/qtrpdf/r_qt0803z.htm.

6 See www.rba.gov.au/publications/bulletin/2010/mar/8.html.

7 While the foreign exchange forward rate market was dominated by thirty banks in 1998, it was dominated by only fourteen banks three years later. According to a 2009 ECB survey, the five largest Credit Default Swaps dealers were involved in half of the total outstanding notional amounts, while the ten largest CDS dealers accounted for 72 per cent of the market turnover (Zingales, 2011).

8 We believe that this transfer of income from the industrial sphere to the financial sphere could be captured with the help of stock-flow consistent frameworks *à la* Lavoie–Godley (Pilkington, 2009).

9 The extreme version of the Ricardo–Barro Equivalence Theorem states that government deficits do not matter at all, as they have no effect on aggregate demand, national saving, real interest rates, exchange rates, current and future output levels. Budget deficits are offset by increased private saving, because rational forward-looking agents optimize their inter-temporal utility functions under (fiscal) constraints, as they understand that government borrowing today necessarily has to be financed later through higher taxes.

10 These considerations will be of utmost importance in our assessment of the impact of the Euro sovereign debt crisis on the NMC (Chapter 15).

11 "More worrying are in fact the deflationary fears; in March 2013, Greece's consumer price indexes have decreased 0.2% (- 0.3% in June 2013), marking the first deflation since 1968."

12 Of course, the Ricardian world comes in sharp contrast with the theory of endogenous money developed by post-Keynesian economists. Woodford was certainly right to

conceptualize fiscal policy anew in a non-Ricardian regime. However, Woodford fails to admit that his recognition of the superiority of non-Ricardian regimes amounts to an intellectual victory for post-Keynesians and endogenous money theorists.

11 The zero bound on nominal interest rates and deflationary fears

1 'In my analysis, you're in a liquidity trap when conventional open-market operations – purchases of short-term government debt by the central bank – have lost traction, because short-term rates are close to zero', Krugman (2010).
2 'The point is that while you can think of things the Fed can do even at the zero lower bound, that lower bound is in practice a major constraint on policy' (ibid.).
3 To the question of knowing how much of the world was in a liquidity trap, Krugman (2010) answered in the *New York Times* that

> [a]lmost all advanced countries [were]. The US, obviously; Japan, even more obviously; the eurozone, because the ECB probably couldn't engage in Fed-style quantitative easing even if it wanted to, given the lack of a single backing government; Britain. Not Australia, I guess. But still: essentially the whole advanced world, accounting for 70 percent of world GDP at market prices, is in a liquidity trap.

4 If it weren't for the lower bound, the current Fed funds rate would be minus 5 percent, and that to achieve the same effect as a further 5 points of Fed funds cuts the Fed would have to expand its balance sheet to $10 trillion.

(Ibid.)

5 'For the moment – or more likely for the next several years – we're living in a world in which none of what you learned in Econ 101 applies' (ibid.). See http://krugman.blogs.nytimes.com/2010/03/17/how-much-of-the-world-is-in-a-liquidity-trap/#.
6 In January 2012, the Fed was being quite optimistic, when it was forecasting growth of up to 2.7 per cent in 2012, up to 3.2 per cent in 2013 and up to 4 per cent in 2014. However, six months later, the Fed cut its forecast of 2 per cent growth in 2012 and 2.3 per cent in 2013. IMF Chief Economist Olivier Blanchard told a news conference that the United States was facing a 'fiscal cliff' with the expiration of Bush-era tax cuts and $1.2 trillion in automatic spending reductions, which could potentially pull back the US into a recession. Blanchard adopted a surprisingly alarmist tone in July 2012: 'We're talking about potentially an enormous shock. So if it were to happen it would be a major, major event.' This striking evolution in the official discourse of political and economic leaders concerning the prospects of the first economy in the world shows how fragile and unreliable growth forecasts (upon which many NMC models had previously been built with their core output gap measures) have become since the beginning of the GFC.
7 Before the GFC, open-market operations in the US were generally conducted at auctions several times a week under the form of variable rate repurchase transactions of US Treasury bonds (with a maturity of one day from ninety days).
8 The first step is a monitoring process of all depository institutions accessing the discount window of the Federal Reserve, in order to ensure their safety and soundness. The second step consists of the identification of systemic institutions, whose characteristics would present sizeable risks to the Federal Reserve in the absence of any control on their access to Federal Reserve lending facilities and other Federal Reserve services. The third step is the communication of policy-relevant information – within Federal Reserve Staff and towards supervisory and regulatory institutions – especially with regard to systemic institutions. The fourth step is the implementation of appropriate risk-mitigating procedures, in order to counteract the threat posed by these entities.

9   During the financial crisis that emerged during the summer of 2007, the Federal
     Reserve took a number of important steps aimed at providing liquidity to
     important financial markets and institutions to support overall financial stability.
     Financial stability is a critical prerequisite for achieving sustainable economic
     growth, and all of the Federal Reserve's actions were directed toward achieving
     the Federal Reserve's statutory monetary policy objectives. Specifically, the
     Federal Reserve implemented a number of programs designed to support the
     liquidity of financial institutions and foster improved conditions in financial
     markets, and also extend credit to certain specific institutions and committed to
     extend credit to support systemically important financial firms.
                  (Board of Governors of the Federal Reserve System, 2011, Appendix B)

10   Rather than erroneously viewing QE as a mere restatement of the old printing press,
     we argue that this unconventional monetary policy tool is best viewed in mere
     accounting (or double-entry bookkeeping) terms, whose macroeconomic impact might
     not necessarily extend to the industrial sphere, and can remain circumscribed to
     the banking system, whenever the lending behaviour of a bank is constrained by the
     sluggishness of growth and the pessimistic expectations of entrepreneurs (Keynes,
     1930a).
11   In post-Keynesian monetary theory (Moore, 1988), money is endogenous, because it
     is credit-driven and demand-determined. Therefore, subdued bank lending is condu-
     cive to moderate money creation. Therefore, the injection of massive amounts of
     liquidities into the financial system by the central bank (by means of extensive pur-
     chases of securities recorded with the help of double entry bookkeeping accounting
     techniques). The conclusion is straightforward: money is indeed endogenous (and not
     exogenous) to the economic system.
12   On Thursday 26 April 2012, Michel Barnier, the EU commissioner for internal
     markets, asked Mrs Andrea Enria, President of the European Banking Authority, to
     investigate the use of the extraordinary three-month loans granted to European banks
     in December 2011 and February 2012. It is feared that banks might have used these
     loans for recapitalization or balance sheet restructuring purposes without boosting
     lending to the real economy.
13   'The U.S. government has a technology, called a printing press (or today, its elec-
     tronic equivalent), that allows it to produce as many U.S. dollars as it wishes at no
     cost' (Bernanke, 2002b).

12 Austerity measures versus growth: a post-crisis conundrum?

1 See www.ilo.org/public/english/bureau/inst/download/wow2012.pdf.
2 The dollar was pegged to gold at $35 per oz in January 1934.
3 *The General Theory* was not published until 1936.
4 See www.roosevelt2012.fr/.
5 See Pierre Larrouturou's article entitled 'We Do Not Want to Die in the Rubbles of
   Neoliberalism', on 30 April 2012 in French newspaper *Le Monde*. See www.lemonde.
   fr/idees/article/2012/04/30/nous-ne-voulons-pas-mourir-dans-les-decombres-du-
   neoliberalisme_1693201_3232.html.
6 *Le Parisien*, 25 August 2007; the economic suicide of Europe is also evoked by Paul
   Krugman.
7 See   www.guardian.co.uk/business/2011/oct/06/britain-financial-crisis-quantitative-
   easing.
8 During his presidential campaign, François Hollande (who was elected French president in May 2012), outlined the need to 'dominate finance' and leave investors 'with
   no space to act'. See 'Francois Hollande Talks Tough on Financial Markets', available at www.bbc.co.uk/news/business-17687759.

9   George Bush Sr, XLI President of the United States, 1989–1993, Remarks Following Discussions with President Vaclav Havel of Czechoslovakia, 20 February 1990. See www.presidency.ucsb.edu/ws/?pid=18166#axzz1tVD12rHx.

10 'Un effort sur les recettes fiscales et sociales de l'ordre de 15 milliards d'euros est nécessaire', Les Echos no. 20712 of 5 July 2010, available at http://archives.lesechos.fr/archives/2010/LesEchos/20712-14-ECH.htm.

11 A requirement, which calls for a renewed reflection on the current mode of governance of ratings agencies, and the possible creation of a new European public rating agency, whose organizational objectives, mode of governance and capital structure would be made transparent to its stakeholders.

12 Our knowledge of taxation matters has been considerably updated since the beginning of the GFC.

13 See 'Q&A: Austerity Measures Derailed?' 24 April 2012, available at www.bbc.co.uk/news/business-17815546.

14 The Netherlands, one of the few along with Germany to maintain an AAA credit rating. Yet, the Dutch economy contracted 0.7 per cent in the fourth quarter of 2011, putting the country officially into recession.

15 See www.bbc.co.uk/news/world-europe-17966333.

16 The European Central Bank decided to leave interest rates unchanged on 3 May 2012. But ECB Chairman Mario Draghi slightly hinted at future rate cuts.

17 See http://ec.europa.eu/news/eu_explained/120702_en.htm.

18 The Spanish and the Irish sovereign debt crises cannot be explained by excessive pre-crisis deficits. The two countries were engaged in large deficit reductions prior to the GFC. Mirroring the US subprime crisis, the two countries had certainly overlooked the destructive effects of their own housing price bubbles.

19 See www.ons.gov.uk/ons/dcp171766_263951.pdf. For Krugman (2012a) writing in the *New York Times*, this is 'an economic report showing that Britain is doing worse in the current slump than it did in the 1930s'.

20 '[Y]outh unemployment rates have increased in about 80 per cent of advanced economies' (ibid., p. viii).

21 See www.econ.nyu.edu/user/debraj/Courses/Readings/BenabouAER.pdf.

22 TINA is a famous acronym that stands for 'There Is No Alternative'. It is often linked to the ideology propounded by Margaret Thatcher.

23 T. Landon, Jr (2012), 'Spain is Still Awaiting the Payoff from Austerity', *New York Times*, 28 April.

24 'Socio-epidemiology' is a new methodological approach integrating sociological and epidemiological perspectives and methodologies, it takes a multidisciplinary approach encompassing epidemiology, biostatistics, mixed method, social marketing, behavioural science and communication science. It fits well into the trans-disciplinary approach to the sovereign debt crisis advocated by Pilkington (2011b).

25 The unemployment rate for people under twenty-five in Spain climbed to 52 per cent in April 2012. These are Great Depression-like figures.

26 See www.bbc.co.uk/news/business-16771939.

13 Quantitative easing: sound policy making or an admission of defeat?

1   See www.investopedia.com/terms/q/quantitative-easing.asp#axzz1tcCojTv3.

2   For Koo, this is a central feature of the balance-sheet recession that afflicted Japan. Koo criticizes the consensual view in economics according to which private firms are always profit-maximizing agents. In a balance-sheet recession, indebted corporations and households prefer to deleverage their balance sheets, rather than make productive bets by borrowing on the credit market.

3 The high-powered money pumped into the Japanese banking system between 2001 and 2006 was equivalent to five times the required reserves.

4 These notorious post-Keynesian economists have been leading heterodox figures in the English-speaking world. Yet, the Franco-Italian circuit school (Schmitt, Parguez, Graziani etc.) has also greatly contributed to the theoretical reflection on endogenous money in Europe and Canada.

5 To be fair, in a typical disclaimer, the paper starts with a footnote stating that the ideas of the two authors do not *necessarily* represent the views of the BIS (Brio and Disyatat, 2009, p. 1, fn 2). The same can be said of all papers published by the BIS. However, we think that widely quoted working papers stamped by the BIS may provide a clear indication of the underlying views that the institution is willing to endorse.

6 A well-articulated critique of the multiplier view of credit creation is spelled out in Ryan-Collins *et al.* (2012).

7 There is an extensive literature on capital crunches in banking theory.

8 See www.federalreserve.gov/boarddocs/speeches/2003/20030531/default.htm.

9 The transmission channel to other substitutable assets is called the portfolio balance channel, which has been the object of numerous discussions since the inception of QE1.

10 This expression questions the NMC transparency mantra discussed in Chapter 4, but it reinforces the game-theoretic approach to central banking (Morris and Shin, 2005).

11 See http://federalreserve.gov/newsevents/press/monetary/20101103a.htm.

12 About the true effects of monetary policy on stock prices, finance professional and Wall Street expert John Nyaradi nonetheless declared on 12 July 2012,

> As we all know, stock prices eventually are based on earnings, and no amount of monetary policy, low interest rates or quantitative easing can add profits to corporate bottom lines. Monetary policy can set the stage for, but cannot create, demand.
>
> (Nyaradi, 2012)

13 Using the medical metaphor, John Nyaradi (2012) summed up this idea: 'Like antibotics fighting a virus, quantitative easing is losing its effect as the virus grows immune and mutates to offset continued attacks.'

14 See www.bloomberg.com/news/2012-05-01/dallas-fed-s-fisher-not-supportive-of-quantitative-easing.html.

14 Revisiting the theory of optimum currency areas

1 Google Scholar mentions 5,276 citations for Mundell's paper (June 2013).

2 In this respect, Mundell shared the ideas of Friedman (1953) and Johnson (1972), who were clearly advocates of flexible exchange rates, although they were clearly resting on very different paradigms.

3 Bayoumi and Eichengreen (1992) pointed out that Europe's periphery had suffered from large idiosyncratic shocks in comparison to core countries, let alone to US regions.

4 See www.eurofound.europa.eu/eiro/studies/tn0803019s/tn0803019s.htm.

5 The German example immediately springs to mind in the European context.

15 Lessons from the Euro sovereign debt crisis

1 As Weisbrot argues,

> The standard analysis in the financial press is that the Germans haven't recovered from the hyper-inflation of 85 years ago, and they are therefore more afraid of inflation than they are of having a second European recession in less than three years.

2 Article 105.2 of the Treaty establishing the European Community.
3 Notes and coins were introduced on 1 January 2002.
4 'Already before the crisis, it was acknowledged that the EU model of cross-border banking was not stable', the European Commission said in a report on Wednesday 30 May 2012.
5 According to the OCDE website, a GDP contraction of 0.6% was forecasted for the euro area in 2013. Source: http://www.oecd.org/eco/outlook/euroareaeconomicfore-castsummary.htm. Last consulted in June 2013.
6 The rhetoric of the Euro sovereign debt crisis was acknowledged by Pilkington (2011b).
7 Atkinson and Andes (2008). Yet, the rhetoric of the newness of the knowledge economy is evident. Peter Drucker (1966, pp. 2–3) wrote that 'the manual worker works with his hands and produces goods or services. In contrast, a knowledge worker works with his or her head not hands, and produces ideas, knowledge, and information.'
8 See www.imf.org/external/pubs/ft/exrp/sdrm/eng/sdrm.pdf.
9 'I guess you guys have to be creative here', is what US President Barack Obama reportedly said to German Chancellor Angela Merkel at the Cannes Summit on 4 November 2011.

16 Post-crisis methodological considerations in central banking theory

1 'The 1987 stock market crash is a real-world example of how monetary policy aimed at macro stability coupled with other types of policy emphasizing financial stability can minimize the economic fallout of a sharp decline in asset prices' (Bernanke, 2002a).
2 The use of this word is criticized by Pilkington (2011a) in his review of dictionary entries devoted to RBC theory.
3 Idem.
4 The controversial role of mathematics in economic theory was discussed earlier in this chapter.
5 For a critique of the efficient market hypothesis in a post-crisis scenario, see Quiggin (2010).
6 The effective loss given default (LGD*) for a collateralized transaction is expressed as $LGD^* = LGD \times (E^*/E)$.
   Where:

   LGD is that of the senior unsecured exposure before recognition of collateral;
   E is the current value of the exposure (i.e. cash lent or securities lent or posted);
   E* should be calculated based on the following formula:
   $E^* = \max\{0, [E \times (1 + He) - C \times (1 - Hc - Hfx)]\}$

   Where:

   E* is the exposure value after risk mitigation;
   E is current value of the exposure;
   He is haircut appropriate to the exposure;
   C is the current value of the collateral received;
   Hc is haircut appropriate to the collateral;
   Hfx is haircut appropriate for currency mismatch between the collateral and exposure.

7 See www.ecb.int/home/html/researcher_swm.en.html.
8 Again, a transdisciplinary approach (Pilkington, 2011b) to the representative agent problem would be much more relevant here.
9 Attributed to Buiter (2009).

10 See for instance CEPREMAP's project for FP7-ICT, which was submitted to the European Commission: available at http://ec.europa.eu/information_society/activities/ egovernment/events/fp7_events/fp7_infoday_nov_2010/presentations/mihoubi_ ferhat_cepremap_proposal_for_fp7_ict_solutions_for_governance_and_policy.pdf.

11 There is a vast literature on models, their relation to reality and their construction. See the papers included in Part III of Mäki (2002), in Morgan and Morrison (1999).

12 'There is no formal way to check whether such interpretations are "true", and the mathematical truth of theorems applied to such models does not warrant claims of "objective truth" concerning the modelled reality' (Hennig, 2010, p. 46).

13 An interesting discussion of the debate between Krugman and Cochrane is provided by Katarina Juselius, available at www.econ.ku.dk/okokj/papers/response%20to%20 Krugman.doc. From an econometric standpoint, cointegrated VAR models (CVAR) are deemed superior to DSGE models, which are criticized for leaving out a number of stochastic trends in the real data. Juselius concludes her paper by stating that 'many economists were indeed blinded by the beauty of their theory models and in my view Krugman was right to point this out to the readers of NY Times'.

14 For instance, the title of a book such as Masood's *The Truth about the Global Financial Crisis* is misleading; available at http://businessperspectives.org/books/Preface_ masood.pdf. In Rorty's fashion, The Global Financial Crisis should be equated to all the facts that observers and commentators refer to as the GFC. The tentative uncovering of a higher level of reality that would cast light on all the hidden mechanisms that could satisfactorily explain the unfolding of the GFC in its entirety, and subsequently dressing this infinitely complex set of interrelations in the clothes of a formal mathematical model, can only constitute an illusory epistemological endeavour: '[t]o believe that the mechanisms of our infinitely complex reality can be pre-specified in a mathematically exact model seems almost absurd'. See www.econ.ku.dk/okokj/ papers/response%20to%20Krugman.doc.

15 A comment attributable to James Galbraith on 'Are Economics PhDs Learning the Wrong Thing?' by Brendan Greeley in *Business Week*, 1 June 2012; available at www.businessweek.com/articles/2012-06-01/are-economics-phds-learning-the-wrong-thing#p2.

16 See www.thefreedictionary.com/model.

17 A reference to the sociology of emotions, an oft-overlooked interdisciplinary research programme could possibly enhance the explanatory power of agent-based models. Emotions are complex scientific phenomena that can be defined as the '"glue" binding people together' (Turner, 2005, p. 1, emphasis in the text).

18   For times of crisis are when economists are most needed. If they cannot get their advice accepted in the clinch – or, worse yet, if they have no useful advice to offer – the whole enterprise of economic scholarship has failed in its most essential duty.
        (speech by Paul Krugman, Nobel Prize in Economics, awarded Doctor Honoris Causa in Lisbon, Aula Magna, 27 February 2012).

References

Abel, A.B. and Bernanke, B.S. (2005), *Macroeconomics*, 5th edn, Harlow, UK: Pearson Addison Wesley.

Aghion, P., Blundell, R., Griffith, R., Howitt, P. and Prantl, S. (2009), 'The Effects of Entry on Incumbent Innovation and Productivity', *Review of Economics and Statistics*, 91(1): 20–32.

Aghion, P., Farhi, E. and Kharroubi, E. (2012), 'Monetary Policy, Liquidity, and Growth', NBER Working Paper No. 18072, May.

Aiyar, Swaminathan S. Anklesaria (2009), 'An International Monetary Fund Currency to Rival the Dollar? Why Special Drawing Rights Can't Play That Role', CATO Institute, Development Policy Analysis no. 10, July.

Allais, M. (1997), 'La formation scientifique, Une communication du Prix Nobel d'économie', address to the Académie des Sciences Morales et Politiques.

Appelbaum, B. (2012), 'Fed Signals that a Full Recovery is Years Away', *New York Times*, 25 January available at www.nytimes.com/2012/01/26/business/economy/fed-to-maintain-rates-near-zero-through-late-2014.html?pagewanted=all.

Arestis, P. (2007), *Is There a New Consensus in Macroeconomics?* Basingstoke, UK: Palgrave Macmillan.

Arestis, P. (2009), 'The New Consensus in Macroeconomics: A Critical Appraisal', in G. Fontana and M. Setterfield (eds), *Macroeconomic Theory and Macroeconomic Pedagogy*, Basingstoke: Palgrave Macmillan.

Arestis, P. and Sawyer, M. (2003), 'On the Effectiveness of Monetary Policy and Fiscal Policy', Levy Economics Institute Working Paper No. 369, January. Available at http://ssrn.com/abstract=382401 or http://dx.doi.org/10.2139/ssrn.38240.

Arestis, P. and Sawyer, M. (2005), 'New Consensus Monetary Policy: An Appraisal', in Philip Arestis, Michelle Baddeley and John McCombie (eds), *The New Monetary Policy: Implications and Relevance*, Cheltenham: Edward Elgar.

Arrighi, G. (1999), 'The Global Market', *Journal of World-Systems Research*, 5: 217–251.

Arrowsmith, J. and Marginson, P. (2008), 'Wage Flexibility in Europe', European Industrial Relations Observatory, available at www.eurofound.europa.eu/eiro/studies/tn0803019s/tn0803019s.htm.

Asso, P.F. and Leeson, R. (2012), 'Monetary Policy Rules: From Adam Smith to John Taylor', in E.F. Koening, R. Leeson and G.A. Kahn (eds), *The Taylor Rule and the Transformation of Monetary Policy*, Stanford, CA: Hoover Institution Press.

Athey, S., Atkeson, A. and Kehoe, P.J. (2004), 'The Optimal Degree of Discretion in Monetary Policy', ECB Working Paper No. 338, 27 April. Published in: *Econometrica*, 73(5): 1431–1475, September 2005.

Atkinson, R. and Andes, S. (2008), 'The 2008 State New Economy Index: Benchmarking Economic Transformation in the States', Information Technology and Innovation Foundation (ITIF), Washington, DC, available at www.itif.org/files/2008_State_New_Economy_Index.pdf.

Auerbach, J. and Gorodnichenko, Y. (2010), 'Measuring the Output Responses to Fiscal Policy', NBER Working Paper No. 16311, August.

Axelrod, R. (1997). *The Complexity of Cooperation: Agent-Based Models of Competition and Collaboration*, Princeton, NJ: Princeton University Press.

Barbaroux, N. (2008), 'The Wicksellian Flavour in Macroeconomics', Perfil de Coyuntura, *Economica*, 11, July–December.

Barro, R.J. and Gordon, D.B. (1983), 'Rules, Discretion and Reputation in a Model of Monetary Policy', *Journal of Monetary Economics*, 12(1): 101–121.

Bayoumi, T. and Eichengreen, B. (1992), 'Shocking Aspects of European Monetary Unification', NBER Working Paper No. 3949.

Bean, C. (2007), 'Is there a New Consensus in Monetary Policy?' 13 April, available at www.bankofengland.co.uk/publications/Documents/other/monetary/bean070413.pdf.

Benassy-Queré, A. and Pisani-Ferry, J. (2011), 'What International Monetary System for a Fast-Changing World Economy? in Jack T. Boorman and André Icard (eds), *Reform of the International Monetary System: The Palais Royal Initiative*, Emerging Markets Forum, New Delhi: Sage.

Berezin, M. (2009), *Illiberal Politics in Neoliberal Times: Culture, Security and Populism in the New Europe*, New York: Cambridge University Press.

Bernanke, B. (2002a), 'Asset-Price "Bubbles" and Monetary Policy – Remarks by Governor Ben S. Bernanke Before the New York Chapter of the National Association for Business Economics', New York, 15 October, available at www.federalreserve.gov/boarddocs/speeches/2002/20021015/default.htm.

Bernanke, B. (2002b), 'Deflation: Making Sure "It" Doesn't Happen Here', Remarks by Governor Ben S. Bernanke, Before the National Economists Club, Washington, DC, 21 November, available www.federalreserve.gov/boarddocs/speeches/2002/20021121/default.htm.

Bernanke, B. (2003), 'Some Thoughts on Monetary Policy in Japan', Remarks by Governor Ben S. Bernanke, Before the Japan Society of Monetary Economics, Tokyo, Japan, 31 May, available www.federalreserve.gov/boarddocs/speeches/2003/20030531/default.htm.

Bernanke, B. (2004a) 'The Great Moderation', Remarks by Governor Ben S. Bernanke at the meetings of the Eastern Economic Association, Washington, DC, 20 February.

Bernanke, B. (2004b), 'What Policymakers Can Learn from Asset Prices', Remarks by Governor Ben S. Bernanke, Before the Investment Analysts Society of Chicago, Chicago, IL, 15 April, available www.federalreserve.gov/boarddocs/speeches/2004/20040415/default.htm#f2.

Bernanke, B. (2010), 'Central Bank Independence, Transparency, and Accountability', Speech of Chairman Ben S. Bernanke at the Institute for Monetary and Economic Studies International Conference, Bank of Japan, Tokyo, Japan, 25 May, available at www.federalreserve.gov/newsevents/speech/bernanke20100525a.htm.

Bernanke, B. (2011a), Testimony before the Senate Banking Committee, 1 March, available www.federalreserve.gov/newsevents/testimony/bernanke20110301a.htm.

Bernanke, B. (2011b), 'The Effects of the Great Recession on Central Bank Doctrine and Practice', Presentation given at the Federal Reserve Bank of Boston 56th Economic Conference, Boston, MA, 18 October.

Bernanke, B. (2012), Transcript of Chairman Bernanke's Press Conference, 25 January, available www.federalreserve.gov/mediacenter/files/FOMCpresconf20120125.pdf.

Bernanke, B. and Gertler, M. (1999), 'Monetary Policy and Asset Price Volatility', Proceedings, Federal Reserve Bank of Kansas City, pp. 77–128.

Bernanke, B. and Gertler, M. (2001), 'Should Central Banks Respond to Movements in Asset Prices?' *American Economic Review*, 91(2): 253–257.

Bernanke, B. and Mishkin, F.S. (1997), 'Inflation Targeting: A New Framework for Monetary Policy?' *Journal of Economic Perspectives, American Economic Association*, 11(2): 97–116.

Bernanke, B., Laubach, T., Mishkin, F. and Posen, A. (1999), *Inflation Targeting: Lessons from the International Experience*, Princeton, NJ: Princeton University Press.

Bernanke, B., Reinhart, V.R. and Sack B.P. (2004), 'Monetary Policy Alternatives at the Zero Bound: An Empirical Assessment', Brookings Papers on Economic Activity, Economic Studies Program, Brookings Institution, 35(2): 1–100.

Bernanke, B.S. and Gertler, M. (1995), 'Inside the Black Box: The Credit Channel of Monetary Policy Transmission', *Journal of Economic Perspectives, American Economic Association*, 9(4): 27–48.

Bini Smaghi, L. (1998), 'The Democratic Accountability of the European Central Bank', Mimeo, European Monetary Institute, May.

Bini Smaghi, L. (2008), 'Careful with the "d" words!', Speech given in the European Colloquia Series, Venice, 25 November.

Bini Smaghi, L. (2009), 'The Euro Area's Exchange Rate Policy and the Experience with International Monetary Coordination during the Crisis', Speech by Lorenzo Bini Smaghi, Member of the Executive Board of the ECB at a conference entitled 'Towards a European Foreign Economic Policy' organized by the European Commission, Brussels, 6 April 2009, available at www.ecb.europa.eu/press/key/date/2009/html/sp090406.en.html.

BIS (2010), Triennial Survey 2010, available www.ecb.int/pub/pdf/other/bistriennialsurvey2010euroareadataen.pdf.

Blanchard, O. and Sheen, J. (2007), *Macroeconomics*, 2nd Australian edn, Frenchs Forest, Australia: Pearson/Prentice-Hall.

Blanchard, O. (2008), 'The State of Macro', NBER Working Papers 14259, National Bureau of Economic Research, Inc.

Bliek, J. and Parguez, A. (2006), *Le Plein Emploi ou le Chaos*, Paris: Economica.

Blinder, A. (1998), *Central Banking in Theory and Practice*, Cambridge, MA: MIT Press.

Blinder, A. (1999), 'Economics Becomes a Science: Or Does It?' in A. Bearn (ed.), *Useful Knowledge: The American Philosophical Society Millennium Program* Philadelphia, PA: American Philosophical Society.

Blinder, A. (2000), 'Central-Bank Credibility: Why Do We Care? How Do We Build It?' *American Economic Review, American Economic Association*, 90(5): 1421–1431.

Blundell-Wignall, A., Lumpkin, S., Schich, S. and Slovik, P. (2011), 'Bank Competition and Financial Stability', OECD, available www.oecd.org/dataoecd/14/49/48501035.pdf.

Board of Governors of the Federal Reserve System (2010), Press Release, 3 November, available http://federalreserve.gov/newsevents/press/monetary/20101103a.htm.

Board of Governors of the Federal Reserve System (2011), 'Monthly Report on Credit and Liquidity Programs and the Balance Sheet', February, available www.federalreserve.gov/monetarypolicy/files/monthlyclbsreport201102.pdf.

Boianovsky, M. and Trautwein, H.-M. (2001), 'An Early Manuscript by Knut Wicksell on the Bank Rate of Interest', *History of Political Economy*, 33(3): 485–507.

Boltho, A. and Carlin, W. (2012), 'The Problems of European Monetary Union: Asymmetric Shocks or Asymmetric Behaviour?' 31 March, available www.voxeu.org/article/problems-eurozone.

Bordo, M. and Jeanne, O. (2002), 'Boom-Bust in Asset Prices, Economic Instability, and Monetary Policy', NBER Working Paper No. 8966, June.

Borio, C. (2006), 'Monetary and Prudential Policies at a Crossroads? New Challenges in the New Century', BIS Working Papers, no. 216, September.

Borio, C. and Disyatat, P. (2009), 'Unconventional Monetary Policies: An Appraisal', BIS Working Papers, No. 292.

Borio, C. and Lowe, P. (2002), 'Asset Prices, Financial and Monetary Stability: Exploring the Nexus', BIS Working Paper No. 114.

Borio, C. and Nelson, W. (2008), 'Monetary Operations and the Financial Turmoil', *BIS Quarterly Review*, March: 31–46.

Bouleau, N. (2011), 'Mathematics and Real-World Knowledge', *real-world economics review*, issue 57, 6 September.

Brady, M.E. and Arthmar, R. (2010), 'A Road Map for Economists, Logicians, Philosophers, Mathematicians, Statisticians, Psychologists and Decision Theorists Seeking to Follow the Mathematical Structure of Keynes's Approach to Specifying Lower and Upper Bounds for Probabilities in the *A Treatise on Probability*, 1921', 31 May, available at SSRN:http://ssrn.com/abstract=1618445.

Brash, T.D. (1999), 'Text of the sixth L K Jha Memorial Lecture given by the Governor of the Reserve Bank of New Zealand, Dr Donald T Brash, in Mumbai on 17 June 1999' to the Trans-Tasman Business Circle, Melbourne, 9 February, available www.bis.org/review/r990706a.pdf.

Brash, T.D. (2000), 'Inflation Targeting in New Zealand, 1988–2000', by Donald T. Brash, Governor of the Reserve Bank of New Zealand, to the Trans-Tasman Business Circle, Melbourne, 9 February, available www.rbnz.govt.nz/speeches/0086932.html.

Brender, A., Gagna, E. and Pisani, F. (2009), 'Can We Understand the Recent Moves of the Euro–Dollar Exchange Rate?' VoxEu, 21 July, available www.voxeu.eu/index.php?q=node/3792.

Brown, V. (1993), 'Decanonizing Discourses: Textual Analysis and the History of Economic Thought', in W. Henderson, T. Dudley-Evans and R. Backhouse (eds), *Economics and Language*, London: Routledge.

Brunner, K. (1981), 'The Art of Central Banking', Center for Research in Government Policy and Business, University of Rochester, Working Paper GPB 81-6.

Bryant, J. (1985), 'Review of Laidler (1982)', *Journal of Economic Literature*, 23(1).

Buchanan, M. (2009), 'Meltdown Modeling: Could Agent-Based Computer Models Prevent Another Financial Crisis?' *Nature*, 460(7256): 680–682.

Buiter, W.H. (2002), 'The Fiscal Theory of the Price Level: A Critique', *Economic Journal, Royal Economic Society*, 112(481): 459–480.

Buiter, W.H. (2005), 'New Developments in Monetary Economics: Two Ghosts, Two Eccentricities, a Fallacy, a Mirage and a Mythos', *Economic Journal, Royal Economic Society*, 115(502): C1–C31, 03.

Buiter, W.H. (2009), 'The Unfortunate Uselessness of Most "State of the Art" Academic Monetary Economics', *Financial Times*, 3 March.

Cafiso, G. (2008), 'The Euro's Influence upon Trade: Rose Effect versus Effect', ECB Working Paper Series No. 941, September, available at www.ecb.int/pub/pdf/scpwps/ecbwp941.pdf.

Cagan, P. (1978), 'Monetarism in Historical Perspective' in T. Mayer (ed.), *The Structure of Monetarism*, New York: W.W. Norton and Co.

Cagliarini, A., Kent, C. and Stevens, G. (2010), 'Fifty Years of Monetary Policy: What Have We Learned?' Available at www.rba.gov.au/publications/confs/2010/cagliarini-kent-stevens.pdf.

Calvo, G. (1978), 'On the Time Consistency of Optimal Policy in a Monetary Economy', *Econometrica*, 46, 1411–1428.

Canzoreni, M.B., Cumby, R.E. and Behzad, T.D. (2000), 'Fiscal Discipline and Exchange Rate Systems', Working Paper, December, available at http://www9.georgetown.edu/faculty/cumbyr/papers/Fiscal_EXRate.PDF.

Carlin, W. and Soskice, D. (2005), 'The 3-Equation New Keynesian Model: A Graphical Exposition', Open Access publications from University College London.

Carlin, W. and Soskice, D. (2006), *Macroeconomics: Imperfections, Institutions and Policies*, Oxford: Oxford University Press.

Castoriadis, C. (1975), *The Imaginary Institution of Society*, Cambridge, MA: MIT Press.

Cecchetti, S.G., Genberg, H. and Wadhwani, S. (2002), 'Asset Prices in a Flexible Inflation Targeting Framework', in W.C. Hunter, G.G. Kaufman and M. Pomerleano (eds), *Asset Price Bubbles: The Implications for Monetary, Regulatory and International Policies*, Cambridge, MA: MIT Press.

CEPREMAP (2010), Project for FP7-ICT, submitted to the European Commission, available at http://ec.europa.eu/information_society/activities/egovernment/events/fp7_events/fp7_infoday_nov_2010/presentations/mihoubi_ferhat_cepremap_proposal_for_fp7_ict_solutions_for_governance_and_policy.pdf.

Chang, Y., Kim, S.-B. and Schorfheide, F. (2011), 'Labor-Market Heterogeneity, Aggregation, and the Policy-(In)variance of DSGE Model Parameters', RCER Working Papers 566, University of Rochester – Center for Economic Research, available at http://rcer.econ.rochester.edu/RCERPAPERS/rcer_566.pdf.

Chant, J., Lai, A., Illing, M. and Daniel, F. (2003), Technical Report No. 95/Rapport technique No. 95, Essays on Financial Stability, Bank of Canada.

Chari, V.V. and Kehoe, P. (2006), 'Modern Macroeconomics in Practice: How Theory is Shaping Policy', *Journal of Economic Perspectives*, 20(4): 3–28.

Chatelain, J.B. and Ralf, K. (2012), 'The Failure of Financial Macroeconomics and What to do About It', Documents de Travail du Centre d'Economie de la Sorbonne, Version 2, 21 May, available at www.gdresymposium.eu/papers/ChatelainJB.pdf.

Chick, V. (1998), 'On Knowing One's Place: The Role of Formalism in Economics', *Economic Journal*, 108(451): 1829–1836.

Chick, V. (2002), 'Keynes's Theory of Investment and Necessary Compromise', in S.C. Dow and J. Hillard (eds), *Keynes, Uncertainty and the Global Economy: Beyond Keynes, Volume Two*, Cheltenham: Edward Elgar Publishing.

Christiano, L.J., Eichenbaum, M. and Evans, C. (2001), 'Nominal Rigidities and the Dynamic Effects of a Shock to Monetary Policy', Working Paper No. 0107, Federal Reserve Bank of Cleveland.

Clarida, R., Galí, J. and Gertler, M. (1998), 'Monetary Policy Rules and Macroeconomic Stability: Evidence and Some Theory', CEPR Discussion Papers 1908.

Clarida, R., Galí, J. and Gertler, M. (1999), 'The Science of Monetary Policy: A New-Keynesian Perspective', *Journal of Economic Literature*, 37: 1661–1707.

Cochrane, J. (2005), 'Money as Stock', *Journal of Monetary Economics*, 52: 501–528.

Cochrane, J. (2011), 'How did Paul Krugman get it so Wrong?' Institute of Economic Affairs, available at http://faculty.chicagobooth.edu/john.cochrane/research/papers/ecaf_2077.pdf.

Colander, D. (1996), *Beyond Micro Foundations: Post-Walrasian Macroeconomics*, Cambridge: Cambridge University Press.

Colander, D. (2006), *Post Walrasian Macroeconomics: Beyond the DSGE Model*, Cambridge: Cambridge University Press.

Colander, D. (2010), 'Moving Beyond the Rhetoric of Pluralism: Suggestions for an Inside the Mainstream Heterodoxy', in R.F. Garnett Jr, E. Olsen and M. Starr (eds), *Economic Pluralism*, London: Routledge.

Colander, D., Föllmer, H., Haas, A., Juselius, K., Kirman, A. and Sloth, B. (2009a), 'Mathematics, Methods and Modern Economics: The Dahlem Group on Economic Modeling', *Real-World Economic Review*, 50: 118–121.

Colander, D., Goldberg, M., Haas, A., Juselius, K., Kirman, A., Lux, T. and Sloth, B. (2009b), 'The Financial Crisis and the Systemic Failure of the Economics Profession', *Critical Review*, 21(2–3): 249–267.

Colander, D., Howitt, P., Kirman, A., Leijonhufvud, A. and Mehrling, P. (2008), 'Beyond DSGE Models: Toward an Empirically Based Macroeconomics', *American Economic Review*, 98(2): 236–240.

Cook, D. and Devereux, M. (2011), 'Sharing the Burden: Monetary and Fiscal Responses to a World Liquidity Trap', Globalization and Monetary Policy Institute Working Paper 84, Federal Reserve Bank of Dallas.

Corsetti, G. (2012), 'Has Austerity Gone too Far?" Voxeu.org, 2 April, available at www.voxeu.org/article/has-austerity-gone-too-far-new-vox-debate.

Crockett, A. (2002), Speech by Andrew Crockett, General Manager of the Bank of International Settlements, on the occasion of the Bank's Annual General Meeting in Basel on 8 July.

Crowe, C. (2010), 'Testing the Transparency Benefits of Inflation Targeting: Evidence from Private Sector Forecasts', *Journal of Monetary Economics*, 57(2): 226–232.

Davidson, P. (1986), 'The Simple Macroeconomics of a Nonergodic Monetary Economy Versus a Share Economy: Is Weitzman's Macroeconomics too Simple?' *Journal of Post Keynesian Economics*, 9(2): 212–225.

Davidson, P. (1992), 'Money: Cause or Effect? Exogenous or Endogenous?' in E.J. Nell and W. Semmler (eds), *Nicholas Kaldor and Mainstream Economics*, New York: St Martin's Press.

DeLong, B. (1995), 'The Inflation of the 1970s, Presentation Notes', University of California at Berkeley and National Bureau of Economic Research, 19 December.

DeLong, J.B. and Summers, L.H. (2012), 'Fiscal Policy in a Depressed Economy: Conference Draft', 22 March, available at http://delong.typepad.com/sdj/2012/03/delong-and-summers-fiscal-policy-in-a-depressed-economy-conference-draft.html.

De Walque, G., Pierrard, O. and Rouabah, A. (2010), 'Financial (In)Stability, Supervision and Liquidity Injections: A Dynamic General Equilibrium Approach', *Economic Journal*, 120(December): 1234–1261.

Dib, A. (2009), 'Banks, Credit Markets Frictions, and Business Cycles', Bank of Canada, Working Paper.

Dicken, P. (1998), *Global Shift: Transforming the World Economy*, 3rd edn, London: Paul Chapman.

Dickerson, A.M. (2004), 'A Politically Viable Approach to Sovereign Debt Restructuring', *Emory Law Journal*, 53: 997–1012.

Dincer, N. and Eichengreen, B. (2007), 'Central Bank Transparency: Where, Why, and with What Effects?' NBER Working Paper No. 13003, March.

Dincer, N. and Eichengreen, B. (2009), 'Central Bank Transparency: Causes, Consequences and Updates', NBER Working Paper Series No. 14791, March.

Directorate General for Internal Policies – Policy Department, Economic and Scientific Policy (2012), 'Non-Standard Policy Measures: A First Assessment', available at www.europarl.europa.eu/document/activities/cont/201204/20120419ATT43528/20120 419ATT43528EN.pdf.

Dosse, F. (1987), *L'Histoire en miettes: Des 'Annales' à la 'nouvelle histoire'*, Paris: La Découverte.

Dow, S. (2008), 'Mainstream Methodology, Financial Markets and Global Political Economy-super- 1', *Contributions to Political Economy*, 27(1): 13–29.

Dow, S.C. (1990), 'Beyond Dualism', *Cambridge Journal of Economics*, 14(2): 143–157.

Doyle, P. (2012), 'Letter to Mr Shalaan, Dean of the IMF Executive Board', 18 June, available at http://cnnibusiness.files.wordpress.com/2012/07/doyle.pdf.

Draghi, M. (2012a), Speech at the European Parliament Economic and Monetary Affairs Committee, Brussels, 31 May.

Draghi, M. (2012b), Hearing at the Committee on Economic and Monetary Affairs of the European Parliament – Introductory statement by Mario Draghi, President of the ECB Brussels, 25 April, available at www.ecb.int/press/key/date/2012/html/sp120425.en. html.

Draghi, M. (2012c), *Wall Street Journal*, 24 February.

Drucker, P. (1966), *The Effective Executive*, New York: HarperCollins.

Duhigg, C. and Kocieniewski, D. (2012), 'How Apple Sidesteps Billions in Taxes', *New York Times*, 28 April.

ECB (2001), 'Issues Related to Monetary Policy Rules', Monthly Bulletin, October 2001: 37–50.

ECB (2008) 'Financial Stability Review', June, available at www.ecb.int/pub/pdf/other/ financialstabilityreview200806en.pdf.

ECB (2011), 'The Monetary Policy of the ECB', available at www.ecb.int/pub/pdf/other/ monetarypolicy2011en.pdf.

Eggertsson, G.B. and Woodford, M. (2003), 'The Zero Bound on Interest Rates and Optimal Monetary Policy', *Brookings Papers on Economic Activity*, Economic Studies Program, Brookings Institution, 34(1): 139–235.

Eichengreen, B. (1997), 'Is Europe an Optimum Currency Area?' in B. Eichengreen, *European Monetary Unification: Theory, Practice, and Analysis*, Cambridge, MA: MIT Press.

Eichengreen, B., El-Erian, M., Fraga, A., Ito, T., Pisani-Ferry, J., Prasad, E., Rajan, R., Ramos, M., Reinhart, C., Rey, H., Rodrik, D., Rogoff, K., Shin, H.S., Velasco, A., Weder di Mauro, B. and Yu, Y. (2011), 'Rethinking Central Banking', Brookings Institution, Washington, DC.

Einstein, A. (1930), 'Religion and Science', *New York Times Magazine*, 9 November 1930, section 5, pp. 1–4.

Eijffinger, S.C.W. and Hoeberichts, M. (2000), 'Central Bank Accountability and Transparency: Theory and Some Evidence', Discussion Paper Series 1: Economic Studies 2000, 06, Deutsche Bundesbank, Research Centre.

Eijffinger, S. and Geraats, P. (2005), 'How Transparent are Central Banks?' available at www.econ.cam.ac.uk/faculty/geraats/tpindex.pdf.

Elliott, L. and Allen, K. (2011), 'Britain in Grip of Worst Ever Financial Crisis, Bank of England Governor Fears', *Guardian*, 6 October, available at www.guardian.co.uk/business/2011/oct/06/britain-financial-crisis-quantitative-easing.

Epstein, J. (2006). 'Growing Adaptive Organizations: An Agent-Based Computational Approach', in J. Epstein (ed.), *Generative Social Science: Studies in Agent-Based Computational Modeling*, Princeton, NJ: Princeton University Press.

European Commission (2013), European Economic Forecast Winter 2013, Commission Staff Working Document, Directorate-General for Economic and Financial Affairs.

European Parliament (2012), 'Non-Standard Policy Measures: A First Assessment', Policy Department (Economic and Scientific Policy), April, available at www.europarl.europa.eu/document/activities/cont/201204/20120419ATT43528/20120419ATT43528EN.pdf.

Fagiolo, G., Moneta, A. and Windrum, P. (2007), 'A Critical Guide to Empirical Validation of Agent-Based Models in Economics: Methodologies, Procedures, and Open Problems', *Computational Economics*, 30: 195–226.

Fahr, S., Motto, R., Rostagno, M., Smets, F. and Tristani, O. (2011), 'Lessons for Monetary Policy Strategies from the Recent Past', in Marek Jarocinski, Frank Smets and Christian Thimann (eds), *Approaches to Monetary Policy Revisited: Lessons from the Crisis*, Proceedings of the sixth ECB central banking conference, Frankfurt am Main: European Central Bank.

Farmer, J. and Foley D. (2009), 'The Economy Needs Agent-Based Modelling', *Nature*, 460(7256): 685–686.

Ferguson, R.W. (2005), 'Remarks by Vice Chairman Roger W. Ferguson, Jr. at a European Central Bank Colloquium in Honor of Tommaso Padoa-Schioppa', European Central Bank, Frankfurt, Germany, 27 April, available at www.federalreserve.gov/boarddocs/speeches/2005/20050427/default.htm.

Ferrell, O.C., Fraedrich, J. and Ferrell, L. (2011), *Business Ethics: Ethical Decision Making and Cases*, 8th edn, Andover, UK: Cengage Learning.

Fiedler, S. (2010), 'Phraseology in a Time of Crisis: The Language of Bank Advertisements Before and During the Financial Crisis of 2008–2010', in K. Kuiper (ed.), *Yearbook of Phraseology* 1, Berlin/New York: de Gruyter.

Financial Times (2003), Interview with Milton Friedman, 7 June.

Fisher, I. (1896), *Appreciation and Interest: A Study of the Influence of Monetary Appreciation and Depreciation on the Rate of Interest with Applications to the Bimetallic Controversy and the Theory of Interest*, New York: Macmillan.

Fisher, R. (2012), Federal Reserve Bank of Dallas President, Bloomberg, available at www.bloomberg.com/news/2012-05-01/dallas-fed-s-fisher-not-supportive-of-quantitative-easing.html.

Federal Open Market Committee (2003), Transcript of the Federal Open Market Committee (FOMC), Meeting on 28 October, available at www.federalreserve.gov/monetary-policy/files/FOMC20031028meeting.pdf.

Fontana, G. (2006), 'The "New Consensus" View of Monetary Policy: A New Wicksellian Connection?' *Intervention. European Journal of Economics and Economic Policies, Metropolis*, 3(2): 263–278.

Fontana, G. (2009), 'Whither New Consensus Economics? The Role of Government and Fiscal Policy in Modern Macroeconomics', in E. Hein, T. Niechoj and E. Stockhammer (eds), *Macroeconomic Policies on Shaky Foundations: Whither Mainstream Economics?* Marburg: Metropolis-Verlag.

Forder, J. (2000), 'Central Bank Independence and Credibility: Is There a Shred of Evidence?' *International Finance*, 3(1): 167–185.

Forder, J. (2004), '"Credibility" in Context: Do Central Bankers and Economists Interpret the Term Differently?' *Econ Journal Watch*, 1(3): 413–426.

Freeland, C. (2012), 'The Rise of Lousy and Lovely Jobs', Reuters.com, 12 April, available at http://blogs.reuters.com/chrystia-freeland/2012/04/12/the-rise-of-lousy-and-lovely-jobs/.

Friedman, B.M and Sims, C.A. (2005), Brookings Papers on Economic Activity, 2, Comments by Benjamin M. Friedman and Christopher A. Sims on 'Central Bank Transparency and the Signal Value of Prices' by Stephen Morris and Hyun Song Shin, available at www.brookings.edu/~/media/Projects/BPEA/Fall%202005/2005b_bpea_morris.PDF.

Friedman, M. and Schwartz, A.J. (1963), *A Monetary History of the United States, 1867–1960*, Princeton, NJ: Princeton University Press.

Friedman, M. (1953), *Essays in Positive Economics*, Chicago, IL: University of Chicago Press.

Friedman, M. (1968), 'The Role of Monetary Policy', *American Economic Review*, 58(1): 1–214.

Friedman, T. (2000), 'The Golden Straightjacket', in T. Friedman (ed.), *The Lexus and the Olive Tree*, New York: Anchor Books.

Fry, M., Julius, D., Mahadeva, L., Roger, S. and Sterne, G. (2000), 'Key Issues in the Choice of Monetary Policy Framework', in L. Mahadeva and G. Sterne (eds), *Monetary Policy Frameworks in a Global Context*, London: Routledge.

Fukuyama, F. (1992), *The End of History and the Last Man*, New York: The Free Press.

Galbraith, J.K. (2008), 'The Collapse of Monetarism and the Irrelevance of the New Monetary Consensus', Levy Institute, Policy Note 2008/1, May, available at www.levyinstitute.org/pubs/pn_08_1.pdf.

Galí, J. (2010), 'The New Keynesian Approach to Monetary Policy Analysis: Lessons and New Directions', in V. Wieland (ed.), *The Science and Practice of Monetary Policy Today*, Heidelberg: Springer.

Galí, J. and Gertler, M. (1999), 'Inflation Dynamics: A Structural Econometric Analysis', *Journal of Monetary Economics*, 44(2): 195–222.

Galí, J. and Gertler, M. (2007), 'Macroeconomic Modeling for Monetary Policy Evaluation', *Journal of Economic Perspectives*, 21(4): 25–46.

Geraats, P.M. (2002), 'Central Bank Transparency', *Economic Journal*, 112: 532–565.

Gerali, A., Neri, S., Sessa, L. and Signoretti, F.M. (2008), 'Credit and Banking in a DSGE Model', Bank of Italy, mimeo.

Giavazzi, F. and Giovannini, A. (2010), 'The Low-Interest-Rate Trap', Voxeu, 19 July, available at www.voxeu.org/index.php?q=node/5309.

Giddis, K. (2010), available at http://money.cnn.com/2010/08/10/news/economy/fed_decision/index.htm.

Gomme, P. (2006), 'Central Bank Credibility', Economic Commentary, Federal Reserve Bank of Cleveland, 1 August.

Goodfriend, M. and King, R. (1997), 'The New Neoclassical Synthesis and the Role of Monetary Policy', Federal Reserve Bank of Richmond, Working papers, No. 98-5, June.

Goodfriend, M. (1997), 'Monetary Policy Comes of Age: A 20th Century Odyssey', *Federal Reserve Bank of Richmond Economic Quarterly*, 83: 1–22.

Goodfriend, M. (2003), 'Interest Rate Policy should Not React Directly to Asset Prices', in W. Hunter, G. Kaufman and M. Pomerleano (eds), *Asset Price Bubbles: The Implications for Monetary Regulatory, and International Policies*, Cambridge, MA: MIT Press.

Goodfriend, M. (2005), *Federal Reserve Bank of St. Louis Review*, 87(2, Part 2): 243–262.

Goodfriend, M. (2007), 'How the World Achieved Consensus on Monetary Policy', *Journal of Economic Perspectives*, 21(4): 47–68.

Goodhart, C. (2004), 'Review of M. Woodford (2003)', *Journal of Economics*, 82: 195–200.

Goodhart, C. (2005a), 'The Future of Central Banking', Financial Markets Group, London School of Economics, Special Paper No. 162, p. 7, available at http://www2. lse.ac.uk/fmg/documents/specialPapers/2005/sp162.pdf.

Goodhart, C. (2005b), 'The Foundation of Macroeconomics: Theoretical Rigour Versus Empirical Realism', Paper presented at the Conference on the History of Macroeconomics, Louvain-la-Neuve, Belgium, January.

Grabner, M. (2002), 'Representative Agents and the Micro-Foundations of Macroeconomics', available at www.econ.ucdavis.edu/graduate/mgrabner/research/microfoundations.pdf.

Greeley, B. (2012), 'Are Economics PhDs Learning the Wrong Thing?' *Business Week*, 1 June.

Greenaway, D. and Shaw, G.K (1988), *Macroeconomics: Theory and Policy in the U.K.*, 2nd edn, Oxford: Basil Blackwell.

Greenspan, A. (2000), The Federal Reserve's report on monetary policy, Before the Committee on Banking, Housing, and Urban Affairs, US Senate, 20 July, available at www.federalreserve.gov/boarddocs/hh/2000/July/testimony.htm.

Greenspan, A. (2004), Testimony of Chairman Alan Greenspan, 'The Economic Outlook', before the Joint Economic Committee, US Senate, 21 April, available at www.federalreserve.gov/boarddocs/testimony/2004/20040421/default.htm.

Greider, W. (1987), *Secrets of the Temple: How the Federal Reserve Runs the Country*. New York: Simon & Schuster.

Gros, D. (2011), 'Can Austerity be Self-Defeating?', Voxeu, 29 November.

Group of Seven (1995), 'Statement of the Group of Seven Finance Ministers and Central Bank Governors', 7 October, available at www.g8.utoronto.ca/finance/fm951007.htm.

Guttmann, R. (2008), 'Central Banking in a Debt-Deflation Crisis: A Comparison of the Fed and ECB', Hofstra University, New York; CEPN, Université Paris 13, available at www.univ-paris13.fr/cepn/IMG/pdf/texte_guttmann_210308.pdf.

Hansen, L.P. and Sargent, T.J. (2008), *Robustness*. Princeton, NJ: Princeton University Press.

Hartley, J.E. (1997), *The Representative Agent in Macroeconomics*, London and New York: Routledge.

Harvey, D. (2005), *A Brief History of Neoliberalism*, Oxford: Oxford University Press.

Hayek, F.A. (1975 [1929]), *The 'Paradox of Saving', Profits, Interest, and Investment*, Clifton, NJ: Augustus M. Kelley.

Hennig, C. (2010), 'Mathematical Models and Reality: A Constructivist Perspective', *Foundations of Science*, 15: 29–48.

Holland, J. and Miller, J.H. (1991), 'Artificial Adaptive Agents in Economic Theory', *American Economic Review*, 81(2): 365–370.

Hommes, C. (2008), 'Interacting Agents in Finance', in *The New Palgrave Dictionary of Economics*, Basingstoke, UK: Palgrave Macmillan.

Hongcai, X. (2012), 'Reform of Monetary System', *China Daily*, 16 June, available at www.chinadailyapac.com.

Howells, P. (2007), 'The Demand for Endogenous Money: A Lesson in Institutional Change', Discussion Papers 0701, Department of Economics, University of the West of England.

Hurson, T. (2008) *Think Better: An Innovator's Guide to Productive Thinking*, New York: McGraw-Hill.

Iacoviello, M. (2005), 'House Prices, Borrowing Constraints and Monetary Policy in the Business Cycle', *American Economic Review*, 95(3): 739–764.

IMF (2009), 'World Economic Outlook: Crisis and Recovery', *World Economic and Financial Surveys*, April.

IMF (2012a), 'Transparency in Monetary and Financial Policies', International Monetary Fund Factsheet, available at www.imf.org/external/np/exr/facts/pdf/mtransp.pdf.

IMF (2012b), 'World Economic Outlook: Growth Resuming, Dangers Remain', available at www.imf.org/external/pubs/ft/weo/2012/01/pdf/text.pdf.

IMF (2012c), 'World Economic Outlook Update: Global Recovery Stalls, Downside Risks Intensify', 24 January, available at www.imf.org/external/pubs/ft/weo/2012/update/01/.

IMF Factsheet (2013), 'Transparency in Monetary and Financial Policies', 15 March, available at www.imf.org/external/np/exr/facts/mtransp.htm.

International Labour Organization (International Institute for Labour Studies) (2012), 'World of Work Report 2012: Better Jobs for a Better Economy', International Institute for Labour Studies, available at http://www.ilo.org/wcmsp5/groups/public/---dgreports/---dcomm/---publ/documents/publication/wcms_179453.pdf.

ISDA (2010), Market Review of OTC Derivative Bilateral Collateralization Practices (2.0), ISDA Collateral Steering Committee, 1 March.

ISDA Collateral Steering Committee (2010), 'Market Review of OTC Derivative Bilateral Collateralization Practices', (2.0), 1 March, available at www.isda.org/c_and_a/pdf/Collateral-Market-Review.pdf.

Issing, O. (2005), 'Communication, Transparency, Accountability: Monetary Policy in the Twenty First Century', *Federal Reserve Bank of Saint Louis Review*, 87: 65–83.

Jaimovich, N. and Siu, H.E. (2012), 'The Trend is the Cycle: Job Polarization and Jobless Recoveries', 31 March, available at http://faculty.arts.ubc.ca/hsiu/research/polar20120331.pdf.

Jeanne, O. (2011), Lecture given by Professor Olivier Jeanne, Johns Hopkins University, Baltimore, Colloque international 'Face aux déséquilibres mondiaux: quelle régulation?' Banque de France, March.

Joffe, J. (2011), 'The Euro Widens the Culture Gap', *New York Times*, 12 September, available at www.nytimes.com/roomfordebate/2011/09/12/will-culture-clash-splinter-the-european-union/the-euro-widened-the-cu.

Johnson, H.G. (1972), 'The Monetary Approach to the Balance-of-Payments-Theory', *Journal of Financial and Quantitative Analysis*, 7(2), reprinted in Frenkel e Johnson (1976).

Jones, S. (2012), 'Hedge Funds Bet Against Eurozone', *Financial Times*, 28 April, available at www.ft.com/intl/cms/s/0/4bb383c4-9068-11e1-8cdc-00144feab49a.html#axzz226hnPdya

Judd, K.L. (2006), 'Computationally Intensive Analyses in Economics', in L. Tesfatsion and K.L. Judd (eds), *Handbook of Computational Economics*, vol. 2, Amsterdam: North Holland.

Kahn, G.A. (2007), 'Communicating a Policy Path: The Next Frontier in Central Bank Transparency', Fed Kansas City, *Economic Review*, 1: 25–51.

Kaldor, N. (1934), 'The Determinateness of Static Equilibrium', *Review of Economic Studies*, February.

Kaldor, N. and Trevithick, J. (1981), 'A Keynesian Perspective on Money', *Lloyds Bank Review*, 139: 1–19.

Kay, J. (2011), 'The Map is Not the Territory: An Essay on the State of Economics', Institute for New Economic Thinking, 26 September.

Keynes, J.M. (1921), *A Treatise on Probability*, 1st edn, London: Macmillan.

Keynes, J.M. (1930a), *A Treatise on Money*, 2 vols, New York: Harcourt Brace.

Keynes, J.M. (1930b), 'Economic Possibilities for Our Grand-Children', in *Essays in Persuasion*, London: Macmillan Press Ltd.

Keynes, J.M. (1931), 'The Future', Essays in Persuasion, Ch. 5, CWJMK, IX, pp. 329–331.

Keynes, J.M. (1936), *The General Theory of Employment, Interest and Money*, London: Macmillan (reprinted 2007).

Keynes, J.M. (1937), 'The General Theory of Employment', *Quarterly Journal of Economics*, 51(2): 209–223.

Keynes, J.M (1973[1921]), A Treatise on Probability in *The Collected Writings of John Maynard Keynes* (CWJMK), vol. VIII, London: Macmillan.

King, M. (2002), 'No Money, No Inflation: The Role of Money in the Economy', *Bank of England Quarterly Bulletin*, Summer: 162–77.

King, M. (2005), 'Monetary Policy: Practice Ahead of Theory (Mais Lecture 2005)', Lecture delivered on 17 May 2005 at the Cass Business School, City, available at www.bankofengland.co.uk/ publications/speeches/2005/speech245.pdf.

King, M. (2008), 'Microfoundations', available at www.boeckler.de/pdf/v_2008_10_31_king.pdf.

King, L., Kitson, M., Konzelmann, S. and Wilkinson, F. (2012), 'Austerity: Making the Same Mistakes Again – Or is This Time Different?' Special Issue of the *Cambridge Journal of Economics*, 36(1): 1–15.

Kirman, A.P. (1992), 'Whom or What does the Representative Individual Represent?' *Journal of Economic Perspectives*, 6(2): 117–136.

Klosa, T. and Nooteboom, B. (2001), 'Agent-based Computational Transaction Cost Economics', *Journal of Economic Dynamics and Control*, 25(3–4): 503–552.

Kocherlakota, N. (2010), 'Inside the FOMC', Speech by The President of The Federal Reserve Bank of Minneapolis, Marquette, Michigan, 17 August.

Koo, R. (2008), *The Holy Grail of Macroeconomics: Lessons from Japan's Great Recession*, Singapore: John Wiley & Sons.

Krueger, A.O. (2002), 'A New Approach to Sovereign Debt Restructuring', International Monetary Fund, Washington, DC, April.

Krugman, P. (1998), 'It's Baaack! Japan's Slump and the Return of the Liquidity Trap', *Brookings Papers on Economic Activity*, 2: 137–187.

Krugman, P. (1999), 'Japan Heads for the Edge', *Financial Times*, 20 January.

Krugman, P. (2000), 'How Complicated Does the Model Have to Be?' *Oxford Review of Economic Policy*, 16(4): 33–42.

Krugman, P. (2007), 'Who was Milton Friedman?' *New York Review of Books*, 15 February, available at www.nybooks.com/articles/archives/2007/feb/15/who-was-milton-friedman/?pagination=false.

Krugman, P. (2009), 'How Did Economists Get It So Wrong?' *New York Times Magazine*, 2 September.

Krugman, P. (2010), 'How Much of the World is in a Liquidity Trap?' *New York Times*, 17 March.

Krugman, P. (2011), 'Keynes was Right', *New York Times*, 29 December.

Krugman, P. (2012a), 'Europe's Economic Suicide', *New York Times*, 15 April.

Krugman, P. (2012b), 'Death of a Fairy Tale', *New York Times*, 26 April, available at www.nytimes.com/2012/04/27/opinion/krugman-death-of-a-fairy-tale.html?partner=rssnyt&emc=rss.

Krugman, P. (2012c), 'The Austerity Agenda', *New York Times*, 31 May.

Krugman, P. and Wells, R. (2010), 'The Slump Goes On: Why?' *New York Review of Books*, 57(14), 30 September.

Kuhn, T.S. (1962), *The Structure of Scientific Revolutions*, Chicago, IL: University of Chicago Press .

Kydland, F.E. and Prescott, E.C. (1977), 'Rules Rather than Discretion: The Inconsistency of Optimal Plans', *Journal of Political Economy*, 85(3), 473–492.

Kydland, F.E. and Prescott, E.C. (1982), 'Time to Build and Aggregate Fluctuations', *Econometrica*, 50(6): 1345–1370.

Laidler, D. (1982), *Monetarist Perspectives*, Cambridge, MA: Harvard University Press.

Laidler, D. (1987), 'Bullionist Controversy', in J. Eatwell, M. Milgate and P. Newman (eds), *The New Palgrave: A Dictionary of Economics*, London: Macmillan.

Laidler, D. (1997), 'Inflation Control and Monetary Policy Rules', in Iwao Kuroda (ed.), *Towards More: Effective Monetary Policy*, New York: Macmillan Press.

Laidler, D. (2004), 'Woodford and Wicksell on Interest and Prices: The Place of the Pure Credit Economy in the Theory of Monetary Policy', Notes for a panel discussion held at the History of Economics Society Meeting in Toronto, 25–28 June.

Laidler, D. (2006), 'Woodford and Wicksell on Interest and Prices: The Place of the Pure Credit Economy in the Theory of Monetary Policy', *Journal of the History of Economic Thought*, 28(02): 151–159.

Laidler, D. (2011), 'The End of the History of Economic Thought and its Future', After-dinner speech, delivered in mid-Bosphorus on 21 May 2011, in acceptance of honorary membership in the European Society for the History of Economic Thought at the Society's annual conference in Istanbul.

Landon, T. Jr (2012), 'Spain is Still Awaiting the Payoff from Austerity', *New York Times*, 28 April.

Larrouturou, P. (2012), 'We Do Not Want to Die in the Rubbles of Neoliberalism', *Le Monde*, 30 April, available at www.lemonde.fr/idees/article/2012/04/30/nous-ne-voulons-pas-mourir-dans-les-decombres-du-neoliberalisme_1693201_3232.html.

Lavoie, M. (1985), 'Credit and Money: The Dynamic Circuit, Overdraft Economics and Post Keynesian Economics', in Marc Jarsulic (ed.), *Money and Macro Policy*, Boston, MA: Kluwer-Nijhoff.

Lavoie, M. (1996), 'Horizontalism, Structuralism, Liquidity Preference and the Principle of Increasing Risk', *Scottish Journal of Political Economy*, Scottish Economic Society, 43(3): 275–300.

Lavoie, M. (2004), 'The New Consensus on Monetary Policy Seen from a Post-Keynesian Perspective', in M. Lavoie and M. Seccareccia (eds) *Central Banking in the Modern World: Alternative Perspectives*, Cheltenham: Edward Elgar.

Lavoie, M. (2005), 'Monetary Base Endogeneity and the New Procedures of the Asset-Based Canadian and American Monetary Systems', *Journal of Post Keynesian Economics*, 27(4): 689–709.

Lavoie, M. (2006a), 'Do Heterodox Theories have Anything in Common? A Post-Keynesian Point of View', *Intervention – Zeitschrift für Ökonomie Journal of Economics*, 3(1): 87–112.

Lavoie, M. (2006b), 'A Post-Keynesian Amendment to the New Consensus on Monetary Policy', *Metroeconomica*, 57(2): 165–192.

Lavoie, M. (2007), 'Endogenous Money: Accomodationist', in P. Arestis and M. Sawyer (eds), *A Handbook of Alternative Monetary Economics*, Northampton, MA: Edward Elgar.

Lavoie, M. and Seccareccia, M. (eds) (2004), *Central Banking in the Modern World: Alternative Perspectives*, Cheltenham: Edward Elgar.

Lawson, N. (1981), Text of a speech given by The Rt Hon Nigel Lawson, MP, Financial Secretary to the Treasury, to the Zurich Society of Economics at the Kongresshaus, Zurich, Wednesday 14 January 1981, published by the Conservative Political Centre.

Lawson, T. (1997), *Economics and Reality*, London: Routledge.

Lawson, T. (2006), 'The Nature of Heterodox Economics', *Cambridge Journal of Economics*, 30(4): 483–505.

Lawson, T. (2009), 'The Current Economic Crisis: Its Nature and the Course of Academic Economics', *Cambridge Journal of Economics*, 33(4): 759–777.

Lawson, T. (2012), 'Mathematical Modelling and Ideology in the Economics Academy: Competing Explanations of the Fallings of the Modern Discipline', *Economic Thought*, 1(1): 3–22.

Layard, R. (1986), *How to beat unemployment*, Oxford: Oxford University Press.

Le Bourva, J. (1962), 'Création de la monnaie et multiplicateur du crédit', *Revue économique*, 23: 243–282.

Le Heron, E. (2003), 'A New Consensus on Monetary Policy?' *Brazilian Journal of Political Economy*, 23(4): 3–27.

Le Heron, E. (2005), 'The Monetary Policy of the ECB and the Fed: Credibility versus Confidence, a Comparative Approach', with E. Carré, in Philip Arestis, Jesus Ferreiro and Felipe Serrano (eds), *Financial Developments in National and International Markets*, London: Palgrave-Macmillan.

Lee, F. (2008), 'Heterodox economics', *The New Palgrave Dictionary of Economics*, 2nd edn, vol. 4, London: Palgrave Macmillan.

Leeper, E.M. and Walker, T.B. (2011), 'Perceptions and Misperceptions of Fiscal Inflation', BIS Working Papers 364, Bank for International Settlements, available at www.bis.org/events/conf110623/leeper.pdf.

Les Echos (2010), 'Un effort sur les recettes fiscales et sociales de l'ordre de 15 milliards d'euros est nécessaire', Gilles Carrez, general rapporteur to the Parliament for the budget, interviewed by Etienne Lefebvre and Lucie Robequain, 5 July, available at http://archives.lesechos.fr/archives/2010/LesEchos/20712-14-ECH.htm.

Leutbecher, M. and Palmer, T.N. (2008), 'Ensemble Forecasting', *Journal of Computational Physics*, 227(7): 3515–3539.

Lucas, R. and Rapping, L. (1969), 'Real Wages, Employment and Inflation', *Journal of Political Economy*, 77(5): 721–754.

Lucas, R.E. Jr (1973), 'Some International Evidence on Output-Inflation Trade-offs', *American Economic Review*, 63, pp. 326–334.

Lucas, R.E. Jr (1976), 'Econometric Policy Evaluation: A Critique', in K. Brunner and A. Meltzer (eds), *The Phillips Curve and Labor Markets*, Carnegie-Rochester Conference Series on Public Policy 1, New York: American Elsevier.

Lucas, R.E. Jr (1980), 'Two Illustrations of the Quantity Theory of Money', *American Economic Review*, 70(5): 1005–1014.

Lucas, R.E. Jr (2003), 'Macroeconomic Priorities', 2003 Presidential Address to the American Economic Association, 10 January.

Lucas, R.E. Jr (2009), 'In Defence of the Dismal Science', *The Economist*, 6 August, available at www.economist.com/node/14165405.

Lybek, T. (2004), 'Central Bank Autonomy, Accountability, and Governance: Conceptual Framework prepared by Tonny Lybek', Write-up for Presentation at LEG 2004 Seminar, 18 August, available at https://www.imf.org/external/np/leg/sem/2004/cdmfl/eng/lybek.pdf.

McCallum, B. (1999), 'Recent Developments in Monetary Policy Analysis: The Roles of Theory and Evidence', *Journal of Economic Methodology*, 6(2): 171–198.

McCallum, B. (2001), 'Monetary Policy Analysis in Models Without Money', *Review*, Federal Reserve Bank of St Louis, July: 145–164.

McCallum, B. (2005), 'What Is the Proper Perspective for Monetary Policy Optimality?' *Monetary and Economic Studies*, Institute for Monetary and Economic Studies, Bank of Japan, 23(S1): 13–24.

McCallum, B.T. (2010), 'Michael Woodford's Contributions to Monetary Economics', in Volker Wieland (ed.), *The Science and Practice of Monetary Policy Today: The Deutsche Bank Prize in Financial Economics 2007*, Heidelberg: Springer.

McCloskey, D.N. (1985), *The Rhetoric of Economics*, Madison, WI: University of Wisconsin Press.

McCloskey, D.N. (1990), *On Narrative: If You're So Smart: The Narrative of Economic Expertise*, Chicago, IL: University of Chicago Press.

McHoul, A.W. and Grace, W. (2002), *A Foucault Primer: Discourse, Power, and the Subject*, London: Routledge.

Mckee, M. (2009), 'Taylor Says Fed gets Rule Right, Goldman Doesn't (Update1)', Bloomberg, 24 July, available at www.bloomberg.com/apps/news?pid=newsarchive&sid=aZ2uJpI.Noj4.

McKinnon, R. (2000), 'Mundell, the Euro and Optimum Currency Areas', Stanford University Working Papers.

Mackintosh, J. (2010), 'The ECB May Yet Turn to QE', *Financial Times*, 12 July.

Mäki, U. (2002), *Fact and Fiction in Economics: Models, Realism and Social Construction*, Cambridge: Cambridge University Press.

Mankiw, N. Gregory (2006), 'The Macroeconomist as Scientist and Engineer', *Journal of Economic Perspectives*, 20(4): 29–46, available at www.economics.harvard.edu/files/faculty/40_Macroeconomist_as_Scientist.pdf.

Meade, J.E. (1985), 'Wage-Fixing Revisited', a revised and expanded text of the fourth Robbins lecture delivered at the University of Stirling, October 1984.

Meese, R.A. and Rogoff, K. (1983a), 'Empirical Exchange Rate Models of the Seventies', *Journal of International Economics*, 14(1–2): 3–24.

Meese, R.A. and Rogoff, K. (1983b), 'The Out-of-Sample Failure of Empirical Exchange Rate Models: Sampling Error or Misspecification?' in J.A. Frenkel (ed.), *Exchange Rates and International Macroeconomics*, Chicago, IL: Chicago University Press.

Meyer, L.H. (2001), 'Does Money Matter?' Remarks by Governor Laurence H. Meyer, the 2001 Homer Jones Memorial Lecture, Washington University, St Louis, Missouri, 28 March, available at www.federalreserve.gov/boarddocs/speeches/2001/20010328/default.htm.

Middleton, P. (1989), 'Economic Policy Formulation in the Treasury in the Post-War Period', *National Institute Economic Review*, February: 46–51.

Miller, M. and Skidelsky, R. (2012), 'How Keynes Would Solve the Eurozone Crisis', *Financial Times*, 15 May, available at www.ft.com/cms/s/2/55d094cc-9e74-11e1-a24e-00144feabdc0.html#axzz2LhV62Dtp.

Mishkin, F. (2000), 'What Should Central Banks Do?', Review, Federal Reserve Bank of St. Louis, November: 1–14.

Mishkin, F. (2004), *The Economics of Money, Banking and Financial Markets*, 7th edn, Boston, MA: Pearson-Addison Wesley.

Mishkin, F. (2007), Keynote Speech: 'Will Monetary Policy Become More of a Science?' at the CFS Symposium 'The Theory and Practice of Monetary Policy Today', Frankfurt am Main, 4 October, Deutsche Bank Prize in Financial Economics, available at www.ifk-cfs.de/fileadmin/images/10_db_prize/Newsletter_Extract_02-07.pdf.

Misir, T.L. (2011), 'The Struggle Against Neoliberal Austerity and the Survival of the European Project', EU Centre in Singapore, Working Paper No. 4, November, available at www.eucentre.sg/articles/336/downloads/WP04.TheStruggleAgainstNeoliberalAusterityandtheSurvivaloftheEuropeanProject.pdf.

Molodtsova, T., Nikolsko-Rzhevskyy, A. and Papel, D.H. (2008), 'Taylor Rules with Real-Time Data: A tale of Two Countries and One Exchange Rate', *Journal of Monetary Economics*, 55: 63–79.

Monetary Policy Committee (1999), 'The Transmission Mechanism of Monetary Policy', Report by Bank of England staff under the guidance of the Monetary Policy Committee in response to suggestions by the Treasury Committee of the House of Commons and the House of Lords Select Committee on the Monetary Policy Committee of the Bank of England, available at www.bankofengland.co.uk/publications/Documents/other/monetary/montrans.pdf.

Moore, B. (1988), *Horizontalists and Verticalists: The Macroeconomics Of Credit Money*, Cambridge: Cambridge University Press.

Moore, B.J. (2001), 'Some reflections on endogenous money', in L.P. Rochon and M. Vernengo (eds), *Credit, Interest Rates and the Open Economy: Essays on Horizontalism*, Cheltenham, UK and Northampton, MA, USA: Edward Elgar.

Moore, B. (2003), 'L'endogénéité de l'offre de monnaie: fixe t-on le 'prix' ou la 'quantité' des réserves?' in P. Piegay and L-P. Rochon (eds), *Théories Monétaires Post Keynésiennes*, Paris: Economica.

Morgan, M.S. and Morrison, M. (1999), 'Models as Mediators', in M.S. Morgan and M. Morrison (eds), *Perspectives on Natural and Social Science*, Cambridge: Cambridge University Press.

Morris, S. and Shin, H.S. (2002), 'Social Value of Public Information', *American Economic Review*, 92(5): 1521–1534.

Morris, S. and Shin, H.S. (2005), 'Central Bank Transparency and the Signal Value of Prices', *Brookings Papers on Economic Activity*, Economic Studies Program, Brookings Institution, 36(2): 1–66.

Mundell, R. (1961), 'A Theory of Optimum Currency Areas', *American Economic Review*, 51(4): 657–665.

Mundell, R. (1968), 'A Theory of Optimum Currency Areas', in R. Mundel, *International Economics*, New York: Macmillan.

Mundell, R. (1973a), 'Uncommon Arguments for Common Currencies', in H.G. Johnson and A.K. Swoboda (eds), *The Economics of Common Currencies*, London: Allen & Unwin.

Mundell, R.A. (1973b), 'A Plan for a European Currency', in H.G. Johnson and A.K. Swoboda (eds), *The Economics of Common Currencies*, London: Allen and Unwin.

Myers, M. (2012), 'Economic Review', Office for National Statistics, 25 April, available at www.ons.gov.uk/ons/dcp171766_263951.pdf.

Nersisyan, Y. (2006–2007), 'Review of Central Banking in the Modern Word: Alternative Perspectives, edited by M. Lavoie and M. Seccareccia (2005)', in *Oeconomicus*, VIII.

Neville, F. (2008), 'Real Business Cycles', in William A. Darity (ed.), *International Encyclopedia of Social Sciences*, 2nd edn, New York: Macmillan.

Nightingale, S., Ossolinski, C. and Zurawski, A. (2010), 'Activity in Global Foreign Exchange Markets', *RBA Bulletin*, December: 45–51.

Nyriadi, J. (2012), 'Dr Bernanke Can't Save Us', Market Watch, *Wall Street Journal*, 12 July, available at www.marketwatch.com/story/dr-bernanke-cant-save-us-2012-07-12.

Obama, B. (2012), President Obama press conference at the White House, 8 June.

Obstfeld, M. and Rogoff, K. (2002), 'Global Implications of Self-Oriented National Monetary Rules', *Quarterly Journal of Economics*, 117, May: 503–536.

Oeffner, M. (2009), 'Agent-based Keynesian Macroeconomics', PhD thesis, Faculty of Economics, University of Würzburg, available at http://dx.doi.org/10.2139/ssrn.1618445.

Orphanides, A. (2007), 'Taylor Rules', Federal Reserve Board, Finance and Economics, Discussion Series No. 2007-18.

Orphanides, A. (2010a), 'Monetary Policy Lessons from the Crisis', Working Papers 2010–1, Central Bank of Cyprus.

Orphanides, A. (2010b), 'Reflections on Inflation Targeting', in D. Cobham, Ø. Eitrheim, S. Gerlach and J.F. Qvigstad (eds), *Twenty Years of Inflation Targeting*, Cambridge: Cambridge University Press.

Orphanides, A. and Wieland, V. (1998), 'Price Stability and Monetary Policy Effectiveness when Nominal Interest Rates are Bounded at Zero', Finance and Economics Discussion Series 1998–35, Board of Governors of the Federal Reserve System.

Page, S. (2008), 'Agent-Based Models', in S.N. Durlauf and L.E. Blume (eds), *The New Palgrave Dictionary of Economics*, 2nd edn, New York: Palgrave Macmillan.

Parguez, A, (1986), 'Au cœur du circuit ou quelques réponses aux énigmes du circuit', in 'Economics et Sociétés', ISMEA, Série Monnaie et Production, no. 3.

Pepper, G.T. and Oliver, M.J. (2001), *Monetarism Under Thatcher: Lessons for the Future*, Cheltenham: Edward Elgar.

Phelps, E.S. (1967), 'Phillips Curves, Expectations of Inflation, and Optimal Unemployment over Time', *Economica*, 34(139): 254–281.

Phillips, A.W. (1958), 'The Relation between Unemployment and the Rate of Change of Money Wage Rates in the United Kingdom, 1861–1957', *Economica*, 25(100): 283–299.

Pigou, A.C. (1943), 'The Classical Stationary State', *Economic Journal*, 53, December: 343–351.

Pilkington, M. (2008), 'Conceptualizing the Shadow Financial System in a Stock-Flow Consistent Framework', *Global Business and Economics Anthology*, II: 268–279.

Pilkington, M. (2009), 'The Financialization of Modern Economies in Monetary Circuit Theory', in Jean-François Ponsot and Sergio Rossi (eds), *The Political Economy of Monetary Circuits: Tradition and Change in Post-Keynesian Economics*, New York: Palgrave Macmillan.

Pilkington, M. (2010), 'Transnational Corporations in a Global Monetary Theory of Production: A World-Systems Perspective', *Journal of World-Systems Research*, XVI(2): 246–265.

Pilkington, M. (2011a), 'Real Business Cycle in Modern Dictionaries', in Daniele Besomi (ed.), *Crises and Cycles in Economic Dictionaries and Encyclopedias*, New York: Routledge.

Pilkington, M. (2011b), 'The Sovereign Debt Crisis: A Transdisciplinary Approach', *International Journal of Pluralism and Economics Education*, 2(4): 369–397.

Pilkington, M. (2012a), 'The French Evolution: France and the Europeanisation of Higher Education', *Journal of Higher Education Policy and Management*, 34(1): 39–50.

Pilkington, M. (2012b), 'Economics as a Polymorphic Discursive Construct: Heterodoxy and Pluralism', *On the Horizon*, 20(3): 239–252.

Plosser, C.I. (1989), 'Understanding Real Business Cycles', *Journal of Economic Perspectives*, American Economic Association, 3(3): 51–77.

Polanyi, K. (1957). *The Great Transformation*, Boston, MA: Beacon Press.

Pounds, W.F. (1965), 'The Process of Problem Finding', Working Paper No. 145-65, Sloan School of Management, MIT, available at http://18.7.29.232/bitstream/handle/1721.1/48769/processofproblem00poun.pdf?sequence=1.

Pricewaterhouse Coopers (2012a), 'Understanding [And Coming to Terms With] "the New Normal"', Final Report PricewaterhouseCoopers Dinner, 21 February, available at www.ceforum.org/upload2/Final_Report_PwC_Dinner_21_Feb_12.pdf.

Pricewaterhouse Coopers (2012b), 'Managing Charities in the New Normal: A Perfect Storm?' Fifth 'Managing in a Downturn' survey report produced by PwC, Charity Finance Group and the Institute of Fundraising.

Quiggin, J. (2010), *Zombie Economics: How Dead Ideas Still Walk Among Us*, Princeton, NJ: Princeton University Press.

Ramsey, F.P. (1922), 'Mr. Keynes on Probability', *Cambridge Magazine*, XI(1): 3–5. Reprinted in *British Journal of the Philosophy of Science*, 40, 219–222 (1989).

Ramsey, F.P. (1926), 'Truth and Probability', in D.H. Mellor (ed.), *Foundations: Essays in Philosophy, Logic, Mathematics, and Economics*, London: Routledge & Kegan Paul (1978).

Rochon, L-P (2001), 'Horizontalism: Setting the record straight' in L.P. Rochon and M. Vernengo (eds), *Credit, Interest Rates and the Open Economy: Essays on Horizontalism*, Cheltenham, UK and Northampton, MA, USA: Edward Elgar.

Rogers, S. (2010), 'Inflation Targeting at 20: Achievements and Challenges', in D. Cobham, Ø. Eitrheim, S. Gerlach and J. Qvigstad (eds), *Twenty Years of Inflation Targeting: Lessons Learned and Future Prospects*, Cambridge: Cambridge University Press.

Romer, C.D. (1992), 'What Ended the Great Depression?' *Journal of Economic History*, 52(4): 757–784.

Romer, D.H. (2000), 'Keynesian Macroeconomics without the LM Curve', *Journal of Economic Perspectives*, 14(2): 149–169.

Roosevelt 2012 Collective (2012), available at www.roosevelt2012.fr/.

Rorty, R. (1987), 'Thugs and Theorists', *Political Theory*, 15(4): 564–580.

Rorty, R. (2000a), 'Response to Davidson', in R. Brandom (ed.), *Rorty and His Critics*, Oxford: Blackwell.

Rorty, R. (2000b), 'Response to Brandom', in R. Brandom (ed.), *Rorty and His Critics*, Oxford: Blackwell.

Rotenberg, J. and Woodford, M. (1997), 'An Optimization-Based Econometric Framework for the Evaluation of Monetary Policy', NBER Macroeconomics Annual.

Ryan-Collins, J., Greenham, T., Werner, R. and Jackson, A. (2012), *Where Does Money Come From? A Guide to the UK Monetary and Banking System*, 2nd edn, London: New Economics Foundation.

Sack, B. (2009), 'The Fed's Expanded Balance Sheet', Brian Sack, Executive Vice President, Federal Reserve Bank of New York, December.

Sargent, T.J. (1983), 'The Ends of Four Big Inflations', in Robert E. Hall (ed.), *Inflation: Causes and Effects*, Chicago, IL: University of Chicago Press, for the NBER.

Sargent, T. (1986), 'Government Debt and Taxes', Working Papers 293, Federal Reserve Bank of Minneapolis.

Say, J.-B. (1971), *A Treatise on Political Economy*, New York: Augustus M. Kelley.

Sbordone, A.M., Tambalotti, A., Rao, K. and Walsh, K. (2010), 'Policy Analysis Using DSGE Models: An Introduction', Federal Reserve Bank of New York Economic Review, October, available at www.newyorkfed.org/research/epr/10v16n2/1010sbor.pdf.

Schmidt-Hebel, K. (2010), 'Inflation Targeting and Emerging Market Economies', in D. Cobham, Ø. Eitrheim, S. Gerlach and J. Qvigstad (eds), *Twenty Years of Inflation Targeting: Lessons Learned and Future Prospects*, Cambridge: Cambridge University Press.

Seppecher, P. (Last update: July 2013), JAMEL software available at http://p.seppecher.free.fr/jamel/javadoc/index.html.

Setterfield, M. (2004), 'Central Banking, Stability and Macroeconomic Outcomes: A Comparative Analysis of New Consensus and Post-Keynesian Monetary Macroeconomics', in M. Lavoie and M. Seccareccia (eds), *Central Banking in the Modern World: Alternative Perspectives*, Cheltenham: Edward Elgar.

Setterfield, M. (2008), 'Path Dependency, Hysteresis and Macrodynamics', Working Paper, October.

Shitatsuka, S. (2009), 'Size and Composition of the Central Bank Balance Sheet: Revisiting Japan's Experience of the Quantitative Easing Policy', IMES Discussion Paper Series, E 25, November.

Shulman, David (1992), 'The Goldilocks Economy: Keeping the Bears at Bay', Salomon Brothers strategy paper.

Sims, C.A. (2006), 'Rational Inattention: Beyond the Linear Quadratic Case', *American Economic Review*, 96(2): 158–163.

Smets, F. (2000), 'What Horizon for Price Stability', Working Paper Series 24, European Central Bank.

Smets, F. and Wouters, R. (2003), 'An Estimated Dynamic Stochastic General Equilibrium Model of the Euro Area', *Journal of the European Economic Association*, 1(5): 1123–1175.

Smets, F. and Wouters, R. (2007), 'Shocks and Frictions in US Business Cycles: A Bayesian DSGE Approach', *American Economic Review*, American Economic Association, 97(3): 586–606.

Smith, R.P. (2009), 'Real-Financial Interactions in Macro-Finance Models', *Quantitative and Qualitative Analysis in Social Sciences*, 3(1): 1–20, available at www.qass.org.uk/2009/Vol_1/paper1.pdf.

Solow, R. (2008), 'Reply to Chari and Kehoe', *Journal of Economic Perspectives*, 22(1): 243–246.

Solow, R. (2011), Robert Solow, Interviewed by Viv Davies, 1 April 2011, available at www.voxeu.org/index.php?q=node/6310.

Somer, J. (2012), 'The Calming Effect of Central Banks', *New York Times*, 28 April.

Soros, G. (1997), 'The Capitalist Threat', *Atlantic Monthly*, February.

Soros, G. (2008), *Reflexivity in Financial Markets, The New Paradigm for Financial Markets: The Credit Crisis of 2008 and What it Means* (1st ed.), New York: Public Affairs.

Spiegel, P. (2012), 'Barroso Pushes EU Banking Union', *Financial Times*, 12 June.

Stark, J. (2007), Speech by Jürgen Stark, Member of the Executive Board of the ECB

Conference on inflation targeting, Magyar Nemzeti Bank (MNB), Budapest, 19 January, available at www.ecb.int/press/key/date/2007/html/sp070119.en.html.

Stark, J. (2010), 'The New Normal', Intervention by Jürgen Stark, Member of the Executive Board of the ECB, at the 13th Euro Finance Week, Frankfurt, 16 November, available at www.ecb.int/press/key/date/2010/html/sp101116_1.en.html.

Stiglitz, J.E. (2011), 'Rethinking Macroeconomics: What Failed, And How To Repair It', *Journal of the European Economic Association*, 9(4): 591–645.

Stock, James, and Watson, Mark W. (2002), 'Has the Business Cycle Changed and Why?' *NBER Macroeconomics Annual 2002*, Cambridge, MA: MIT Press.

Strachman, E. and Fucidji, J.R. (2010), 'The Current Financial and Economic Crisis: Empirical and Methodological Issues', MPRA Paper 27130, available at http://mpra.ub.uni-muenchen.de/27130/1/MPRA_paper_27130.pdf.

Stuckler, D., Kentikelenis, A., Papanicolas, I., Karanikolos, M., Basu, S. and McKee, M. (2011), 'Health Effects of Financial Crisis: Omens of a Greek Tragedy', *Lancet*, 378(9801): 1457–1458, 22 October, available at www.thelancet.com/journals/lancet/article/PIIS0140-6736%2811%2961556-0/fulltext.

Sugden, R. (2000), 'Credible Worlds: The Status of Theoretical Models in Economics', *Journal of Economic Methodology*, 7(1): 1–31.

Sugden, R. (2002), 'Credible Worlds: The Status of the Theoretical Models in Economics', in Uskali Mäki (ed.), *Fact and Fiction in Economics: Models, Realism, and Social Construction*, Cambridge: Cambridge University Press.

Summers, L.H (1991), 'The Scientific Illusion in Empirical Macroeconomics', *Scandinavian Journal of Economics*, 93(2): 129–148.

Svensson, L. (2000), 'Does the P* Model Provide Any Rationale for Monetary Targeting?' *German Economic Review*, 1 February: 69–81.

Svensson, L. (2001), 'Price Stability as a Target for Monetary Policy: Defining and Maintaining Price Stability', Deutsche Bundesbank (ed.), *The Monetary Transmission Process: Recent Developments and Lessons for Europe*, New York: Palgrave.

Tamborini, R. (2006), 'Back to Wicksell? In Search of the Foundations of Practical Monetary Policy', Department of Economics Working Papers 0602, Department of Economics, University of Trento, Italia.

Taylor, C. (2011), *A Macroeconomic Regime for the 21st Century: Towards a New Economic Order*, New York: Routledge.

Taylor, J. (1993). 'Discretion Versus Policy Rules in Practice', Carnegie-Rochester Conference Series on Public Policy, 39: 195–214.

Taylor, J. (1999), 'A Historical Analysis of Monetary Policy Rules', NBER Chapters, in J.B Taylor (ed.), *Monetary Policy Rules*, National Bureau of Economic Research, Chicago, IL: University of Chicago Press.

Taylor, J. (2000), 'Teaching Modern Macroeconomics at the Principles Level', *American Economic Review*, American Economic Association, 90(2): 90–94.

Taylor, J. (2009a), 'Economic Policy and the Financial Crisis: An Empirical Analysis of What Went Wrong', *Critical Review*, 21(2–3): 341–364.

Taylor, J. (2009b), *Getting Off Track: How Government Actions and Interventions Caused, Prolonged, and Worsened the Financial Crisis*, Stanford, CA: Hoover Institution Press Publication.

Taylor, J. (2011), available at http://johnbtaylorsblog.blogspot.fr/2011/03/lessons-learned-from-ben-bernankes.html.

Tesfatsion, L. (2002), 'Agent-Based Computational Economics: Growing Economies from the Bottom Up', *Artificial Life*, 8(1): 55–82.

Tesfatsion, L. (2003), 'Agent-based Computational Economics: Modeling Economies as Complex Adaptive Systems', *Information Sciences*, 149(4): 262–268.

Tesfatsion, L. (2006), 'Agent-Based Computational Economics: A Constructive Approach to Economic Theory', in L. Tesfatsion and K.L. Judd (eds), *Handbook of Computational Economics*, vol. 2, part 2, Amsterdam: North-Holland.

Thornton, D.L (2010), 'How Did We Get to Inflation Targeting and Where Do We Need to Go to Now? A Perspective from the US Experience', in David P. Cobham (ed.), *Twenty Years of Inflation Targeting: Lessons Learned and Future Prospects*, New York, Cambridge: Cambridge University Press.

Tinbergen, J. (1952), 'On the Theory of Economic Policy', 2nd edn, Vol. 1 of *Contributions to Economic Analysis*, Amsterdam: North Holland.

Tomljanovich, M. (2007), 'Does Central Bank Transparency Impact Financial Markets? A Cross-Country Econometric Analysis', *Southern Economic Journal*, 73(3): 110–123.

Torres, R. (2012), 'Editorial', 'World of Work Report 2012: Better Jobs for a Better Economy', International Labour Organization (International Institute for Labour Studies), available at http://www.ilo.org/wcmsp5/groups/public/---dgreports/---dcomm/---publ/documents/publication/wcms_179453.pdf

Trichet, J.C. (2004), 'Current Challenges for the ECB-Sustainable Non-Inflationary Growth and Financial Stability', Speech by Jean Claude Trichet, President of the ECB, at a conference in Hamburg, 13 May, BIS Paper, available at www.bis.org/review/r040518c.pdf?frames=0.

Turner, J.H. (2005), *The Sociology of Emotions*, Cambridge: Cambridge University Press.

United Kingdom (1959), Report of the Committee on the Workings of the Monetary System, available at http://discovery.nationalarchives.gov.uk/SearchUI/details?Uri=C13896.

Veron, N. (2011), 'Europe needs Institutional Creativity', *Globe and Mail*, 16 November.

Viñals, J. (2001), 'Monetary Policy in a Low Inflation Environment', Banco de España Working Paper, No. 0107.

Wadhwani, S. (2008), 'Should Monetary Policy Respond to Asset Price Bubbles? Revisiting the Debate', FMG Special Papers sp180, Financial Markets, available at www2.lse.ac.uk/fmg/documents/specialPapers/2008/sp180.pdf.

Waller, C.J. (2011), 'Independence + Accountability: Why the Fed is a Well-Designed Central Bank', *Federal Reserve Bank of St Louis Review*, 93(5): 293–302.

Wallerstein, I. (2008), 'The Demise of Neoliberal Globalization', *Monthly Review*, available at www.monthlyreview.org/mrzine/wallerstein010208.html.

Walsh, C.E. (1995), 'Optimal Contracts for Central Bankers', *American Economic Review*, 85(1): 150–167.

Walsh, C.E. (2002), 'Teaching Inflation Targeting: An Analysis for Intermediate Macro', *Journal of Economic Education*, 33(4): 333–347.

Walsh, C.E. (2003), *Monetary Theory and Policy*, 2nd edn, Cambridge, MA: MIT Press.

Walsh, C.E. (2005), 'Interest and Prices: A Review Essay, a Review of Mike Woodford's Interest and Prices: Foundations of a Theory of Monetary Policy', *Macroeconomic Dynamics*, 9(2005): 462–468.

Webb, T. (2010), 'World Gripped by "International Currency War"', *Guardian*, 28 September.

Weisbrot, M. (2012), Interview with Mark Weisbrot on 'The Eurozone: Self-Inflicted Depression', New Left Project, available at www.newleftproject.org/index.php/site/article_comments/the_eurozone_self_inflicted_depression.

Wicksell, K. (1898), *Geldzins und Güterpreise: Eine Untersuchung über die den Tauschw-*

ert des Geldes bestimmenden Ursachen, Jena: Gustav Fischer (tr. 1936: *Interest and Prices: A Study of the Causes Regulating the Value of Money*, London: Macmillan).

Wicksell, K. (1922), *Vorlesungen über Nationalökonomie*, Band 2, Jena: Gustav Fischer.

Wilson, D.J (2012), 'Government Spending: An Economic Boost', Federal Reserve Bank of San Francisco, 6 February, available at www.frbsf.org/publications/economics/letter/2012/el2012-04.html.

Wilson, J. and Oakley, D. (2010), 'ECB's Bond Purchases Slow Sharply', *Financial Times*, 12 July.

Wolf, M. (2012), 'Why Quantitative Easing is the Only Game in Town', *Financial Times*, 15 March, available at www.ft.com/intl/cms/s/0/de9be724-6df6-11e1-baa5-00144feab 49a.html#axzz1tWINbaYe.

Wolf, M. (2013), 'Why the Euro Crisis is Not Yet Over', *Financial Times*, 19 February, available at www.ft.com/intl/cms/s/0/74acaf5c-79f2-11e2-9dad-00144feabdc0.html# axzz2LhV62Dtp.

Woodford, M. 1995), 'Price-Level Determinacy without Control of a Monetary Aggregate', *Carnegie-Rochester Conference Series on Public Policy*, 43(1): 1–46.

Woodford, M. (1996), 'Control of the Public Debt: A Requirement for Price Stability?' NBER Working Papers 5684, National Bureau of Economic Research.

Woodford, M. (1998), 'Public Debt and the Price Level', manuscript, Princeton University, 7 July.

Woodford, M. (2000), Chapter 4, 'A Neo-Wicksellian Framework for the Analysis of Monetary Policy', mimeo.

Woodford, M. (2001), 'Fiscal Requirements for Price Stability', *Journal of Money, Credit and Banking*, 33(3): 669–728.

Woodford, M. (2003), *Interest and Prices: Foundations of a Theory of Monetary Policy*, Princeton, NJ: Princeton University Press.

Woodford, M. (2006), 'How Important is Money in the Conduct of Monetary Policy?' 30 October, available at www.ecb.eu/events/pdf/conferences/cbc4/Woodford.pdf.

Woodford, M. (2008), 'Convergence in Macroeconomics: Elements of the New Synthesis', Prepared for the session 'Convergence in Macroeconomics?' at the annual meeting of America's Economics Association, New Orleans, 4 January.

Woodford, M. (2010), 'The Case for Forecast Targeting as a Monetary Policy Strategy', in Volker Wieland (ed.), *The Science and Practice of Monetary Policy Today: The Deutsche Bank Prize in Financial Economics 2007*, Berlin: Springer.

Woodford, M. (2011), 'What's Wrong with Economic Models?' Columbia University, 3 October.

Woodford, M. (2013), 'Principled Policymaking in an Uncertain World,' In Rethinking Expectations The Way Forward for Macroeconomics, Edited by Roman Frydman, Edmund S. Phelps, Princeton: Princeton University, Press, pp. 389-414.

Woolley, J.T. (1984), *The Federal Reserve and the Politics of Monetary Policy*, Cambridge: Cambridge University Press.

World Bank (2009), World Bank Data, available at http://data.worldbank.org/.

World Federation of Exchanges Aggregate (2009), WFE 2009 Market Highlights, available at www.world-exchanges.org/statistics.

Wray, R. (1998), *Understanding Modern Money: The Key to Full Employment and Price Stability*, Cheltenham: Edward Elgar.

Wray, R. (2004), 'The Fed and the New Monetary Consensus, The Case for Rate Hikes, Part Two', Public Policy Brief No. 80, Levy Economics Institute, available at www.levyinstitute.org/pubs/hili80A.pdf.

Wray, R. (2007), 'A Post-Keynesian View of Central Bank Independence, Policy Targets, and the Rules-versus-Discretion Debate', Working Paper No. 510, Levy Economics Institute, available at www.levyinstitute.org/pubs/wp_510.pdf.

Wray, R. (2011), 'The Fall of the New Monetary Consensus', ASSA conference in Denver, USA, 6 January, available at www.creditwritedowns.com/2011/01/fall-of-new-monetary-consensus.html.

Wyplosz, C. (2012a), 'Fiscal Rules: Theoretical Issues and Historical Experiences', Graduate Institute, Geneva.

Wyplosz, C. (2012b), 'The Coming Revolt Against Austerity', Voxeu.org, available at www.voxeu.org/article/coming-revolt-against-austerity.

Zingales, L. (2011), 'The Derivatives Market's Helpful Enemies', Project Syndicate, 18 May, available at www.project-syndicate.org/commentary/the-derivatives-market-s-helpful-enemies.

Index

For Product Safety Concerns and Information please contact our
EU representative GPSR@taylorandfrancis.com Taylor & Francis
Verlag GmbH, Kaufingerstraße 24, 80331 München, Germany